T - S
So.ge -t22
H -tr
v. 1

Geography Alive!

Regions and People

Lesson Guide 1

Teachers' Curriculum Institute

Program Directors
Bert Bower
Jim Lobdell

Program Advisors
National Council for
Geographic Education

Curriculum Developers
Julie Cremin
Erin Fry
Amy George
Colleen Guccione
Steve Seely
Kelly Shafsky
Lisa Sutterer

Author
Diane Hart

Contributing Writers
Wendy Frey
Erin Fry
Brent Goff
Holly Melton
Hilarie Staton
Ellen Todras
Julie Weiss

Director of Development: Liz Russell
Editorial Project Manager: Laura Alavosus
Content Editors: John Bergez, John Burner
Production Editors: Mali Apple, Beverly Cory
Editorial Assistant: Anna Embree
Art Director: John F. Kelly
Production Manager: Lynn Sanchez
Senior Graphic Designer: Christy Uyeno
Graphic Designers: Katy Haun, Paul Rebello, Don Taka
Photo Edit Manager: Margee Robinson
Art Editor: Eric Houts
Audio Director: Katy Haun

TCi® Teachers' Curriculum Institute
P.O. Box 50996
Palo Alto, CA 94303

ISBN13: 978-1-58371-428-7   ISBN10: 1-58371-428-6
5 6 7 8 9 10 -ML- 12 11 10 09 08

Praise for *Geography Alive! Regions and People*

I am excited about the development of this new geography program, *Geography Alive! Regions and People*, which incorporates many of the approaches used in TCI's successful *History Alive!* programs. The innovative, hands-on lessons challenge students to use the tools of geography to view, analyze, and understand the world around them while building on their content area reading skills.

Most world geography texts move from region to region in a predictable sequence, often with superficial coverage. *Geography Alive!* uses a case study approach, allowing students to study geographic issues in greater depth. Each case study, aligned with the National Geography Standards, is framed by an essential question and built around an interactive classroom activity. The activity is tightly integrated with the corresponding chapter in the text and provides students with opportunities to explore and wrestle with geographic concepts and issues. Students examine such topics as spatial inequality in Mexico City, resource consumption in the United States, the impact of the monsoon on South Asia, competing land interests in the Amazon, and the role of women micro-entrepreneurs in Africa.

Embedded in each case study are opportunities for students to develop skills in geographic analysis and geographic inquiry. In addition to providing student editions at both the sixth and ninth grade reading levels, the program includes a mapping lab for each region, a digital teacher resource CD-ROM, and an impressive array of high-quality maps, diagrams, and graphs.

An important component of each case study is the section on Global Connections. Here, students examine the broader global context of issues that arise in the case study. For example, the case study on Japan focuses on how population density affects the way people live. After analyzing how population density impacts transportation, land use, housing, and health in that country, students examine factors contributing to the well-being of people in other countries with a high population density, such as Bangladesh, Singapore, and the Netherlands.

What sets this program apart is that is asks students to use real geographers' skills and strategies to look at critical contemporary geographic issues. This program is a welcome relief from the mind-numbing encyclopedic tour of world regions, still prevalent in many current world geography classes.

Gwenda H. Rice
NCGE President 2004
Chair, Division of Teacher Education
College of Education
Western Oregon University

Contents

Using the *Geography Alive!* Program

Through case studies of geographic issues, *Geography Alive! Regions and People* leads students to explore the physical and human geography of each of seven world regions. The program components are designed to maximize teachers' time and creativity, providing insightful and stimulating classroom experiences for students and teachers alike.

Using the Lesson Guide

Overview offers a snapshot of what students will experience in the lesson.

Materials lists items needed for the lesson.

Preview activities help students build on their prior knowledge and connect new ideas to their own experiences. The Lesson Guide provides directions for quick and simple execution of the Preview pages in the Interactive Student Notebook.

Essential Question and *Geoterms* provides a transition from the Preview activity and introduces the main concepts of the lesson. This section focuses on leading students through the Essential Question that appears on the first page of each chapter and on using the Geoterms defined in that chapter.

Classroom activity for each lesson uses one of six interactive TCI teaching strategies to tap students' multiple intelligences and help geography come alive. The Lesson Guide provides simple, step-by-step procedures and reproducible student and teacher materials that make activities easy to implement in the classroom.

Global Connections provides additional information for enriching the classroom discussion around this feature, which appears at the end of every chapter.

Processing assignments wrap up lessons for students by asking them to apply what they've learned in an authentic task. The Lesson Guide provides directions for completing the Processing assignments, which appear in the Interactive Student Notebook.

Online Resources directs teachers to the Web site www.teachtci.com, where they will find links to other sites related to the chapter content.

Assessment masters accompany each lesson in the Lesson Guide. Each three-page test contains standards-based multiple-choice questions and constructed-response items that invite students to apply their knowledge of geography. Each section of the test is complete on its own page, allowing for flexibility in administering the test. Answer keys and scoring rubrics are provided for each assessment.

Guide to Reading Notes provides annotations to help teachers quickly check students' work in the Interactive Student Notebook.

Student Handouts and ***Information Masters*** follow many lessons in the Lesson Guide. The materials list for each lesson alerts teachers to these masters and indicates the suggested number of copies and any preparation required.

Processing assignment to apply learning often appears on the last page of the lesson in the notebook.

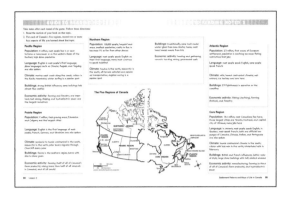

Using the Supporting Components

Additional components provide multisensory dimensions to the classroom experience. Each component is an integral part of its lesson, and directions for use appear in each lesson of the Lesson Guide.

Using the Interactive Student Notebook

The Interactive Student Notebook is a keystone component of the *Geography Alive!* program. Here all the parts of the integrated lesson come together for the student to form a personal record of learning.

Preview activity to ignite student interest often fills the first page of each lesson in the notebook.

Geoterms on the second page promotes better reading comprehension by having students both define and illustrate key terms.

Reading Notes are the central organizing tools for the content of every chapter. Graphically organized, they structure learning by helping students access and record main ideas and supporting details.

Transparencies and ***Placards*** provide visual information to support the program.

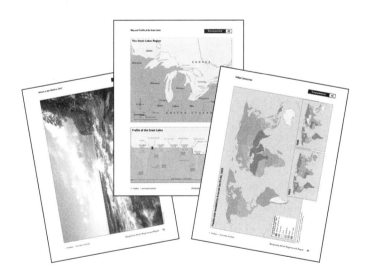

Sounds of Geography CD contains dramatic readings, musical recordings, and other audio effects to enhance the drama and realism of many student activities.

Digital Teacher Resources CD-ROM includes an editable assessment bank and digital versions of the Lesson Guide, Interactive Student Notebook, and transparencies provided with the program.

Using the Student Edition

Each unit in *Geography Alive! Regions and People* explores one of the seven world regions. Unit introductions provide useful background information on the physical and human geography of the region. Each case study chapter within the unit begins with an opening image that provides a visual introduction for students. The written introduction organizes the main ideas of the chapter and introduces key concepts.

Reading *Geography Alive! Regions and People* is an essential part of the classroom activities. To complete each activity, students must carefully read and consider each section of each chapter. The text is presented in clear sections that are numbered for easy reference.

To support different reading abilities, the student text is available at both middle and high school reading levels. Images and content are the same page for page in the two editions.

Geoterms are important geography terms highlighted in color and defined in each chapter. This easy access to definitions of unfamiliar words significantly improves students' reading comprehension. All highlighted terms and their definitions are also found in the Glossary at the back of the book.

Photographs, maps, graphs, diagrams, and tables support **visual learning** throughout the chapters. Captions focus students on the important points of the case study. The graphics and captions provide a way for readers at all levels to comprehend the key concepts of the chapter.

Beginning to Think Globally and **Global Connections** appear at the end of each chapter. After reviewing the chapter's key concepts, students explore the Essential Question on a worldwide level. Three critical thinking questions, supported by maps and graphics, provide the impetus for in-depth classroom discussions.

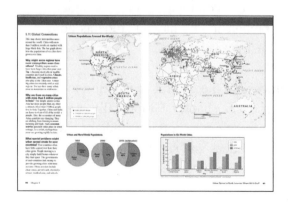

Using the Mapping Labs

Mapping Labs explore seven world regions. Each region's Mapping Lab contains a Mapping Lab Lesson Guide, Lab Manual, transparencies, and placards.

A *Mapping Lab Lesson Guide* consists of five separate activities called *challenges*. The challenges are carefully spiraled from simpler to more complex, though it is not necessary to do all five. Teachers should read through the procedures to see which of the challenges are most appropriate for their students. Each challenge will require at least a full class period.

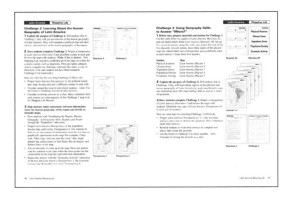

The *Lab Manual* contains the student pages for all seven Mapping Labs in one easy-to-use book. Teachers can direct students to the individual challenges they want to use.

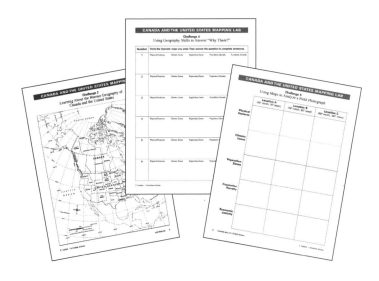

Each Mapping Lab contains seven *transparencies*—six regional maps and a field photograph—and three sets of *placards* that provide five colorful specialty maps of the region. Teachers use the transparencies and placards to set up stations around the room for students to visit as they complete the challenge activities. The Lesson Guide provides instructions for using the placards, each of which is an integral part of the lesson.

The *Geography Alive!* Assessment Program

When most people hear the word *assessment,* they automatically think *testing.* The two words are often viewed as interchangeable. In *Geography Alive!* you will find that assessment and testing are complementary, but not identical, activities.

Assessment is the process of gathering information about students and their learning. Throughout this program, you will be gathering such information by directly observing students as they work through lesson activities and complete their Reading Notes in the Interactive Student Notebook.

Testing is one means of assessment. It provides you with a snapshot of what students know and can do at a point in time. Like any snapshot, a test has its limitations. It cannot show everything that might be captured about a given student at a specific moment. With that in mind, the tests developed for this program have been designed to do four things with reasonable efficiency:

- measure your students' understanding of key content and concepts
- assess your students' mastery of geographic skills
- challenge your students to use what they have learned to complete authentic assessment tasks
- prepare your students for the breadth and depth of geographic questions and tasks that they are likely to encounter on state-mandated assessments

A Flexible Chapter Assessment System

You will find four pages of assessment masters at the end of each lesson in the Lesson Guide. These assessments can also be found on the Digital Teacher Resources CD. For best graphic quality, print these pages from the Digital Teacher Resources CD rather than photocopying them from the Lesson Guide.

Each of the four pages has a specific purpose. You can use them all together or separately to meet your specific testing needs. You may also choose to use some elements as in-class activities or homework assignments, rather than as parts of a formal chapter test.

Mastering the Content
The first page contains eight multiple-choice questions that check a student's understanding of the main concepts and content introduced in the chapter. These questions range from simple recall to application, analysis, and evaluation. They use the wording and formats most commonly found on standardized tests. By using them regularly, you will be embedding test preparation into your assessment program.

Applying Geographic Skills The second page has short-answer tasks designed to assess how well your students have mastered a wide range of geographic skills. On these pages students are asked to read, compare, and analyze a great variety of graphics including maps, diagrams, graphs, tables, and cartoons. These skill assessments are scaffolded to guide students from simple tasks, such as identifying data, to more complex critical thinking tasks.

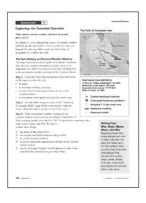

Exploring the Essential Question

The third page takes students back to the Essential Question they encountered at the beginning of each chapter, asking them to use what they have learned to complete a constructed-response task that relates to that question. Each task is accompanied by a visual prompt that provides information for students to draw upon. It is also carefully scaffolded to help students gather and organize the information they will need to complete the task. The final work product may be a written piece or a visual representation of information. Most work products are similar to those called for in state assessments that include constructed-response tasks.

Scoring Information

The final page contains an answer key for the multiple-choice questions and scoring rubrics for the *Applying Geography Skills* and *Exploring the Essential Question* tasks. In addition, you will find sample responses for these tasks. This page can be used both by teachers in assessing student work and by students in evaluating their own or each other's work. The sample responses also serve as realistic models of what "good" looks like. They are included to help students see how they might raise their own work to this level.

Test Terms Glossary Throughout the assessments, you will see test terms defined for students at point of use. Experience has shown that many students fail to respond well to assessment tasks not from lack of knowledge, but because they do not understand what they are being asked to do. By focusing attention on common assessment terms, such as *identify* and *explain,* you can help your students become better test takers.

Writing Tips and Design Tips Many of the *Exploring the Essential Question* tasks are also supported with *Writing Tips* or *Design Tips*. These tips are designed to reinforce what students are learning about communicating ideas in their other content classes, such as language arts. The tips also reflect Teacher Curriculum Institute's commitment to helping all students develop the visual and writing skills they will need to be effective communicators throughout their lives.

Assessing Students with Special Needs

Many teachers are tempted to exempt students with special needs from classroom tests for fear that their performance levels will be too low or that students will experience too much frustration. As a result, special needs students are often far less well prepared for mandated state tests than other students.

The Geography Alive! assessments have been designed to work with the broad spectrum of students found in many social studies classrooms. Reading levels have been kept low. Directions are clearly written. Terms that students need to know are defined at point of use. Each task is scaffolded in such a way that students at almost every ability level can enter the task and receive at least some credit.

The Geographer's World

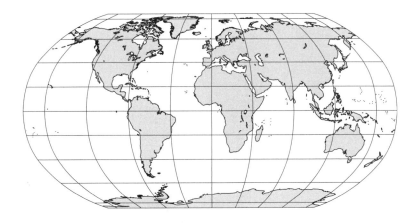

The Tools of Geography

Overview

In this lesson, students acquire the basic map-reading skills they will need for success in this program. Working in pairs, students study maps in a **Social Studies Skill Builder,** learning the difference between absolute and relative location; locating major parallels and meridians; determining location with lines of latitude and longitude; measuring distance using scale; reviewing hemispheres, continents, and oceans; and learning about Earth-sun relations and the relative merits of various map projections.

Objectives

Students will

- define and explain the importance of these key geographic terms: *absolute location, distortion, map projection, relative location.*
- understand the difference between absolute and relative location.
- locate major parallels and meridians.
- use latitude and longitude to determine absolute location.
- measure distance using scale.
- identify continents and oceans for a given hemisphere.
- understand how Earth-sun relations cause seasons.
- understand the relative merits of five map projections (Mercator, Eckert IV, Robinson, Goode's Homolosine, and Lambert Equal-Area).
- design a map with basic map components (title, legend, compass rose, grid system, scale).

Materials

- *Geography Alive! Regions and People*
- Interactive Student Notebooks
- Transparencies 1A–1I
- Student Handout 1A (3 copies)
- Student Handout 1B (17 copies)
- Student Handouts 1C and 1D (2 copies of each)
- Student Handout 1E (1 per student)
- Student Handouts 1F–1K (2 copies of each, cut apart)
- CD Track 1
- masking tape
- colored pencils or markers

Preview

1 Prepare materials. On the back of each of the 3 copies of *Student Handout 1A: Gold Deposits,* write any number from 1 to 20. On the back of each of the 17 copies of *Student Handout 1B: Dirt,* write the remaining numbers from 1 to 20. Use each number only once.

Student Handouts 1A–1D

2 Arrange the classroom. Create a grid in the classroom by evenly spacing one set of coordinates cut from *Student Handout 1C: Latitude Coordinates* in order along the right wall and the second set along the left wall. Then evenly space the coordinates cut from *Student Handout 1D: Longitude Coordinates* in order along the front and back walls. (**Note:** It is important that these coordinates can be seen by but are not necessarily obvious to students. When students enter the room, do not point them out.) Tape each copy of Student Handout 1A, face up, to the floor at three exact coordinates of your choice.

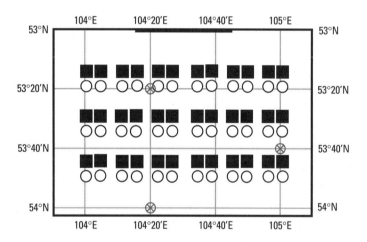

⊗ gold placed at exact coordinates

3 Meet with students outside the classroom and divide them into mixed-ability pairs. In each pair, designate a Cartographer and a Geologist. Explain that the classroom has been transformed into a "Siberian wilderness" that contains valuable deposits of gold. The students will enter the site at different times. Cartographers will enter first. Their task will be to map the site for the Geologists. Cartographers will then give their maps to the Geologists, who will enter the room and use the maps to search for the gold deposits.

4 Pass out *Student Handout 1E: About Gold.* Explain that, while Geologists are waiting outside the classroom, they must read and take notes on the handout, which contains important hints that could help them locate gold deposits. (**Note:** The handout will also serve to keep students busy while their partners are in the classroom.)

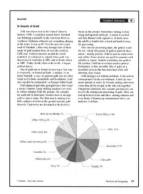

Student Handout 1E

5 **Have Cartographers enter the classroom to map the site.**
Give each Cartographer a sheet of paper, and explain that they
can use any method they like to map the locations of the three
gold deposits they discover. They will have five minutes. Their
maps must be as accurate as possible because they are what the
Geologists will use to search for the gold. To create a more
realistic atmosphere, play CD Track 1, "Siberia Sound Effects,"
and project *Transparency 1A: Siberian Wilderness* as you allow
Cartographers to enter the room and begin making their maps.
(**Note:** It is likely that most students will not think of using the
coordinates on the walls to add a grid to their maps.)

Transparency 1A

6 **Have Cartographers leave the classroom.** After five minutes, have Cartographers stop drawing and exit the classroom.
Ask them to record their own and their partner's names on their
maps. Collect the maps, and have Cartographers begin reading
Student Handout 1E. Tell students not to talk with their partners.

7 **Rearrange the classroom.** Move some of the desks and chairs
to look as though a snowstorm has hit the site. Turn each copy
of Student Handout 1A over, retaping them to the floor at the
same coordinates. Place several copies of Student Handout 1B
face down and clustered nearby. Arrange the remaining copies
of Student Handout 1B face down throughout the classroom.
Tape the sheets to the floor so students cannot lift them up. You
may even want to move desks or chairs over some of the papers.

8 **Have Geologists enter the classroom to search for gold.**
Tell students that a terrible snowstorm has covered the landscape with snow and debris. Then tell Geologists they will have
only one minute to explore the site. When they enter the site,
they will use their maps to select and write down the three numbers that they think represent the gold deposits. Distribute the
maps to the Geologists, and allow them to enter the room. Play
CD Track 1 and project Transparency 1A to create a more realistic atmosphere. Geologists may walk around the classroom,
but explain that they may not touch the sheets of paper as they
are "covered in snow." Expect most students to struggle with
following their partners' maps. The one or two students who
used the coordinates to add a grid to their maps should easily
locate the gold deposits.

9 **Have Cartographers enter the classroom.** After one minute,
ask Geologists to stop searching, and invite Cartographers to
rejoin their partners. Expect the Cartographers to be confused
when they see the classroom after the "snowstorm" that has hit
the site.

10 **Reveal where the gold deposits are located.** Have students stand along the walls of the room as you reveal the locations of the gold deposits. Move any furniture covering the papers. One at a time, remove the tape from the papers and show students what is on the other side. Finally, call attention to the pairs of students who correctly identified some or all of the gold deposits.

11 **Debrief the experience.** Encourage students to share their maps as you lead a discussion about the experience using these questions:

- *Ask Geologists:* How did it feel to use your partner's map to search for the gold? What was helpful about the map? How could it have been improved? How did it feel to rely on a map that someone else drew? Which teams located the most gold deposits? What made them successful?

- *Ask Cartographers:* What methods did you use to map the site? Did any of you use the numbers on the walls? If so, did it help the Geologists to find the gold? What other helpful components did you include on your maps? If you had to draw another map of the site, what would you do differently?

- *Ask the class:* What do the numbers on the walls represent? Where have you seen latitude and longitude before? Why do you think using latitude and longitude to find location is helpful to geologists and other people? What other components make maps easier to use?

(**Note:** After the debriefing, you may want to conduct the activity again to allow all Cartographers to use the coordinates to add a grid to their maps. This may be especially useful if students struggled with the third set of questions above.)

12 **Explain the connection between the Preview and the upcoming activity.** Tell students that geographers have many ways to show location on a map. One is by using lines of latitude and longitude. With these, geographers can show the exact, or absolute, location of something even if the landscape changes in some way. Point out that the maps that used the numbers on the classroom walls clearly indicated the locations of the gold deposits even after the snowstorm hit. In the upcoming activity, students will learn how to use latitude and longitude to find absolute location. They will also discover the importance of other map components, such as scale.

Essential Question and Geoterms

1 **Introduce Chapter 1 in** *Geography Alive! Regions and People.* Explain that in this chapter, students will learn how to read maps. Have them read Section 1.1. Then ask,

- In what ways are today's geographers similar to the explorers Lewis and Clark?
- How do today's geographers use maps?

2 **Introduce the Graphic Organizer and the Essential Question.** Have students examine the illustration, which is a physical map of the world. Ask,

- What do you see?
- How did the maker of this map choose to draw the world?
- Why do you think the mapmaker would draw the world in this way?
- What components does this map have?
- What other components make maps useful?

Have students read the accompanying text. Make sure they understand the Essential Question, *How do geographers show information on maps?* You may want to post the Essential Question in the classroom or write it on the board for the duration of this activity.

3 **Have students read Section 1.2.** Then have them work individually or in pairs to complete Geoterms 1 in their Interactive Student Notebooks. Have them share their answers in pairs, or have volunteers share their answers with the class.

Geoterms 1

Social Studies Skill Builder

Note: This activity has six phases, covering six topics: (1) basic map components, (2) latitude and longitude, (3) scale, (4) hemispheres, continents, and oceans, (5) Earth-sun relations, and (6) map projections. You may want to allow one class period to teach each skill. Alternatively, you might modify or eliminate a phase depending on your students' skill level.

1 **Prepare materials and arrange the classroom.** Before class, cut apart two copies each of *Student Handouts 1F–1K.* Place the cards in six piles, one for each phase of the activity.

2 **Divide students into mixed-ability pairs.** Have students arrange their desks so that pairs can easily talk among themselves and clearly see the projected transparencies.

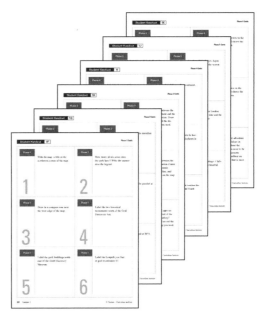

Student Handouts 1F–1K

Phase 1: Map Titles and Symbols

1 Project *Transparency 1B: Basic Map Components.*
Explain that students will now learn the basic components of a
map, which you will introduce by asking a series of questions.
Have students turn to Section 1.3 of Reading Notes 1 in their
Interactive Student Notebooks. Have several volunteers respond
to these questions as you point to various parts of the map:

Transparency 1B   **Reading Notes 1**

- Which map component tells us the subject of the map?
  *The title tells us this is the Marshall Gold Discovery State
  Historic Park.*

- Which map component tells us the pieces of information we
  can learn from this map? *The legend tells us that we can
  learn the locations of paved roads, footpaths, picnic areas,
  historical monuments, and park buildings.*

- Put your pencil on your map so that it points north. Now
  point it south, east, and then west. What do we call these
  four points? *cardinal directions*

- Put your pencil on your map so that it points southeast,
  northeast, southwest, and then northwest. What do we call
  these four points? *intermediate directions*

- What map component indicates direction? *the compass rose*

- (Point to the grid lines.) What do we call this map component? *the map grid*

- (Point to the Gold Discovery Museum.) How can we use
  the map grid to give the location of the Gold Discovery
  Museum? *State the grid coordinates E5 or E6.*

- (Point to the Gold Discovery Museum and then to the
  Sawmill Replica.) How can you tell someone to get to the
  Gold Discovery Museum from the Sawmill Replica without
  using the map grid? *Possible answer: Go left along the footpath, cross Main Street, and continue on the footpath until
  you see the museum.*

- (Point to the Gold Discovery Museum and then to the
  Thomas House.) How can you tell someone to get to the
  Gold Discovery Museum from the Thomas House without
  using the map grid? *Possible answer: Go left on High Street,
  and turn left onto Back Street. At the intersection of Back
  and Bridge streets, you will see the museum.*

- Why are these directions different if the location of the Gold
  Discovery Museum has not changed? *We are giving directions relative to our starting point. Explain that this is called
  relative location.*

- Why is the map grid helpful? *The map grid gives exact, or
  absolute, location.*

2 Have students read Section 1.3.

3 Have students respond to cards cut from *Student Handout 1F: Phase 1 Cards.* Give one card to each pair of students. Have them respond to the cards by labeling the map in their Reading Notes in the correct locations with (1) the number of the card and (2) the answer.

4 Check students' work. When a pair finishes with a card, have both students raise their hands. Use Guide to Reading Notes 1 to check their answers and award them points (optional). Continue until most pairs have had a chance to respond to all of the cards.

Phase 2: The Global Grid: Latitude and Longitude

1 Project *Transparency 1C: Parallels of Latitude and Meridians of Longitude.* Tell students that they will now learn how to use latitude and longitude to determine absolute location. Introduce the skill by asking this series of questions:

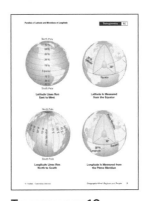

Transparency 1C

- What are the lines that circle Earth called? *Parallels of latitude. Explain that they have this name because the distance between them is always the same.*

- In what direction do parallels circle Earth? *east to west*

- (Point to the equator.) What is this parallel called? Why is it important? *The equator; it serves as a reference when measuring parallels of latitude.*

- How do we measure parallels of latitude? *With degrees. Explain that parallels are measured in degrees because they are angular measurements. If you move north from the equator, a parallel of latitude is x degrees north, or x°N. If you move south from the equator, a parallel of latitude is x degrees south, or x°S. As you move away from the equator in either direction, the parallels of latitude become higher in number because the angles get larger. The farthest point north is 90°N, which is the North Pole. The farthest point south is 90°S, which is the South Pole.*

- What are the lines that run from the North Pole to the South Pole called? *Meridians of longitude. Explain that, unlike parallels of latitude, the distance between them varies.*

- (Point to the prime meridian.) What is this meridian called? Why is it important? *The prime meridian; it serves as a reference when measuring meridians of longitude.*

- How do we measure meridians of longitude? *With degrees. Point out that these are also angular measurements. If you move east from the prime meridian, a meridian of longitude is x°E. If you move west from the prime meridian, a meridian of longitude is x°W. As you move away from the prime meridian in either direction, the meridians of longitude become higher in number because the angles get larger. The farthest point east is 180°E. The farthest point west is 180°W, which is*

the same line as 180°E. This line is called the International Date Line.

2 **Project** *Transparency 1D: Latitude and Longitude.* **Have** students turn to Section 1.4 of their Reading Notes, and continue the discussion by asking this second series of questions:

- (Point to the grid lines on the map.) What do we call this map component? *A map grid. Explain that this is a special grid system, called the global grid, with unique characteristics that you will now review.*

- What do we call the lines that run east to west on a map? *parallels of latitude*

- Where do we begin and end the measuring of parallels of latitude? *We begin at the equator and end 90° north and south of the equator.*

- What do we call the lines that run north to south? *meridians of longitude*

- Where do we begin and end the measuring of meridians of longitude? *We begin at the prime meridian and end 180° east and west of the prime meridian.*

- (Point to the spot at coordinates 45°N, 105°W.) How can you use longitude and latitude to identify this location? *Use the coordinates 45 degrees north latitude, 105 degrees west longitude.*

- What will you find at 30°S, 135°E? *Australia*

3 **Repeat Steps 2–4 from Phase 1.** Have students read Section 1.4. As before, have pairs complete the cards cut from *Student Handout 1G: Phase 2 Cards.*

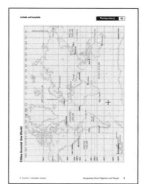 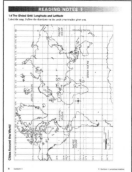

Transparency 1D   **Reading Notes 1**

Phase 3: Dealing with Distances: Map Scale

1 **Project** *Transparency 1E: Scale.* Tell students they will now learn how to measure distance using scale. Have students turn to Section 1.5 of their Reading Notes, and introduce the concept by asking this series of questions:

Transparency 1E   **Reading Notes 1**

- What is similar about these two maps? *Possible answer: Both show Washington, D.C., and Route 395.*

- What is different about the maps? *Possible answer: The lower map has more streets labeled.*

- If both maps show Washington, D.C., why are they different? *They use different scales.*

- What does the scale tell us? *It tells how the map size compares to the real size of the landscape. It also allows us to measure distance.*

- What is the scale of the upper map? *A distance of $1\frac{5}{8}$ inches represents about 10 miles. A distance of 1 inch represents about 10 kilometers.*

- What is the scale of the lower map? *A distance of $1\frac{1}{4}$ inches represents about 0.5 mile. A distance of $\frac{3}{4}$ inch represents about 0.5 kilometer.*

- Which map is more useful in finding the distance between Arlington, Virginia, and Washington, D.C.? Why? *The upper map because it has a smaller scale. It shows Washington, D.C., and its surrounding areas.*

- Which map is more useful in finding the distance between the Lincoln and Jefferson memorials? Why? *The lower map because it has a larger scale. It shows a more focused area of Washington, D.C.*

- (Demonstrate how to use a straightedge, such as an index card, to measure distance. Align the straightedge to the scale, and mark the scale on the card with a pencil. Use your markings to measure the distance between two locations.) What is the distance between the U.S. Capitol Building and the White House? Which map did you use? *Use the lower map to find that the distance is about 1.5 miles, or 2.5 kilometers.*

2 **Repeat Steps 2–4 from Phase 1.** Have students read Section 1.5. Then have pairs complete the cards cut from *Student Handout 1H: Phase 3 Cards.*

Phase 4: Hemispheres, Continents, and Oceans

1 **Project** *Transparency 1F: Hemispheres, Continents, and Oceans.* Tell students they will now review hemispheres, continents, and oceans. Have students turn to Section 1.6 of their Reading Notes, and introduce the concepts by asking this series of questions:

- (Point to the compass rose.) What is this used for? *It indicates the directions north, south, east, and west.*

- (Point to the equator.) What is this line called? Why is it important? *The equator; it divides Earth into the Northern and Southern hemispheres.*

- (Point to the prime meridian.) What is this line called? Why is it important? *The prime meridian; it divides Earth into the Eastern and Western hemispheres.*

- How many continents are shown on this map? What are their names? *seven; North America, South America, Africa, Asia, Europe, Australia, and Antarctica*

- How many oceans are shown on this map? What are their names? *four; the Pacific, Arctic, Atlantic, and Indian*

2 **Repeat Steps 2–4 from Phase 1.** Have students read Section 1.6. Then have pairs complete the cards cut from *Student Handout 1I: Phase 4 Cards.*

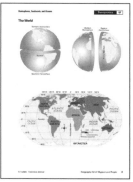

Transparency 1F

Reading Notes 1

Phase 5: Earth and the Sun

1 Project *Transparency 1G: Earth-Sun Relations.* Tell students they will now learn about the relationship between Earth and the sun. Have students turn to Section 1.7 of their Reading Notes, and introduce the concept by asking this series of questions:

- (Point to North America on each of the four globes.) Why is North America in sunlight only half of the time? *When North America faces the sun, it is daytime there. When North America is turned away from the sun, it is night there. This is caused by Earth's rotation.*

- How long does it take Earth to complete one rotation? *approximately 24 hours*

- (Point to each of the four globes again.) Besides rotation, how else does Earth move? *Earth moves around the sun in a nearly circular path called an orbit. One complete trip around the sun is called a revolution.*

- How long does it take Earth to complete one revolution? *$365\frac{1}{4}$ days, which is an Earth year*

- (Point to the Northern Hemisphere on each globe.) Throughout the year, do the sun's rays shine equally on the Northern and Southern hemispheres? *No. Explain that this is caused by the tilt of Earth's axis.*

- (Point to the Tropic of Cancer on each globe.) On what date do the sun's rays shine straight down on the Tropic of Cancer? *June 21 or 22*

- What season begins in the Northern Hemisphere on June 21 or 22? *Summer. Explain that this is because the Northern Hemisphere is tilted toward the sun.*

- (Point to the Southern Hemisphere on the globe for June 21 or 22.) What season begins in the Southern Hemisphere on June 21 or 22? *Winter. Explain that unlike the Northern Hemisphere on that date, the Southern Hemisphere is tilted away from the sun.*

- What causes seasons to occur? *Throughout the year, different parts of Earth receive more sunlight than others. When the North Pole is tilted toward the sun, the Northern Hemisphere receives more sunlight than the Southern. It is summer in the Northern Hemisphere and winter in the Southern. As Earth revolves halfway around the sun, the Southern Hemisphere receives more sunlight than the Northern. It is summer in the Southern Hemisphere and winter in the Northern.*

2 **Repeat Steps 2–4 from Phase 1.** Have students read Section 1.7. Then have pairs complete the cards cut from *Student Handout 1J: Phase 5 Cards.*

Transparency 1G   Reading Notes 1

Phase 6: Understanding Map Projections

1 Project *Transparency 1H: Three Map Projections of the United States.* Tell students they will now learn about map projections. Have volunteers respond to these questions:

Transparency 1H

- (Point to each of the three colored outlines of the United States.) Which of these three outlines is an accurate map of the United States? *None of the outlines is a completely accurate map.*

- What model could give a more accurate map of the United States? *A globe shows the most accurate map.*

- What are the challenges of using a globe? *Globes do not show a lot of detail, they are expensive, and they are not easy to carry around.*

- What happens when you try to represent the surface of the globe on a flat map? *The surface of the globe will break around the North and South Poles. If you don't want the surface to break, you must stretch it. This is called distortion.* (**Note:** You may want to use an orange peel to demonstrate how the surface of a globe would break if it were flattened. Also, you may want to refer students to the explanation in Section 1.2 of *Geography Alive! Regions and People* of how the surface of the globe would stretch if it were flattened.)

2 Project *Transparency 1I: Map Projections.* Have students turn to Section 1.8 of their Reading Notes, and continue the discussion by asking this second series of questions:

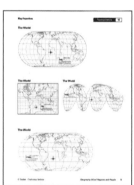 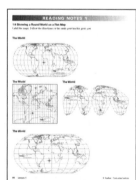

Transparency 1I   **Reading Notes 1**

- (Point to each map projection.) What does each map show? *the world*

- If they are all world maps, why does each look different? *Each map shows the surface of the globe as a flat map but in a different way. Explain that they are different map projections.*

- What is similar about all four map projections? *Possible answer: They all show North America, South America, Europe, Africa, Asia, and Australia.*

- What is different about the map projections? *Possible answer: The sizes of some landmasses look larger or smaller on the various projections.*

- (Point to Greenland on the Mercator projection.) Why might Greenland look so large on this map projection? *Explain that to make this projection, the mapmaker had to stretch the size of Greenland. This type of distortion is called area distortion because Greenland is not actually this large in comparison to the rest of Earth.* (**Note:** You may want to use a globe to show students the true relative size of Greenland.)

- (Point to South America on the Eckert IV projection.) Why might South America have a different shape on this map projection? *Explain that to make this projection, the mapmaker had to stretch the shape of South America. This type of distortion is called shape distortion; South America is not actually this shape.* (**Note:** You may want to use a globe to show students the correct shape of South America.)

- If all of these map projections have some distortion, is one more useful than another? *It depends on what you are using the map for. A Mercator projection, for example, is helpful for determining direction. An Eckert IV projection is helpful for getting an accurate view of the relative sizes of various places.*

3 Repeat Steps 2–4 from Phase 1. Have students read Section 1.8. Then have pairs complete the cards cut from *Student Handout 1K: Phase 6 Cards.*

Processing

Have students complete Processing 1 in their Interactive Student Notebooks. Review the directions, and answer any questions they have. Allow adequate time for them to complete their maps. They may need rulers or yardsticks to create an accurate scale. (**Note:** You may want to assign this as homework. If so, change the instructions to have students map a room in their home, such as their bedroom, instead of the classroom.)

Processing 1

Online Resources

For more information on the tools of geography, refer students to Online Resources for *Geography Alive! Regions and People* at www.teachtci.com.

Assessment

Masters for assessment appear on the next three pages followed by answers and scoring rubrics.

Mastering the Content

Shade in the oval by the letter of the best answer for each question.

1. What does the relative location of a place tell you?
   ○ A. the longitude and latitude of a place
   ○ B. which symbol shows a place on a map
   ○ C. where a place is compared to another place
   ○ D. the map projection being used to show a place

2. Which two continents are located entirely in the Western Hemisphere?
   ○ A. Europe and Africa
   ○ B. Asia and Antarctica
   ○ C. North America and Australia
   ○ D. North America and South America

3. Maps cannot represent the exact size or shape of Earth's features because of
   ○ A. tilt.
   ○ B. scale.
   ○ C. rotation.
   ○ D. distortion.

4. What do geographers use to indicate the absolute location of any place on Earth?
   ○ A. a global grid
   ○ B. a map legend
   ○ C. a map scale
   ○ D. a compass rose

5. A meridian of longitude is an imaginary line that runs
   ○ A. parallel to the Arctic Circle.
   ○ B. parallel to the Tropic of Cancer.
   ○ C. from the North Pole to the South Pole.
   ○ D. from the Prime Meridian to the International Date Line.

6. Which of the following is the **main** advantage of the type of map projection shown below?

The World

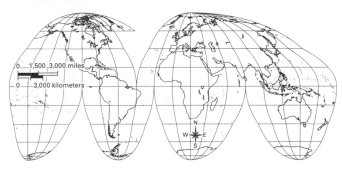

   ○ A. It shows the area of oceans more accurately.
   ○ B. It shows distances between places more accurately.
   ○ C. It shows relative locations of places more accurately.
   ○ D. It shows the size and shapes of continents more accurately.

7. What causes the changing of seasons throughout the year?
   ○ A. the rotation of Earth around its axis
   ○ B. the tilt of Earth's axis toward the sun
   ○ C. the distance between the sun and Earth
   ○ D. the division of Earth into hemispheres

8. What does a map's scale compare?
   ○ A. direction on a map with direction on Earth
   ○ B. distance on a map with distance on Earth
   ○ C. location on a map with location on a globe
   ○ D. distortion on a map with distortion on a globe

Applying Geography Skills:
Identifying Elements of a Map

Use the map and your knowledge of geography to complete the task below.

Step 1. Identify the map elements marked A–E on the chart below.

Step 2. Briefly describe what each element tells a map user.

Letter	Map Element	What This Element Tells a Map User
A		
B	global grid of longitude and latitude	
C		
D		what the symbols on the map stand for
E		

Test Terms Glossary

To **identify** means to tell what something is.

To **describe** means to provide details about something, such as what is it for.

© Teachers' Curriculum Institute

Exploring the Essential Question

How do geographers show information on maps?

In Chapter 1, you explored a variety of ways that geographers show information on maps. Now you will use what you learned. Use the information on the map below and your knowledge of geography to complete this task.

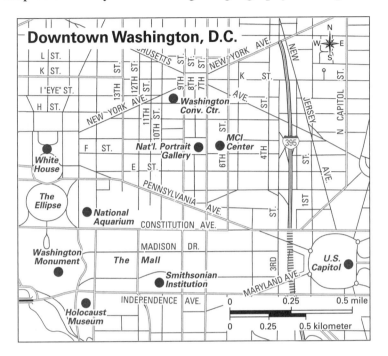

The Task: Writing Directions from a Map of Washington, D.C.

This map is a large-scale map of Washington, D.C. It shows streets and landmarks that are found in our nation's capital. Your task is to help someone find the way from the National Aquarium to the National Portrait Gallery.

Step 1. On the map, locate the National Aquarium. Draw a route a person could use to walk from there to the National Portrait Gallery.

Step 2. Use the route you marked to write directions for this walk. Write your directions on another piece of paper using complete sentences. In your directions, be sure to do these four things:

A. Give your directions a title.
B. Describe the relative location of the National Aquarium compared to the National Portrait Gallery using the map's scale and compass rose.
C. Describe your route street by street. At each turn, indicate which way the person should be walking. Use cardinal directions (north, south, east, or west).
D. Describe the location of the National Portrait Gallery at the end of your route.

Writing Tips: Giving Directions
Every sentence should have a subject and a verb. Directions usually use "you" as the subject. Often, however, "you" is not included in the sentence. Instead, it is understood to be there. The subject "you" is understood in this example:

Go to the corner of Fifth Avenue and Grand Street.

Test Terms Glossary
To **describe** means to provide details about something, such as how to get from place to place.

Applying Geography Skills: Sample Responses

Letter	Map Element	What This Element Tells a Map User
A	title	the topic of a map
B	global grid of longitude and latitude	the absolute location of places on a map
C	compass rose	cardinal directions on a map
D	legend or key	what the symbols on the map stand for
E	scale	how distances on a map compare to distances on Earth

Exploring the Essential Question: Sample Response

Step 1. Map should show a route from the National Aquarium to the National Portrait Gallery. Routes may vary, but the written directions should follow the route drawn on the map.

Step 2. Directions should include the four elements listed in the prompt. These elements are identified by letter in the response below.

A. Directions from the National Aquarium to the National Portrait Gallery

B. The National Aquarium is located southwest of the National Portrait Gallery. It is about half a mile from one building to the other.

C. To get to the National Portrait Gallery, exit the National Aquarium on Constitution Avenue. Turn left and walk east on Constitution Avenue.

C. Turn left onto 7th Street. Walk north along 7th Street.

D. The National Portrait Gallery is on 7th Street, north of F Street.

Mastering the Content Answer Key

1. C	2. D	3. D	4. A
5. C	6. D	7. B	8. B

Applying Geography Skills Scoring Rubric

Score	General Description
2	Student responds to all parts of the task. Response is correct and clear.
1	Student responds to some parts of the task. Response is mostly correct.
0	Response does not match the task or is incorrect.

Exploring the Essential Question Scoring Rubric

Score	General Description
3	Student responds to all parts of the task. Response is correct, clear, and supported by details.
2	Student responds to most or all parts of the task. Response is generally correct but may lack details.
1	Student responds to at least one part of the task. Response may contain errors and lack details.
0	Response does not match the task or is incorrect.

53°N

53°20′N

53°40′N

54°N

104°E

104°20′E

104°40′E

105°E

In Search of Gold

Gold was discovered in the United States in January 1848. A carpenter named James Marshall was building a sawmill on the American River in Northern California when he saw something shining in the water. It was gold! Over the next two years, word of Marshall's discovery brought tens of thousands of gold seekers from all over the world to California. Gold production around the world exploded. It continued to expand when gold was discovered in Australia in 1851 and in South Africa in 1886. Today, South Africa is the world's largest gold producer.

Ores of gold can be formed in two ways. One way is *exogenetic,* or formed at Earth's surface. As in James Marshall's case, exogenetic gold ores are often found in riverbeds, streambeds, and floodplains. Gold ores can also be *endogenetic,* or formed within Earth.

Gold mining begins after geologists have discovered a surface deposit. Large drilling machines are used to collect samples from the ground. The samples are analyzed to determine whether there is enough gold to open a mine. The first step in mining is to drill a pattern of holes in the ground near the gold deposits. Explosives are detonated in the holes to break up the ground. Sometimes mining is done using underground methods. A tunnel is created and then blasted with explosives. In both cases, the rubble is loaded into a truck and hauled away for processing.

After several processing steps, the gold is ready for use. About 85 percent of gold is used for decoration—mostly jewelry. Gold is used in some wires and cables. Some doctors use gold for patients with arthritis or cancer. Dentists sometimes use gold to fill cavities. Gold has even been used to protect firefighters. A thin, invisible film of gold on a facemask protects the face from heat while still allowing clear vision.

Gold mining is not without problems. It has serious consequences for the environment. It uses an enormous amount of water. In Nevada, mining uses more water than all the people in the state put together! Dangerous chemicals like cyanide and mercury are used in the mining and processing of gold. They can end up in local rivers and lakes, causing sickness and even death. Cleaning up contaminated sites costs millions of dollars.

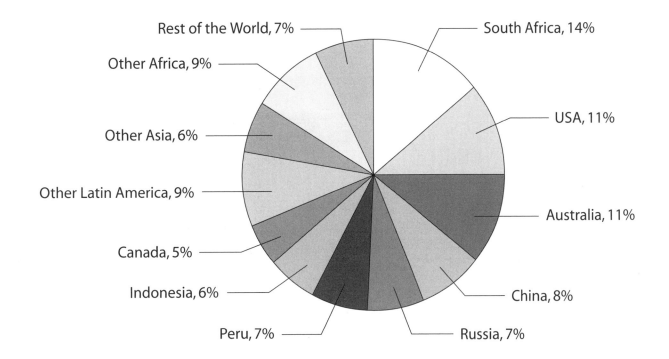

Rest of the World, 7%
Other Africa, 9%
Other Asia, 6%
Other Latin America, 9%
Canada, 5%
Indonesia, 6%
Peru, 7%
Russia, 7%
China, 8%
Australia, 11%
USA, 11%
South Africa, 14%

Phase 1

Write the map's title in the northwest corner above the map.

1

Phase 1

How many picnic areas does the park have? Write the answer near the legend.

2

Phase 1

Draw a compass rose near the west edge of the map.

3

Phase 1

Label the two historical monuments south of the Gold Discovery Site.

4

Phase 1

Label the park buildings northeast of the Gold Discovery Museum.

5

Phase 1

Label the footpath you find at grid coordinates F1.

6

Phase 1

Label the park building whose absolute location is G6.

7

Phase 1

Trace two routes—each in a different color—from the Mill Site to the Jail Ruins.

8

Phase 1

What direction is Emmanuel Church from the Olde Coloma Theatre? Write the direction near the church.

9

Phase 1

What direction is St. John's Church from the schoolhouse? Write the direction near the church.

10

Phase 2

Write the name of the parallel at 0° latitude.

1

Phase 2

Write the name of the meridian at 0° longitude.

2

Phase 2

Write the name of the parallel at $23\frac{1}{2}°$ north latitude and the name of the parallel at $23\frac{1}{2}°$ south latitude.

3

Phase 2

Write the name of the parallel at $66\frac{1}{2}°$ north latitude.

4

Phase 2

Label the city located at 47°N, 71°W.

5

Phase 2

Label the city located at 38°S, 145°E.

6

Phase 2

Label the city located at 41°N, 29°E.

7

Phase 2

Label the city located at 19°N, 73°E.

8

Phase 2

Label the two cities located north of 15° north latitude and east of 105° east longitude.

9

Phase 2

Label the five cities located south of 30° north latitude and west of 15° east longitude.

10

Phase 3

Find the distance between Washington, D.C., and New Carrollton. Draw a line between the two places, and write the distance on the line.

1

Phase 3

Find the distance between the Washington Monument and the Smithsonian Institution. Draw a line between the two places, and write the distance on the line.

2

Phase 3

Find the distance between Potomac and College Park. Draw a line between the two places, and write the distance on the line.

3

Phase 3

Find the distance between the Washington Convention Center and the National Portrait Gallery. Draw a line between the two places, and write the distance on the line.

4

Phase 3

What will you find approximately 3 miles north of Falls Church? Draw a line between the two places, and write the distance on the line.

5

Phase 3

What will you find approximately 0.75 mile west of the National Portrait Gallery? Draw a line between the two places, and write the distance on the line.

6

Phase 3

What will you find approximately 10 miles east of Alexandria? Draw a line between the two places, and write the distance on the line.

7

Phase 3

What will you find approximately 1.25 miles southeast of the National Aquarium? Draw a line between the two places, and write the distance on the line.

8

Phase 3

Which map will help you find your friend's apartment on New York Avenue? Write "find an apartment" near the map you would use.

9

Phase 3

Which map will help you to decide if you should walk or take a taxi to Washington, D.C., from Arlington? Write "decide to walk or take a taxi" near the map you would use.

10

Phase 4

Label the largest continent.

1

Phase 4

Label the smallest continent.

2

Phase 4

Locate the United States. Within its borders, label the two hemispheres in which it is located.

3

Phase 4

Locate Africa. Within its borders, label the hemispheres in which it is located.

4

Phase 4

Label the continent directly north of Africa.

5

Phase 4

Label the ocean that touches the shores of Europe and South America.

6

Phase 4

Label the three continents that the equator runs through.

7

Phase 4

Label the ocean that lies north of Europe.

8

Phase 4

Label the ocean that touches the shores of both Asia and South America.

9

Phase 4

Label the ocean the lies to the south of Asia.

10

Phase 5

It is March 30 in St. Petersburg, Russia. Label the date and the season near that city.

1

Phase 5

It is June 30 in Tokyo, Japan. Label the date and the season near that city.

2

Phase 5

It is September 30 in Quebec City, Canada. Label the date and the season near that city.

3

Phase 5

It is December 30 in London, England. Label the date and the season near that city.

4

Phase 5

It is summer in Melbourne, Australia. Label the season in Rio de Janeiro, Brazil.

5

Phase 5

It is summer in Santiago, Chile. Label the season in Istanbul, Turkey.

6

Phase 5

It is winter in Shanghai, China. Label the season in Tehran, Iran.

7

Phase 5

It is winter in London, England. Label the season in Cape Town, South Africa.

8

Phase 5

Find the four tropical zone cities in the Southern Hemisphere. Label each of them *tropical zone*.

9

Phase 5

Find the two temperate zone cities that are in both the Northern and the Western hemispheres. Label each of them *temperate zone*.

10

Phase 6

Label each map projection with its name. (**Clue:** Look very carefully at the differences between the Robinson and Eckert IV projections.)

1

Phase 6

Color in North America on the map projection that shows the most area distortion.

2

Phase 6

Draw an equal sign in North America on the map projection that does not distort area.

3

Phase 6

Circle North America on the map projection that shows the most shape distortion.

4

Phase 6

Find the map projection that has a balance between area and shape distortion without affecting the oceans. Outline and draw an equal sign in North America on that map projection.

5

Phase 6

You own an outdoor adventure company that specializes in sailing trips throughout the Atlantic Ocean. You need to be able to determine accurate direction. Draw a sailboat on the map projection that is most helpful to you.

6

Phase 6

7

You work for the United Nations studying how many people live per square mile in various countries. You need to be able to determine the accurate size of land. Draw a stick figure of a person on the map projection that is most helpful to you.

Phase 6

8

You work for a book publisher that has to present a fairly accurate picture of the world. You need to avoid a lot of area or shape distortion. Draw a book on the map projection that is most helpful to you.

Phase 6

9

You study ocean life along the coast of Antarctica. You need to be able to see a continuous view of the ocean along the coast. Draw a fish with an X through it on the map projection that is least helpful to you.

1.3 Map Titles and Symbols

Label the map. Follow the directions on the cards your teacher gives you.

1. Marshall Gold Discovery State Historic Park

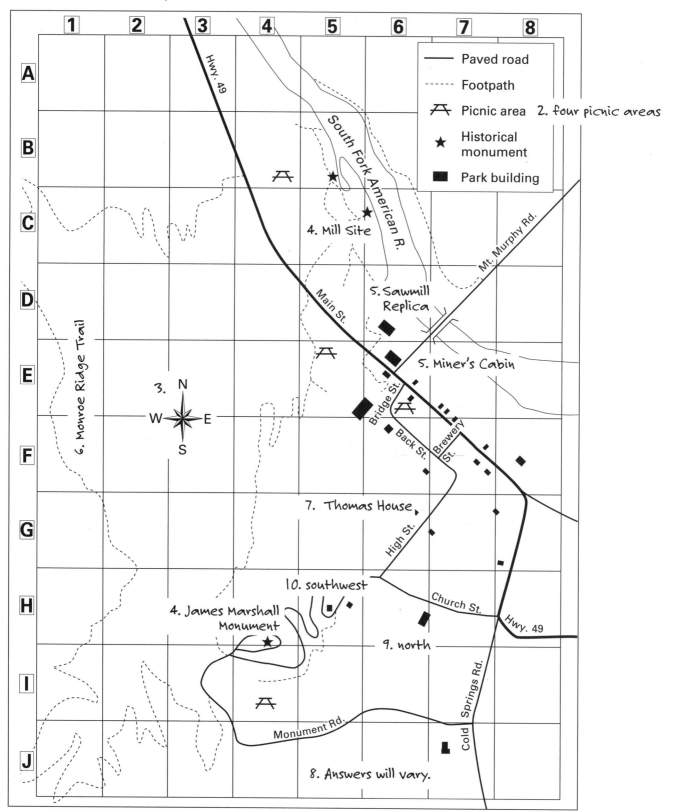

1.4 The Global Grid: Longitude and Latitude

Label the map. Follow the directions on the cards your teacher gives you.

Cities Around the World

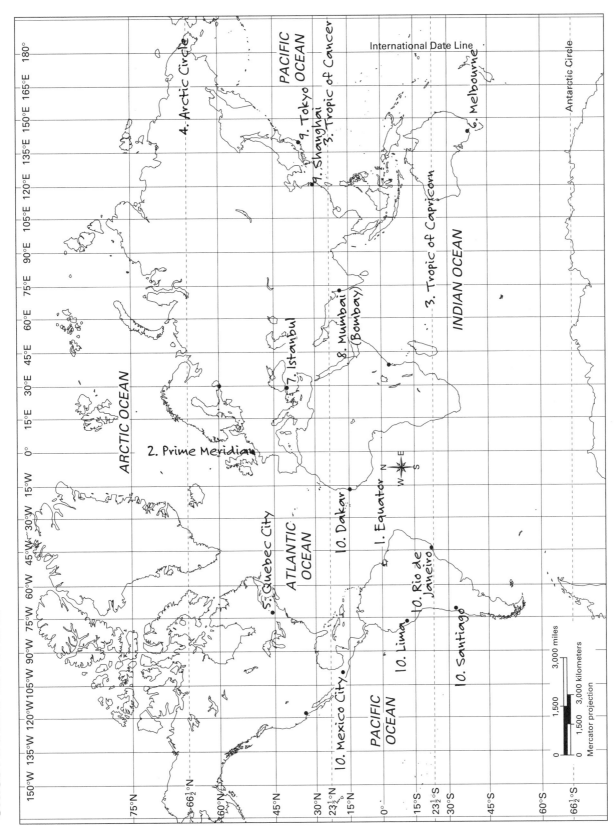

4. Arctic Circle

PACIFIC OCEAN

9. Tokyo

9. Shanghai

3. Tropic of Cancer

International Date Line

6. Melbourne

3. Tropic of Capricorn

INDIAN OCEAN

Antarctic Circle

8. Mumbai (Bombay)

7. Istanbul

ARCTIC OCEAN

2. Prime Meridian

5. Quebec City

ATLANTIC OCEAN

10. Dakar

1. Equator

10. Mexico City

10. Rio de Janeiro

10. Lima

10. Santiago

PACIFIC OCEAN

3,000 miles

1,500

3,000 kilometers

1,500

Mercator projection

180° 165°E 150°E 135°E 120°E 105°E 90°E 75°E 60°E 45°E 30°E 15°E 0° 15°W 30°W 45°W 60°W 75°W 90°W 105°W 120°W 135°W 150°W

75°N

66½°N

60°N

45°N

30°N

23½°N

15°N

0°

15°S

23½°S

30°S

45°S

60°S

66½°S

1.5 Dealing with Distances: Map Scale

Label the maps. Follow the directions on the cards your teacher gives you.

Washington, D.C., and Surrounding Areas

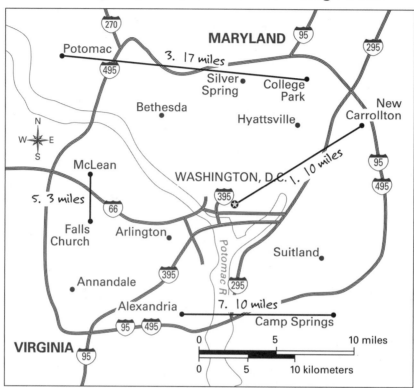

10. decide to walk or take a taxi

Downtown Washington, D.C.

9. find an apartment

1.6 Hemispheres, Continents, and Oceans

Label the map. Follow the directions on the cards your teacher gives you.

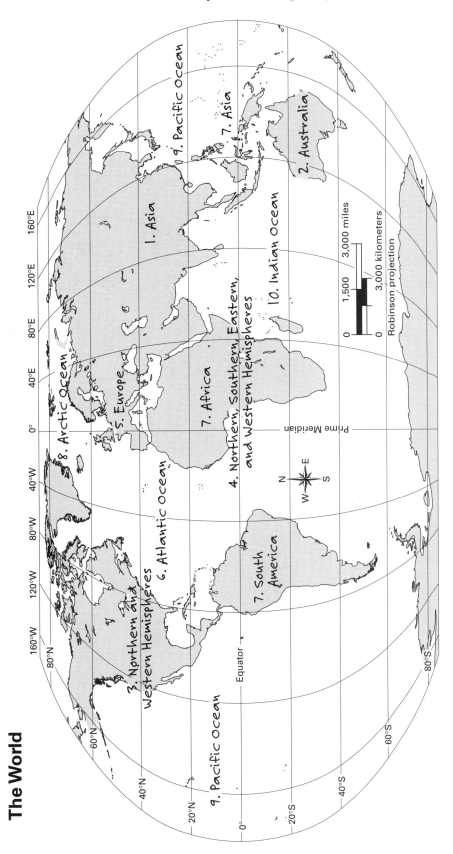

The World

9. Pacific Ocean

7. Asia

2. Australia

1. Asia

10. Indian Ocean

5. Europe

7. Africa

4. Northern, Southern, Eastern, and Western Hemispheres

8. Arctic Ocean

6. Atlantic Ocean

3. Northern and Western Hemispheres

7. South America

9. Pacific Ocean

Prime Meridian

Equator

3,000 miles

3,000 kilometers

1,500

0

0

Robinson projection

160°E 120°E 80°E 40°E 0° 40°W 80°W 120°W 160°W

80°N 60°N 40°N 20°N 0° 20°S 40°S 60°S 80°S

1.7 Earth and the Sun

Label the map. Follow the directions on the cards your teacher gives you.

Cities Around the World

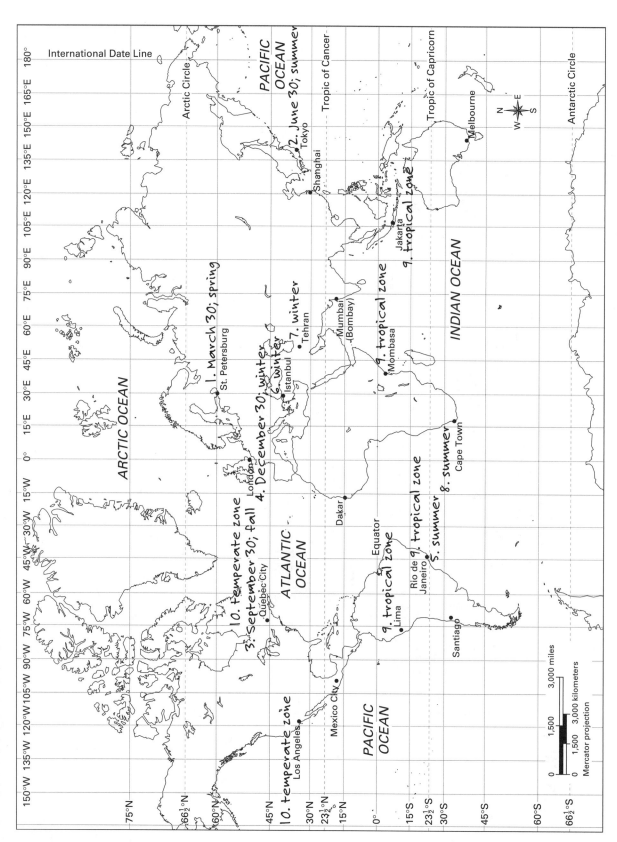

1.8 Showing a Round World on a Flat Map

Label the maps. Follow the directions on the cards your teacher gives you.

The World

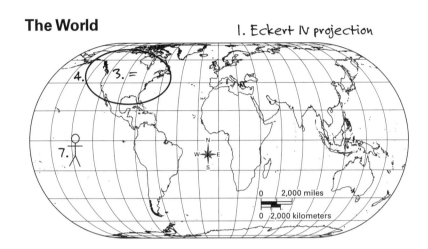

1. Eckert IV projection

The World

1. Mercator projection

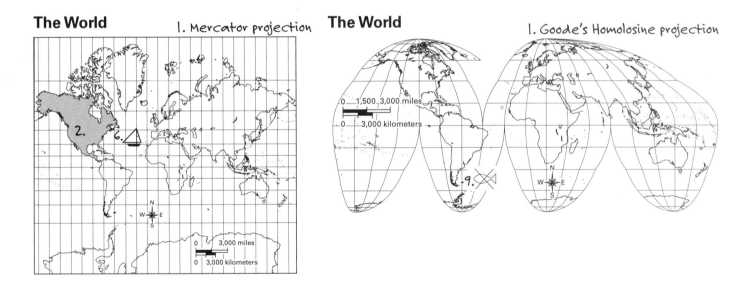

The World

1. Goode's Homolosine projection

The World

1. Robinson projection

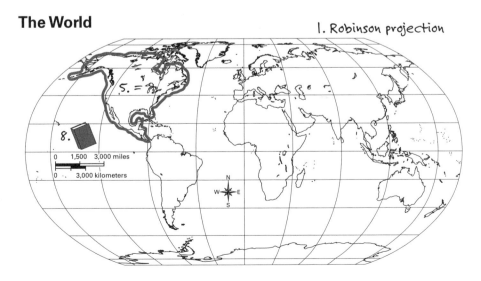

Seeing the World Like a Geographer

Overview

In this **Visual Discovery** activity, students learn to read and analyze various types of thematic maps that geographers use to represent the world. Using six different world maps, students learn how to get information about physical features, climate, vegetation, population density, economic activity, and regions. They read about the maps and their legends, take notes, and dramatize three of the maps. Students then apply their understanding by using all six thematic maps to create a poem about a country of their choice.

Objectives

Students will

- define and explain the importance of these key geographic terms: *climate, economic activity, landform, physical feature, population density, region, thematic map, vegetation.*

- define the terminology specific to six types of thematic maps: physical features, climate zones, vegetation zones, population density, economic activity, and regions.

- analyze six thematic maps to gather information about the world.

Materials

- *Geography Alive! Regions and People*
- Interactive Student Notebooks
- Transparencies 2A–2F
- Student Handouts 2A–2C (1 of each for every 3 students)

Preview

1 Have students complete Preview 2 in their Interactive Student Notebooks. Ask several students to share their advertisements.

2 Explain the connection between the Preview and the upcoming activity. Tell students that there are many characteristics one can use to describe a place. Some, like landscape, weather, and plant life, are physical features. Some, like population and job opportunities, are human features. In this lesson, students will learn more about how to describe a place by its physical and human features. They will also learn how to read and analyze thematic maps—of physical features, climate, vegetation, population density, economic activity, and regions—that show this information.

Preview 2

Essential Question and Geoterms

1 Introduce Chapter 2 in *Geography Alive! Regions and People.* Explain that in this chapter, students will learn about the various thematic maps that geographers use to study the world. Have students read Section 2.1. Then ask,

- What information did John Snow show on his map of London?
- How did his map help to show how cholera was spread?
- What do geographers call this type of map?

2 Introduce the Graphic Organizer and the Essential Question. Have students examine the map legend. Then ask,

- What is this item?
- Where do you usually see a map legend?
- What is a map legend used for?
- What types of information might we learn from a map legend?
- Why might a map legend be important when looking at a thematic map?

Have students read the accompanying text. Make sure they understand the Essential Question, *Why do geographers use a variety of maps to represent the world?* You may want to post the Essential Question in the classroom or write it on the board for the duration of the activity.

3 Have students read Section 2.2. Then have them work individually or in pairs to complete Geoterms 2 in their Interactive Student Notebooks. Have them share their answers with another student, or have volunteers share their answers with the class.

Geoterms 2

Visual Discovery

Note: This activity has six phases, covering six types of thematic maps: (1) world physical features, (2) world climate, (3) world vegetation, (4) world population density, (5) world economic activity, and (6) world regions. You may want to allow one class period to cover each type of map. Alternatively, you might modify or eliminate a phase depending on your students' skill level.

1 Prepare materials. Make one copy of each of Student Handouts 2A–2C for every three students.

2 Divide students into mixed-ability groups of three. Have them arrange their desks so that groups can easily talk among themselves and clearly see the projected transparencies. You may want to prepare a transparency that shows them where and with whom to sit.

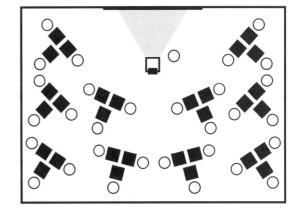

Phase 1: World Physical Features Map

1 Project *Transparency 2A: World Physical Features Map.* Help students carefully analyze the image by asking,

- What do you see?
- What do the colors on the map represent?
- Where are the highest elevations in the world? How do you know?
- What physical features have some of the highest elevations in the world?
- What other physical features does this map show?
- What patterns do you see between types of physical features and elevation?
- What other patterns do you see in locations of various physical features? What might cause these patterns?
- What questions do you have after looking at this world physical features map?

Transparency 2A

2 Have students read Section 2.3 and complete the corresponding section of Reading Notes 2. When they have finished, use Guide to Reading Notes 2 to review the answers with the class. (**Note:** Alternatively, throughout this activity, complete the Reading Notes as a class until you are confident that groups can complete them on their own.)

3 Have students prepare to bring the map terminology to life by conducting an act-it-out. Give each group a copy of *Student Handout 2A: Directions for the Physical Features Act-It-Out.* Assign each group a physical feature from the list, and

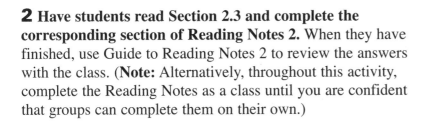  

Reading Notes 2   **Student Handout 2A**

give them a few minutes to complete the steps on the handout. For example, to model a delta, students might lie in a line on the floor, making the sounds of a river, with the student at the end spreading his or her arms out wide. To model a plateau, students might get on their hands and knees next to each other, with their heads down and their backs straight.

4 Conduct the act-it-out. Call up one group to stand in front of the map and arrange their bodies to model their assigned physical feature. Ask the audience to identify the physical feature being modeled by the group. Repeat for the remaining groups.

Delta   Plateau

Phase 2: World Climate Map

1 Project *Transparency 2B: World Climate Map.* Help students analyze the image by asking,

- What do you see?
- What do the colors on the map represent?
- Where are the tropical climates of the world? Near which parallels of latitude are most tropical climates located?
- Where are the ice cap and tundra climates of the world? Near which parallels of latitude are most ice cap and tundra climates located?
- Why do you think tropical climates are located near the equator while colder climates are located in higher latitudes?
- Where are the highlands climates located? What do you think influences this type of climate?
- What other patterns do you see in the locations of various climates? Besides latitude and elevation (altitude), what else might cause these patterns?
- What questions do you have after looking at this world climate map?

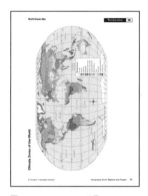

Transparency 2B

2 Have students read Section 2.4 and work in their groups to complete the corresponding Reading Notes. Review the answers with the class.

3 Have students prepare to bring the map terminology to life by conducting an act-it-out. Give each group a copy of *Student Handout 2B: Directions for the Climate Act-It-Out.* Assign each group a climate zone, and have them complete the steps on the handout.

4 Conduct the act-it-out. Have one group stand in front of an appropriate area on the map and perform its weather report. Ask the audience to identify the climate zone reported on by the group. Repeat with the remaining groups.

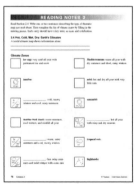

Reading Notes 2   **Student Handout 2B**

Phase 3: World Vegetation Map

1 Project *Transparency 2C: World Vegetation Map.* Help students analyze the image by asking,

- What do you see?
- What do the colors on the map represent?
- Where is desert scrub vegetation found? Generally, what type of climate is found there? (**Note:** You may want to project Transparency 2B again.)
- What types of vegetation are found near the equator? Generally, what type of climate is found there?
- Why do you think desert scrub is found in arid climates while tropical grassland and broadleaf evergreen forest are located in tropical climates?
- (Point to the Nile River.) What type of vegetation do you find along the Nile? What might influence the vegetation here?
- What other patterns do you see in the locations of various vegetation types? Besides climate, what else might help cause these patterns?
- What questions do you have after looking at this world vegetation map?

2 **Have students read Section 2.5 and work in their groups to complete the corresponding Reading Notes.** Review the answers with the class.

Transparency 2C

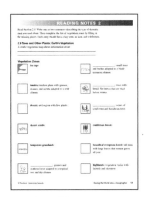

Reading Notes 2

Phase 4: World Population Density Map

1 Project *Transparency 2D: World Population Density Map.* Help students analyze the image by asking,

- What do you see?
- What do the colors on the map represent?
- Which continent has the lowest average population density? How do you know?
- What other information can you learn from this map?
- What are some of the most populated cities in the world?
- What patterns do you see between the most populated cities and population density?
- What other patterns do you see in the areas of dense population? What do you think causes these patterns?
- What questions do you have after looking at this world population density map?

2 **Have students read Section 2.6 and work in their groups to complete the corresponding Reading Notes.** Review the answers with the class.

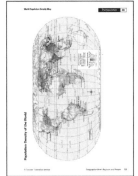 

Transparency 2D   **Reading Notes 2**

Phase 5: World Economic Activity Map

1 Project *Transparency 2E: World Economic Activity Map.*
Help students analyze the image by asking,

* What do you see?
* What do the colors represent? What do the symbols represent?
* Where do you find trade and manufacturing? How do you know?
* Where do you find coal? How do you know?
* Why do you think trade and manufacturing are located near places where coal is found?
* What other patterns do you see in the locations of types of land use? In the locations of resources? What might cause those patterns?
* What questions do you have after looking at this world economic activity map?

2 **Have students read Section 2.7 and work in their groups to complete the corresponding Reading Notes.** Review the answers with the class.

3 **Have students prepare to bring the map terminology to life by conducting an act-it-out.** Give each group a copy of *Student Handout 2C: Directions for the Economic Activity Act-It-Out.* Assign each group a land use, and have them complete the steps on the handout. To show subsistence farming, for example, they might pretend to be working on small plots of land. For commercial farming, they might pretend to be working with farm machinery on large tracts of land.

4 **Conduct the act-it-out.** Have the students in one group take their places in front of an appropriate area on the map. Ask them each of the questions in Step 3 of the handout. Then ask the audience to identify the land use dramatized by the group. Repeat with the remaining groups.

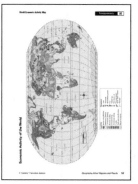

Transparency 2E

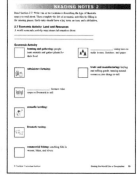

Reading Notes 2

Student Handout 2C

Phase 6: World Regions Map

1 Project *Transparency 2F: World Regions Map.* Help students analyze the image by asking,

- What do you see?
- How many regions does this map show?
- Why do you think the regions were created in this way?
- What do you think are some of the common characteristics for each region?

2 **Have students read Section 2.8 and work in their groups to complete the corresponding Reading Notes.** Review the answers with the class.

Transparency 2F

Reading Notes 2

Processing

Have students complete Processing 2 in their Interactive Student Notebooks. Direct them to the world maps in the Resources section of *Geography Alive! Regions and People.* Have them use the world political map to choose their countries. If time permits, you may want to have them share their poems in a poetry reading. (**Note:** You may want to have students use tracing paper to trace an outline of their country from the world map. The outline will serve as an overlay when reading the other thematic maps.)

Processing 2

Online Resources

For more information on the work of geographers, refer students to Online Resources for *Geography Alive! Regions and People* at www.teachtci.com.

Assessment

Masters for assessment appear on the next three pages followed by answers and scoring rubrics.

Mastering the Content

Shade in the oval by the letter of the best answer for each question.

1. A map that shows population density is a type of
   - ○ A. physical map.
   - ○ B. political map.
   - ○ C. regional map.
   - ○ D. thematic map.

2. What kind of information is shown on this map of North Africa?

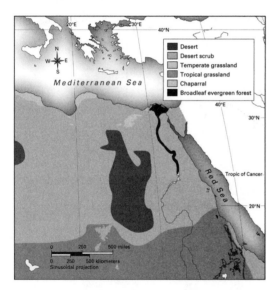

   - ○ A. climate zones
   - ○ B. population density
   - ○ C. vegetation zones
   - ○ D. economic activity

3. Which of the following will you find on a map that shows physical features?
   - ○ A. businesses
   - ○ B. landforms
   - ○ C. population
   - ○ D. vegetation

4. Which term means the pattern of weather over a long period of time?
   - ○ A. climate
   - ○ C. region
   - ○ B. density
   - ○ D. vegetation

5. What are coal, iron, uranium, and petroleum?
   - ○ A. land uses
   - ○ B. vegetation zones
   - ○ C. natural resources
   - ○ D. economic activities

6. What does an economic activity map of a country show?
   - ○ A. where its people live
   - ○ B. what kind of climate it has
   - ○ C. how high its mountains are
   - ○ D. how its people make a living

7. Use this graph to answer the question below.

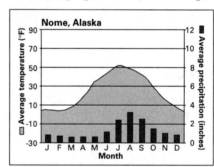

   What kind of information about Nome, Alaska, is shown on the graph?
   - ○ A. climate pattern
   - ○ B. vegetation zones
   - ○ C. economic activity
   - ○ D. population density

8. What do geographers call an area with one or more features that set it apart from other areas?
   - ○ A. a city
   - ○ B. a region
   - ○ C. a landform
   - ○ D. a climate zone

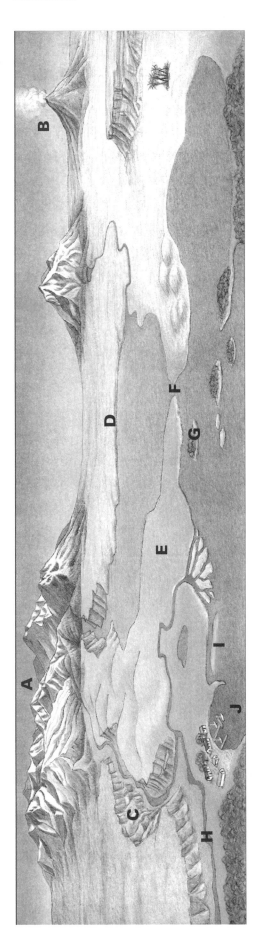

Applying Geography Skills: Identifying Landforms and Water Bodies

Use this diagram and your knowledge of geography to complete the task below.

Landforms and water bodies are marked A to J on the diagram. Label them below, using the terms in the Word Bank.

Test Terms Glossary
To **label** something means to attach identification to it.

Word Bank
bay
canyon
coast
island
mountain range
plain
reef
strait
tributary
volcano

A _____

B _____

C _____

D _____

E _____

F _____

G _____

H _____

I _____

J _____

Exploring the Essential Question

Why do geographers use a variety of maps to represent the world?

In Chapter 2, you explored a variety of maps. Now you will use what you learned as a geographer would. Use the information on the map below and your knowledge of geography to complete this task.

Economic Activity of Australia

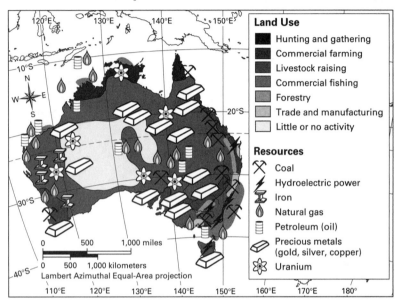

Writing Tips: Sentence Basics
Every sentence should begin with a capital letter and end with punctuation. The punctuation can be a period, a question mark, or an exclamation point. The initial capital letter signals the reader that the writer is beginning a new idea or thought. Punctuation signals the end of that thought. Here's an example:

The town of Alice Springs is located in the center of Australia. Why would people want to visit this town?

The Task: Writing a Description of Australia

This economic activity map shows information about natural resources and land use in Australia. Your task is to write a brief description of economic activity in that country based on the map.

Step 1: Find the compass rose and scale on the map. Use these tools to estimate the size of Australia from north to south and from east to west.

Step 2: Look at the natural resource symbols on the map. Circle the three or four most common resources you see on the map legend.

Step 3: Study the land use patterns shown on the map. Note what parts of the country have little or no activity. Note what parts have a variety of land uses.

Step 4: Use the information from Steps 1–3 to write a short description of Australia. Write your description on another piece of paper using complete sentences. Give your description a title. You can use the same title as the map. In your description, provide details about these three subjects:

A. the general size and shape of Australia
B. the most common natural resources of Australia
C. where most economic activity takes place in Australia

Test Terms Glossary
To **estimate** means to make a rough calculation of something.

Applying Geography Skills: Correct Responses

A. mountain range

B. volcano

C. canyon

D. coast

E. plain

F. strait

G. island

H. tributary

I. reef

J. bay

1. D	2. C	3. B	4. A
5. C	6. D	7. A	8. B

Exploring the Essential Question: Sample Response

Economic Activity of Australia

Australia is shaped like a kidney bean. It stretches about 2,000 miles from east to west. It is about 1,000 miles from north to south. Australia's most common natural resources are precious metals, coal, petroleum, and natural gas. Most economic activity takes place near the coast. The center of Australia has little or no economic activity.

**Applying Geography Skills
Scoring Rubric**

Score	General Description
2	Student responds to all parts of the task. Response is correct and clear.
1	Student responds to some parts of the task. Response is mostly correct.
0	Response does not match the task or is incorrect.

**Exploring the Essential
Question Scoring Rubric**

Score	General Description
3	Student responds to all parts of the task. Response is correct, clear, and supported by details.
2	Student responds to most or all parts of the task. Response is generally correct but may lack details.
1	Student responds to at least one part of the task. Response may contain errors and lack details.
0	Response does not match the task or is incorrect.

Act Out a Physical Feature

You will work with your group to bring to life one aspect of the world physical features map. All members of your group must participate in the act-it-out.

Step 1 Circle the physical feature your group has been assigned.

basin	isthmus	plateau
bay	lake	river
canyon	mountain range	strait
delta	peninsula	
gulf	plain	

Step 2 Your group members will arrange their bodies to model your assigned physical feature. You may use sounds or movement to make your presentation more realistic. For example, to model a river, you might lie on the floor in a line and make the sounds of water flowing by. Your presentation must be geographically accurate and clearly demonstrate your assigned feature.

To prepare, talk about these questions with your group:
- Does this feature represent the shape of land, something on land, or a body of water?
- What are the characteristics of your feature?
- What makes this feature unique?

Step 3 Practice arranging your bodies to model your physical feature. Remember, you may use sounds or movement to make your model more realistic.

Act Out a Climate Zone

You will work with your group to bring to life an aspect of the world climate map. All members of your group must participate in the act-it-out.

Step 1 Circle the climate zone your group has been assigned.

tropical wet	Mediterranean	highlands
tropical wet and dry	humid subtropical	subarctic
semiarid	humid continental	tundra
arid	marine west coast	ice cap

Step 2 Your group will create a one-minute weather report that highlights your climate zone. Your report must be geographically accurate and clearly demonstrate the characteristics of your assigned zone.

To prepare, talk about these questions with your group:
- In what parts of the world is this climate zone found?
- What are the main characteristics of this climate zone?
- How would the climate in this zone impact people's daily lives (clothing, housing, leisure activities)?

Step 3 Create and practice your weather report. Your weather report should include information on the following:
- your location
- current conditions, such as temperature and precipitation, that influence climate in your location
- how people's lives are impacted by this climate (what they should wear, what they do for fun, and so on)

You may use visuals and other props to make your weather report more realistic.

Act Out an Economic Activity

You will work with your group to bring to life an aspect of the world economic activity map. All members of your group must participate in the act-it-out.

Step 1 Circle the land use your group has been assigned.

hunting and gathering   nomadic herding

forestry   subsistence farming

livestock raising   trade and manufacturing

commercial farming   commercial fishing

Step 2 Your group will demonstrate the activities of the people who use the land in the way of your assigned land use. For example, to model commercial fishing, you might rock side to side as if on a boat and pretend you are lifting heavy nets full of fish. Your presentation must be geographically accurate and clearly demonstrate your assigned land use.

To prepare, talk about these questions with your group:
- In what parts of the world is this land use found?
- How does the land look, sound, or smell?
- What types of jobs would people have?

Step 3 Practice your act-it-out. Pantomime the activities of people who live where your land use is found. When asked by your teacher, you will have to answer the questions below without directly naming your assigned land use. (For example, if your assigned land use is subsistence farming, do not say you see a farm. Instead, you might say you see fields.) Assign one question to each group member.
- In what part of the world are you?
- What are the sights, sounds, and smells of this location?
- What are you doing?

You may use visuals and other props to make your act-it-out more realistic.

Read Section 2.3. Write one or two sentences describing the type of thematic map you read about. Then match the physical features in the Word Bank to their correct locations on the illustration. An example is done for you.

2.3 Mapping Earth's Physical Features

A world physical features map shows information about
the names, locations, and shapes of landforms and water bodies.

Physical Features

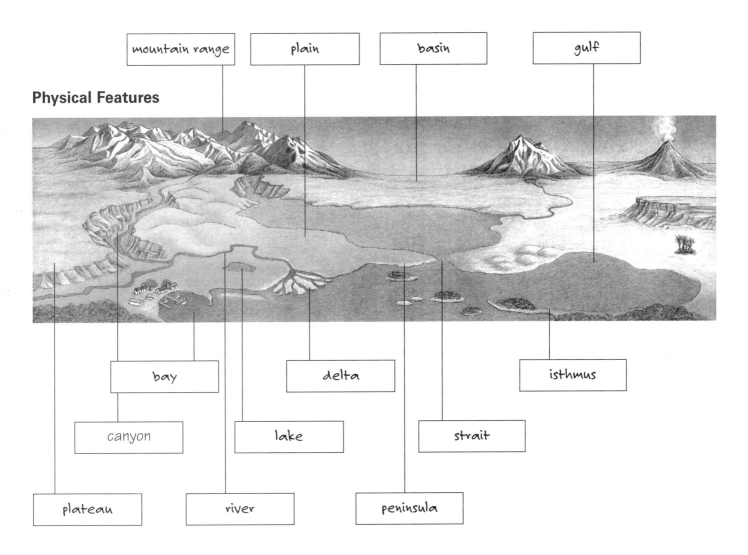

| mountain range | plain | basin | gulf |

bay   delta   isthmus

canyon   lake   strait

plateau   river   peninsula

Word Bank: basin bay delta gulf isthmus lake

mountain range peninsula plain plateau river strait

Read Section 2.4. Write one or two sentences describing the type of thematic map you read about. Then complete the list of climate zones by filling in the missing pieces. Each entry should have a key term, an icon, and a definition.

2.4 Hot, Cold, Wet, Dry: Earth's Climates

A world climate map shows information about
Earth's climate zones. Each zone has a particular pattern of precipitation
and temperature.

Climate Zones   Drawings will vary.

 ice cap: very cold all year with permanent ice and snow

 tundra: very cold winters, cold summers, and little rain or snow

 subarctic: cold, snowy winters and cool, rainy summers

 marine west coast: warm summers, cool winters, and rainfall all year

 humid continental: warm, rainy summers and cool, snowy winters

 humid subtropical: hot, rainy summers and mild winters with some rain

 Mediterranean: warm all year with dry summers and short, rainy winters

 arid: hot and dry all year with very little rain

 semiarid: hot, dry summers and cool, dry winters

 tropical wet and dry: hot all year with rainy and dry seasons

 tropical wet: hot and rainy all year

 highlands: temperature and precipitation vary with latitude and elevation

Read Section 2.5. Write one or two sentences describing the type of thematic map you read about. Then complete the list of vegetation zones by filling in the missing pieces. Each entry should have a key term, an icon, and a definition.

2.5 Trees and Other Plants: Earth's Vegetation

A world vegetation map shows information about where plants grow by dividing the world into vegetation zones. In each zone, a certain mix of plants has adapted to similar conditions.

Vegetation Zones   Drawings will vary.

 ice cap: permanent ice and snow; no plant life

 chaparral: small trees and bushes adapted to a Mediterranean climate

 tundra: treeless plain with grasses, mosses, and scrubs adapted to a cold climate

 deciduous forest: trees with broad, flat leaves that are shed before winter

desert: arid region with few plants

 mixed forest: a mix of coniferous and deciduous trees

 desert scrub: small trees, bushes, and other plants adapted to a dry climate

 coniferous forest: evergreen trees with needles and cones

 temperate grassland: short and tall grasses adapted to cool climates

broadleaf evergreen forest: tall trees with large leaves that remain green all year

 tropical grassland: grasses and scattered trees adapted to a tropical wet and dry climate

 highlands: vegetation varies with latitude and elevation

Read Section 2.6. Write one or two sentences describing the type of thematic map you read about. Then complete the list of population densities by filling in the missing pieces. Each entry should have a key term, an icon, and a definition.

2.6 Where People Live: Population Density

A world population density map shows information about population density, or how crowded places are. It also shows information about population patterns.

Population Density   Drawings will vary.

more than 250 people per square mile: an average of more than 250 people live in every square mile

125–250 people per square mile: an average of 125 to 250 people live in every square mile

25–125 people per square mile: an average of 25 to 125 people live in every square mile

2–25 people per square mile: an average of 2 to 25 people live in every square mile

fewer than 2 people per square mile: an average of fewer than 2 people live in every square mile

Read Section 2.7. Write one or two sentences describing the type of thematic map you read about. Then complete the list of economic activities by filling in the missing pieces. Each entry should have a key term, an icon, and a definition.

2.7 Economic Activity: Land and Resources

A world economic activity map shows information about land use, which is how people use land to meet their needs. It might also show the locations of important resources.

Economic Activity   Drawings will vary.

 hunting and gathering: people hunt animals and gather plants for their food

 forestry: using trees to make homes, furniture, and paper

 subsistence farming: small farmers grow crops to feed their own families

 trade and manufacturing: buying and selling goods; turning natural resources into things to sell

 commercial farming: farmers raise crops or livestock to sell

 nomadic herding: people move around to find food and water for their herds and use the animals' milk and other products

 livestock raising: raising cattle, sheep, or goats on huge ranches

 commercial fishing: catching fish in oceans, lakes, and rivers

Read Section 2.8. Write one or two sentences describing the type of thematic map you read about. Then color and label each of the seven world regions.

2.8 Organizing Earth's Surface: Regions

A world regions map shows information about
the patterns geographers use to organize Earth's surface.

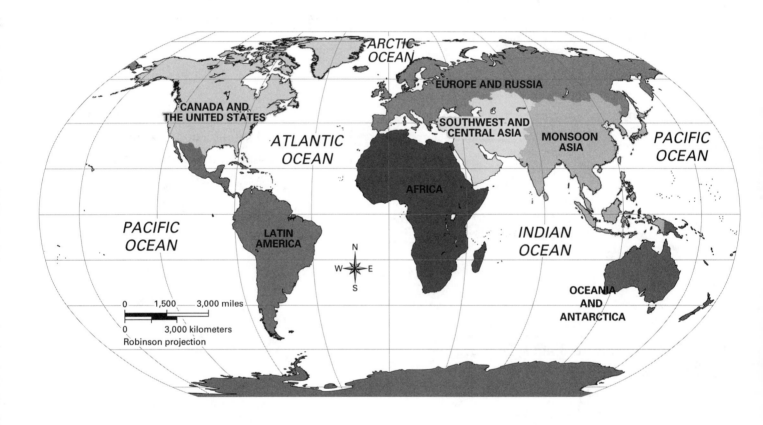

UNIT 2

Canada and the United States

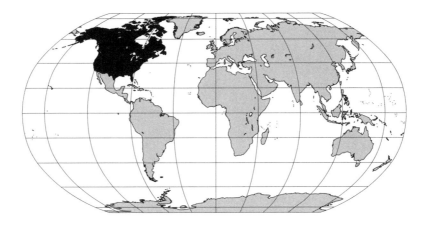

Lesson 3
Settlement Patterns and Ways
of Life in Canada

Lesson 4
The Great Lakes:
The U.S. and Canada's Freshwater Treasures

Lesson 5
Urban Sprawl in North America:
Where Will It End?

Lesson 6
National Parks: Saving the Natural Heritage
of the U.S. and Canada

Lesson 7
Consumption Patterns in the United States:
The Impact of Living Well

Lesson 8
Migration to the United States:
The Impact on People and Places

Settlement Patterns and Ways of Life in Canada

Overview

In this lesson, students explore how location influences life in the varied regions of Canada. In a **Social Studies Skill Builder,** students play a fast-paced board game that requires them to match tokens representing various aspects of life—population, climate, language, buildings, or economic activity—to one of the five regions of Canada. Students check their token placement as they read about life in Canada from the Atlantic to the Pacific. Finally, they create an annotated map of their own community showing how *where* they live influences *how* they live.

Objectives

Students will

- define and explain the importance of these key geographic terms: *ecumene, plural society, rural, urban.*

- analyze the characteristics of each of the five regions of Canada.

- explain how location affects ways of life in those five regions.

- evaluate the importance of location on ways of life around the world.

Materials

- *Geography Alive! Regions and People*
- Interactive Student Notebooks
- Transparencies 3A–3C
- Student Handouts 3A and 3B (1 copy of each for every 2 students)
- Information Masters 3A–3E (1 transparency of each)
- scissors
- envelopes (5 for every 2 students)
- transparent tape
- masking tape

Preview

1 Before class, create a floor map of Canada. Use masking tape to roughly outline Canada's political boundaries, as shown below. Make the floor map as large as possible.

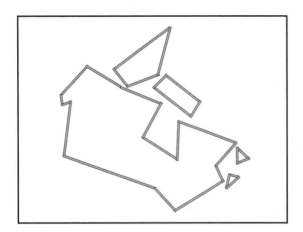

2 Introduce students to Canada's physical features. Project *Transparency 3A: Canada's Physical Features,* and briefly review the country's major physical features with the class. Then ask students to decide where in Canada they would most want to live based on the physical features of the area and to stand on the floor map in the location. Once all students are standing on the map, ask these questions:

- What factors led you to choose your location?
- What factors made you choose *not* to settle in other locations?

Transparency 3A

3 Project *Transparency 3B: Canada's Population Density.* Help students examine the map by asking,

- Which areas appear to have the most people? The fewest?
- Most of Canada's population lives within 100 miles of the country's southern border. Why do you think that is?
- How do you think life along Canada's southern border is different from life in the far northern part of the country?
- How do you think life in the eastern part of the country is different from life in the western part?

Transparency 3B

4 Make connections between the Preview and the upcoming activity. Tell students that Canada is the second largest country in the world in area, and yet most people live in only a small part of it. Canada is an incredibly varied place, with five very different regions. In the upcoming activity, students will examine the similarities and differences among these five regions that make life in each region distinctive.

Essential Question and Geoterms

1 Introduce Chapter 3 in *Geography Alive! Regions and People.* Explain that in this chapter, students will learn about Canada's five regions and how people's lives in each region are influenced by where they live. Have them read Section 3.1.

2 Introduce the Graphic Organizer and the Essential Question. Have students examine the map of Canada. Ask,

- What do you see?
- How many different regions is Canada divided into?
- What factors do you think might lead to differences in the way people live in these regions?

Have students read the accompanying text. Make sure they understand the Essential Question, *How does where you live influence how you live?* You may want to post the Essential Question in the room or write it on the board for the duration of the activity.

3 Have students read Section 3.2 for a general background on the settlement of Canada. Then have them work individually or in pairs to complete Geoterms 3 in their Interactive Student Notebooks. Ask them to share their answers with another student, or have volunteers share their answers with the class.

Geoterms 3

Social Studies Skill Builder

1 Explain the game. Tell students that they will now play a game with a partner to learn about settlement patterns and ways of life in Canada. They will use a map of Canada as a game board as they examine the population, language, climate, buildings, and economic activity of each of the five regions. As they explore each topic, they will take notes highlighting key aspects of each region.

2 Arrange students in mixed-ability pairs. You may want to prepare a transparency showing students who their partners are and where they will sit.

3 Have students read Section 3.3. Have pairs review the map and regional descriptions in Section 3.3 to orient themselves to the five regions of Canada. Make sure they understand which provinces and territories make up each region, and answer any questions they have about the map before they begin the activity.

4 Assemble the game boards. Give each pair a copy of *Student Handout 3A: Where in Canada? Game Board.* Have them cut out and then tape together the two parts of the map of Canada to create their game boards.

5 Prepare the game pieces. Have students cut the game pieces from the three pages of *Student Handout 3B: Where in Canada? Game Pieces* and put them in envelopes labeled by topic: *population, language, climate, buildings,* and *economic activity.* (**Note:** Alternatively, cut out the game pieces yourself before class and reuse them for each class that does this activity.) Explain that pairs will use each set of game pieces in one of the five rounds of the game.

6 Have students play Round 1, which explores the topic of population. Project Transparency 3B for this round of the game only. Follow these steps to conduct the game:

- Have pairs place each of their population game pieces on the game board in the region they think has the given population. Tell them that they must have a reason for the placement of each game piece, such as, "This region is so far north that it is probably very cold and most people wouldn't want to live there." Students may consult the map in Section 3.3 of *Geography Alive! Regions and People* if they need to.

- When pairs are finished, discuss the placement of their game pieces. Ask, *Which regions do you think have the highest populations, and why? The lowest? What factors would make someone want to live, or not live, in each region?*

- Have students read Section 3.4 of *Geography Alive! Regions and People* and reposition any game pieces that were placed incorrectly.

- Project *Information Master 3A: Map for Round 1* and have students check the placement of their game pieces. Answer any questions they have about Canada's population.

- Have students open their Interactive Student Notebooks to Reading Notes 3 and complete the notes for population by recording two key things they learned—from the game or the reading—about that topic for each region of Canada.

- Have students return the population game pieces to their envelopes.

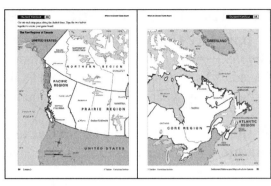

Student Handout 3A

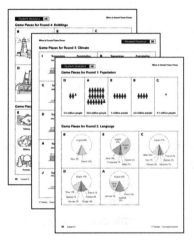

Student Handout 3B

Information Master 3A

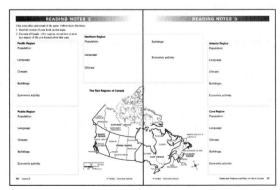

Reading Notes 3

7 Have students play Round 2 of the game. Repeat Step 6 for the topic of language, with these modifications:

- When discussing the placement of students' game pieces, ask, *What do you think are the two official languages of Canada? Why do you think so many different languages are spoken in each region? How might language and the various cultures of these people influence how people live in these different regions?*

- Have students read Section 3.5.

- Project *Information Master 3B: Map for Round 2* to have students check the placement of their game pieces.

Information Master 3B

8 Have students play Round 3 of the game. Repeat Step 6 for the topic of climate, with these modifications:

- When discussing the placement of students' game pieces, ask, *Which areas are likely to have the coldest temperatures? The warmest? How do you think climate affects how people live in these different regions?*

- Have students read Section 3.6.

- Project *Information Master 3C: Map for Round 3* to have students check the placement of their game pieces.

Information Master 3C

9 Have students play Round 4 of the game. Repeat Step 6 for the topic of buildings, with these modifications:

- When discussing the placement of students' game pieces, ask, *Why do you think buildings are different in each region? What factors are likely to influence these differences? How do you think people's location affects the types of homes and other structures that they build?*

- Have students read Section 3.7.

- Project *Information Master 3D: Map for Round 4* to have students check the placement of their game pieces.

Information Master 3D

10 Have students play Round 5 of the game. Repeat Step 6 for the topic of economic activity, with these modifications:

- When discussing the placement of students' game pieces, ask, *Which regions are most likely to have fishing? Forestry? Manufacturing? Mining? Hydroelectric power? Hunting and gathering? Why? How do you think people's location affects what kinds of jobs they have?*

- Have students read Section 3.8.

- Project *Information Master 3E: Map for Round 5* to have students check the placement of their game pieces.

Information Master 3E

11 Have each pair write two *Where Do I Live?* questions for playing a second game. Each question must describe three characteristics of the life of a student in one of Canada's five regions. Use this example to demonstrate how to phrase the questions: "My father works at a store that sells fish. We are one of a few families in my area that speak French at home. We can see boats out on the ocean from my classroom. Where do I live?" Answer: the Atlantic region.

12 Use students' questions to play *Where Do I Live?* Once each pair has written two questions, have pairs take their questions and Reading Notes and join together to form groups of four. Each pair will ask their questions of the other pair and see if they can give the correct region. Once each pair has asked their questions, the pairs will partner with new pairs, forming a new group of four. Repeat this process as many times as is useful for students to review this information.

13 Debrief the activity. Ask students to make connections between where people live and how that influences the way they live. Ask,

- What factors help determine *where* people in Canada live, or settle?
- What factors help determine *how* people in Canada live?
- What characteristics did you notice that are exclusive to each region?

Global Connections

1 Introduce the Global Connections. Have students read Section 3.9. Tell them that they will now see how some of the issues they encountered in the activity exist in other areas of the world.

2 Project *Transparency 3C: Global Connections.* Help students analyze the map by asking the questions below. Use the additional information given to enrich the discussion.

- **What interesting details do you see?**

- **What do the shaded regions represent?**

- **What can you say about the location of the ecumene?**
  The ecumene tends to be located in temperate climate zones where it is neither too hot nor too cold, too wet nor too dry. It also tends to be near coastal areas, rivers, and lakes.

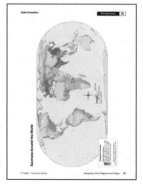

Transparency 3C

3 Have students read Section 3.10 and examine the rest of the information in the section. Then lead a discussion of these questions:

- **What climate zones are likely to be found in the global ecumene?**

- **What physical features are likely to lie outside the global ecumene?**

- **What might life be like for people who live outside the ecumene?**
  Some people live in areas that are not part of the ecumene. For example, in the Sahara there are oases, areas where water is plentiful. People can live in this desert by living near an oasis. Life outside the ecumene can be difficult, but people in these areas make adaptations in the way they live.

Processing

Have students complete Processing 3 in their Interactive Student Notebooks. Review the directions, and answer any questions they have. You might want to provide them with an outline map of your state to help facilitate this assignment.

Online Resources

For more information on settlement patterns, refer students to Online Resources for *Geography Alive! Regions and People* at www.teachtci.com.

Assessment

Masters for assessment appear on the next three pages followed by answers and scoring rubrics.

Processing 3

Assessment **3**

Mastering the Content

Shade in the oval by the letter of the best answer for each question.

1. An ecumene is a region that is well suited to permanent settlement. Which of these **best** defines Canada's ecumene?
   ○ A. the plains region
   ○ B. the border region
   ○ C. the tundra region
   ○ D. the subarctic region

2. Ice skating on a frozen canal in winter is an example of how Canadians in Ottawa have
   ○ A. created economic activity.
   ○ B. adapted to their environment.
   ○ C. celebrated their plural society.
   ○ D. preserved native peoples' culture.

3. The graph below shows the languages that are spoken in which region of Canada?

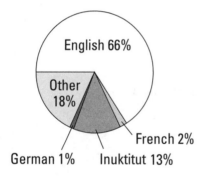

   ○ A. Core Region
   ○ B. Prairie Region
   ○ C. Pacific Region
   ○ D. Northern Region

4. Why were lighthouses first built in the Atlantic Region?
   ○ A. to store grain
   ○ B. to attract tourists
   ○ C. to generate electricity
   ○ D. to prevent shipwrecks

5. The castle-like buildings found in the Pacific Region show the influence of which of Canada's founding peoples?
   ○ A. Asian immigrants
   ○ B. British settlers
   ○ C. French colonists
   ○ D. Native Americans

6. Each person below represents one million people. Which graph represents the population of Canada's Core Region?

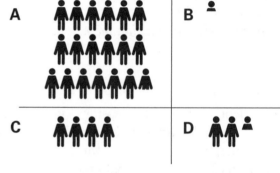

   ○ A. Graph A   ○ C. Graph C
   ○ B. Graph B   ○ D. Graph D

7. Which of these is the **main** reason why so few people live in Canada's Northern Region?
   ○ A. dense forests
   ○ B. few resources
   ○ C. harsh winters
   ○ D. rugged mountains

8. The illustration below shows buildings **most** often found in which kind of region?

   ○ A. rural
   ○ B. urban
   ○ C. mining
   ○ D. manufacturing

Applying Geography Skills:
Reading a Population Change Map

Use the map and your knowledge of geography to complete the tasks below.

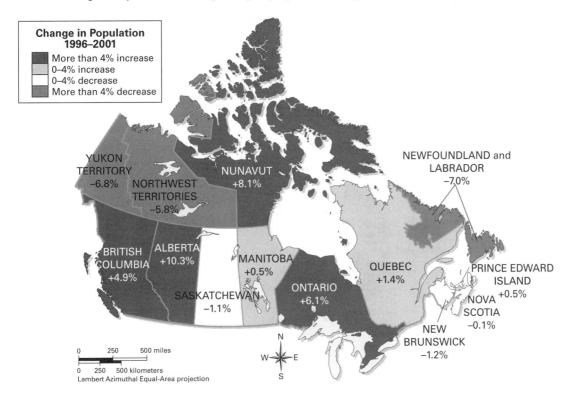

This map shows how Canada's population changed between 1996 and 2001.

1. Briefly describe two different ways this map shows that an area gained or lost people.

2. Identify the area that gained the most people as a percent of its population.

3. Identify the area that lost the most people as a percent of its population.

Test Terms Glossary

To **describe** means to provide details about something, such as how it works.

To **identify** means to name something that matches what is asked for in a task.

Exploring the Essential Question

How does where you live influence how you live?

In Chapter 3, you explored how Canadians are influenced by the region in which they live. Now you will use what you learned. Use the information below and your knowledge of geography to complete this task.

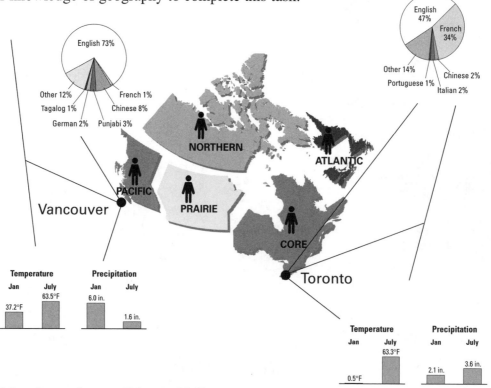

The Task: Linking Location to Ways of Life

These drawings show information about climate, languages, and economic activity in two of Canada's regions. Put yourself in one of those regions. Then answer questions about your life there.

Step 1: Choose the region you will write about. Draw a circle around the person symbol that represents you in that region.

Step 2: On a separate piece of paper, answer the following questions about your life in that region. Write your answers in complete sentences.

A. What is your name?
B. In which region do you live?
C. What language or languages do you speak at home and in school?
D. What does your family do to make a living?
E. What is the climate like where you live?
F. What do people where you live do for fun in the winter?

Writing Tips: Proper Nouns

Be sure to capitalize all proper nouns in your response. A proper noun is the name of a specific person, place, or thing. Proper nouns include these things:

• names of people
• names of places
• names of languages
• holidays
• days of the week
• months of the year

Applying Geography Skills: Sample Responses

1. This map shows population change by shading areas that gained or lost people using different amounts of shading. Also, each area is labeled with its percent gain or loss.

2. The area with the largest percentage gain was Alberta.

3. The area with the largest percentage loss was Newfoundland and Labrador.

Exploring the Essential Question: Sample Response

Step 1: Student should have drawn a circle around the person symbol in the region he or she chose to write about.

Step 2: Answers will vary depending on the student and the region chosen to write about.

A. My name is Kim Lee.
B. I live in the Pacific Region of Canada.
C. I speak Chinese at home and English in school.
D. My family works in the shipping industry. Ships from this region carry products from Canada all over the world.
E. The climate in this region is warmer than in most of Canada. Most days are cool, and there is a lot of rain.
F. A lot of people like to ski in the winter. Some people go surfing. I like to play ice hockey.

Mastering the Content Answer Key

1. B	2. B	3. D	4. D
5. B	6. A	7. C	8. A

Applying Geography Skills Scoring Rubric

Score	General Description
2	Student responds to all parts of the task. Response is correct and clear.
1	Student responds to some parts of the task. Response is mostly correct.
0	Response does not match the task or is incorrect.

Exploring the Essential Question Scoring Rubric

Score	General Description
3	Student responds to all parts of the task. Response is correct, clear, and supported by details.
2	Student responds to most or all parts of the task. Response is generally correct but may lack details.
1	Student responds to at least one part of the task. Response may contain errors and lack details.
0	Response does not match the task or is incorrect.

Cut out each half of the map along the dashed lines. Tape the two pieces together to create your game board.

The Five Regions of Canada

UNITED STATES

YUKON TERRITORY

NORTHWEST TERRITORIES

• Whitehorse

NORTHERN REGION

Great Bear Lake

NUNAVUT

PACIFIC REGION

Great Slave Lake

140°W

50°N

Lake Athabasca

Fort St. John •

Churchill •

ALBERTA

MANITOBA

BRITISH COLUMBIA

PRAIRIE REGION

PACIFIC OCEAN

Lake Winnipeg

• Vancouver

• Calgary

SASKATCHEWAN

N
W E
S

130°W

UNITED STATES

0   250   500 miles

0   250   500 kilometers

Lambert Azimuthal Equal-Area projection

Game Pieces for Round 1: Population

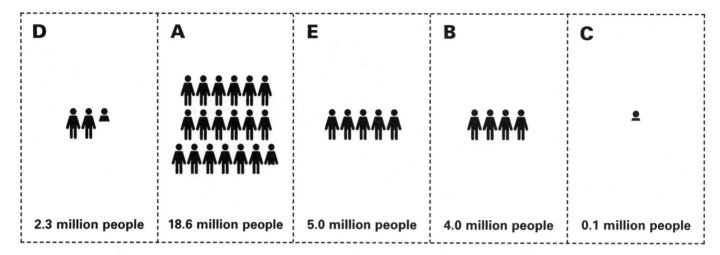

D	A	E	B	C
2.3 million people	18.6 million people	5.0 million people	4.0 million people	0.1 million people

Game Pieces for Round 2: Language

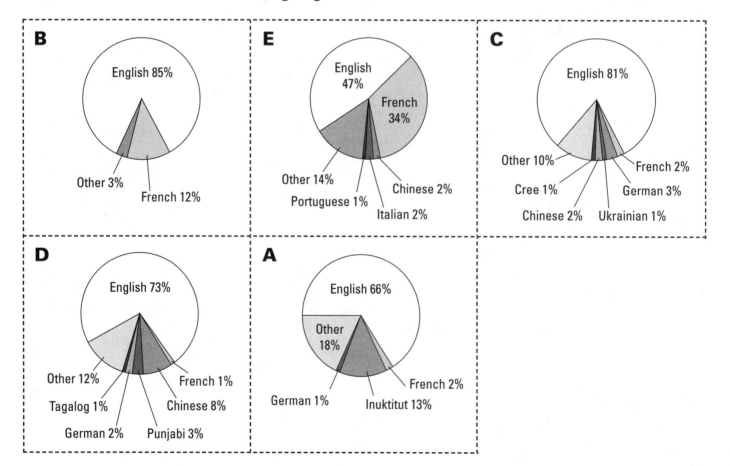

B
English 85%
Other 3%
French 12%

E
English 47%
French 34%
Other 14%
Portuguese 1%
Italian 2%
Chinese 2%

C
English 81%
Other 10%
Cree 1%
Chinese 2%
Ukrainian 1%
German 3%
French 2%

D
English 73%
Other 12%
Tagalog 1%
German 2%
Punjabi 3%
Chinese 8%
French 1%

A
English 66%
Other 18%
German 1%
Inuktitut 13%
French 2%

Game Pieces for Round 3: Climate

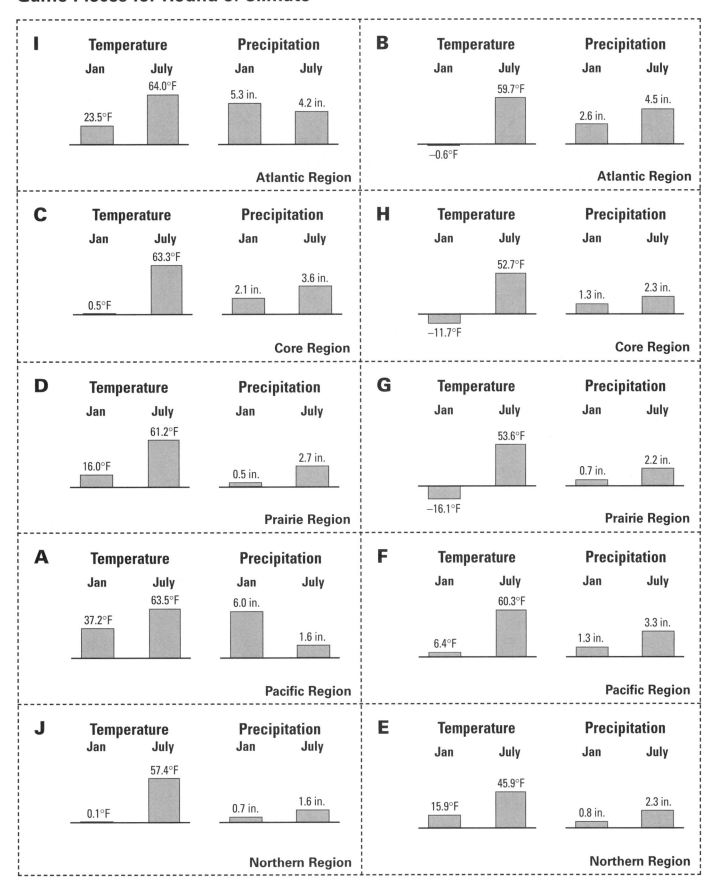

I

Temperature
Jan   July
                    64.0°F
23.5°F

Precipitation
Jan   July
5.3 in.
                    4.2 in.

Atlantic Region

B

Temperature
Jan   July
                    59.7°F
−0.6°F

Precipitation
Jan   July
                    4.5 in.
2.6 in.

Atlantic Region

C

Temperature
Jan   July
                    63.3°F
0.5°F

Precipitation
Jan   July
2.1 in.   3.6 in.

Core Region

H

Temperature
Jan   July
                    52.7°F
−11.7°F

Precipitation
Jan   July
1.3 in.   2.3 in.

Core Region

D

Temperature
Jan   July
                    61.2°F
16.0°F

Precipitation
Jan   July
0.5 in.   2.7 in.

Prairie Region

G

Temperature
Jan   July
                    53.6°F
−16.1°F

Precipitation
Jan   July
0.7 in.   2.2 in.

Prairie Region

A

Temperature
Jan   July
                    63.5°F
37.2°F

Precipitation
Jan   July
6.0 in.
                    1.6 in.

Pacific Region

F

Temperature
Jan   July
                    60.3°F
6.4°F

Precipitation
Jan   July
1.3 in.   3.3 in.

Pacific Region

J

Temperature
Jan   July
                    57.4°F
0.1°F

Precipitation
Jan   July
0.7 in.   1.6 in.

Northern Region

E

Temperature
Jan   July
                    45.9°F
15.9°F

Precipitation
Jan   July
0.8 in.   2.3 in.

Northern Region

Game Pieces for Round 4: Buildings

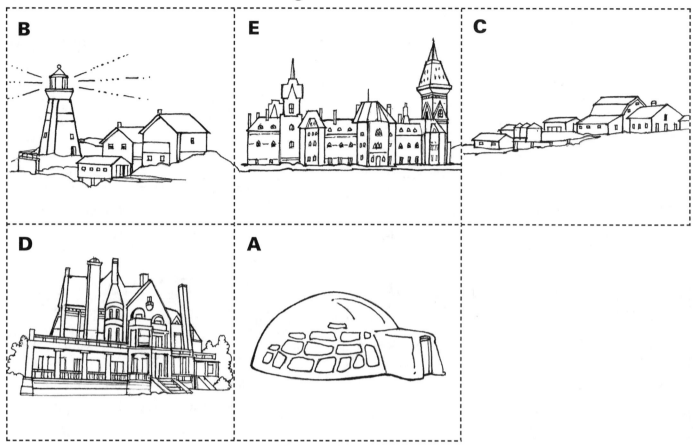

B   **E**   **C**

D   **A**

Game Pieces for Round 5: Economic Activity

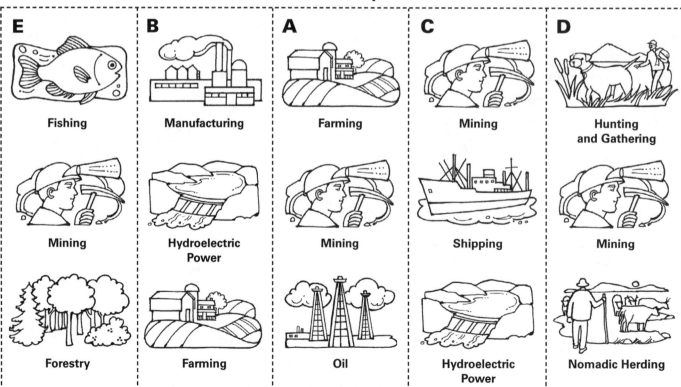

E	B	A	C	D
Fishing	Manufacturing	Farming	Mining	Hunting and Gathering
Mining	Hydroelectric Power	Mining	Shipping	Mining
Forestry	Farming	Oil	Hydroelectric Power	Nomadic Herding

Population in the Five Regions of Canada

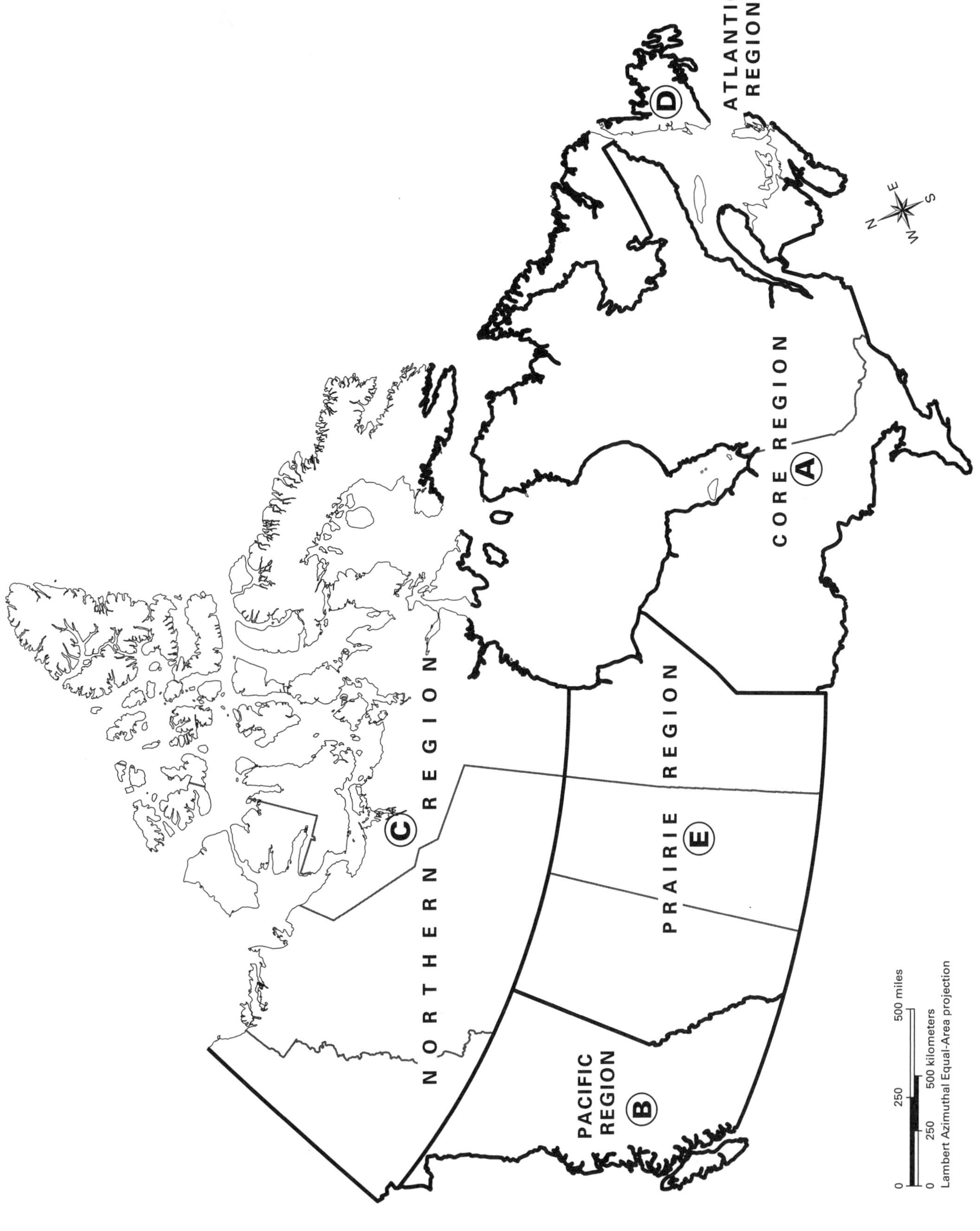

ATLANTIC REGION

(D)

CORE REGION

(A)

NORTHERN REGION

(C)

PRAIRIE REGION

(E)

PACIFIC REGION

(B)

500 miles

500 kilometers

Lambert Azimuthal Equal-Area projection

250

250

0

0

Languages in the Five Regions of Canada

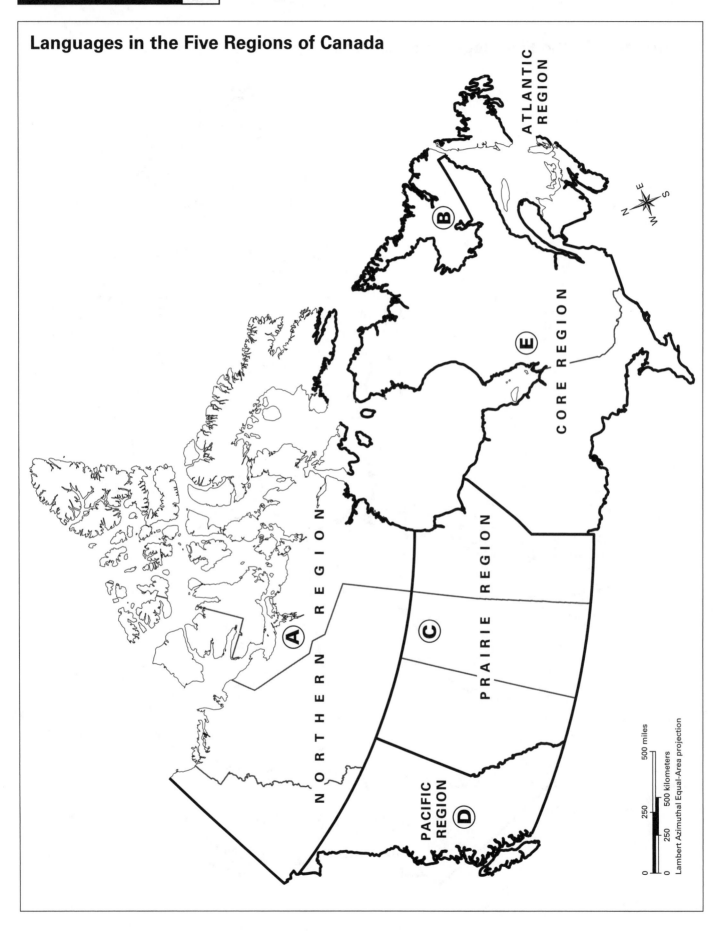

Climate in the Five Regions of Canada

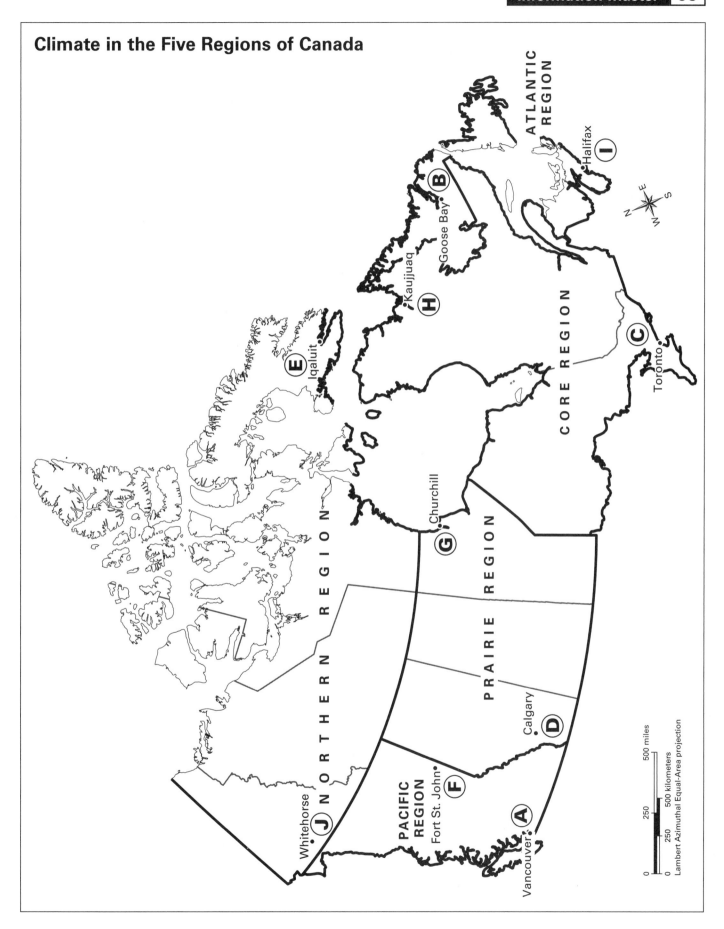

Buildings in the Five Regions of Canada

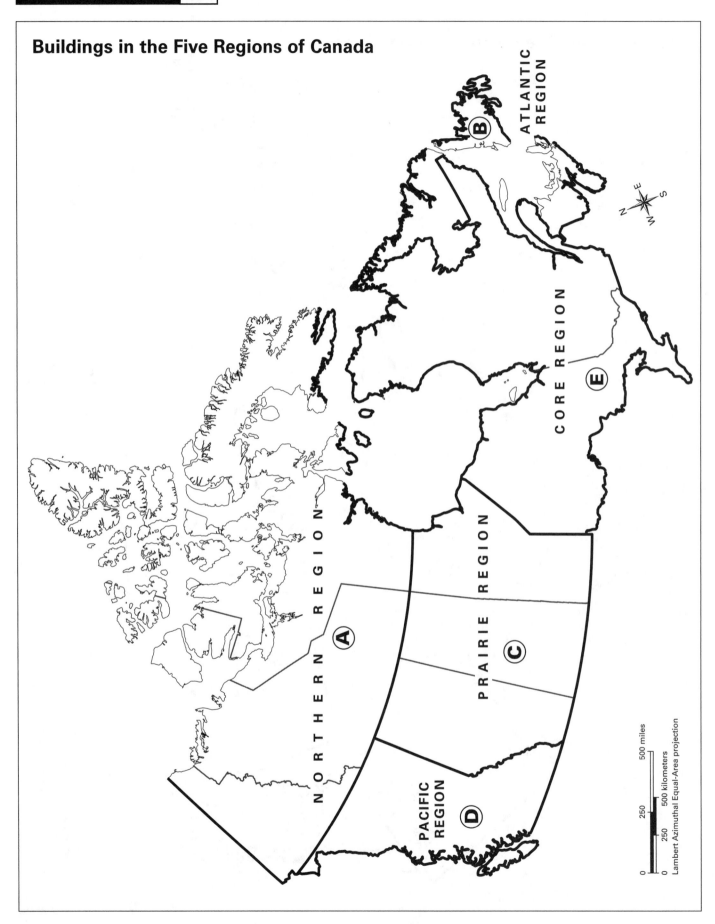

Economic Activity in the Five Regions of Canada

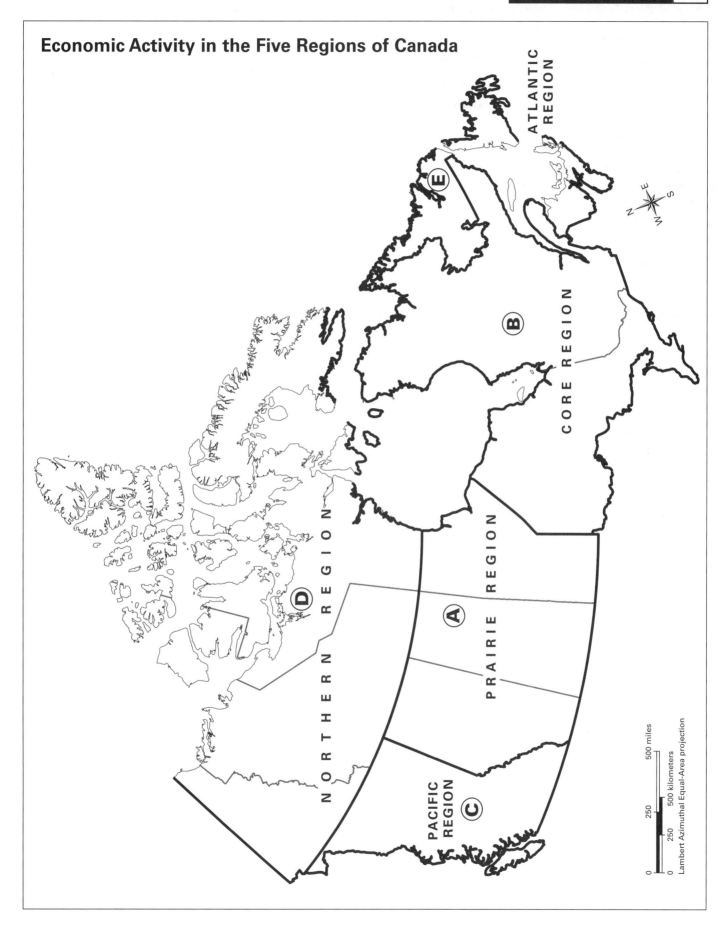

Take notes after each round of the game. Follow these directions:

1. Read the section of your book on that topic.
2. For each of Canada's five regions, record two or more key aspects of life you learned about that topic.

Pacific Region

Population: 4 million; most people live in or near Victoria or Vancouver or on the western slopes of the Rockies; high Asian population

Language: English is most people's first language; Asian languages such as Chinese, Punjabi, and Tagalog are also spoken

Climate: marine west coast along the coast; colder in the Rocky Mountains; winter surfing is a popular sport

Buildings: strong British influence; some buildings look almost like castles

Economic activity: farming and forestry are important, but mining, shipping, and hydroelectric power are the largest industries

Prairie Region

Population: 5 million; fast-growing area; Edmonton and Calgary are the largest cities

Language: English is the first language of most people; French, German, and Ukrainian are also spoken

Climate: semiarid to humid continental in the south, subarctic in the north; polar bears migrate through Churchill every year

Buildings: farms in the southern region; barns with silos to store grain

Economic activity: farming (half of all of Canada's farm products), mining (more than half of all minerals in Canada), and oil (oil sands)

Northern Region

Population: 100,000 people; largest land area, smallest population; costly to live in because it's so far from other places

Language: most people speak English as their first language; many Inuit continue to speak Inuktitut

Climate: tundra in the north, subarctic in the south; all-terrain vehicles are popular as transportation; dog sled racing is a popular sport

The Five Regions of Canada

Buildings: traditionally, some Inuit made winter igloos from snow blocks; today most have houses made from kits

Economic activity: hunting and gathering, nomadic herding, mining, government work

Atlantic Region

Population: 2.3 million; first areas of European settlement; population is declining because fishing restrictions limit jobs

Language: most people speak English; some people speak French

Climate: mild, humid continental climate; wet winters; ice hockey was born here

Buildings: 275 lighthouses in operation on the coastline

Economic activity: fishing (declining), farming (limited), and forestry

Core Region

Population: 18.6 million; most Canadians live here; three largest cities are Toronto, Montreal, and capital city of Ottawa; many jobs here

Language: in Ontario, most people speak English; in Quebec, most speak French; both are official languages of Canada; Chinese, Italian, and Portuguese are also spoken

Climate: humid continental climate in the south; colder with less rain in the north; Winterlude held in February

Buildings: British and French influences; Gothic revival style; large stone buildings with tall, pointed windows

Economic activity: manufacturing, farming (a third of all of Canada's farm products), and hydroelectric power

Iqaluit

Kuujjuaq

Goose Bay

NEWFOUNDLAND & LABRADOR

QUEBEC

PRINCE EDWARD ISLAND

ONTARIO

ATLANTIC REGION

CORE REGION

Halifax

NOVA SCOTIA

NEW BRUNSWICK

Toronto

N
E
W
S

The Great Lakes: The U.S. and Canada's Freshwater Treasures

Overview

In this lesson, students learn about the Great Lakes, including environmental threats to this freshwater ecosystem and efforts to manage the lakes. In a **Writing for Understanding** activity, students analyze data that illustrate the state of the Great Lakes today, such as bald eagle numbers, wetland areas remaining, and pollution levels. They then debate the data from the perspective of "Great Lakes Boosters" and "Great Lakes Doomers." Students apply what they've learned by writing an editorial about the lakes' current status and future prospects.

Objectives

Students will

- define and explain the importance of these key geographic terms: *ecosystem, food chain, food web, freshwater, watershed.*
- evaluate the environmental health and management of the Great Lakes freshwater ecosystem.
- examine the environmental challenges facing global freshwater ecosystems and the impending crisis in freshwater supplies.

Materials

- *Geography Alive! Regions and People*
- Interactive Student Notebooks
- Transparencies 4A–4C
- Placards 4A–4F (2 sets)
- Station Materials 4A–4C (2 copies of each)
- Information Masters 4A and 4B (1 transparency of each)
- Student Handout 4 (1 per student)
- CD Tracks 2 and 3

Preview

1 Introduce the game *Where in the World Is This?* Ask students to gather in a semicircle around the screen with a sheet of paper and a pencil. Explain that they will now play a game called *Where in the World Is This?* The goal is to guess the geographic location of a photograph you will project, with the fewest number of clues. Explain the rules: You will read 10 facts about the location, one at a time. After each fact, students will have an opportunity to write down their guess of the photograph's location. If they think they know the location, they are to write down the fact number and their guess and then fold their papers in half. Blurting out answers is not allowed. Each student may write only one guess, and once an answer has been recorded it may not be changed. The student or students who correctly guess the location with the fewest facts win the game.

2 Play the game. Play CD Track 2, "Great Lakes Sound Effects," and project *Transparency 4A: Where in the World Is This?* Read the facts below one at a time, and monitor students as they record their guesses.

Transparency 4A

- *Fact 1:* This feature has more than 11,000 miles of coastline. This distance is almost half Earth's circumference.
- *Fact 2:* This feature contains 35,000 islands.
- *Fact 3:* This feature is young. It took its present form just 3,000 years ago.
- *Fact 4:* This feature is 1,200 miles across at its widest point.
- *Fact 5:* At its deepest point, this feature is 1,333 feet deep.
- *Fact 6:* This feature is the size of Scandinavia (Norway, Sweden, Finland, and Denmark).
- *Fact 7:* One of every 4 Canadians and 1 of every 10 Americans live near this feature.
- *Fact 8:* One U.S. state near this feature has more lighthouses than any other state.
- *Fact 9:* This feature holds nearly 20% of the world's fresh water and 90% of the fresh water in the entire United States—a total of 6 quadrillion gallons! That amount of water could cover the entire United States to a depth of nearly 10 feet.
- *Fact 10:* The cities of Green Bay, Milwaukee, Chicago, Detroit, Cleveland, Buffalo, Hamilton, and Toronto all sit along this feature's shores.

3 Debrief the game. Reveal the correct answer: the Great Lakes. Then ask,

• How many of you wrote down an incorrect answer? What facts led you to reach a false conclusion?

• How many of you wrote down the correct answer? What facts helped you to reach the right answer?

• What facts surprised you about the Great Lakes?

• What do you now know about the Great Lakes that you didn't know before?

4 Explain the connection between the game and the upcoming activity. Tell students that in the upcoming activity they will study the Great Lakes, one of Earth's most distinctive and important physical features. Millions of people from two nations—plus thousands of animal and plant species—depend on the water in these lakes. Fresh water is essential to the survival of the human species. Unfortunately, it has often been a victim of human activity. Today, freshwater ecosystems are threatened by air and water pollutants and the increasing demands of billions of people around the world. Fortunately, many thoughtful people are asking the same question—the Essential Question for this lesson: *How can people best use and protect Earth's freshwater ecosystems?* A study of the Great Lakes has much to teach us about how to answer that question.

5 Have students complete Preview 4. Put students in mixed-ability pairs, and have them open their Interactive Student Notebooks to Preview 4. Project *Transparency 4B: Map and Profile of the Great Lakes,* and review the directions with them. When they have finished, use Transparency 4B and the following information to review the answers to the questions:

• *Preview page 1:* Lake Superior is the largest Great Lake; Lake Ontario is the smallest. Eight U.S. states and one Canadian province border the lakes. The United States controls more of the Great Lakes. The distance from the St. Lawrence to Duluth, as the crow flies, is about 800 miles.

• *Preview page 2:* Lake Superior is the deepest Great Lake; Lake Erie is the shallowest. Water flows from Lake Superior into the St. Lawrence River and out to the Atlantic because of the drop in elevation. People could probably most quickly pollute Lake Erie because it is relatively small and shallow.

Transparency 4B

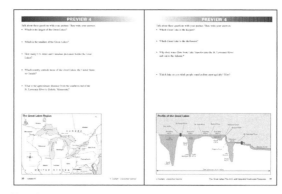

Preview 4

Essential Question and Geoterms

1 Introduce Chapter 4 in *Geography Alive! Regions and People.* Explain that in this chapter, students will learn about the uses and management of the Great Lakes ecosystem. Have them read Section 4.1. Then ask them to identify two details in the satellite photograph of the Great Lakes that relate to what they just read.

2 Introduce the Graphic Organizer and the Essential Question. Have students examine the illustration of how people use the Great Lakes. Then ask,

- What do you see?
- What are some of the ways people use the Great Lakes?
- How might these uses affect the Great Lakes ecosystem?

Have students read the accompanying text. Make sure they understand the Essential Question, *How can people best use and protect Earth's freshwater ecosystems?* You may want to post the Essential Question in the room or write it on the board for the duration of the activity.

3 Have students read Section 4.2. Then have them work individually or in pairs to complete Geoterms 4 in their Interactive Student Notebooks. Ask them to share their answers with another student, or have volunteers share their answers with the class.

Geoterms 4

Writing for Understanding

1 Prepare the classroom. Post *Placards 4A–4F* and *Station Materials 4A–4C* on the walls to create six stations around the room. Set up two of each of these three stations:

- *Pollution:* Post Placards 4A and 4B and Station Materials 4A at each station.
- *Invasive Species:* Post Placards 4C and 4D and Station Materials 4B at each station.
- *Habitat Loss:* Post Placards 4E and 4F and Station Materials 4C at each station.

Space the items at each station about two feet apart to accommodate two or three pairs of students at a station.

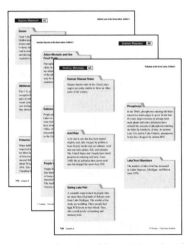

Station Materials 4A–4C

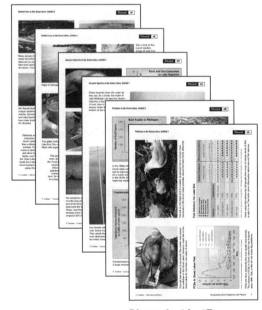

Placards 4A–4F

2 Introduce students to the context of the activity. Have students read the opening paragraph of Section 4.3 in *Geography Alive! Regions and People*. Then play CD Track 3, "The Sad State of Our Once-Great Lakes," as students follow along with the simulated news article in Section 4.3. When the recording ends, ask these questions:

- What problems did the Great Lakes face in 1969?
- How did the condition of the lakes get so bad?
- What actions might people have taken to better manage the lakes? Do you think any of these actions were taken?
- Do you think the Great Lakes are better or worse off today?

3 Have teams conduct research in preparation for the debate. Follow these steps:

- Project a transparency of *Information Master 4A: Preparing for a Debate*. Review the instructions for how students will conduct their investigation of the Great Lakes to prepare for the debate that follows. (**Note:** You may want to leave the directions projected for the duration of the investigation.)

- Assign half of the class to be "Boosters" and half to be "Doomers." Then divide each team into pairs to conduct their research.

- Emphasize that every student will be responsible for helping their team to do their best in the debate. Their goal should be to quickly and thoroughly gather a variety of evidence to support their side during the debate.

- Assign one third of the pairs to begin with each of the three topics—pollution, invasive species, and habitat loss. (**Note:** Based on students' skill level and the amount of time you have allotted for the activity, decide how long to give students to gather evidence. To save classroom time, you might have students read Sections 4.4, 4.5, and 4.6 individually or ahead of time rather than during the preparation for the debate.)

- Have pairs conduct their investigation by reading each section (Section 4.4, 4.5, or 4.6), visiting the related station ("Pollution," "Invasive Species," or "Habitat Loss"), and taking notes in the appropriate section of Reading Notes 4. When they reach the T-chart in each Reading Notes section, they should focus on recording evidence that will support their team's arguments during the upcoming debate.

Information Master 4A

Reading Notes 4

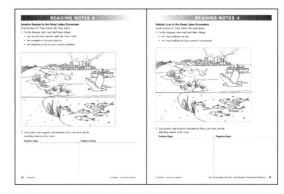

Reading Notes 4

4 Conduct and moderate the debate. When students have finished their research, project a transparency of *Information Master 4B: Participating in a Debate*. Review the instructions for how the two teams will debate the state of the Great Lakes, including the rules for the debate. Elect a team captain for each side, and conduct the debate. (**Note:** You might have teams come to the debate with a simple sign featuring a slogan, such as, "The Great Lakes Are in Great Shape!" or "The Great Lakes Are a Great Mess!" They could also chant the slogans at the beginning of the debate. You may want to leave the directions projected for the duration of the debate.)

Information Master 4B

5 Debrief the debate. Ask students,

- Step outside your role. Which side do *you* believe made the best arguments?
- What can be said about the state of the Great Lakes today?
- How do people affect freshwater ecosystems in positive ways?
- How do people affect freshwater ecosystems in negative ways?
- What lessons can we learn about what to do and what not to do to protect and preserve Earth's freshwater resources?

6 Have students gather information to prepare to write an editorial about the Great Lakes. Form groups of four students, each with representatives from both sides of the debate. Have groups share information to complete Reading Notes 4 so that every student has both positive and negative information on the state of the Great Lakes to use in their editorials. Everyone should have at least three pieces of evidence on both sides for each of the three pages of Reading Notes.

7 Distribute *Student Handout 4: Writing an Editorial* to each student. Explain that students will use their Reading Notes to create an editorial on the state of the Great Lakes. Review the guidelines, and have students create their editorials.

Student Handout 4

Global Connections

1 Introduce the Global Connections. Have students read Section 4.7. Tell them that they will now see how some of the issues they encountered in the activity play out on a global scale.

2 Project *Transparency 4C: Global Connections.* Help students analyze the maps by asking,

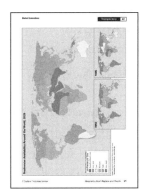

Transparency 4C

- **What are these maps about?**

- **What do the colored regions represent?**

- **What story do these maps tell?**

- **Which world regions had an abundance of fresh water in 1995? Which had a freshwater shortage in 1995? Which regions will face shortages in the future?**

- **What factors account for a shortage of fresh water?** *Climate, lack of water-collection technologies, and population growth are the key factors that account for a shortage of fresh water.*

3 Have students read Section 4.8 and examine the rest of the information in the section. Then lead a discussion of these questions:

- **What additional concerns did the reading raise?**

- **How can people best use and manage the world's freshwater resources?**

Processing

There is no Processing assignment for this activity. The editorial functions as a Processing assignment.

Online Resources

For more information on the Great Lakes region, refer students to Online Resources for *Geography Alive! Regions and People* at www.teachtci.com.

Assessment

Masters for assessment appear on the next three pages followed by answers and scoring rubrics.

Mastering the Content

Shade in the oval by the letter of the best answer for each question.

1. How were the Great Lakes created?
   - ○ A. by the clearing of forests
   - ○ B. by the damming of rivers
   - ○ C. by the melting of glaciers
   - ○ D. by the shrinking of oceans

2. Which of these terms is **best** defined as a geographic area that includes all of the rivers and streams that flow into a lake or sea?
   - ○ A. basin
   - ○ B. landmass
   - ○ C. plateau
   - ○ D. watershed

3. Read the description below. Then decide which of the terms below **best** fits what is being described.

   Insects feed on the algae and plants that grow in the Great Lakes. Tiny fish eat the insects. Larger fish feed on the small fish. Eagles and otters eat the larger fish.

   - ○ A. Great Lakes habitat
   - ○ B. Great Lakes watershed
   - ○ C. Great Lakes food chain
   - ○ D. Great Lakes freshwater ecosystem

4. Which of the following suffered **most** from DDT poisoning in the Great Lakes region?
   - ○ A. fish-eating birds
   - ○ B. large fish
   - ○ D. small fish
   - ○ D. tiny organisms

5. The sea lamprey and zebra mussel are part of which of these Great Lakes ecosystem problems?
   - ○ A. wetland loss
   - ○ B. invasive species
   - ○ C. algae explosions
   - ○ D. point-source pollution

6. Which of the following conclusions about Michigan is **best** supported by the graph below?

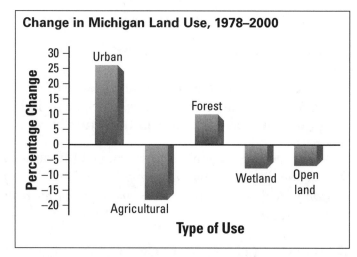

   - ○ A. Housing areas are expanding.
   - ○ B. Dairy farms are a leading industry.
   - ○ C. The lumber industry is shrinking.
   - ○ D. Wetlands are becoming more polluted.

7. What is the **main** difference between point-source and non-point-source pollution?
   - ○ A. how toxic the pollution is
   - ○ B. where the pollution comes from
   - ○ C. what time of year the pollution occurs
   - ○ D. what animals are harmed by the pollution

8. Which of these is a **major** reason for a growing water shortage in many countries?
   - ○ A. habitat loss
   - ○ B. invasive species
   - ○ C. shrinking glaciers
   - ○ D. population growth

Applying Geography Skills:
Reading a Fish Advisory Table

Use the fish advisory table and your knowledge of geography to complete the tasks below.

Fish Advisory for Lake Erie

Legend:
- ▲ Unlimited consumption
- ▼ One meal per week
- ● One meal per month
- ■ Six meals per year
- ◆ Do not eat these fish.

Species	Contaminants	General Population – Length (inches)									Women and Children – Length (inches)								
		6–8	8–10	10–12	12–14	14–18	18–22	22–26	26–30	30+	6–8	8–10	10–12	12–14	14–18	18–22	22–26	26–30	30+
Carp, Catfish	PCBs, Dioxins	◆	◆	◆	◆	◆	◆	◆	◆	◆	◆	◆	◆	◆	◆	◆	◆	◆	◆
Chinook Salmon	PCBs			▲	▲	▲	▲	▲	▲	▲			●	●	●	●	●	●	●
Coho Salmon	PCBs			▲	▲	▲	▲	▲	▲	▲			●	●	●	●	●	●	●
Freshwater Drum	PCBs	▲	▲	▲	▲	▲	▲	▲	▲	▲	▼	▼	▼	▼	▼	▼	▼	▼	▼
Lake Trout	PCBs			▲	▲	▲	▲	▲	▲	▲			■	■	■	■	■	■	■

Great Lakes fish advisories tell people how much of certain fish can be safely eaten. Answer the following questions based on this information.

1. Which kind of fish is unsafe for anyone to eat?

2. Which kind of fish is safe for most adults but should not be eaten by children and women more than six times a year?

3. Which fish are safe for *everyone* to eat if limited to one meal a week?

4. Based on this chart, what conclusion can you draw about the safety of eating fish from Lake Erie?

Test Terms Glossary
A **conclusion** is a judgment reached after looking at the facts.

Assessment | **4**

Exploring the Essential Question

How can people best use and protect Earth's freshwater ecosystems?

In Chapter 4, you explored what has happened to the Great Lakes freshwater ecosystem. Now you will use what you learned. Use the information on the diagram below and your knowledge of geography to complete this task.

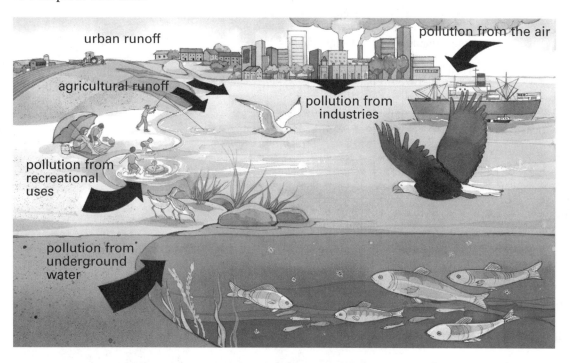

The Task: Creating a Great Lakes Pollution Billboard

This diagram shows many sources of water pollution in the Great Lakes watershed. Use it to design a billboard that shows one thing people can do to protect this freshwater ecosystem.

Step 1: Choose one source of pollution to show in your billboard. Circle your choice on the diagram.

Step 2: Think of one thing people might do to help reduce that source of pollution. Write your idea here:

Step 3: On another sheet of paper, design a billboard that shows your idea about reducing water pollution. Your billboard should have these things:

A. images or words that identify the pollution source you circled
B. images or words that communicate your idea for reducing pollution

Design Tips
A billboard should be so simple that people can get the message as they drive by at high speeds. Get your point across quickly using large images and as few words as possible.

Applying Geography Skills: Sample Responses

1. Carp/catfish is unsafe for anyone to eat.
2. Lake trout are safe for most adults but should not be eaten by children and women more than six times a year.
3. Freshwater drum are safe for everyone to eat if limited to one meal a week.
4. People should be very careful about eating fish from Lake Erie because many are polluted with toxic chemicals such as PCBs and dioxins.

Exploring the Essential Question: Sample Response

Step 1: Student should circle one source of pollution on the diagram. Example: Agricultural runoff

Step 2: Student should think of one thing people might do to help reduce that source of pollution, such as:
- use fewer pesticides on crops
- water less to reduce runoff

Step 3: Designs will vary but should clearly identify one source of pollution and one way such pollution might be reduced.

Mastering the Content Answer Key

1. C	2. D	3. C	4. A
5. B	6. A	7. B	8. D

Applying Geography Skills Scoring Rubric

Score	General Description
2	Student responds to all parts of the task. Response is correct and clear.
1	Student responds to some parts of the task. Response is mostly correct.
0	Response does not match the task or is incorrect.

Exploring the Essential Question Scoring Rubric

Score	General Description
3	Student responds to all parts of the task. Response is correct, clear, and supported by details.
2	Student responds to most or all parts of the task. Response is generally correct but may lack details.
1	Student responds to at least one part of the task. Response may contain errors and lack details.
0	Response does not match the task or is incorrect.

Human Disease Rates

Human disease rates in the Great Lakes region are pretty similar to those in other parts of the country.

Phosphorus

In the 1960s, phosphorus entering the lakes caused too much algae to grow. In the last 20 years, improvements in sewage treatment plants and other industries have reduced the amount of phosphorus entering the lakes by hundreds of tons. In western Lake Erie and in Lake Ontario, phosphorus levels have dropped by almost 80%.

Acid Rain

Acid rain is rain that has been turned slightly acid, like vinegar, by pollution from factory smoke and car exhaust. Acid rain can harm plants, fish, and animals. The United States and Canada have made progress in reducing acid rain. Since 1980, the air pollution that causes acid rain has dropped by more than 35%.

Lake Trout Numbers

The number of lake trout has increased in Lakes Superior, Michigan, and Huron since 1970.

Eating Lake Fish

A scientific study looked at people who ate more than 24 pounds of fish per year from Lake Michigan. The results of the study are troubling. These people had high PCB levels in their blood. They also scored poorly on learning and memory tests.

Zebra Mussels and the Food Chain

Phytoplankton form the base of the food chain in the Great Lakes. Some people are afraid that zebra mussels eat too much of the phytoplankton in the lakes. They may be taking food away from other creatures.

Chubs, Ducks, and Zebra Mussels

By the early 1950s, a fish called the *silver chub* was nearly extinct. Now their numbers are increasing. They love to eat zebra mussels. Some birds—like diving ducks—also eat zebra mussels. Their numbers are rising too. Zebra mussels can accumulate toxic chemicals at a rate 300,000 times higher than concentrations in the environment. These chemicals become more concentrated in animals as they move up the food chain.

Salmon

People put Pacific salmon in the Great Lakes to replace native fish species that were lost to the sea lamprey. The salmon have done very well. According to the Office of the Great Lakes, this was a successful introduction of a new species in the Great Lakes ecosystem.

Sea Lampreys

Sea lampreys kill more lake trout today than commercial fishing and sport fishing combined.

Purple Loosestrife

Purple loosestrife is an invasive plant that hurts the Great Lakes ecosystem. It is being successfully controlled with the introduction of the Galerucella beetle. The beetle eats the roots, stems, and flowers of the plant.

Dunes

Great Lakes sand dunes are in trouble. Habitat destruction from the building of homes and businesses is the biggest threat to them. Sand mining also affects them. And recreational use by people walking and driving off-road vehicles damages vegetation and erodes the sand dunes.

Restoration Projects

The Great Lakes Coastal Program supports projects that help the ecosystem. In 2001, projects under this program restored or protected more than 900 acres of coastal habitat. This helps local fish and wildlife immensely.

Wetlands

The U.S. and Canadian governments recognize the value of wetlands. The pace of wetland loss has declined in recent years. Builders must now create new wetland to replace the acres that they destroy.

Great Lakes Habitats

Some Great Lakes habitats are found nowhere else in the world. The lakes are home to more than 100 rare plants and animals. These include tiny prairie flowers and enormous sturgeon.

Fisheries on the Great Lakes

Water habitats in the Great Lakes have improved since 1970. Commercial fishers there catch about 110 million pounds of fish every year. The Canadian commercial fishery in Lake Erie caught about 50 million pounds of fish in 1991. This brought in about 59 million Canadian dollars.

Prepare for a Debate on the State of the Great Lakes Today

Follow these steps to prepare for a debate on the state of the Great Lakes:

Step 1: Learn about your role. Your teacher will assign you one of two roles for the debate:

Great Lakes Booster: You work to promote the natural beauty and clean environment of the Great Lakes region. Your job is to attract businesses and visitors to the area. You believe that the Great Lakes have improved since 1969. You have very few concerns about the lakes. You love any good news about them. You tend to downplay or disregard any bad news about them.

Great Lakes Doomer: You volunteer for a citizens group. The group raises awareness about the environmental problems in the Great Lakes watershed. Every chance you get, you speak at public gatherings. You talk to public agencies and school groups. You are saddened by the current state of the lakes. You believe that the lakes are in grave danger. You are alarmed by any bad news about the lakes. You tend to downplay or disregard any good news about them.

Step 2: Gather evidence for the debate. Three stations in the room contain evidence about the state of the Great Lakes today. For each station, read the matching section (Section 4.4, 4.5, or 4.6) of *Geography Alive! Regions and People*. Record evidence you find on the appropriate page of Reading Notes 4. For example, when you visit the "Pollution" station, you will record evidence in Section 4.4 of your Reading Notes, which is devoted to pollution. The more useful evidence you record, the better your team will do during the debate.

Participate in a Debate on the State of the Great Lakes Today

Follow these steps to participate in a debate on the state of the
Great Lakes:

Step 1: Arrange the room. Place desks on opposite sides of the room
so that the two teams are facing each other.

Step 2: Learn the rules of the debate.
- *Rule 1:* Students must raise their hands if they wish to speak. They
  may speak only when called on by the teacher.
- *Rule 2:* Students may present only one piece of evidence each time
  they are called on.
- *Rule 3:* Your team will receive 1 point for each solid and relevant piece
  of evidence you present. Your teacher will decide if the evidence
  deserves a point. Your team will lose 1 point for arguing with the
  teacher or for repeating evidence. Listen carefully!
- *Rule 4:* Your team will receive 10 bonus points if every student on
  the team presents at least once.
- *Rule 5:* Students may pass notes with evidence written on them to
  others on their team.
- *Rule 6:* Teams may call two 3-minute breaks to gather additional
  information, share information, or talk about strategy. The team
  captain decides when to call them.

Step 3: Debate the state of the Great Lakes today. Listen to the
following debate questions as your teacher reads them. After each
question, your teacher will ask students on each team to present evidence
about the question. Debate according to the rules.

Debate Question 1: How well are people managing the effects of
pollution on the Great Lakes watershed?

Debate Question 2: How well are people managing invasive species in
the Great Lakes watershed?

Debate Question 3: How well are people protecting Great Lakes habitat?

Write an Editorial About the State of the Great Lakes

Take on the role of a Canadian or U.S. scientist living along the shores of the Great Lakes. You want to raise awareness about the condition of the lakes. You decide to write an editorial.

Use your book and your Reading Notes to help you. Your editorial must have these things:

- a headline that shows your point of view about the state of the Great Lakes
- 250 to 500 words
- these five sections:

  Introduction: Tell who you are, where you live, and why you are qualified to write the editorial.

  Paragraph 2: Make your case for how serious the problem of pollution is in the Great Lakes.

  Paragraph 3: Make your case for how serious the invasive species problem is in the Great Lakes.

  Paragraph 4: Make your case for how serious the loss of habitat is in the Great Lakes.

  Conclusion: End your editorial with five points under the heading "What Should Be Done." Explain what you think should be done to preserve and protect the Great Lakes ecosystem.

Pollution in the Great Lakes Ecosystem

Read Section 4.4. Then follow the steps below.

1. On the diagram, draw and label these things:

   - two examples of point-source pollution sewage treatment plant, industrial discharge

   - one example of non-point-source pollution runoff, toxic dumps, air pollution, sediment

   - two ways that pollution is still a problem in the Great Lakes runoff, toxic dumps, air pollution, toxic sediments

2. List positive and negative information from your book and the matching station in the room.

Positive Signs Possible answers:	**Negative Signs** Possible answers:
• The Cuyahoga River stopped being flammable. • Algae growth in the lakes was reduced. • The lakes turned blue again. • PCBs and DDT declined in the food chain. • The bald eagle made a comeback.	• Non-point-source pollution is still a serious problem. • Toxic waste dumps contain poisons that get in the water. • Pollution from the air, like mercury, still pollutes the lakes. • Toxic sediments are another source of pollution.

Invasive Species in the Great Lakes Ecosystem

Read Section 4.5. Then follow the steps below.

1. On the diagram, draw and label these things:

   - one way invasive species enter the Great Lakes ballast water from ships, hitching rides on ships
   - two examples of invasive species sea lamprey, Asian carp, zebra mussels, alewife
   - two solutions to the invasive species problem treat ballast water, barriers to nonnative species, stock lakes with predators of invasive species

2. List positive and negative information from your book and the matching station in the room.

Positive Signs Possible answers:	**Negative Signs** Possible answers:
• Regulations on ballast water keep invasive species out.	• There are over 170 invasive species in the Great Lakes.
• Barriers keep invasive species out.	• Invasive species have already damaged the Great Lakes ecosystem.
• Governments have introduced new species, like the Pacific salmon, to control invasive species.	• The Asian carp threatens to invade the lakes.
• Alewife numbers are down.	
• Native fish are beginning to recover.	

Habitat Loss in the Great Lakes Ecosystem

Read Section 4.6. Then follow the steps below.

1. On the diagram, draw and label these things:

   • two ways habitat was lost farms, logging, factories, cities, development

   • two ways habitat has been restored or protected low-impact logging,
     replanting, creating nature preserves

2. List positive and negative information from your book and the
   matching station in the room.

Positive Signs Possible answers:	**Negative Signs** Possible answers:
• Timber companies now use practices that are not as harmful.	• Almost half of the original forests of the Great Lakes are gone.
• Great Lakes forests are now expanding instead of shrinking.	• More people are moving to the Great Lakes, putting pressure on habitats.
• Wetlands are being protected.	• More than half of Great Lakes wetlands have disappeared.
• Public and private groups are creating nature preserves on existing wetlands.	
• Builders in some areas are required to restore wetlands to replace what they destroy.	

Urban Sprawl in North America: Where Will It End?

Overview

In this **Experiential Exercise,** students explore the debate surrounding urban sprawl by working in policy-planning groups to make recommendations about how to best address impending growth in three urban areas: Portland, Toronto, and Atlanta. Within their policy-planning groups, each student assumes a role representing an interest group with strong opinions about how to deal with urban sprawl. Groups debate possible urban sprawl policies and prepare policy recommendations before learning how each city actually dealt with sprawl. Finally, students develop a plan to deal with urban sprawl in an area near them.

Objectives

Students will

- define and explain the importance of these key geographic terms: *metropolitan area, rural fringe, suburb, urban core, urban fringe, urban sprawl.*
- analyze the causes of, consequences of, and various solutions to urban sprawl.
- identify the effects of urban sprawl policies implemented in three North American cities.
- analyze the implications of global urban patterns and international solutions to sprawl.

Materials

- *Geography Alive! Regions and People*
- Interactive Student Notebooks
- Transparencies 5A and 5B
- Student Handout 5 (1 set for every 5 students plus 1 additional set)
- Information Master 5 (1 transparency)
- colored pencils or markers

Preview

1 **Project the 1955 aerial photograph and map of Phoenix on *Transparency 5A: Land Use in Metropolitan Phoenix.*** Have students analyze it by asking,

- How would you describe this area?

- How much of this land is developed?

- Do you think a lot of people live here? Why or why not?

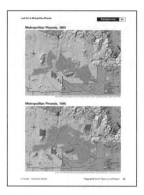

Transparency 5A

2 **Now project both the 1955 and 1995 maps.** Ask,

- How is the 1995 map different from the 1955 map?

- How would you describe this area now?

- How much of this land is developed?

- Which type of land use has increased the most? What might this mean in terms of how many people now live in this area? How might this affect other forms of land use in this area?

- What are some things that might be positive about these changes? What are some things that might be negative about these changes?

3 **Have students complete Preview 5.** Ask students to open their Interactive Student Notebooks to Preview 5 and, with a partner, follow the directions for brainstorming some of the outcomes of urban growth. Remind them that some outcomes might be positive while some might be negative.

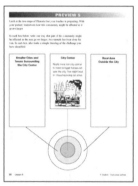

Preview 5

4 **Connect the Preview to the upcoming activity.** Tell students that the maps they just saw demonstrate the phenomenon of urban sprawl. In 1955, Phoenix was a small city in the Arizona desert, encompassing only 17 square miles and having a population of only 107,000 people. By 1994, it had grown to about 450 square miles with a population of nearly 1,100,000. This means that Phoenix's 1994 population was about 10 times its 1955 population, while the city's area was more than 26 times larger. In fact, by 1995 Phoenix was rapidly expanding into the desert at the rate of one acre per hour! This phenomenon, called *urban sprawl,* is not new to North America. However, people in this region are considering, more than ever before, some of the consequences and potential solutions to sprawl.

Essential Question and Geoterms

1 Introduce Chapter 5 in *Geography Alive! Regions and People*. Explain that in this chapter, students will learn about how cities have expanded in the United States and Canada over the past 50 years. They will look at the causes of this sprawl as well as some of the consequences and proposed solutions. Have them read Section 5.1. Then ask them to identify three details in the photograph of housing developments in Las Vegas that relate to what they just read.

2 Introduce the Graphic Organizer and the Essential Question. Have students examine the diagram of urban sprawl. Then ask,

- What do you see?
- What is the center of this area called? What types of buildings and facilities might you find if you visited the urban core?
- What is the area around the urban core called? What might you find if you visited the urban fringe?
- What is the area around the urban fringe called? What might you find if you visited the rural fringe?
- Which of these areas do you think has the greatest population?

Have students read the accompanying text. Make sure they understand the Essential Question, *How does urban sprawl affect people and the planet?* You may want to post the Essential Question in the room or write it on the board for the duration of the activity.

3 Have students read Section 5.2. This will give them a general background on the history of growth in metropolitan areas. Then have them work individually or in pairs to complete Geoterms 5 in their Interactive Student Notebooks. Ask them to share their answers with another student, or have volunteers share their answers with the class.

Geoterms 5

Experiential Exercise

1 Prepare the classroom. Create groups of five desks where students will meet in their policy-planning groups. In addition, at five well-spaced locations along the walls of the room, post signs with the names of the five interest groups in this activity (cut from a copy of *Student Handout 5: Interest Group Roles*): *Planning Commissioner, Smart Growth Advocate, Suburban Housing Developer, Environmentalist,* and *Citizen for Affordable Housing.* Also post the corresponding concerns and ideas of each interest group (cut from the handout) at each location.

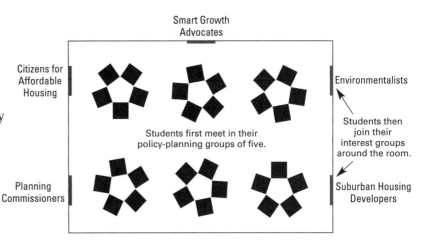

Smart Growth Advocates

Citizens for Affordable Housing

Environmentalists

Students then join their interest groups around the room.

Students first meet in their policy-planning groups of five.

Planning Commissioners

Suburban Housing Developers

2 Explain the activity. In this activity, each student will represent an interest group with strong opinions about how to deal with urban sprawl. During the activity, students from these various perspectives will meet in policy-planning groups to decide what to do about sprawl in three urban areas: Portland, Toronto, and Atlanta. They will work in their policy-planning groups to make recommendations about how best to plan for growth in these three areas.

3 Have students read Section 5.3. This section introduces some of the arguments for and against urban sprawl. When students have finished the reading, check their understanding of the material by asking,

• What are some of the arguments in favor of urban sprawl?

• What are some of the arguments against urban sprawl?

4 Place students in groups of five and assign them to interest groups. Explain that students are now in their policy-planning groups. Then distribute all five pages of Student Handout 5 to each policy-planning group and assign a role to each student in each group: Planning Commissioner, Smart Growth Advocate, Suburban Housing Developer, Environmentalist, or Citizen for Affordable Housing.

5 Have students learn about their roles. Give students a few minutes to become familiar with their roles and to learn the goals of their interest groups. The key to this activity is how well students understand their roles; you may want to spend time reviewing the five roles to check for understanding. Explain that during the activity, students with the same role will meet to talk through their position on each case of urban sprawl that they examine.

Student Handout 5

6 Have students decorate and display their nameplates. Have students fold their handouts in half and quickly decorate their nameplates. Tell them to create a symbol and a slogan to help others understand their position on urban sprawl. For example, Environmentalists might draw a house with a large X through it and write "Save the Environment: No New Houses!"

7 Guide students through the activity. Project *Information Master 5: Steps for Determining Policy to Address Sprawl,* and review the steps with the class. Begin the activity by having students read Section 5.4. These tips will help you execute the activity effectively:

- *Step 1:* At the end of Section 5.4, students will read about three proposed policy options for dealing with urban sprawl in Portland. These are the options they will discuss with their interest groups at Step 2 and their policy-planning groups at Step 4. Have students complete the Reading Notes for Section 5.4 independently.

- *Step 2:* Have students meet with their interest groups at the signs posted around the room. Create a sense of urgency by having students adhere to the 3-minute time limit to construct their arguments. Then give students, within their interest groups, a few minutes to record in their Reading Notes the policy they decide on and three reasons for it.

- *Step 3:* Have students reconvene in their policy-planning groups and state their positions. Stay on top of the 30-second time limit to ensure that all points of view are expressed; you might use a bell or whistle to alert students when their 30 seconds are up and it is time for the next student to speak.

- *Step 4:* Once all members have all shared their ideas, give the policy-planning groups 5 minutes to agree on a plan.

- *Step 5:* Have the Planning Commissioner from each group stand and explain that group's decision and the reasons behind it.

- *Step 6:* Have students complete the Reading Notes for Section 5.5 with the members of their policy-planning groups. You might want to facilitate a brief discussion about how Portland's actual decision differs from or matches what their groups decided and about which interest group they think had the largest influence on the decision-making process.

Follow a similar procedure for Toronto (Sections 5.6 and 5.7) and Atlanta (Sections 5.8 and 5.9).

8 Debrief the activity. Help students begin to think about the larger issue of global sprawl by asking,

- Which interest group's ideas do you think are best for the environment? For homebuyers? For communities?
- Why do you think there are so many opinions on urban sprawl?

Information Master 5

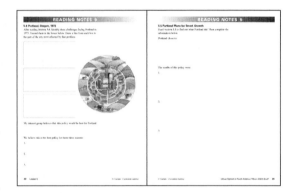

Reading Notes 5

Global Connections

1 Introduce the Global Connections. Have students read Section 5.10. Tell them that they will now see how some of the issues they encountered in the activity play out on a global scale.

2 Project *Transparency 5B: Global Connections.* Help students analyze the map by discussing the questions below, which are designed to help them begin to think about the complex issues regarding urban sprawl around the world. Use the additional information given to enrich the discussion.

Transparency 5B

• **What interesting details do you see on this map?**

• **What do the different colored dots represent?**

Purple dots represent urban areas with 100,000 to 1,000,000 people. Red dots represent urban areas with 1,000,000 to 5,000,000 people. Black dots represent urban areas with over 5,000,000 people.

• **Which areas appear to have the most urban areas? The fewest?**

Europe appears to have the greatest number of urban areas, followed by Asia, North America, and South America. India, the United States, China, Brazil, and Japan appear to have the greatest number of urban areas in an individual country. Most of the urban areas with over 5,000,000 people are in Asia. Africa and Australia have the fewest.

• **Why might there be such differences in different areas?**

Areas with high populations typically have large urban areas. Developed countries also tend to have more urban areas because most jobs are located in cities. The amount of inhabitable land in a country is also a big factor in urban sprawl. Areas that are too cold, like Antarctica and the far northern parts of North America, Europe, and Asia, have fewer urban areas. The same is true of areas that are too arid, like northern Africa, the Arabian Peninsula, and much of central Australia. Also, areas high in mountains or in dense forest or jungles are unlikely to have many large urban areas.

3 **Have students read Section 5.11 and examine the rest of the information in the section.** Then lead a discussion of these questions:

- **Why do you think there are so many large cities in the world?**

- **Why do you think there are so many urban areas of over 5 million people in Asia?**

- **What challenges do you think metropolitan areas face because of this growth?**

Processing

Have students complete Processing 5 in their Interactive Student Notebooks. It may be helpful to start this assignment as a class and to have maps of your local area available to students while completing this assignment.

Online Resources

For more information on urban sprawl, refer students to Online Resources for *Geography Alive! Regions and People* at www.teachtci.com.

Assessment

Masters for assessment appear on the next three pages followed by answers and scoring rubrics.

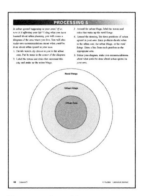

Processing 5

Assessment 5

Mastering the Content

Shade in the oval by the letter of the best answer for each question.

1. Which of the following is a **major** concern of people who oppose urban sprawl?
   - ○ A. habitat loss
   - ○ B. affordable housing
   - ○ C. subsistence farming
   - ○ D. point-source pollution

2. The dark places on the map below are **best** defined as which of the following?

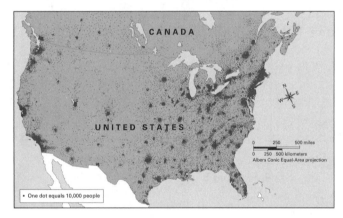

   - ○ A. urban cores
   - ○ B. rural fringes
   - ○ C. metropolitan areas
   - ○ D. transportation districts

3. Where is the suburb of a city **most likely** to be located?
   - ○ A. on the urban fringe
   - ○ B. inside the urban core
   - ○ C. in a mixed-use neighborhood
   - ○ D. outside the urban growth boundary

4. Which of these is **not** part of Portland's smart growth approach to land use planning?
   - ○ A. mixed-use developments
   - ○ B. a well-planned transit system
   - ○ C. a pedestrian-friendly downtown
   - ○ D. single-family homes on large lots

5. In 1973, Oregon placed growth boundaries around its urban areas. What was the **main** purpose of these boundaries?
   - ○ A. to expand public transit systems
   - ○ B. to make housing more affordable
   - ○ C. to stop development of farmland
   - ○ D. to reduce traffic jams on highways

6. Toronto's Official Plan encourages infill instead of urban sprawl. Which of these is the **best** example of infill?
   - ○ A. constructing a new airport on nearby farm fields
   - ○ B. building a new transit system to link city suburbs
   - ○ C. filling in wetlands to create space for a new shopping mall
   - ○ D. replacing an abandoned factory with a new apartment building

7. Atlanta has been called "the fastest-spreading human settlement in history." Where has **most** of this settlement taken place since the 1990s?
   - ○ A. on the rural fringe
   - ○ B. within the urban core
   - ○ C. inside the growth boundary
   - ○ D. near hiking and biking trails

8. In 1950, about 29 percent of the world's people lived in cities. By 2030, that percentage is expected to more than double. Choose the graph that **best** represents the world's urban and rural population in 2030.

   ○ A.

   ○ B.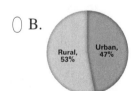

   ○ C.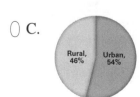

   ○ D.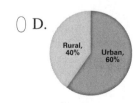

Applying Geography Skills:
Analyzing an Urban Growth Diagram

Use the diagram and your knowledge of geography to complete the tasks below.

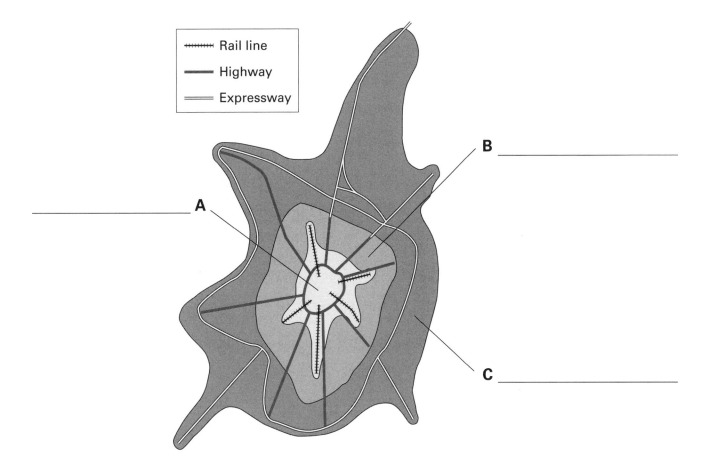

This diagram shows how a city grows.

1. Label Parts A, B, and C with these terms: *urban fringe, urban core, rural fringe.*

2. Notice the lines that start near the center of the diagram and lead to its edges. What do those lines represent?

3. Explain how those lines affect life in a metropolitan area.

Test Terms Glossary

To **explain** means to make the relationship between two things clear.

Exploring the Essential Question

How does urban sprawl affect people and the planet?

In Chapter 5, you explored urban sprawl in three cities. Now you will use what you learned. Use the information on the maps below and your knowledge of geography to complete this task.

Metropolitan Phoenix, 1955

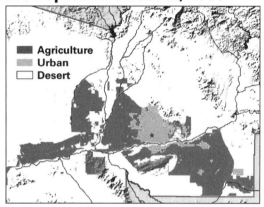

Metropolitan Phoenix, 1995

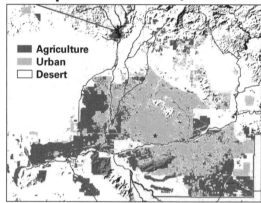

The Task: Looking at Urban Growth from Different Points of View

These maps show urban sprawl around the city of Phoenix, Arizona, in two different years. Your job is to look at these changes from the point of view of one of the people listed below.

Step 1: Circle the person below through whose eyes you will view changes to the Phoenix area.
- a parent looking for a home in this area
- a farmer looking for farmland in this area
- a city planner in charge of meeting water needs in this area
- a construction worker who builds roads in this area

Step 2: Compare the 1955 and 1995 maps. List two changes that you see.

Step 3: On a separate piece of paper, write an e-mail to a friend about the Phoenix area. In your e-mail, do the following:
A. Describe how the Phoenix area has changed since 1955. Use details from the maps.
B. Tell how these changes have affected you, your family, or your job.
C. State whether you think growth should or should not be controlled in the future. Defend your position with at least one fact or reason.

Writing Tips: Point of View
When you adopt another person's point of view, you write as if you were that person. Using personal pronouns such as *I*, *my*, and *me* will help you do this.

Test Terms Glossary
To **compare** means to show how two things are alike and different.

To **defend** means to support a position with facts, reasons, or examples.

Applying Geography Skills: Sample Responses

1. A = urban core; B = urban fringe; C = rural fringe
2. These lines represent forms of public transportation, such as highways and rail lines.
3. Answers will vary. Possible answer: Most city growth follows transportation lines out of the urban core and into the urban fringe. Transportation lines make it possible for people to live outside the urban core but get into the city center for work and shopping.

Exploring the Essential Question: Sample Response

Step 1: Students should circle one of the four people.

Step 2: Answers will vary; for example:
- The Phoenix metropolitan area expanded greatly between 1955 and 1995.
- A great deal of farmland has been lost to development.
- Development has pushed into the desert.
- Some new farmland has opened up.

Step 3: The e-mail should include all the elements listed in the prompt.

> You would not believe how much Phoenix has grown since 1955. Development has taken over huge areas that were once farms. It has also moved into the desert north of the city. All of this growth has affected my job as a city planner. As this area grows, its water needs grow also. But because Phoenix is located in a desert, water supplies are limited. Finding water and bringing it to new developments seems to get harder every year. I believe that we need to control future growth in this area. I know people want new houses that they can afford. But if we don't slow growth soon, we won't have enough water to meet everyone's needs.

Mastering the Content Answer Key

1. A	2. C	3. A	4. D
5. C	6. D	7. A	8. D

Applying Geography Skills Scoring Rubric

Score	General Description
2	Student responds to all parts of the task. Response is correct and clear.
1	Student responds to some parts of the task. Response is mostly correct.
0	Response does not match the task or is incorrect.

Exploring the Essential Question Scoring Rubric

Score	General Description
3	Student responds to all parts of the task. Response is correct, clear, and supported by details.
2	Student responds to most or all parts of the task. Response is generally correct but may lack details.
1	Student responds to at least one part of the task. Response may contain errors and lack details.
0	Response does not match the task or is incorrect.

Planning Commissioner

Major Concerns

- You want to make sure any new development is good for your community as a whole.
- You want the planning commission to be fair to everyone who appears before it.
- You want people to know you are doing your best to improve your community.

Ideas About Development

- You think that people need homes and jobs in the community.
- You believe development is good because it creates more places to live. It also creates jobs for the people who build new homes and for local businesses.

Ideas About the Environment

- Your main concern is not protecting the environment. However, you want to make sure your community is a clean and pleasant place to live.

Ideas About Planning for Future Growth

- You want your community to be a place where people want to live.
- You are concerned about the cost of new roads, water, sewer systems, and schools in newly developed areas. You know that people are unhappy if taxes have to be raised to pay for such improvements.

Smart Growth Advocate

- -

Major Concerns

- You are worried about the environment being harmed by uncontrolled growth.
- You want towns and cities to be friendly places where people know their neighbors.

Ideas About Development

- You believe that urban sprawl needs to be slowed or stopped.
- You think people should not build on undeveloped lands.
- You support mixed-use development. This means developing neighbor-hoods with a mix of shops, schools, libraries, restaurants, and housing.

Ideas About the Environment

- You believe that the best way to protect the environment is to limit urban growth.
- You believe that smart growth strategies will reduce pressure to develop open spaces.

Ideas About Planning for Future Growth

- You want new development to focus on mixed-use development.
- You support infill, or development of abandoned or run-down areas, over development in the rural fringe.

Suburban Housing Developer

Major Concerns

- You want to make a good living by building homes for people.
- You want to continue building large homes in the suburbs because they are easy to sell.

Ideas About Development

- You believe that people should be able to build and buy homes wherever they want to.
- You prefer building on undeveloped land at the edge of the city instead of infill projects. Developing new areas is less expensive than building in a city. Also, many people want homes with yards.

Ideas About the Environment

- The environment is not your major concern. You think environmentalists may be exaggerating their concerns. You know there are still hundreds of millions of acres of undeveloped land in the United States.

Ideas About Planning for Future Growth

- Planning for future growth is not your major concern. Your responsibility is to build solid, affordable homes for people who want to move to your area.

Environmentalist

Major Concerns

- You believe the environment is being harmed by growing cities.
- You worry about health problems caused by pollution.

Ideas About Development

- You think urban sprawl must be stopped. You think more people need to live in already developed metropolitan areas.
- You support mixed-use development. This means developing neighborhoods with a mix of shops, schools, libraries, restaurants, and housing.

Ideas About the Environment

- You believe the best way to protect the environment is to leave as much land as possible as open space.
- You are concerned about pollution from cars. You support development that does not make people depend on their cars to get to work and stores.

Ideas About Planning for Future Growth

- You think communities need to do more to get people out of cars. This means providing walking and biking paths and more public transportation.
- You support policies that protect rural areas and open space from development. Such policies include urban growth boundaries that limit where new housing can be built.

Citizen for Affordable Housing

- -

Major Concerns

- You are worried about the rising cost of housing.
- You want to make sure affordable housing is available for everyone.

Ideas About Development

- You want cities to have a mix of housing at different prices. This way, everyone could find a place to live.
- You are not against sprawl if it helps to provide affordable housing.

Ideas About the Environment

- Your main concern is not protecting the environment. It is helping people find housing.
- You worry that people with nice homes in the suburbs sometimes use environmental concerns to prevent new houses from being built near them.

Ideas About Planning for Future Growth

- You do not oppose mixed-use development. But you worry that it often means less house for more money.
- You believe people should be able to build and buy single-family homes in the suburbs and rural fringe.
- You oppose limitations on development that are likely to make housing more expensive.

Develop Plans for Dealing with Urban Sprawl

You are a member of a policy-planning group. You will work with your group to develop a plan for dealing with urban sprawl in three cities.

Step 1: Read Section 5.4 in *Geography Alive! Regions and People*. This will introduce you to the issues Portland, Oregon, was facing in the early 1970s. Label the diagram in your Reading Notes for Section 5.4.

Step 2: Briefly meet with your interest group. Quickly meet in the area your teacher has designated for your interest group. You have 3 minutes to construct an argument that every member of your interest group will bring back to their policy-planning meeting. Your argument must

- explain your interest group's position on urban sprawl.
- explain the policy you think is best for this city.
- give three reasons why this is the best policy for the city to adopt.

Work with your interest group to record your argument and your reasoning in your Reading Notes.

Step 3: Meet with your policy-planning group and make your argument. Each person in your policy-planning group has 30 seconds to make his or her argument. When it is your turn, state which policy you think will best address the issue of urban sprawl in this city and explain why.

Step 4: Create a plan with your policy-planning group. Your group now has 5 minutes to agree on a plan to deal with urban sprawl in this city. The plan should satisfy as many members of your group as possible. It may be one of the three possible plans you read about, or it may be a combination of ideas. You may need to compromise or to vote to come to an agreement.

Step 5: Report your plan to the class. Your Planning Commissioner will be asked to explain the policy your group chose and the reasons behind it.

Step 6: Read Section 5.5. Complete the Reading Notes for this section.

Repeat this process for Toronto and Atlanta. Use Sections 5.6 and 5.7 for Toronto and Sections 5.8 and 5.9 for Atlanta.

5.4 Portland, Oregon, 1973

After reading Section 5.4, identify three challenges facing Portland in 1973. Record them in the boxes below. Draw a line from each box to the part of the city most affected by that problem.

Portland was a beautiful city, but in the 1960s and 1970s its population grew very fast.

People began moving outside the city and building homes in the urban fringe.

Urban sprawl might take over too many farms and forests.

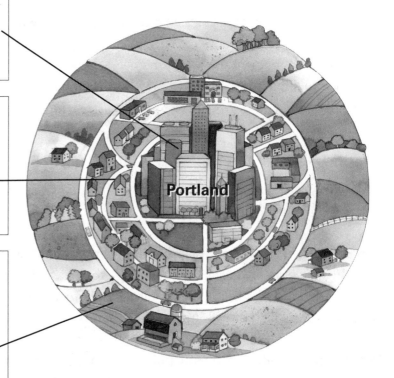

My interest group believes that this policy would be best for Portland:
Answers will vary.

We believe this is the best policy for these three reasons:

1. Answers will vary.

2.

3.

5.5 Portland Plans for Smart Growth

Read Section 5.5 to find out what Portland did. Then complete the information below.

Portland chose to: create land use planning laws. They created an urban growth boundary that separated urban land from rural land and limited development to inside the boundary.

The results of this policy were:

1. Portland focused on smart growth by making better use of land they could build on. They built mixed-use developments that combine homes and businesses in one area.

2. Portland created a pedestrian-friendly downtown with beautiful parks and open spaces.

3. Portland created a well-planned public transit system using buses and a light rail system so people could get around without using cars.

5.6 Toronto, Ontario, 1999

After reading Section 5.6, identify three challenges facing Toronto in 1999. Record them in the boxes below. Draw a line from each box to the part of the city most affected by that problem.

By the 1960s, this area was run down.

In the 1980s and 1990s, Toronto began to sprawl outward. Traffic clogged the suburban highways and led to pollution.

Sprawl took over farmland, forests, and wetlands.

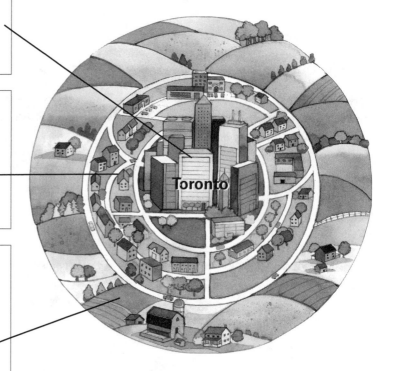

My interest group believes that this policy would be best for Toronto:

Answers will vary.

We believe this is the best policy for these three reasons:

1. Answers will vary.

2.

3.

5.7 Toronto Plans for 30 Years of Growth

Read Section 5.7 to find out what Toronto did. Then complete the information below.

Toronto chose to: create an Official Plan that allowed growth to continue in about 25% of the city but limited growth in the rest of the city.

The results of this policy were:

1. Toronto limited growth in 75% of the city, including residential neighborhoods, waterways, parks, and open space.

2. Toronto focused on infill in 25% of the city. They planned to use mixed-use building that would bring new homes, shops, and businesses to the urban core.

3. Toronto improved public transportation to link growth areas so people could travel within the city without always relying on cars.

5.8 Atlanta, Georgia, 1998

After reading Section 5.8, identify three challenges facing Atlanta in 1998. Record them in the boxes below. Draw a line from each box to the part of the city most affected by that problem.

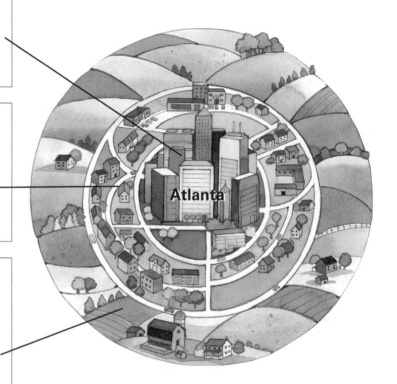

> Atlanta boomed in the 1990s, leading the nation in new jobs, homes, and highways. There was not enough room for all the people moving there to live within the city.

> New homes were built at a rapid pace, and people who bought them relied on cars to get around. Air around the Atlanta area grew incredibly polluted. There were traffic jams day and night.

> Hundreds of acres of forest were cut down each week to make room for new homes. The urban fringe sprawled into the rural fringe.

My interest group believes that this policy would be best for Atlanta:

Answers will vary.

We believe this is the best policy for these three reasons:

1. Answers will vary.

2.

3.

5.9 Atlanta Fights Pollution with Public Transit

Read Section 5.9 to find out what Atlanta did. Then complete the information below.

Atlanta chose to: focus on public transit to help decrease people's dependence on their cars and to meet Clean Air Act standards.

The results of this policy were:

1. Atlanta created the Georgia Regional Transportation Authority to reduce traffic, reduce air pollution from cars, and reduce poorly planned development.

2 Atlanta created some mixed-use development neighborhoods so people could walk to shops and jobs.

3. Atlanta expanded MARTA train and bus lines and the regional subway system and built new bike trails, footpaths, and rail lines.

National Parks: Saving the Natural Heritage of the U.S. and Canada

Overview

In this lesson, students learn about the unique topography and characteristics of North American national parks that make them worth preserving. In a **Response Group** activity, students work in groups to represent adventure tour companies and use topographic maps to plan tours highlighting the flora, fauna, and physical features of three national parks: Waterton-Glacier, Prince Edward Island, and Yosemite. Students then discuss the merits and drawbacks of each tour before identifying the challenges to preserving national parks today.

Objectives

Students will

- define and explain the importance of these key geographic terms: *conservationist, fauna, flora, topographic map.*
- demonstrate an ability to read and use topographic maps.
- identify the features of national parks in North America that make the parks special and worth preserving.
- identify the challenges to national parks in the 21st century.

Materials

- *Geography Alive! Regions and People*
- Interactive Student Notebooks
- Transparencies 6A–6F
- Information Masters 6A and 6B (1 transparency of each)
- 11″ x 17″ sheets of paper (1 for every 3 students)
- index cards (1 for every 3 students)

Preview

1 **Project the top half of** *Transparency 6A: Using Contour Lines.* Have students analyze this aerial photograph by asking,

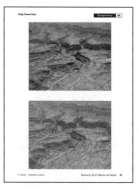

- What physical features do you see in this image?

- Where do you think this is? Give one piece of evidence from the photograph to support your answer.

- Why do you think this place has been set aside as a national park?

- Suppose you wanted to go hiking in the Grand Canyon and you had this aerial photograph. Can you see a route you might use to get from the rim of the canyon to the bottom? How far do you think the rim of the canyon is from the bottom? How would you decide on the best way down?

- What additional information would you want to know about the land before hiking here?

Transparency 6A

2 **Reveal the bottom half of Transparency 6A.** Contour lines showing the elevations of the area have been added to the aerial photograph. Ask,

- Take a look at the lines that have been added to the photograph. What do you think the numbers on the lines represent?

- What do you think these lines are telling us?

- What additional information can we tell about the land by looking at these lines?

- Why would these lines help you to plan a hike through the Grand Canyon?

3 **Project** *Transparency 6B: Topographic Map of Grand Canyon National Park* **and explain the purpose of topographic maps.** Tell students that geographers have a precise way of showing information about land. Explain that this is a topographic map. Once students understand how to read it, it will help them get anywhere they want to go in the park by telling them about distance, elevation, roads, trails, and waterways. Tell students that they will be planning adventure tours of three national parks during the upcoming activity and will need to understand how to use a topographic map.

Transparency 6B

4 **Introduce students to the skill of reading topographic maps.** Have students open *Geography Alive! Regions and People* to Chapter 6. Tell them that they will use the topographic map of the Grand Canyon in their books to figure out how to read such maps. Have them work individually or with a partner to answer the questions below. You might invite students to come up to the projector and answer each question by pointing out important features or details.

- How many miles is it across this map from east to west? North to south? How can you tell?

- If you wanted to go from Point A to Point B on this map, how many miles would that be?

- What are the wavy lines all over the map called? How can you tell?

- What do contour lines tell us about the land?

- How high is Point A? Point B?

- What is the change in elevation between each pair of adjacent contour lines? How can you tell?

- What information can we find out about the map by reading the symbols in the legend? On the map, find one example of each symbol.

5 Help students better understand contour lines. Display the transparency of *Information Master 6A: Examining Contour Lines,* which shows the topographic view and the profile view of a mountain.

- Point out Trails X and Y in the topographic and profile views. Ask, *What is the change in elevation along Trail X? Along Trail Y?* (Both are 40 feet.)

- Help students to understand how incline is related to contour line spacing. Say, *Suppose you walked along Trail X and then along Trail Y. How does the steepness of the incline along these two trails differ?* (Trail X is less steep than Trail Y. The closer the contour lines, the steeper the incline.)

- Display Transparency 6B again, and point out the slightly darker contour lines. Explain that these index contour lines are spaced farther apart and are often labeled with their elevation. Index contour lines can make reading a topographic map easier. Ask, *What is the elevation change between index contour lines on this map?* (400 feet)

6 Have students complete Preview 6 in their Interactive Student Notebooks. The Preview shows a small section of a topographic map and a partially completed elevation profile of a section of Grand Canyon National Park. Across the map is a line, with Point A at one end and Point B at the other. Tell students they need to complete the elevation profile for a trip along this line. Remind them that the elevation change between contour lines and between index contour lines will help them determine distances when creating the elevation profile. (**Note:** The first half mile of the trip is done for students. You might consider making a transparency of Preview 6 and constructing the next half mile as a class to make sure students understand how to translate the map information onto an elevation profile.)

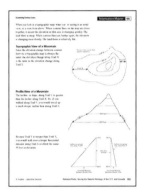

Information Master 6A

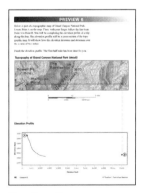

Preview 6

When students finish, have them compare their work to the elevation profile shown in Section 6.2 of *Geography Alive! Regions and People*.

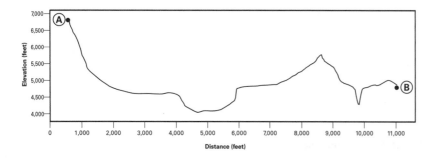

7 **Explain the connection between the Preview and the upcoming activity.** Tell students that understanding topographic maps is essential to planning trips in wilderness settings. In this activity, they will use topographic maps to create adventure tours through wilderness areas that were set aside as national parks.

Essential Question and Geoterms

1 **Introduce Chapter 6.** Explain that in this chapter, students will learn about the unique landscape of some of North America's national parks. Have students read Section 6.1. Then ask them to identify at least three details on the topographic map of the Grand Canyon that represent ideas in the reading.

2 **Introduce the Graphic Organizer and the Essential Question.** Have students examine the topographic map legend. Ask,

- What do you see?
- What does this type of map legend tell us about the land shown on the map?
- How might this map legend help us answer the Essential Question?

Have students read the accompanying text. Make sure they understand the Essential Question, *What features make national parks special and worth preserving?* You may want to post the Essential Question in the room or write it on the board for the duration of the activity.

3 **Have students read Section 6.2.** Then have them work individually or in pairs to complete Geoterms 6 in their Interactive Student Notebooks. Ask them to share their answers with another student, or have volunteers share their answers with the class.

Geoterms 6

Response Group

1 Place students in mixed-ability groups of three. You may want to prepare a transparency that shows them with whom they will work and where they will sit.

2 Explain the activity. Tell groups that they are now adventure tour companies trying to plan exciting yet realistic tours of three national parks in North America: Waterton-Glacier, Prince Edward Island, and Yosemite. Groups will map a route and create an itinerary, or plan, advertising the highlights of each tour. The class will then compare all of the groups' routes and tour plans before holding a class discussion on two of the tours. Finally, students will elect one group—based on how adventurous, realistic, and desirable their tour is—to be the adventure guides for the "class trip" through that park. Project *Information Master 6B: Sample Tour Plan,* and have the class examine the sample tour plan for Grand Canyon National Park. It is also reproduced in Reading Notes 6 of their Interactive Student Notebooks.

Information Master 6B

3 Have groups create a company name and logo. Give groups about five minutes to design and create a company name and logo on an 11-by-17-inch sheet of paper. Names and logos should not be specific to any one park, since companies will plan trips in all three parks. Have groups post their signs on the wall as close as possible to their workstations. (**Note:** You might have groups present their company names and logos to the class.)

4 Have students read Section 6.3. The reading contains information on the topography, flora, and fauna of Waterton-Glacier International Peace Park. After they read the section, project *Transparency 6C: Topographic Map of Waterton-Glacier International Peace Park* and ask,

- What flora and fauna will tourists see on their tour of this park?
- What special places or physical features will you want tourists to visit? (**Note:** You might ask students to point out the locations of the various features they mention.)
- How would you describe the terrain in this park?
- What do you think makes this park worth preserving?

Transparency 6C

5 Have students follow the directions in their Interactive Student Notebooks to create their tours. Review the directions with students. Remind students to use the sample Grand Canyon tour plan as a guide for creating their own tours. Monitor groups' progress as they prepare their first tour. Students might have many questions, at first, about how to design their routes and choose activities and transportation methods. (**Note:** To keep the activity moving, you might set a time limit for groups to complete their tours.)

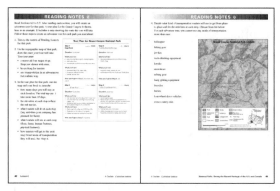

Reading Notes 6

6 Have students choose the adventure tour the class will take. First, have each group write the name of their tour company on an index card. Collect the cards, holding them face down so you can't see the names. Then follow these steps:

- Draw two to four index cards, depending on the class size.
- Have the chosen groups present their tours to the class, using Transparency 6C to show their tour routes and explaining what makes their tours exciting and realistic.
- Have students decide which of the presented tours the class should take by discussing this question: *Which group did the best job of showcasing the features that make national parks special and worth preserving?*
- Allow groups a few minutes to state their tour choice and reasons to the class. Then have the class vote to choose one tour to take.
- Congratulate the winning tour company.

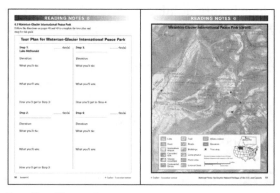

Reading Notes 6

7 Repeat Steps 4–6 for Prince Edward Island National Park. During Step 4, have students read Section 6.4, and use *Transparency 6D: Topographic Map of Prince Edward Island National Park.*

8 Repeat Steps 4–6 for Yosemite National Park. During Step 4, have students read Section 6.5, and use *Transparency 6E: Topographic Map of Yosemite National Park.*

Transparency 6D   **Transparency 6E**

9 Debrief the activity. Have students read Section 6.6 to learn about some of the other parks in the region. Then help them return to the Essential Question by asking,

- Why do you think the governments of the United States and Canada want to preserve these places?
- Which features in each park do you think are unique?
- What would make people want to visit these parks?
- Are these parks worth preserving? Why or why not?

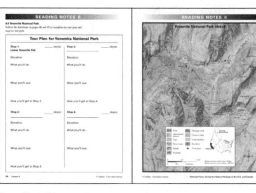

Reading Notes 6

Global Connections

1 **Introduce the Global Connections.** Have students read Section 6.7. Then explain that they will see how some of the issues they encountered in the activity exist in other areas of the world.

2 **Project** *Transparency 6F: Global Connections.* Have students analyze the map by discussing and sharing their answers to the questions below, which will encourage students to begin to think about the complex issues surrounding land preservation. Use the additional information given to enrich the discussion.

Transparency 6F

- **What interesting details do you see on this map?**

- **What does each color on the map represent?**

- **Which countries appear to have preserved the most land?**

- **Which appear to have preserved the least land?**

- **Why might there be such differences between areas?**
  Many factors affect how much land a country protects. One is the expense of preservation. Some countries are better equipped to handle the financial burden of national parks, marine reserves, national monuments, and so on. Another factor is population density. Countries with a large population and relatively little land often find it more difficult to set aside land because it is needed for living space. Other factors have to do with the amount of arable land that can be used to grow food and to live on, whether citizens believe that preserving land is a valuable use of their resources, and the willingness of citizens to give up access to land so that it can be preserved.

3 **Have students read Section 6.8 and examine the rest of the information in the section.** Then lead a discussion of these questions:

- **What problems make it difficult for some countries to set land aside for parks?**

- **What challenges do countries face in protecting preserved land?**

- **Has the world done a good job of setting aside unique lands for preservation?**

Processing

Have students complete Processing 6 in their Interactive Student Notebooks. Encourage them to use the Internet for researching an endangered park that interests them. If time permits, have them share their posters so that the class can learn more about the national parks in the United States and Canada.

Online Resources

For more information on national parks, refer students to Online Resources for *Geography Alive! Regions and People* at www.teachtci.com.

Assessment

Masters for assessment appear on the next three pages followed by answers and scoring rubrics.

Processing 6

Mastering the Content

Shade in the oval by the letter of the best answer for each question.

1. What kind of information is shown on a topographic map?
   - A. flora and fauna
   - B. natural resources
   - C. population density
   - D. landforms and elevation

2. Which of these is the **major** reason for creating national parks?
   - A. to reduce water pollution
   - B. to preserve special places
   - C. to develop natural resources
   - D. to encourage summer vacations

3. People come to Waterton-Glacier International Peace Park to see
   - A. Half Dome.
   - B. Green Gables.
   - C. the Grizzly Giant.
   - D. the Continental Divide.

4. Which of these created the "skeleton forests" found in Prince Edward Island National Park?
   - A. toxic waste
   - B. air pollution
   - C. migrating dunes
   - D. invasive species

5. The unique flora of Yosemite National Park includes
   - A. sequoia trees.
   - B. grizzly bears.
   - C. bighorn sheep.
   - D. sawgrass prairies.

6. Which national park is suffering from lower water levels because of development of nearby lands?
   - A. Denali
   - B. Everglades
   - C. Prince Edward Island
   - D. Great Smoky Mountains

7. What is **most likely** to bring visitors to Wapusk National Park?
   - A. geysers
   - B. glaciers
   - C. polar bears
   - D. mountain goats

8. Based on the map below, which two South American countries have done the **best** job of protecting lands from development?

   - A. Brazil and Bolivia
   - B. Chile and Paraguay
   - C. Argentina and Suriname
   - D. Colombia and Venezuela

Assessment | 6

Applying Geography Skills: Reading a Topographic Map

Use the map and your knowledge of geography to complete the tasks below.

Topography of Prince Edward Island National Park

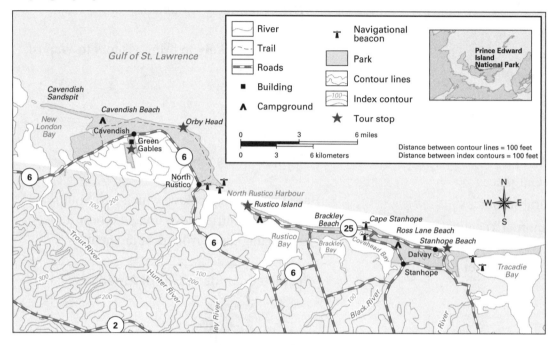

This topographic map is of Prince Edward Island National Park.

1. Locate Cavendish Beach Campground and the Cape Stanhope navigational beacon. Circle both of these landmarks on the map.

2. Estimate the distance between these two landmarks "as the crow flies." This means measuring the shortest distance between them. Draw a straight line between the two points. Then use the map scale to find the distance.

3. Determine the shortest route by road from Cavendish Beach Campground to the Cape Stanhope navigational beacon. Mark it on the map with a pencil or highlighter.

4. Use the map scale to estimate the distance by road between these two landmarks.

Test Terms Glossary

To **estimate** means to make a rough calculation of something.

To **determine** means to find something out, usually after examining some data.

Exploring the Essential Question

What features make national parks special and worth preserving?

In Chapter 6, you explored several national parks and what makes them special places. Now you will use what you learned. Use the information below and your knowledge of geography to complete this task.

Seasonal Data About the Inner Gorge of the Grand Canyon

Data	Jan	Feb	Mar	Apr	May	Jun	Jul	Aug	Sep	Oct	Nov	Dec
Average High (°F)	56	63	71	83	91	101	106	103	99	86	68	57
Average Low (°F)	36	40	46	55	62	71	77	74	68	58	45	36
Hours of Daylight	10	11	12	13	14	15	14	13	12	11	10	9

Sources: www.grand.canyon.national-park.com, www.nps.gov, www.scenic.com.

Bright Angel Trail Information

Distance from South Rim Trailhead to Colorado River: 7.9 miles

Elevation drop from trailhead to river: 4,385 feet

Trail conditions: steep and mostly sunny; limited water availability

Safest summer hiking times: before 10:00 A.M. and after 4:00 P.M.

Travel time: Allow one hour to hike two miles. Add another hour for each thousand feet of elevation you climb. Add extra time for hot weather.

Campgrounds: Indian Garden: halfway down; Bright Angel: near the river

The Task: Planning a Trip Down Into the Grand Canyon

In 2005, a travel channel listed a trip down into the Grand Canyon as one of "99 Things to Do Before You Die." Your job is to plan a trip on Bright Angel Trail to the bottom of the canyon and back.

Step 1: Examine the seasonal data table. Decide which month would be best for your trip. Circle it on the table.

Step 2: Based on the trail information, calculate about how many hours it will take to hike down to the river. Also calculate how many hours it will take to hike back up to the canyon rim.

Step 3: Write out a plan for your trip down into the Grand Canyon. Your plan should include this information:
A. what month you plan to go and why that is a good time
B. how long your trip will be
C. what you will wear and why
D. what you will need to carry with you

Applying Geography Skills: Sample Responses

1. Students should have circled Cavendish Beach Campground and the Cape Stanhope navigational beacon.
2. The distance between the two landmarks "as the crow flies" is about 14 miles. Accept any answer between 12 and 16.
3. Students should have marked a road route between Cavendish Beach Campground and the Cape Stanhope navigational beacon.
4. The distance by road between the two landmarks is about 20 miles. Accept any answer between 18 and 22 miles.

Exploring the Essential Question: Sample Response

Step 1: Answers will vary.

Step 2: It will take about 4 or more hours to hike down to the river. It will take about 8 or more hours to hike back up to the canyon rim.

Step 3: The trip plan should include all of the elements in the prompt.

I plan to make my trip down into the Grand Canyon in April. I chose that month because the weather is not too hot and the days are getting longer, so there will be more daylight. My trip will take two days, one to hike down to the river and the other to hike back. I will wear shorts and a T-shirt because the days will be warm. I will need to wear good hiking shoes because the trail is steep. I will need a warm jacket because the nights are still cool in April. I will need to carry food for two days, camping gear such as a sleeping bag and tent, and a lot of water to drink. I'll also take a flashlight and a star map for looking at the night sky from the bottom of the Grand Canyon.

**Mastering the Content
Answer Key**

1. D	2. B	3. D	4. C
5. A	6. B	7. C	8. D

**Applying Geography Skills
Scoring Rubric**

Score	General Description
2	Student responds to all parts of the task. Response is correct and clear.
1	Student responds to some parts of the task. Response is mostly correct.
0	Response does not match the task or is incorrect.

**Exploring the Essential
Question Scoring Rubric**

Score	General Description
3	Student responds to all parts of the task. Response is correct, clear, and supported by details.
2	Student responds to most or all parts of the task. Response is generally correct but may lack details.
1	Student responds to at least one part of the task. Response may contain errors and lack details.
0	Response does not match the task or is incorrect.

Reading a Topographic Map

When you look at a topographic map, what you're seeing is an aerial view, or a view from above. When contour lines on the map are closer together, it means the elevation in that area is changing quickly. The land there is steep. When contour lines are farther apart, the elevation is changing more slowly. The land there is relatively flat.

Topographic View of a Mountain

Since the elevation change between contour lines on a topographic map is always the same, the elevation change along Trail X is the same as the elevation change along Trail Y.

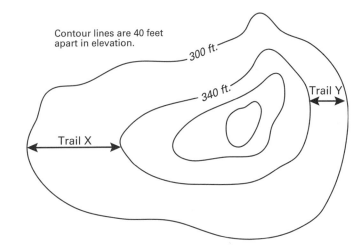

Contour lines are 40 feet apart in elevation.

300 ft.

340 ft.

Trail Y

Trail X

Profile View of a Mountain

The incline, or slope, along Trail Y is greater than the incline along Trail X. So, if you walked along Trail Y, you would travel up a much steeper incline than along Trail X.

Because Trail Y is steeper than Trail X, you would walk over a longer horizontal distance along Trail X to climb the same 40 feet in elevation.

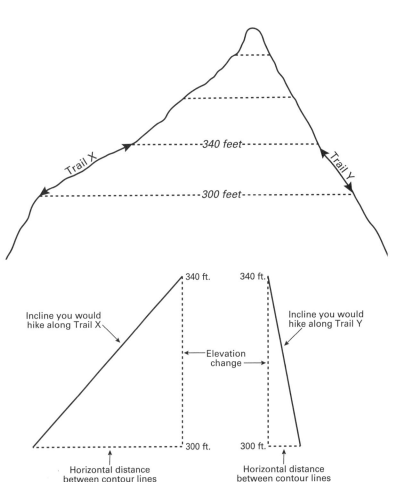

Trail X

Trail Y

340 feet

300 feet

340 ft.

340 ft.

Incline you would hike along Trail X

Incline you would hike along Trail Y

Elevation change

300 ft.

300 ft.

Horizontal distance between contour lines

Horizontal distance between contour lines

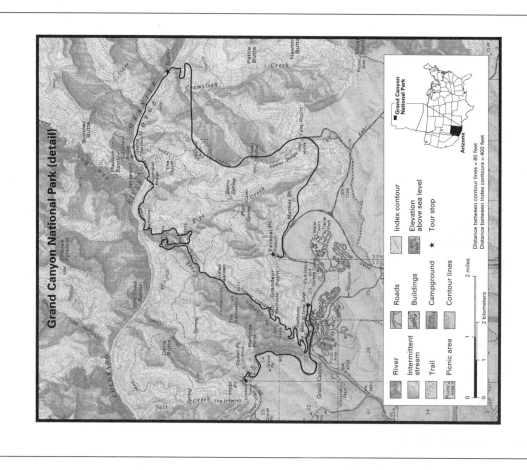

Grand Canyon National Park (detail)

Tour Plan for Grand Canyon National Park

Stop 1:
Hopi Point _____1_____ day(s)

Elevation: 6,500 feet

What you'll do:
- Rappel down Hopi Wall using rock-climbing equipment
- Visit Lookout Tower
- Drive along the South Rim in a four-wheel-drive vehicle

What you'll see:
- spectacular views of the canyon walls
- the dramatic cliffs of the Inferno
- Hopi Wall and Salt Creek

How you'll get to Stop 2: four-wheel-drive vehicle

Stop 2:
El Tovar Hotel _____2_____ day(s)

Elevation: 6,900 feet

What you'll do:
- Have dinner and spend the night at the El Tovar Hotel
- Take a horseback tour down Bright Angel Trail along Garden Creek
- Hike Plateau Point and then continue on horseback to the Suspension Bridge on the Colorado River

What you'll see:
- Bright Angel Trail winding down 2,000-foot cliffs
- Garden Creek at the bottom of the canyon
- buildings and shops surrounding the South Rim

How you'll get to Stop 3: horseback

Stop 3:
Granite Gorge _____2_____ day(s)

Elevation: 2,000 feet

What you'll do:
- White-water rafting on the Colorado River through Granite Gorge

What you'll see:
- suspension bridges spanning the river
- rapids along the River Trail and through Granite Gorge

How you'll get to Stop 4: raft

Stop 4:
Yavapai Point _____1_____ day(s)

Elevation: 6,520 feet

What you'll do:
- Raft through the rapids
- Take a helicopter tour over the Colorado River, the Natural Arch, O'Neill Butte, Yaki Point, and Mather Point
- Land at Yavapai Point and visit the museum there

What you'll see:
- stunning aerial views of the canyon
- exhibits on geology and theories on how the Grand Canyon was formed at the Yavapai Point Museum

Consumption Patterns in the United States: The Impact of Living Well

Overview

This lesson introduces students to consumption patterns in the United States and around the world. After reflecting on consumption patterns in the United States, students participate in a **Response Group** activity. They analyze a series of four cartograms depicting global consumption patterns and gross domestic product and identify reasons for those patterns. They then use what they've learned to make predictions about future challenges posed by the growing global consumer class.

Objectives

Students will

- define and explain the importance of these key geographic terms: *consumption, developed country, developing country, gross domestic product (GDP), per capita.*
- demonstrate an ability to read and interpret cartograms.
- identify current consumption patterns in the United States.
- compare U.S. consumption patterns with those of other countries around the world.
- evaluate the effects and predict the future impact of growing levels of consumerism.

Materials

- *Geography Alive! Regions and People*
- Interactive Student Notebooks
- Transparencies 7A–7G
- Student Handout 7A (1 copy)
- Student Handout 7B (1 per student)
- Information Master 7 (1 transparency)

Preview

1 Prepare for the Preview activity. Choose four students to participate in the act-it-out in Step 3 of this Preview, and give each of them one role card cut from *Student Handout 7A: Preview Role Cards*. Ask them to read over their role cards and think of possible answers to the questions, from their characters' perspective. Explain that during the act-it-out, the class will analyze a photograph of a shopping mall. The four students will then be "interviewed" based on the information and questions on their role cards.

Student Handout 7A

2 Project *Transparency 7A: Preview 7.* Have students carefully analyze the image by asking,

- What interesting details do you see?
- Where do you think these people are? What evidence from the photograph supports your conclusion?
- What country do you think this shopping mall is in? Why do you think so?
- What are some of the reasons that all of these people might be in a shopping mall?
- Do you think that people in every country go to malls like this to shop? Why or why not?

Transparency 7A

3 Bring the image to life by conducting an act-it-out. Line up at least four chairs in front of the projected image so that the backs of the chairs form the "handrails" of the escalator. Ask the four actors to come forward and get on the "escalator." Explain to the class that you are a reporter for a local TV station doing a report on patterns of consumption and attitudes among U.S. shoppers. One at a time, ask the actors questions based on their role cards, such as these:

- Who are you?
- Why are you at the mall today? How often do you come here?
- What are you planning to purchase today? Do you already own something like what you are buying today? If so, why are you buying more?
- Do you think most Americans can afford to shop for the goods you are purchasing? Why or why not?
- Do you think that people in other parts of the world have the ability to shop like you do? If yes, who? If no, why not?

4 Explain the connection between the Preview and the upcoming activity. Tell students that in the upcoming activity, they will learn about consumption patterns in the United States and compare them to those of other countries. They will also learn why consumption patterns vary greatly around the globe.

Essential Question and Geoterms

1 Introduce Chapter 7 in *Geography Alive! Regions and People.* Have students read Section 7.1. Afterward, ask them to identify at least two ways in which the shopping-mall act-it-out relates to what they have just read.

2 Introduce the Graphic Organizer and the Essential Question. Have students examine the world population cartogram. Then ask,

- How would you describe this map? In what ways is this map different from other world maps you have seen?
- What interesting details do you see?
- Some regions are portrayed larger than others on this map. Why do you think this is?

Tell students that this is a cartogram. A cartogram is a specialty map, usually drawn with straight lines, in which countries or regions are sized based on a set of data, such as population figures, rather than land mass. The general shapes and relative locations of countries or regions are drawn similar to a regular map. On this population cartogram, regions with larger populations are bigger. Tell students that in the upcoming activity, they will be using cartograms to understand consumption patterns around the world.

Have students read the accompanying text. Make sure they understand the Essential Question, *How do American consumption patterns affect people and the planet?* You may want to post the Essential Question in the room or write it on the board for the duration of the activity.

3 Have students read Section 7.2. This reading will give them a general background on consumption patterns in the United States. Then have them complete Geoterms 7 in their Interactive Student Notebooks. Have them share their answers in pairs, or have volunteers share their answers with the class.

Geoterms 7

Response Group

1 Place students in mixed-ability groups of four. You may
want to prepare a transparency that shows them who is in their
group and how to arrange their desks.

2 Review the concept of a cartogram. Project *Transparency 7B:
World Population Cartogram,* and remind students that a cartogram is a visual representation of statistical data. Help them
begin analyzing this cartogram by asking,

Transparency 7B

- What kind of statistical data does this cartogram show?
  How do you know?

- According to this cartogram, which countries have the
  largest populations?

- Which continent appears to have the most people living on it?

Explain other interesting facts related to the cartogram, such as,

- China has the world's largest population, but India is close
  behind. Experts predict that by 2050, India will have the
  world's largest population.

- The United States has the world's third largest population
  but is *far* behind that of India and China. China's population
  is more than four times that of the United States.

- The United States is predicted to remain the third most
  populous country until at least 2015.

3 Teach students more about cartograms. Give each student
a copy of *Student Handout 7B: Understanding Cartograms,* and
review the information about per capita food consumption and
the U.S. food consumption cartogram with them. Then help students create a per capita food consumption cartogram for India
using the given data. (**Note:** You may want to make a transparency of the handout to complete along with students.)

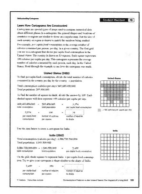

Student Handout 7B

4 Project *Transparency 7C: Food Consumption Cartogram*
to introduce the topic of food consumption. Help students
understand the cartogram by asking,

- What does one square on this cartogram represent?

- What are some of the countries that consume the most food
  per capita? The least?

- What are some of the factors that might account for
  differences in per capita food consumption among these
  countries? *Possible factors include a geographic location
  that makes food production possible, the amount of food
  produced in each country, the population of each country
  relative to the amount of food produced, and the wealth
  necessary to purchase the food that is produced or to import
  additional food from other countries.*

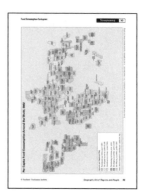

Transparency 7C

5 Have groups read about and discuss food consumption.
Have groups read Section 7.3 and complete Reading Notes 7 for that section. Then quickly assign half of the groups to represent a developed country of the world and the other half to represent a developing country. Allow them to chose which specific country they will represent. Explain that they will now participate in a discussion of consumption patterns around the world. Project *Information Master 7: Discussion Guidelines,* and review the guidelines for the discussion. Give students three minutes to discuss Question 1 in their groups from their country's point of view. Then lead groups through a discussion of the question following the guidelines on Information Master 7.

Reading Notes 7   **Information Master 7**

6 Project *Transparency 7D: Oil Consumption Cartogram* **to introduce the topic of oil consumption.** Help students understand the cartogram by asking,

• What does one square on this cartogram represent?

• What are some of the countries that consume the most oil per capita? The least?

• What are some of the factors that might account for differences in per capita oil consumption among these countries? *Possible factors include the need for oil (developed countries tend to need more oil to support their industries and provide gasoline for vehicles), the location of oil production (countries in the Middle East, where most of the world's current oil supply is located, tend to consume a lot of oil per capita), and the wealth necessary to purchase oil.*

Transparency 7D

7 Have groups read about and discuss oil consumption.
Repeat Step 5 for oil consumption, with these modifications:

• Have students read and complete the Reading Notes for Section 7.4.

• Have groups switch roles for Question 2 on Information Master 7; those who represented developing countries in the previous discussion will now represent developed countries, and vice versa.

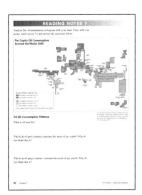

Reading Notes 7

8 Project *Transparency 7E: Personal Computer Consumption Cartogram* **to introduce the topic of personal computer consumption.** Help students understand the cartogram by asking,

• What does one square on this cartogram represent?

• Which countries consume the most personal computers per capita? The least?

• What are some of the factors that might account for differences in per capita computer consumption among these countries? *Possible factors: the demand for personal computers*

Transparency 7E

(developed countries tend to use them in business, and there is a high demand for household personal computers in the developed world) and the wealth necessary to purchase them

9 **Have groups read about and discuss personal computer consumption.** Repeat Step 5 for personal computer consumption, with these modifications:

- Have students read and complete the Reading Notes for Section 7.5.

- Have groups switch roles for Question 3 on Information Master 7.

Reading Notes 7

10 **Project** *Transparency 7F: Gross Domestic Product Cartogram* **to introduce the topic of gross domestic product.** Help students understand the cartogram by asking,

- Which countries have the highest GDP per capita? The least?

- Why do you think GDP is an important indicator of consumption? *People in countries with a high per capita GDP are able to consume more because they have the wealth necessary to buy the things they want.*

- What comparisons can you make between this cartogram of GDP and the other consumption cartograms you saw? *Countries with a high per capita GDP, like the United States, Canada, Japan, Australia, and most of Western Europe, tend to consume more. Countries with a low per capita GDP, like many of those in Africa, Asia, and Latin America, tend to consume less.*

Transparency 7F

11 **Have groups read about and discuss GDP.** Repeat Step 5 for GDP, with these modifications:

- Have students read and complete the Reading Notes for Section 7.6.

- Have groups switch roles for Question 4 on Information Master 7.

12 **Debrief the activity.** Have students focus on the future challenges of patterns of consumption by asking,

- Why do developed countries consume relatively more goods and services?

- Why do developing countries generally consume relatively few goods and services?

- What might happen if developing countries followed the same consumption patterns as developed countries?

- What might be some of the costs—financial, ecological, psychological—of such high levels of consumption?

Reading Notes 7

Global Connections

1 Introduce the Global Connections. Have students read Section 7.7. Then help them identify some of the potential problems associated with the consumption levels of the world's developed countries and possible consequences that may arise as developing nations try to emulate these consumption patterns. Also help them identify actions that all countries might take to help reduce or prevent some of these problems. Then explain that they will now see how one of the by-products of consumption, waste, affects the world.

2 Project *Transparency 7G: Global Connections.* Have students analyze the map by asking the questions that follow. Use the additional information given to enrich the discussion.

Transparency 7G

- **What does this map show?**
  It shows how much municipal waste is produced, per capita, per year, by some countries of the world.

- **What interesting details do you see?**
  Answers will likely include the observation that many countries apparently have no data on municipal waste available.

- **Why do you think so many countries have no data on this topic?**
  Possible answer: Some of these countries might not have organized waste collection or might not keep track of how much waste is collected.

3 Have students read Section 7.8 and examine the rest of the information in the section. Then facilitate a discussion of these questions:

- **Which countries appear to produce the most waste?**

- **How effective is recycling as a way to reduce trash?**

- **How can recycling help people and our planet?**

Processing

Have students complete Processing 7 in their Interactive Student Notebooks. (**Note:** You may want to provide sample political cartoons to help students envision their final product.) If time permits, have students post their political cartoons so that the class can view the various interpretations of what will happen if every country consumed like the United States.

Online Resources

For more information on consumption patterns in the United States, refer students to Online Resources for *Geography Alive! Regions and People* at www.teachtci.com.

Assessment

Masters for assessment appear on the next three pages followed by answers and scoring rubrics.

Processing 7

Mastering the Content

Shade in the oval by the letter of the best answer for each question.

1. Which statement is **most likely** to be true of a developing country?
   - A. Most adults earn enough money to own cars.
   - B. Most adults consume more than 3,000 calories a day.
   - C. Most adults live in rural areas and work in agriculture.
   - D. Most adults live in cities and work in factories or offices.

2. Which term means the total value of goods and services a country produces in a year?
   - A. consumption
   - B. per capita income
   - C. economic activity
   - D. gross domestic product

3. What is the **main** cause of hunger in the world?
   - A. poverty
   - B. pollution
   - C. crop failures
   - D. food shortages

4. Which of these countries leads the world in oil consumption?
   - A. India
   - B. China
   - C. Canada
   - D. United States

5. Which term **best** describes a country with a high per capita GDP?
   - A developed
   - B. developing
   - C. rural
   - D. urban

6. Which of these conclusions is **best** supported by the graph below?

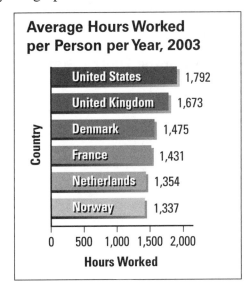

Average Hours Worked per Person per Year, 2003

   - A. American workers use more technology than workers in European countries.
   - B. American workers earn less money than workers in European countries.
   - C. American workers have a stronger work ethic than workers in European countries.
   - D. American workers have more years of schooling than workers in European countries.

7. Which of the following defines members of the global consumer class?
   - A. They have college educations.
   - B. They earn at least $7,000 a year.
   - C. They eat less than 2,700 calories a day.
   - D. They have computers at work or at home.

8. Which of these is **not** an immediate benefit of recycling?
   - A. It saves natural resources.
   - B. It reduces municipal waste.
   - C. It increases gross national product.
   - D. It keeps toxic materials out of dumps.

Applying Geography Skills: Analyzing a Bar Graph

Use the bar graph and your knowledge of geography to complete the tasks below.

Recycling Rates in the United States, 2003

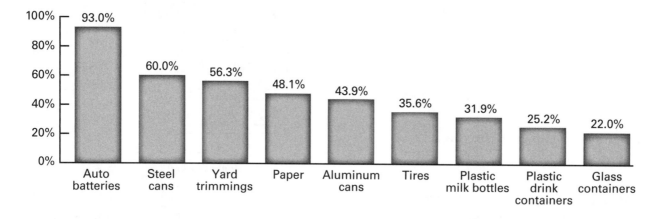

This bar graph shows how much Americans recycled in 2003.

1. Look at the labels on the horizontal axis, or bottom edge, of the graph. What do they indicate about the bars on the graph?

2. Look at the numbers on the vertical axis, or upright edge, of the graph. What do they indicate about the bars on the graph?

3. Identify which material had the highest recycling rate in 2003.

4. Explain why you think this material had such a high recycling rate.

Test Terms Glossary
To **explain** means to give reasons for something.

© Teachers' Curriculum Institute

Exploring the Essential Question

How do American consumption patterns affect people and the planet?

In Chapter 7, you explored consumption patterns in developed and developing countries. Now you will use what you learned to complete the task below.

The Task: Analyzing Global Consumer Class Statistics

You read that most people in the developing world would like to consume much like people in wealthy countries do. Your task is to figure out how large its consumer class would be if the developing world suddenly got rich.

Step 1: Use the information on the graph to fill in the table below. (**Hint:** To calculate the percentages, divide the number of people in the consumer class by the total number of people. Round the answer to two digits. Use a calculator if one is available.)

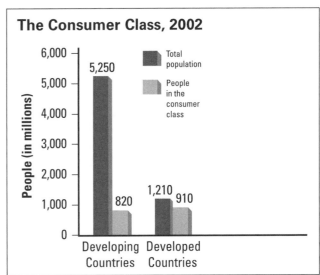

Area	People in the Consumer Class (in millions)	Total Number of People (in millions)	Percent of Population in the Consumer Class
Developed World, 2002			%
Developing World, 2002			%

Step 2: Suppose that the developing world suddenly grew as rich as the developed world in 2002. Calculate about how large its consumer class would become as a result. Use your answer to add a new bar representing this large new consumer class to the graph above. (**Hint:** Multiply the number of people in the developing world by the percent of people in the consumer class in the developed world. Use a decimal point in front of the percent when you do your math. Round your answer to the nearest 10 million people.)

Step 3: List three problems that the world might face if that new large consumer class consumed like Americans do today.

Assessment | **7**

Applying Geography Skills: Sample Responses

1. The labels on the horizontal axis indicate what type of waste material the bar represents.
2. The numbers on the vertical axis indicate what percent of each type of waste material is recycled.
3. Auto batteries had the highest recycling rate in 2003, at 93 percent.
4. Accept any reasonable response. Some students may speculate that most states require battery recycling. Others may note that batteries are filled with toxic chemicals that should not be dumped in landfills and this makes people more likely to recycle them.

Exploring the Essential Question: Sample Response

Student responses should look like the table and graph shown below.

Step 1:

Area	People in the Consumer Class (in millions)	Total Number of People (in millions)	Percent of Population in the Consumer Class
Developed World, 2002	910	1,210	75%
Developing World, 2002	820	5,250	16%

Step 2:

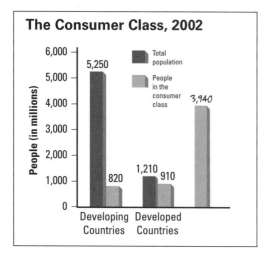

Step 3: Answers might include any of the following:
- shortages of food, oil, and water
- increased air pollution from burning fossil fuels
- increased levels of trash
- increased water pollution from toxic waste materials
- health problems due to overeating or pollution
- conflicts over the distribution of scarce resources

Mastering the Content Answer Key

1. C	2. D	3. A	4. D
5. A	6. C	7. B	8. C

Applying Geography Skills Scoring Rubric

Score	General Description
2	Student responds to all parts of the task. Response is correct and clear.
1	Student responds to some parts of the task. Response is mostly correct.
0	Response does not match the task or is incorrect.

Exploring the Essential Question Scoring Rubric

Score	General Description
3	Student responds to all parts of the task. Response is correct, clear, and supported by details.
2	Student responds to most or all parts of the task. Response is generally correct but may lack details.
1	Student responds to at least one part of the task. Response may contain errors and lack details.
0	Response does not match the task or is incorrect.

Role 1: Teenager

- You are a student.
- You are at the mall today shopping and hanging out with friends. You come to the mall about once a week, usually on weekends.
- Today you are shopping for new sneakers. You already own three pairs, but you want the style that all your friends are buying.
- The sneakers you are buying cost $150. Your parents gave you money to buy them. This is about average for what you spend on sneakers. However, you think there might be other people who cannot afford to spend that much.
- Think about this question: *Do people in other parts of the world have the ability to buy what you will buy today? If yes, who? If no, why not?*

Role 2: Mall Employee

- Two years ago, you moved to America from a small Latin American country. Now you work full-time at a clothing store in the mall.
- You are here today, and almost every day, to work.
- You are not planning to purchase anything today, except for lunch during your shift. Sometimes you find it difficult to work in the mall because there are so many things you want to buy.
- Working in a mall annoys you because there are so many people around all the time. And people are sometimes rude to you when they shop in your store. You wonder if everyone in America is like this, but you are not sure.
- Think about this question: *Do people in other parts of the world have the ability to buy what you will buy today? If yes, who? If no, why not?*

Role 3: Adult Woman

- You are a 30-year-old mother. You have a 2-year-old girl and a 9-year-old boy.

- You are at the mall today doing some holiday shopping. You come to the mall whenever you want to buy clothes for someone in your family. You also come to buy make-up, sporting equipment, and gifts.

- Today you are shopping for holiday gifts for your children. Your 2-year-old wants more toys. She already has more toys than you have a place for in your home. Your 9-year-old wants new hockey equipment and a few CDs. You think his old hockey equipment is fine, but he insists on the newest skates. He also already has a large CD collection, but he wants new CDs that recently came out. Even though you don't think your children "need" these things, you plan to buy them because they are gifts.

- You realize that there are Americans who probably cannot afford to spend as much money as you will spend at the mall today. But since you have the money, you are going to spend it on your children.

- Think about this question: *Do people in other parts of the world have the ability to buy what you will buy today? If yes, who? If no, why not?*

Role 4: Recent College Graduate

- You are 22 years old. You recently graduated from college. You just got a new job making a lot of money.

- You visit the mall about twice a month. You are at the mall today shopping for new clothes for work. You already have many clothes. But now that you make so much money, you want to dress better.

- You think that most Americans with good jobs can afford to shop for new clothes. However, you realize that people who do not make a lot of money probably cannot afford to buy new clothes as often as you do.

- Think about this question: *Do people in other parts of the world have the ability to buy what you will buy today? If yes, who? If no, why not?*

Learn How Cartograms Are Constructed

Cartograms are special types of maps used to compare numerical data about different places. In a cartogram, the general shapes and locations of countries or regions are similar to those on a regular map. But the size of each country or region is drawn to match the numbers being studied.

For example, *per capita food consumption* is the average number of calories consumed per person, per day, in a given country. The first grid you see is a cartogram that shows per capita food consumption in the United States. The country is drawn as 33 squares. Each square represents 100 calories per capita per day. This cartogram represents the average number of calories consumed by each person, each day, in the United States. Read through the example to see how the cartogram was made.

United States (2002)

To find per capita food consumption, divide the total number of calories consumed in the country per day by the country's population.

Total consumption (calories per day): 969,687,600,000
Total population: 287,400,000

To find the number of squares to shade, divide the answer by 100. Each shaded square will then represent 100 calories per capita per day.

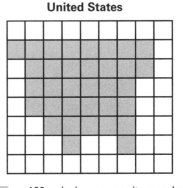

United States

969,687,600,000	÷	287,400,000	=	3,374
total consumption		total population		per capita food consumption

3,374	÷	100	=	34
per capita food consumption		number of calories per square		number of squares to shade

□ = 100 calories per capita per day

Use the data below to draw a cartogram for India.

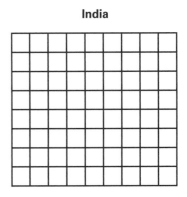

India

India (2002)

Total consumption (calories per day): 2,580,720,500,000
Total population: 1,049,500,000

2,580,720,500,000	÷	1,049,500,000	=	2,459
total consumption		total population		per capita food consumption

On the grid, shade squares to represent India's per capita food consumption. Try to give your cartogram a shape similar to the shape of India.

2,459	÷	100	=	
per capita food consumption		number of calories per square		number of squares to shade

Participate in a Discussion of Consumption Patterns

You will take part in a discussion of consumption patterns around the world. For each question, your group will play the part of either a developed country or a developing country.

Guidelines for Discussing Each Question
Follow these steps to discuss each question below:

- In your group, talk about the question from your country's perspective.
- Alternate the role of Presenter within your group. Each Presenter will represent your group's opinion during the discussion of one of the questions.
- Stand up when speaking.
- Refer to the previous speaker by saying, *"(Name of previous speaker), our group agrees/disagrees with you because…"*
- Support your argument with at least one piece of evidence from the reading or the cartogram.
- Before you sit down, call on the next Presenter by name.

Discussion Questions
Question 1 (Section 7.3)
How does your country feel about the food consumption patterns represented on the cartogram? Why?

Question 2 (Section 7.4)
How does your country feel about the oil consumption patterns represented on the cartogram? Why?

Question 3 (Section 7.5)
How does your country feel about the personal computer consumption patterns represented on the cartogram? Why?

Question 4 (Section 7.6)
How does your country feel about the GDP patterns represented on the cartogram? Why? How does this cartogram and the reading help explain the consumption patterns seen on the first three cartograms?

© Teachers' Curriculum Institute

Analyze the food consumption cartogram with your class. Then, with your group, read Section 7.3 and answer the questions below.

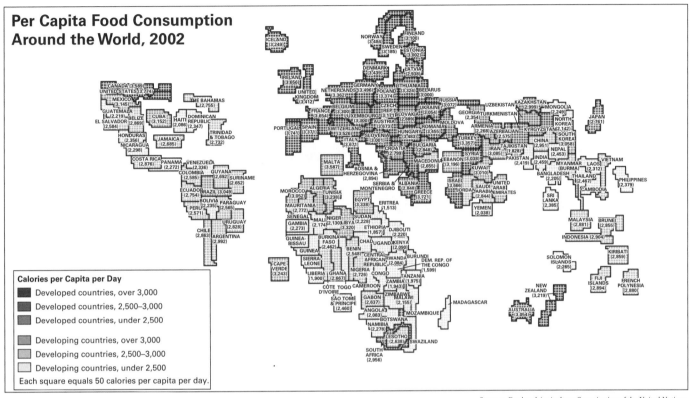

Per Capita Food Consumption Around the World, 2002

Calories per Capita per Day
- Developed countries, over 3,000
- Developed countries, 2,500–3,000
- Developed countries, under 2,500
- Developing countries, over 3,000
- Developing countries, 2,500–3,000
- Developing countries, under 2,500

Each square equals 50 calories per capita per day.

Sources: *Food and Agriculture Organization of the United Nations,* "Food Balance Sheet 2002," faostat.fao.org/faostat/. *Population Reference Bureau,* www.prb.org.

7.3 Food Consumption Patterns

How many calories per day does the average person need to live a healthy life? To live a healthy life, the average person needs about 2,700 calories per day.

List three countries that consume a high amount of calories per capita, per day. What type of country tends to consume more calories per capita? Why do you think that is? Possible answer: The United States, Israel, and France. People in developed countries tend to consume more food. This is probably because they can afford to buy more food.

List three countries that consume a low amount of calories per capita, per day. What type of country tends to consume fewer calories per capita? Why do you think that is? Possible answer: Eritrea, Haiti, and Tajikistan. People in developing countries tend to consume less food, often less than that needed to live a healthy life. There is usually enough food to feed everyone in these countries, but not everyone has enough money to buy it.

Analyze the oil consumption cartogram with your class. Then, with your group, read Section 7.4 and answer the questions below.

Per Capita Oil Consumption Around the World, 2003

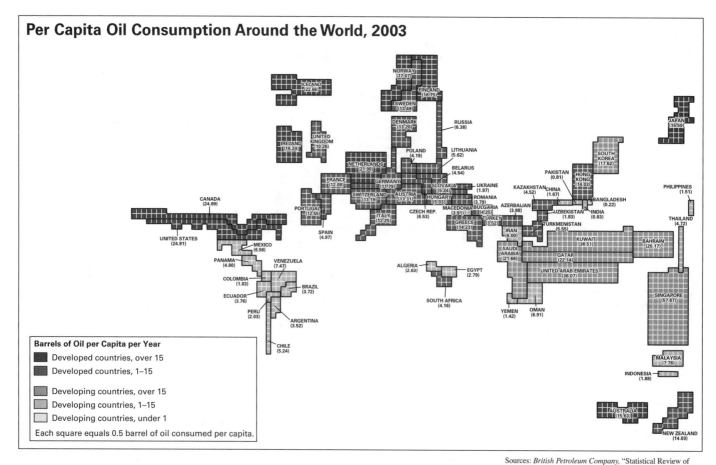

Barrels of Oil per Capita per Year

- Developed countries, over 15
- Developed countries, 1–15
- Developing countries, over 15
- Developing countries, 1–15
- Developing countries, under 1

Each square equals 0.5 barrel of oil consumed per capita.

Sources: *British Petroleum Company*, "Statistical Review of World Energy," www.bp.com. *Population Reference Bureau*, "2004 World Population Data Sheet," www.prb.org. *World Bank, World Development Indicators 2003*, Washington, D.C.: World Bank, 2003.

7.4 Oil Consumption Patterns

What is oil used for? Oil is refined into gasoline. It is also used to make asphalt, plastics, nylon, and other products.

Which developed countries consume the most oil per capita? Why do you think that is? The United States, Japan, and the Netherlands use large quantities of oil per capita. Their cars, trains, and planes need oil for fuel. Power plants burn oil to generate electricity, and oil is used to heat buildings in winter.

Which developing countries consume the most oil per capita? Why do you think that is? Kuwait, Saudi Arabia, and the United Arab Emirates consume large quantities of oil per capita. Oil is found in abundance in many countries in the Middle East and is used as a fuel source there. Other developing countries, like Singapore and South Korea, often import fuel for their industries.

Analyze the computer consumption cartogram with your class. Then, with your group, read Section 7.5 and answer the questions below.

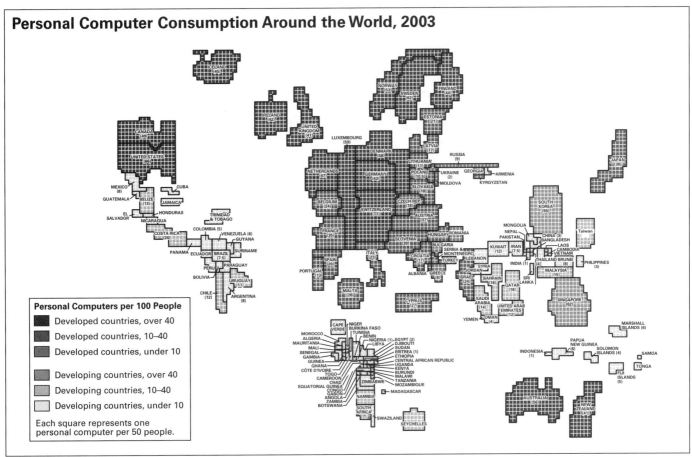

Personal Computer Consumption Around the World, 2003

Sources: *International Telecommunication Union,* "Internet Indicators: Hosts, Users, and Number of PCs," www.itu.int/. *Population Reference Bureau,* www.prb.org.

7.5 Computer and Internet Use Patterns

What are computers and the Internet used for? Governments and businesses use computers to store and manage information. Businesses use the Internet to reach customers. Families use email to stay in touch with relatives.

Which countries have the most access to technology? Why do you think that is? Developed countries, especially the United States, have the most access to technology. Computers and the Internet were invented in the United States. And people and businesses in developed countries have the money to buy computers.

Which countries have the least access to technology? Why do you think that is? Developing countries (such as Chad, Bangladesh, and Samoa) have less access to computers and the Internet than developed countries. This is probably because people and businesses in these countries often do not have enough money to buy computers.

Analyze the gross domestic product (GDP) cartogram with your class.

Then, with your group, read Section 7.6 and answer the questions below.

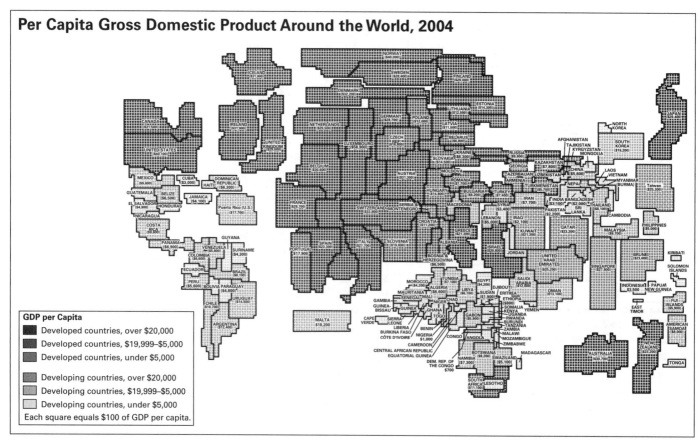

Per Capita Gross Domestic Product Around the World, 2004

GDP per Capita
- Developed countries, over $20,000
- Developed countries, $19,999–$5,000
- Developed countries, under $5,000

- Developing countries, over $20,000
- Developing countries, $19,999–$5,000
- Developing countries, under $5,000

Each square equals $100 of GDP per capita.

Sources: *Central Intelligence Agency*, "The World Factbook," www.cia.gov. *Population Reference Bureau*, www.prb.org.

7.6 The World's Greatest Producers

What three important factors contribute to the United States' high GDP? Abundant natural resources, advanced technologies, and highly skilled workers allow the United States to have a high GDP.

How does education affect GDP in the United States? Educated workers are more skilled. Many people in the United States have completed college. Many adult Americans return to school to learn new skills. This means they can do many types of work.

How does the American work ethic affect GDP? Americans generally believe that work is good for people. Many grow up believing they can be successful. These beliefs lead Americans to work hard. On average, Americans work longer hours and take less vacation than people in other developed countries. All this helps Americans to produce more.

How do you think a country's GDP affects its citizens' ability to consume? Possible answer: Producing goods provides jobs, allowing people to earn the money needed to consume goods. If a country has a high GDP, its workers probably make enough to consume many types of goods. If a country has a low GDP, its workers probably only make enough money to buy basic necessities like food.

Migration to the United States: The Impact on People and Places

Overview

In this lesson, students learn about the push and pull factors that cause people to migrate to the United States. In an **Experiential Exercise,** they assume the roles of seven recent U.S. immigrants and participate in a series of interviews. They then read about the impact of migration on both the United States and the countries that immigrants leave behind.

Objectives

Students will

- define and explain the importance of these key geographic terms: *emigrate, immigrate, migration stream, pull factor, push factor, refugee.*
- understand the primary reasons people emigrate from their country of birth and immigrate to the United States.
- identify key ways in which migration impacts the United States, immigrants, and the countries left behind.
- learn about other important migration streams around the world.

Materials

- *Geography Alive! Regions and People*
- Interactive Student Notebooks
- Transparency 8
- Information Masters 8A and 8B (1 transparency of each)
- Student Handout 8A (1 immigrant biography for every 2 students)
- Student Handout 8B (1 per student)
- CD Track 4
- colored markers

Preview

1 Ask students to complete Preview 8 in their Interactive Student Notebooks. Give students time to draw several arrows on their maps. They may need to consult other maps to locate particular countries. Have students share their answers with a partner. (**Note:** You may want to make a transparency of the map in Preview 8, project it onto a bulletin board covered with white paper, and have students attach lengths of colored yarn with pushpins to show the migration routes.)

2 Explain the connection between the Preview and the upcoming activity. Explain that just as the people that students named on their maps moved from one place to another and had various reasons for doing so, the same is true for people around the world. In the upcoming activity, students will learn about the reasons people migrate to the United States and the impact this has on the United States, the immigrants, and the countries they leave behind.

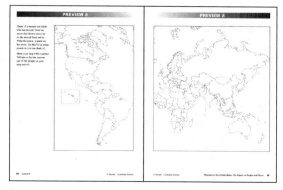

Preview 8

Essential Question and Geoterms

1 Introduce Chapter 8 in *Geography Alive! Regions and People.* Have students read Section 8.1. Then ask them to identify four details in the photograph that relate to what they just read.

2 Introduce the Graphic Organizer and the Essential Question. Have students examine the map showing migration routes to the United States. Ask,

- What do you see?
- What do the arrows represent? What does the thickness of the arrows represent?
- Where are the arrows going to, and where are they coming from?
- For what reasons might people come to the United States?
- What are some ways that the United States might be affected by all of this migration?
- How might the countries where the arrows begin be affected by this migration?

Have students read the accompanying text. Make sure they understand the Essential Question, *How does migration affect the lives of people and the character of places?* You may want to post the Essential Question in the room or write it on the board for the duration of the activity.

3 Have students read Section 8.2. Then have them work individually or in pairs to complete Geoterms 8 in their Interactive Student Notebooks. Ask them to share their answers with another student, or have volunteers share their answers with the class.

Experiential Exercise

Phase 1: Preparing for the Immigrant Interviews

1 Put students in mixed-ability pairs. You may want to prepare a transparency to show them who their partners are and where they will sit.

Geoterms 8

2 Introduce students to the causes of migration to the United States. Have them read Sections 8.3 and 8.4 of *Geography Alive! Regions and People* and, with their partners, complete the corresponding Reading Notes. Afterward, have volunteers share some of their examples of push and pull factors.

3 Introduce the activity. Explain that students will now learn about the push and pull factors affecting one of seven recent immigrants to the United States and then take turns playing the roles of the immigrants in a series of interviews. Give each pair of students one biography from *Student Handout 8A: Biographies of Recent U.S. Immigrants* and one copy of *Student Handout 8B: Immigrant Name Card.*

Reading Notes 8

4 Project a transparency of *Information Master 8A: Preparing for the Interviews.* Review the steps for preparing for the immigrant interviews, and answer any questions students have. You may want to keep the information master projected while students work.

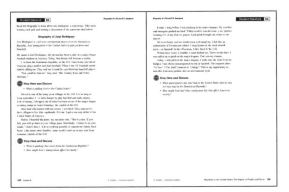

Student Handout 8A

Student Handout 8B

Information Master 8A

5 Allow pairs adequate time to prepare. As students are preparing and practicing for the immigrant interviews, circulate around the room to make sure they are

- answering each question thoroughly.
- including interesting details in their answers.
- using immigrant "artifacts" to help answer the questions.

Phase 2: Conducting the Immigrant Interviews

1 Prepare the classroom for the interviews. Create interview stations by placing desks in face-to-face pairs around the perimeter of the room.

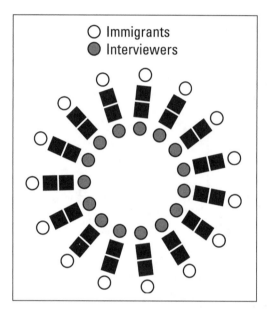

○ Immigrants
● Interviewers

2 Have each pair sit at one of the interview stations, and explain the activity. Tell pairs to decide who will first play the role of the immigrant and who will be the interviewer, and give them a minute to prepare materials for their roles. Immigrants should arrange their completed name cards and artifacts on their desks. Interviewers should have their Interactive Student Notebooks and a pencil. Project a transparency of *Information Master 8B: Conducting the Interviews* and review the directions with students. Interviewers will speak with two immigrants and then share notes with their partners. Partners will then exchange roles, and the new interviewers will interview two "new" immigrants and then return to their partners to share notes. Keep the master projected during the activity for interviewers to refer to.

3 Have interviewers conduct two interviews. Have the first set of interviewers conduct two interviews. Following are some tips for executing this activity effectively.

Information Master 8B   Reading Notes 8

- *Step 1:* Play part of CD Track 4, "Music from Around the World," each time interviewers move around the room to find a new immigrant to interview. Explain that these musical selections come from the countries these immigrants left behind. Remind interviewers that they will have about one minute to find an immigrant they have not yet interviewed and that you will stop the music once all interviewers are again seated. Interviewers must work *together* to make sure each has a "new" immigrant to interview. This task will become a little more difficult with each new interview; however, this is a dynamic way to have students find a new immigrant for every interview.

- *Steps 3 and 4:* Remind immigrants to answer questions thoroughly, to include interesting details in their answers, and to use their artifacts to help them answer the questions.

- *Step 6:* Before interviewers leave their first immigrant, remind them that they have to find a "new" immigrant (one they have not yet interviewed) for their second interview.

4 Have interviewers return to their original partners. After the second interview, have interviewers return to their original stations. Give them about five minutes to share their interview notes with their partners, who will add what they learn to their Reading Notes.

5 Conduct the third and fourth interviews. Have partners reverse roles. The new interviewers will interview two immigrants they have not interviewed or learned about before, and then share notes about the interviews with their partners.

6 Debrief the interviews. Once pairs have completed their interviews and added to each section of their Reading Notes, ask students,

- How did it feel to play the role of a recent immigrant?
- Which specific push factors did you identify in your interviews? Pull factors? Mention the names of immigrants you met in the interviews.
- What did you learn about how immigration affects the United States?
- What did you learn about how emigration affects the countries immigrants leave behind?

7 Have students learn more about how migration affects both the United States and immigrants' home countries. Have them read Sections 8.5 and 8.6 and add additional examples to their Reading Notes.

Global Connections

1 Introduce the Global Connections. Have students read Section 8.7. Tell them that they will now see how some of the issues they encountered in the activity play out on a global scale.

2 Project *Transparency 8: Global Connections.* Have students analyze the map by discussing and sharing their answers to the following questions. Use the additional information given to enrich the discussion.

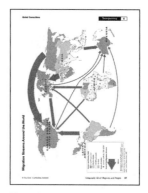

Transparency 8

- **What interesting details do you see?**

- **What do the arrows represent? What does the thickness of the arrows represent?**

  The arrows represent migration streams (large numbers of migrants) coming from major areas of the world and going to others. The thicker the arrow, the greater the net migration.

- **What do the colors and symbols in the countries represent?**

  The colors represent the wealth or poverty of a country. The starbursts represent countries that have experienced armed conflict from 1990 to 2005.

- **What might this map tell us about the relationship between where most migrants leave from and where most move to?**

  Most migrants tend to leave less economically developed, war-prone areas of the world. They tend to enter more economically developed and less war-ridden areas of the world.

3 Have students read Section 8.8 and examine the rest of the information in the section. Encourage them to try to discover relationships among the various types of information given in the map. Then lead a discussion of these questions:

- **Why might some regions "push" more migrants than they "pull"?**

- **Why might some regions "pull" more migrants than they "push"?**

- **How does migration affect both "push" and "pull" countries?**

Processing

Have students complete Processing 8 in their Interactive Student Notebooks.

Online Resources

For more information on immigration to the United States, refer students to Online Resources for *Geography Alive! Regions and People* at www.teachtci.com.

Assessment

Masters for assessment appear on the next three pages followed by answers and scoring rubrics.

Processing 8

Mastering the Content

Shade in the oval by the letter of the best answer for each question.

1. Which term **best** describes people from other countries who enter the United States to start new lives?

   ○ A. consumers

   ○ B. emigrants

   ○ C. immigrants

   ○ D. refugees

2. All of the following are major push factors that cause people to leave their home countries **except**

   ○ A. hunger.

   ○ B. poverty.

   ○ C. violent conflict.

   ○ D. economic opportunity.

3. Which of these statements about immigration to the United States in 2002 is **best** supported by the table below?

   Top Five Countries of Origin of U.S. Immigrants, 2002

Country	Number of Immigrants	Percentage of All U.S. Immigrants
Mexico	115,864	16.4%
India	50,372	7.1%
Philippines	45,397	6.4%
China	40,659	5.8%
El Salvador	28,296	4.0%

   ○ A. China had a larger brain drain to the U.S. than any other country.

   ○ B. Mexico lost more than twice as many people to the U.S. than any other country.

   ○ C. More political refugees came to the U.S. from El Salvador than from any other country.

   ○ D. More newcomers from India later returned to their homeland than immigrants from any other country.

4. Which of the following is **not** a major pull factor drawing people to the United States?

   ○ A. family

   ○ B. schools

   ○ C. freedom

   ○ D. persecution

5. Immigrants **most** help to build the U.S. economy by

   ○ A. using public services.

   ○ B. serving in the military.

   ○ C. starting new businesses.

   ○ D. learning to speak English.

6. What do the three holidays listed below have in common?

   • St. Patrick's Day

   • Cinco de Mayo

   • Chinese New Year

   ○ A. They started in the United States.

   ○ B. They came to the United States with immigrants.

   ○ C. They mark important events in U.S. history.

   ○ D. They are celebrated only by immigrants in the United States.

7. Which is the **best** definition of a brain drain?

   ○ A. the loss of skilled workers who move to other countries

   ○ B. the loss of war refugees who seek safety in other countries

   ○ C. the loss of aging parents who join children in other countries

   ○ D. the loss of good students who attend college in other countries

8. What are payments sent by immigrants to family members in their home country called?

   ○ A. consumption

   ○ B. economic activity

   ○ C. migration streams

   ○ D. remittances

Applying Geography Skills: Analyzing a Flow Map

Use the map and your knowledge of geography to complete the tasks below.

Migration Streams Around the World

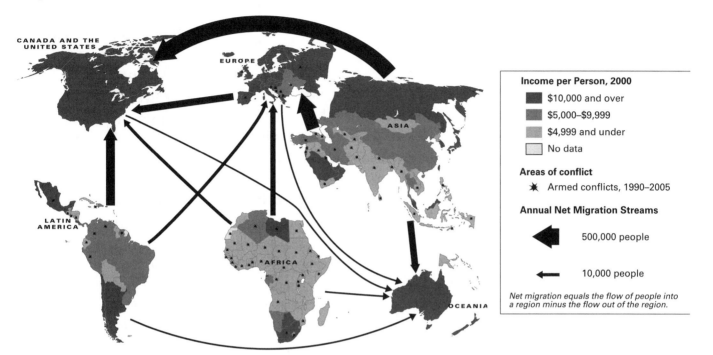

This map shows migrations streams around the world.

1. Circle one arrow on the map. Describe where it begins and where it ends. Tell what the arrow represents. Use the map legend to help you.

2. Identify two push factors shown on the map.

3. Identify one pull factor shown on the map.

4. Determine which region received the most migration streams. Did this region receive the most immigrants? Explain your answer.

> **Test Terms Glossary**
> To **explain** means to give reasons for something.

Exploring the Essential Question

How does migration affect the lives of people and the character of places?

In Chapter 8, you explored why people immigrate. Now you will use what you learned. Use the passage below and your knowledge of geography to complete this task.

The "Lost Boys of Sudan"

Cousins Michael Mach Paul and Abraham Anyieth were 6 and 7 when they fled their burning village in 1987. A brutal war in their homeland, the African country of Sudan, had left the boys without homes or families.

The cousins became part of a group of refugees known as the "Lost Boys of Sudan." The boys walked for hundreds of miles in search of safety. Many died of hunger and thirst along the way. Those who survived finally reached a refugee camp in the country of Kenya.

In 2001, some of the "Lost Boys" began another long journey. This one took them to the United States. Here they were safe and had enough to eat. Still, adjusting to life in a new land was hard. At first they were homesick. They also had much to learn. They had never shopped for food. They had never seen a stove or a microwave. Nor had they experienced cold winters.

In 2005, the cousins began a new walk together. This time, it was across a stage to receive degrees from a community college in Pennsylvania. They had faced many challenges to get here. One was learning how to type. "The professor said our papers had to be typed or we would fail," Anyieth recalls. "I came from a village with no electricity, no telephone. I had never seen a computer before. It took me five hours to type my first page." But the cousins are used to overcoming challenges. As Paul told a reporter, "Nothing could ever be as hard as what we've been through."

The Task: Summarizing an Immigrant Experience

The passage above is about two refugees from Sudan. Your task is to summarize how immigration has changed their lives.

Step 1: Read the passage. Circle two details that describe the boys' lives in Africa. Underline two details about their lives in the United States.

Step 2: Write a paragraph that summarizes how coming to the United States changed the lives of these two "Lost Boys." Include the following in your summary:

A. a topic sentence that introduces your subject
B. details about the refugees' lives in Africa and the United States
C. a conclusion that summarizes how immigration changed their lives

Writing Tips: Creating Topic Sentences

A topic sentence should tell what your paragraph is about. Often you can create a topic sentence by restating the writing prompt.

Prompt: *Write a paragraph that summarizes how coming to the United States changed these two "Lost Boys."*

Topic sentence: *The lives of two of Sudan's "Lost Boys" changed dramatically when they came to the United States.*

Test Terms Glossary

To **summarize** means to briefly present the main points.

Applying Geography Skills: Sample Responses

1. Circled arrows will vary. Student should identify where their choice begins and ends and about how many immigrants it represents. Example: The arrow begins in Africa and ends in Oceania. It represents a migration stream of about 10,000 people from Africa to Oceania in 2000.

2. The two push factors shown on the map are low income per person (poverty) and armed conflicts.

3. The pull factor shown on the map is high income per person. Also accept lack of conflict, or peace, as a pull factor.

4. Oceania received the most migration streams. It did not, however, receive the most immigrants. The arrows going to North America are much thicker than those going to Oceania.

Exploring the Essential Question: Sample Response

Step 1: Circled details may include *burning village, brutal war, without homes or families, hunger and thirst, refugee camp.* Underlined details may include *safety, enough to eat, shopping, stove, microwave, cold winters, receiving degrees, computers.*

Step 2: The paragraph should include all the elements listed in the prompt.

The lives of two of Sudan's "Lost Boys" changed dramatically when they came to America. In Africa, they were homeless and often hungry. They lived in a camp for refugees. After coming to the United States, they had to learn how to use things Americans take for granted, like supermarkets and stoves. They were able to go to school and graduate from college. It was not easy, but these "Lost Boys" were able to build new lives for themselves in their adopted country.

Mastering the Content Answer Key

1. C	2. D	3. B	4. D
5. C	6. B	7. A	8. D

Applying Geography Skills Scoring Rubric

Score	General Description
2	Student responds to all parts of the task. Response is correct and clear.
1	Student responds to some parts of the task. Response is mostly correct.
0	Response does not match the task or is incorrect.

Exploring the Essential Question Scoring Rubric

Score	General Description
3	Student responds to all parts of the task. Response is correct, clear, and supported by details.
2	Student responds to most or all parts of the task. Response is generally correct but may lack details.
1	Student responds to at least one part of the task. Response may contain errors and lack details.
0	Response does not match the task or is incorrect.

Prepare for the Immigrant Interviews

Follow these steps to prepare for the immigrant interviews. Have your teacher initial each step as you complete it.

_____ **Step 1: Read the immigrant's biography carefully.** Talk about the "Stop Here and Discuss" questions with your partner.

_____ **Step 2: Work together to complete the immigrant's name card.**

• Fold the card so that the map appears on one side and the questions appear on the other.

• On the map side of the card, write the immigrant's name in large, bold letters. With a colored marker, draw an arrow from your immigrant's home country to the United States.

• On the other side of the card, write answers that your immigrant would give to the four interview questions. Include interesting details from the immigrant's story. You will use these notes to help you during your interviews later.

• Brainstorm and record ideas for artifacts your immigrant could show during the interviews. These should be simple items you have at home or that you can make, such as photographs or other meaningful family objects. Decide who will bring in the artifacts on the day of the interviews.

_____ **Step 3: Practice the interview.**

• Have one partner play the immigrant and the other be the interviewer.

• The interviewer should practice asking the four questions on the card.

• The immigrant should thoroughly tell the immigrant's story by answering the questions and explaining the artifacts.

• Reverse roles and practice again. Each interview should last 3 to 5 minutes.

Conduct the Immigrant Interviews

Follow these steps to conduct the interviews:

Step 1: Your teacher will play music from the countries these immigrants migrated from. When the music starts, immigrants should hold up their name cards. Interviewers should walk around the room to find an immigrant they have not met before. The music will stop when all interviewers are seated in front of a new immigrant.

Step 2: Interview partners introduce themselves to each other. Immigrants should tell where they are from and show their migration routes on the front of their name cards.

Step 3: Interviewer asks the immigrant, *What push factors drove you to leave your country?* The immigrant answers the question, using artifacts to help. The interviewer takes notes in his or her Reading Notes.

Step 4: Interview pairs repeat Step 3 for these three questions:
- *What pull factors drew you to the United States?*
- *How has your immigration affected you and the United States?*
- *How has your emigration affected the country you left behind?*

Step 5: Interviewers thank the immigrants and prepare for their next interview.

Step 6: Conduct a second interview by repeating Steps 1–5.

Read this biography to learn about one immigrant's experience. Take turns reading each part and leading a discussion of the questions that follow.

Biography of José Rodriguez

José Rodriguez is a 22-year-old baseball player from the Dominican Republic. José immigrated to the United States to play professional baseball.

My name is José Rodriguez. My dream has been to play in a major league baseball stadium in America. Today, that dream will become a reality.

I'm from the Dominican Republic, or the D.R. Back home, just about everyone plays sandlot and club baseball. When I was 15, baseball scouts started calling me. They told me I could be a professional baseball player.

"You could be famous," they said, "like Sammy Sosa and Pedro Martinez."

 Stop Here and Discuss

- *What is pulling José to the United States?*

I lived in one of the many poor villages in the D.R. For as long as I can remember, I've had a hunger to play baseball and make money. Lots of money. I dropped out of school to train at one of the major league scouting camps in Santo Domingo, the capital of the D.R.

Most kids who trained with me weren't recruited. They returned to their villages to live like vagabonds. Not me. I got a one-way ticket to the United States of America.

Before I boarded the plane, my recruiter said, "This is a test. If you fail, you will go back to your village poor. Your family's future is in your hands." I knew then I'd do everything possible to support my family back home. Like many other families, mine would count on money sent from someone outside of the D.R.

 Stop Here and Discuss

- *What is pushing José away from the Dominican Republic?*
- *How might José's immigration affect his family?*

It wasn't long before I was pitching in the minor leagues. My coaches and managers pushed me hard. Within weeks I was the team's ace pitcher, winning five of my first six games. Each pitch brought me closer to the majors.

My host family and the whole town welcomed me. I felt like an ambassador of Dominican culture. I sang hymns in the local church choir—in Spanish! In the off-season, I flew back to the D.R.

Within three years, a Double-A team drafted me. Three weeks later, I was called up to pitch in the major leagues. This was my chance.

Today, I will pitch in the major leagues. I walk onto the field from the bullpen. Fans shout encouragement to me in Spanish. The organist plays "El Toro" ("The Bull") instead of "Charge!" This is my opportunity to turn this American pastime into an international sport.

 Stop Here and Discuss

- *What opportunities has José had in the United States that he may not have had in the Dominican Republic?*
- *How might José and other immigrants like him affect American society?*

Read this biography to learn about one immigrant's experience. Take turns reading each part and leading a discussion of the questions that follow.

Biography of Ricardo Flores

Ricardo Flores is a 42-year-old rancher from Mexico. He immigrated to the United States with his family of six children.

I am Ricardo Flores, a husband and father. My family of six children once lived on a very poor ranch near Guanajuato, Mexico. I couldn't afford the Mexican government's fees to dig the wells needed to save my crops from drought. So I abandoned my ranch, a tough decision. Today I live 1,200 miles away in Garden City, Kansas. I work at a meatpacking plant and earn $15 an hour. That's more than one day's pay in Mexico!

I came alone to the United States. Pedrito, my youngest son, cried, "Please don't leave me! I want to live in America too!" I was separated from my family for 13 years. I saw them only twice a year. This was difficult. But eventually I was able to save enough money for them to legally migrate to the United States. This was what I could give my children: visas to the U.S. Here, they could seek their futures.

 Stop Here and Discuss

- *What pushed Ricardo and his family to leave Mexico?*
- *What pulled them to the United States?*

Not once did my wife and I consider crossing the border illegally. Immigrants who swim across the Rio Grande to avoid the border patrol live in fear of being deported (sent back). It would have been far too risky for a family of eight.

Getting visas for seven was difficult as well. It typically takes 13 years to get an application processed. Finally, we were scheduled for an immigration interview. Even then, the 1,000-mile journey stretched us financially. We had to pay for motel rooms, bus fares, and Mexican passports. We also had to pay for medical exams and application fees.

I worried that my income and that of our U.S. sponsor's might not be enough to support my whole family in the United States. Fortunately, a cousin living in the United States decided to sponsor us too. Our visas were approved.

Stop Here and Discuss

- *What challenges did Ricardo and his family experience in trying to immigrate?*
- *What do you think the role of a U.S. sponsor is?*

We enjoy our life in Garden City. Twenty years ago, 90 percent of the students in schools here were native-born English speakers. Today, more than half are from immigrant families. All my children, even 18-year-old Nora, are enrolled in school. They are hardworking and loved by their teachers. Slowly they are mastering the English language.

I have joined a hometown organization. Nearly 100 workers in the Garden City area meet once a week. Each of them gives $10, $20, sometimes $30 to our treasurer. He sends this money back to Guanajuato. They hope to build a cafeteria for the town's kindergarten. For our next project, we'd like to collect money for a new ambulance. It is our way of helping those in Mexico who cannot realize their dreams in America, as we have.

 Stop Here and Discuss

- *How are immigrants like Ricardo and his family affecting their communities in the United States?*
- *How are immigrants like Ricardo affecting the Mexican communities they left behind?*

Read this biography to learn about one immigrant's experience. Take turns reading each part and leading a discussion of the questions that follow.

Biography of Rachel Tang

Rachel Tang is a 23-year-old medical student at the University of Southern California. She emigrated from China to the United States as a child.

My name is Rachel Tang. I was not born with this name. But when my parents brought me to this country, my teacher could not pronounce my Chinese name, Xiaojun. So she suggested to my mother the American name Rachel. From then on, that was what I was called: Rachel Tang.

I was only a small child when my parents demonstrated in Tiananmen Square. With many others, they cried for freedom and democracy in China. Instead, the government responded with bullets. Many protesters were killed. My parents were not. But they decided it was time to come to America to experience democracy and expose me to the best education possible.

 Stop Here and Discuss

- *What pushed Rachel's family to leave China?*
- *What pulled them to the United States?*

At first, it seemed an impossible dream. Because we lived in a Communist country, we would have to sneak out of China. But a relative of my father who lived in the United States sent us a letter. He urged us to come and sent us a tiny bit of money.

It was decided that my father should go first. For two years, I did not see him. My mother and I waited eagerly for his letters. They were filled not only with news but also with money we would need to make the journey.

When we had enough, my mother bought fake papers for us to use when we traveled. But we did not fly straight to America. We flew first to Thailand. When a customs agent asked where we were going, we made sure not to say America.

From Thailand, we flew to Canada. Then we boarded a bus to take us across the border. At the border, they barely looked at us. But still my mother held her breath, afraid we would be sent back to China. It was a joyous reunion we had with my father in San Francisco, California!

Stop Here and Discuss

- *Why do you think Rachel's father came to the United States first without his family?*
- *How might the Chinese communities that Rachel and other immigrants left be affected by their departure?*

I worked hard in my new school. Every day, my mother made me memorize new words from the dictionary. Once I got a B in history. My mother cried that day. I was told again and again that I must succeed. I must help my family's lives become better. Like most Chinese immigrants, I did what was expected of me. When I graduated from high school, I accepted a full scholarship to Stanford University. This year I transferred to the University of Southern California's medical school. I hope to become a doctor.

I visit my parents often. They live in a community that is primarily made up of other Chinese immigrants. They own a small restaurant in a strip mall with other Chinese business owners. My mother cooks for me, and I am reminded of the tastes and smells of my childhood. I still feel "foreign" despite having lived here for more than 10 years. I also feel American, but others still see me as different, an outsider. I hope to become a citizen someday soon. Maybe then I will be accepted into this American culture completely.

 Stop Here and Discuss

- *What kinds of challenges does Rachel face in her new country?*
- *How are Rachel and other Chinese immigrants affecting their communities in the United States?*

Read this biography to learn about one immigrant's experience. Take turns reading each part and leading a discussion of the questions that follow.

Biography of Olanre Nwidor

Olanre Nwidor is a 40-year-old engineer from Nigeria, in West Africa. Olanre immigrated to the United States after violence broke out in his village.

My wife, two children, and I, Olanre Nwidor, are members of the small Ogoni tribe in Nigeria. For many years, the government permitted a U.S. company to drill oil near our village. With an environmental catastrophe growing, many Ogonis, including myself, protested this drilling. The military responded violently. They executed our leader and eight others. I was then denied a job as a chemical engineer in Nigeria's oil industry.

Surrounded by increasing violence, my family fled to a refugee camp. Eventually, the United Nations acknowledged our persecution and helped us to resettle in a large American city.

 Stop Here and Discuss

- *What pushed Olanre and his family to leave Africa?*
- *What pulled Olanre and his family to the United States?*

I expected an easy and prosperous life in America. It has not come. Government agencies initially gave us food, health care, and shelter. But now we struggle on our own, with low-paying jobs and health problems. High blood pressure nearly forced me to quit my factory job. In addition, my wife is a tuberculosis carrier. Working the night shift as a hotel maid, attending nursing school, and caring for our children exhausts her. She misses the community and her family back home.

I continue to be pressured by family to send money back to Nigeria. Unfortunately, it will have to be my children who provide that kind of support. I am doing all I can to survive in this new and unfriendly world.

In the refugee camp, there was no running water. I remember thinking, "When I get to America, there will be running water. I will sleep in a soft bed. I will be accepted. Blacks in America are free and not discriminated against."

This has not always proven to be true. I sometimes feel like I'm not treated as well as other people who are not immigrants.

Stop Here and Discuss

- *How are immigrants like Olanre affecting villages back home in Nigeria?*
- *What kinds of challenges have Olanre and his family faced in the United States?*

There have been a few highpoints to my life here. I recently quit my job to become a caseworker helping women who have no homes or money. I am also enrolled in nursing school. I have dreams for my kids' futures. They feel that America is their home. Not long ago, my wife gave birth to our new son, Karm. He's a true American. I'm Nigerian. You see two countries living in the same home.

If an Ogoni man asked me about immigrating to America, I would tell him to not have high hopes. America is not a second heaven.

 Stop Here and Discuss

- *How are African immigrants like Olanre and his family affecting their communities in the United States?*
- *What opportunities has Olanre been given in America?*

Read this biography to learn about one immigrant's experience. Take turns reading each part and leading a discussion of the questions that follow.

Biography of Anna Vinski

Anna Vinski is a 37-year-old professor. She emigrated from Latvia to the United States to find a better-paying job.

I sometimes wonder if I made a mistake coming here. To America, I mean. It is true that I did not make much money teaching at the university in Latvia. I made barely enough to survive. And my husband, an engineer who also taught at the university, did little better. But at least in Latvia we were respected. Back home, people in Riga knew us, and we went to dinner parties sometimes. Here we are nobody.

Like my husband, I have tried to get a job at one of the many universities here in Los Angeles, California. I teach mathematics. But the interviewers tell me that my English is not good enough. And so I work as a playground aide at the elementary school my daughter attends. The kids teach me English, and I also take classes at night.

My husband wanted us to come to America. He has needed surgery on his knee for many years now. His brother works as a nurse at a large hospital in Los Angeles. He has urged my husband to come to America to have his surgery. "There are many well-educated, highly trained doctors here," he has told my husband often.

We both believed that there would be more opportunities for our children here. But I've seen the kids on the playground tease my daughter about her accent. I want to hug her, but in front of her friends, I cannot.

 Stop Here and Discuss

- *What pushed Anna's family to leave Latvia?*
- *What pulled them to the United States?*

My children, despite struggling to learn this language, have adjusted quickly. They love American movies and television. Twice already they have begged us to go to Disneyland. They have made a few friends. My oldest son, though, he tells me, "Mom, kids here are not as mature as those in Latvia. They talk of silly things, like who wears what kind of shoes. I miss my friends back home."

But most of his friends really *aren't* back home anymore. They, too, have found new homes in America, Germany, or Israel. Too many honest, intelligent Latvians are finding that they cannot support their families in Latvia.

 Stop Here and Discuss

- *What are some of the challenges Anna and her children are facing in America?*
- *What are some things about America that they enjoy?*

Other immigrants have settled near us, and we have become friends. There are families from Russia, Poland, Croatia, and Hungary. All are people who lived to see Communism fall. They gather at my house for picnics and speak in halting English. Many of us can still speak Russian and sometimes that is easier than English. I enjoy cooking foods that remind us of home. My specialty is Latvian *piragi,* or buns filled with bacon. My neighbors tell me to open a bakery. Maybe someday I will.

My daughter, she plays the piano. It is her dream to someday go to the Juilliard School of Music in New York City. I tell her she can do this if she works hard. I think it is a dream she can reach. And this— this chance to fulfill a dream—this is why we came to America.

 Stop Here and Discuss

- *How are immigrants like Anna affecting their communities in the United States?*
- *What opportunities does Anna's daughter have in America?*

Read this biography to learn about one immigrant's experience. Take turns reading each part and leading a discussion of the questions that follow.

Biography of Sumatra Singh

Sumatra Singh is a 35-year-old software developer in Madison, Wisconsin. He emigrated from India to the United States to excel in his career.

My name is Sumatra Singh. When I was a child in Bombay, India, I used to dream of living like the Americans I saw in Hollywood films. The fast cars, the glitzy stores, the muscled, smooth-talking men… this seemed like the life for me. America seemed so different from Bombay. In Bombay, there were always crowded streets. More and more people from the country-side were moving to Bombay to find better jobs. The dirty sidewalks seemed a far cry from the elegant Hollywood I dreamed about.

Of course, it wasn't Hollywood that brought me to America. It was technology. As a software developer, I could make much more money in America than India. I could come over on an H1B visa. This is the kind of visa they give only to highly skilled immigrants. That way, I could live in the U.S. for 100 weeks, learn all I could about technology, and return to India an expert in my field.

 Stop Here and Discuss

- *What pushed Sumatra to leave India?*
- *What pulled Sumatra to the United States?*

The America I came to was not the same America I saw in the movies. I had to get a very cheap apartment in San Francisco, California. My wife did not get a work visa, so she quickly became bored sitting in our apartment all day. She watched TV and started to become more like American women. At first it was difficult for me. I was not used to think-ing of my wife as an equal. But soon we were shopping together and sharing the household chores like American couples do.

There were other changes. I had to learn to drive on the "wrong" side of the road. In India, we drive on the left. I had to work long hours to move ahead in my job. Even then, I was laid off many times. A tech-nology firm in Madison, Wisconsin, finally hired me. But this meant moving across the country. My wife and I spent many days overcome with homesickness. We missed the large family network that had surrounded us in India.

Stop Here and Discuss

- *What are some of the challenges Sumatra and his wife faced in America?*
- *In what ways have Sumatra and his wife had to adapt to a new American life?*

Even still, there were traces of Indian culture around us. We found a small community of Indian Americans in Wisconsin. They celebrate Indian Independence Day once a year with a parade. My wife wore her *sari* and her *bindi* (a dot on her forehead) for the festival. She looked as beautiful as the day I married her. There were several Indian restaurants nearby that we visited often. We even saw American teenagers with henna tattoos. We laughed at how they'd made a fad out of our traditional Indian custom.

But always in the backs of our minds was the day we would return to India. My mother did not believe we would return. "That American lifestyle will seduce you, maybe even corrupt you!" she would tell me on the phone.

But my wife and I knew we would go home. Near the end of my 100 weeks, I flew back to California to attend the SiliconIndia Career Fair. Recruiters from Indian companies told us of technology jobs back in India. I would return to India to use my experience in the U.S. to help the country of my birth.

 Stop Here and Discuss

- *How are Indian immigrants affecting their communities in the United States?*
- *In what ways do Indian technology immigrants affect their communities back home?*

Read this biography to learn about one immigrant's experience. Take turns reading each part and leading a discussion of the questions that follow.

Biography of Ahmed Al-Mokalla

Ahmed Al-Mokalla is a 38-year-old police officer from Yemen in the Middle East. Ahmed immigrated to the United States after a violent civil war tore his country apart.

When I was 14 and living in Yemen, soldiers came to my house. They took me away and forced me to join the army. I served for three years and fought in Yemen's civil war. When I got out of the army, I came to the United States. Yemen took my childhood. They would not get my adulthood too.

My name is Ahmed Al-Mokalla. I have a wife and a daughter, Laila. Laila was born in the United States. She has had a much different child-hood here than she would have had in Yemen. In Yemen, girls have very little freedom. In school, if she had missed a fact on her multiplication tables, she would have been hit on the head. Here she can go to school without fear. She hopes to go to medical school in a few more years.

 Stop Here and Discuss

- *What pushed Ahmed to leave Yemen?*
- *What pulled Ahmed to the United States?*

When my wife and I first arrived in New York City, I waited tables while I put myself through college. In Yemen, as a boy, I had watched many American "cop" shows. I decided long ago that I wanted to be one of the "good guys." I joined the New York Police Department when I was 24. Finally, I was a good guy, though it didn't always feel like it.

On September 11, 2001, I was stationed at Ground Zero. How to explain what I felt that day? Sadness. When my wife went to pick up Laila from school, another parent yelled at her from his car, "Go back where you came from, terrorist!" It was a difficult time for us, and for all Arab Americans. I am American 100 percent. But I am also Arabic 100 percent. I can't change where I came from, but America is my home.

Stop Here and Discuss

- *What opportunities have Ahmed and his family been given in America?*
- *What challenges have Ahmed and his family faced in America?*

Soon after the events of September 11, 2001, I moved my family to Dearborn, Michigan. The large Arab American community here welcomed us. My wife can speak Arabic all day without ever having to use English if she wants. There are eight mosques near us. A billboard on the freeway near our home used to read, "Attend the church of your choice." But many Muslims in my community voiced concerns over this. Today it reads, "Attend the church, synagogue, or mosque of your choice." This is good.

But not all is good in America. My daughter is made fun of at school for wearing her *massar,* the scarf that covers her head. Teenage boys threw a brick through the window of a business owned by my Arab neighbors. We hear of hate crimes against Arab Americans often.

I hope soon to get a job with the Detroit Police Department, to be a "good guy" once more. Until then, I work in a car factory. My brothers would like to bring their families to America. But my wife and I have no citizenship papers, only green cards. We cannot sponsor them. I tell them to be patient. There will be a new life for them in America when it is time.

 Stop Here and Discuss

- *How are immigrants like Ahmed affecting their communities in the United States?*
- *How has being a Muslim impacted Ahmed and other American Muslims since September of 2001?*

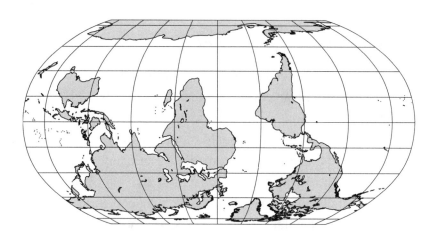

My Name

_____

How has your immigration affected you and the United States?

Artifact for this part of your interview:

How has your emigration affected the country you left behind?

Artifact for this part of your interview:

What push factors drove you to leave your country?

Artifact for this part of your interview:

What pull factors drew you to the United States?

Artifact for this part of your interview:

Follow these steps to complete your Reading Notes:

1. Read Sections 8.3 and 8.4. List examples of each push and pull factor you read about.

2. During the interviews, add any new examples of push and pull factors you learn about to your notes. You might also learn about how immigration affects the United States and the countries left behind. List those examples in your notes for Sections 8.5 and 8.6.

3. After the interviews, read Sections 8.5 and 8.6. Add any new examples you read about to your notes.

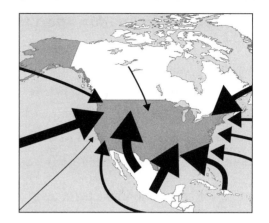

8.3 What Push Factors Drive Emigration?

Examples of political push factors:

- war, persecution
- Cubans feared being jailed for disagreeing with their dictator leader, Fidel Castro.

Examples of environmental push factors:

- drought
- Irish people faced starvation when a fungus destroyed their potato crops.
- People from the Ukraine area were unsafe when the Chernobyl nuclear power plant exploded.

Examples of economic push factors:

- Early U.S. immigrants were poor farmers and working people in Europe who wanted to improve their lives.
- Many people immigrate in hopes of making a better future for themselves.

8.4 What Pull Factors Draw Immigration?

Examples of quality-of-life pull factors:

- The "Lost Boys of Sudan" gained safety, schooling, and jobs.
- Jewish immigrants found the freedom to worship without fear.
- The "American Dream" is the belief that people in America can make a better life for themselves and their children.

Examples of family pull factors:

- Many people join relatives already living in the U.S.

Examples of education pull factors:

- People migrate so their children can attend good schools.

8.5 How Does Immigration Affect the U.S.?

Examples of economic impacts (jobs):

- Immigrant labor helped build America and fight its wars.
- Many immigrants work low-paying jobs that native-born workers don't want, such as farmwork and house cleaning.
- Some are highly skilled, such as doctors, professors, and programmers.
- Some start new businesses or work as athletes or artists.

Examples of economic impacts (taxes):

- Working immigrants pay taxes that support schools, libraries, and health clinics.
- Some immigrants need services such as English language classes, welfare, and health care.

Examples of cultural impacts (neighborhoods, foods, and holidays):

- Immigrant neighborhoods like Chinatown and Little Italy enrich American cities.
- Immigrant foods such as pizza, bagels, and tacos become popular.
- People from many backgrounds celebrate St. Patrick's Day, Chinese New Year, and Cinco de Mayo.
- Immigrants expand Americans' knowledge of the world.

8.6 How Does Emigration Affect the Homelands People Leave Behind?

Examples of economic impacts (brain drain and gain):

- Home countries lose the training and talent of skilled emigrants.
- Many immigrants send money, or remittances, back to their families.
- Some immigrants go to school or work and then return to their homeland to share their new skills and experience.

Examples of social impacts (divided families, community improvements):

- When people leave to find jobs, families are splintered, sometimes for years.
- Remittances may be used to help family members pay for health care and schooling and to help communities pay for wells, schools, and other improvements.

Examples of political impacts (working for better government):

- Some U.S. immigrants work for democracy in their homelands.
- Lithuanian immigrant Valdas Adamkus returned home to be elected president of his newly democratic country.

UNIT 3 Latin America

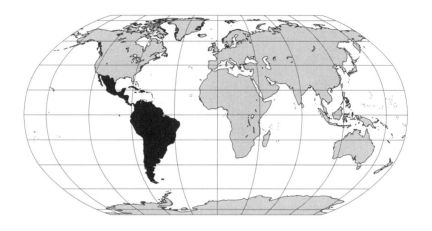

Spatial Inequality in Mexico City: From Cardboard to Castles

Overview

In this lesson, students learn about the process of urbanization and the patterns of inequality that exist in urban areas. In a **Writing for Understanding** activity, students assume the role of exchange students attending a university in Mexico City. They "travel" to four neighborhoods to survey people from four social classes about their experiences living in Mexico City. After discussing their survey results, students conclude their exchange program by writing a newspaper article describing the extreme inequalities evident in Mexico City.

Objectives

Students will

- define and explain the importance of these key geographic terms: *rural decline, spatial inequality, standard of living, urbanization.*
- identify causes and consequences of urbanization.
- explain how spatial inequality affects people living in Mexico City.
- examine standard of living around the world to understand that spatial inequality exists on a global scale.

Materials

- *Geography Alive! Regions and People*
- Interactive Student Notebooks
- Transparencies 9A–9G
- Information Master 9 (1 transparency)
- Student Handout 9 (1 for every 2 students)
- CD Tracks 5–10

Preview

1 **Have students complete Preview 9 in their Interactive Student Notebooks.** When they are finished, ask them to share the variety of features they included in their drawings and some of the best and worst characteristics of cities that they listed.

2 **Explain the connection between the Preview and the upcoming activity.** Tell students that cities around the world share many similarities. Cities are often political, economic, and cultural centers that offer jobs, education, and social services. At the same time, many cities are experiencing problems like those students may have mentioned, such as air pollution, high crime rates, and poverty. In this lesson, students will explore Mexico City, one of the world's most populated cities. They will learn about the opportunities and benefits that have attracted a large population to Mexico City—and explore some of the problems associated with the city's high population and rapid rate of growth.

Preview 9

Essential Question and Geoterms

1 **Introduce Chapter 9 in** *Geography Alive! Regions and People.* Have students examine the aerial photograph of Mexico City and read Section 9.1. Afterward, ask them for four adjectives that might describe life in Mexico City. Encourage them to consider both the photograph and what they learned in the reading.

2 **Introduce the Graphic Organizer and the Essential Question.** Have students examine the map. Ask,
- What do you see?
- What do the divisions on the map have in common? What differences do you notice among them?
- What do the locations pictured in the photographs have in common? What differences do you notice among them?
- What relationship might exist between the map and the photographs?

Have students read the accompanying text. Make sure they understand the Essential Question, *Why does spatial inequality exist in urban areas?* You may want to post the Essential Question in the room or write it on the board for the duration of the activity.

3 **Have students read Section 9.2.** Then have them work individually or in pairs to complete Geoterms 9 in their Interactive Student Notebooks. Have them share their answers with another student, or have volunteers share their answers with the class.

Geoterms 9

Writing for Understanding

Phase 1: Visiting Four Neighborhoods in Mexico City

1 Arrange your classroom. Move the desks to the edges of the room. Create "taxis" by arranging pairs of chairs facing the front of the room as shown in the diagram. (**Note:** Consider using one chair per pair instead of two to re-create the experience of riding in small Mexico City taxis.) Leave enough space for students to gather at the front of the room during their neighborhood visits. (**Note:** You may want to familiarize yourself with CD Tracks 5–10 before conducting the lesson. The tracks are recorded as dual-language interviews, in Spanish and English.)

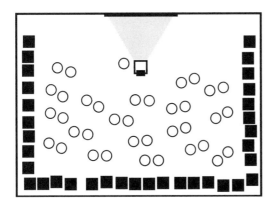

2 Introduce the activity. Put students in mixed-ability pairs, and have each pair pretend to open the doors of a taxi and enter it. Then explain that they are geography students in an exchange program with a university in Mexico City. The purpose of the program is for them to learn about Mexico City's growth as an urban area and the spatial inequalities that exist there. Students will "survey" four people in neighborhoods of varying social classes to learn about their lives. These neighborhood visits will prepare them to write an article for their own school's newspaper at the end of the exchange program.

3 Have students meet their university guides. Explain to students that they will be "joined" in the taxis by two university students who will serve as their guides during the neighborhood visits. Project *Transparency 9A: Your Guides to Mexico City,* and explain that these are the university students who will be their guides. Then play CD Track 5, "Welcome to Mexico City," in which the guides introduce themselves.

Transparency 9A

4 **Project the top half of** *Transparency 9B: Neighborhood Visit 1* **while students read Section 9.3 and complete Part 1 of the Reading Notes for that section.** Project the first photograph on the transparency, and tell students that this is the first neighborhood they will visit. Explain that while they are traveling in their taxis to this neighborhood, they will read Section 9.3 to learn about the reasons people move to Mexico City. Have them complete Part 1 of the Reading Notes for Section 9.3. Use Guide to Reading Notes 9 to check their answers.

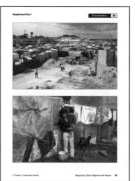 

Transparency 9B   **Reading Notes 9**

5 **Project the bottom half of Transparency 9B, and have students exit their taxis.** Tell students that they will now "meet" this woman, a recent migrant to this neighborhood in Mexico City. Students should bring their Interactive Student Notebooks and pencils with them to record information for their surveys. Invite them to gather at the front of the room as if they are meeting the interviewee in person.

6 **Conduct the first interview.** Play CD Track 6, "Interview 1," in which the two university students "interview" the woman in the photograph. Tell students to listen carefully and to record information for their surveys in Part 2 of their Reading Notes. Explain that the person being interviewed will answer some, but not all, of the survey questions. (**Note:** You may want to pause the CD periodically to make sure students get the necessary information for their surveys.)

7 **Have students reenter the taxis to complete Part 3 of the Reading Notes.** Pass out both pages of *Student Handout 9: Information on the Federal District* to each pair, and have students complete their notes for Section 9.3. Then ask several volunteers to share their responses. Use the Guide to Reading Notes to check their answers. (**Note:** Possible answers are provided; any answers that are well supported should be accepted.)

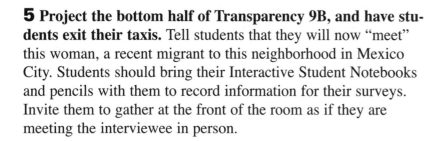

Student Handout 9

8 **Repeat Steps 4 through 7 for the remaining three neighborhoods.** Make these adjustments:

- For the second visit, to meet someone from Mexico City's middle class, use *Transparency 9C: Neighborhood Visit 2* and CD Track 7, "Interview 2." Students read Section 9.4 to learn about problems resulting from Mexico City's rapid growth.

- For the third visit, to meet someone from Mexico City's lower class, use *Transparency 9D: Neighborhood Visit 3* and CD Track 8, "Interview 3." Students read the first part of Section 9.5, "The 'Have Nots' Struggle to Survive," to learn about the living conditions of Mexico City's poor.

Transparencies 9C–9E

- For the fourth visit, to meet someone from Mexico City's upper class, use *Transparency 9E: Neighborhood Visit 4* and CD Track 9, "Interview 4." Students read the second part of Section 9.5, "The 'Haves' Live Well," to learn about the living conditions of Mexico City's wealthy.

Phase 2: Preparing an Article on Life in Mexico City

1 Arrange the classroom. Create a "street cafe" in the Zona Rosa, Mexico City's shopping district, by placing groups of four desks together to create tables. Project *Transparency 9F: A Street Cafe in the Zona Rosa.*

2 Seat two pairs of students at each table. Explain that they are now sitting with their university guides in a street cafe in the Zona Rosa, Mexico City's famous shopping district, to talk about the results of their surveys.

Transparency 9F

3 Play CD Track 10, "Discussing the Survey Results," and have students discuss the questions. Students will be prompted by their guides to answer the following questions. After each question is asked, pause the CD to allow students a few minutes to discuss the question with the others at their tables. Expect them to struggle as the questions become more challenging. (**Note:** You may want to allow more or less time for each question, depending on students' knowledge level and interest.)

- What was the most interesting part of your neighborhood visits?
- What surprised you most when completing the survey in each neighborhood? What didn't surprise you?
- What do you think causes spatial inequality in Mexico City?
- Does life in Mexico City have to be this way? If not, who is responsible for changing it?
- Is spatial inequality fair? Does where people live determine how they will live?
- What about life in Mexico City seems similar to or different from life in your own community?

4 Have students write articles about life in Mexico City. Return the room to its regular configuration, and project a transparency of *Information Master 9: Writing a Newspaper Article.* Review the directions. Give students time in class or as homework to write their first drafts. Review their work, and have them write their final drafts.

Information Master 9

Global Connections

1 Introduce the Global Connections. Have students read Section 9.6. Then explain that they will now see how spatial inequality occurs on a global scale.

2 Project *Transparency 9G: Global Connections.* Help students analyze the map by asking,

Transparency 9G

- **What interesting details do you see?**

- **What color is the United States? What do you think it means to have a "very high" standard of living?**

- **What color is Mexico? What do you think it means to have a "high" standard of living?**

- **What do you think it means to have a "medium" standard of living? "Low"? "Very low"?**

3 Have students turn to Section 9.7. Independently or as a class, have them read the text on the left and analyze the other information in the section. Then facilitate a class discussion by asking the questions that follow. Use the additional information given to enrich the discussion.

- **What does the Human Development Index measure?**
  Since 1993, the United Nations has used the HDI to measure the well-being of people in countries around the world. The HDI considers three areas: a long and healthy life, knowledge, and standard of living. A long and healthy life is measured by life expectancy at birth. Knowledge is measured by a combination of adult literacy rate (weighted two thirds) and school enrollment rate (weighted one third). Standard of living is measured by per capita GDP. Each year, the HDI is published in a UN report that is translated into more than a dozen languages.

- **Why do some countries have a higher HDI rank than might be expected?**
  In some countries, the differences between rich and poor are not great, and many of these countries provide education and health care to all citizens. Cuba is a good example of a country with a higher HDI rank than its GDP might lead one to think. In 2002, the per capita GDP of US$5,259 placed Cuba at 91 of the 175 countries recorded. However, Cuba's life expectancy and school enrollment rates are somewhat surprising. In that year, life expectancy was 76.7 years, placing Cuba at 28 of 177 countries recorded, and school enrollment was 78%, placing the country at 56 of 176 countries recorded.

Since 1959, the government has worked to provide a more equitable distribution of income, housing, services (including health care and education), and employment.

- **Why do some countries have a lower HDI rank than might be expected?**

There is likely a large gap between rich and poor in these countries. The rich live well; the poor have limited access to schools and health care. Saudi Arabia is a good example of a country with a lower HDI rank than its GDP might lead one to think. In 2002, the per capita GDP of US$12,650 placed Saudi Arabia at 44 of the 175 countries recorded. However, in that same year, life expectancy was 72.1 years (67 of 177 countries) and school enrollment was 57% (135 of 176 countries).

Though differences between rich and poor may explain some of these statistics, more revealing are the differences between men and women. Though the government has extended free education to all children, the educational system continues to be divided by gender. Women are expected to marry and raise families, and few Saudi women work outside the home. In fact, in 2002, not one woman served in the Saudi parliament, and less than 1% of Saudi administrators and managers were female.

- **Why do patterns of spatial inequality change over time?**

The UN report publishes HDI trends, showing how a country's well-being can change over time. Countries that once had low HDI ranks can achieve higher ranks; those with high HDI ranks can fall to lower ranks. Often such changes reflect government policies.

Zimbabwe has seen a decline in its HDI since the mid 1980s. The white population controls most of the country's land but accounts for only 1% of the population. The government has promised to redistribute land to landless black peasants. Additionally, in an effort to reduce the country's growing debt, the government has reduced its spending since 1990.

The decline in HDI cannot be attributed entirely to the government. Zimbabwe has seen a sharp drop in life expectancy due to deaths from AIDS. Though the government has launched an educational campaign, life expectancy at birth was estimated at 38 years in 2004, down from 59 years in 1985.

Malaysia has seen its HDI steadily increase. Like Zimbabwe, there are inequalities among ethnic groups. After riots in 1969, the government instituted a series of programs to try to equalize income differences among various ethnic groups,

*with some success: in 1970, the poverty rate was 57%; by
1990, it had dropped to 17%. Even so, a wide income gap
still existed among ethnic groups. In 1990, the government
launched a new series of programs that, among other things,
aimed to reduce the income gap by encouraging more business
ownership among ethnic groups with traditionally lower wages.*

Processing

The newspaper article serves as a Processing assignment for
this lesson.

Online Resources

For more information on spatial inequality, refer students to
Online Resources for *Geography Alive! Regions and People*
at www.teachtci.com.

Assessment

Masters for assessment appear on the next three pages followed
by answers and scoring rubrics.

Mastering the Content

Shade in the oval by the letter of the best answer for each question.

1. The movement of large numbers of people to cities is known as
   ○ A. emission.
   ○ B. distortion.
   ○ C. immigration.
   ○ D. urbanization.

2. What do geographers call the unequal distribution of wealth and resources in a specific geographic area?
   ○ A. economic activity
   ○ B. population density
   ○ C. relative location
   ○ D. spatial inequality

3. Which of these is a **major** cause of rural decline in Mexico?
   ○ A. crowding and pollution
   ○ B. loss of communal lands
   ○ C. rising standards of living
   ○ D. poverty and unemployment

4. Which of these is a **major** effect of rural decline in Mexico?
   ○ A. falling crime rates
   ○ B. rising living standards
   ○ C. increased urbanization
   ○ D. decreased spatial inequality

5. Which of these is the **most** important "pull factor" that draws farm families to Mexico City?
   ○ A. apartment living
   ○ B. communal land
   ○ C. economic opportunity
   ○ D. spatial inequality

6. Which group in Mexico City enjoys the **highest** standard of living?
   ○ A. the "haves"
   ○ B. the "have nots"
   ○ C. the middle class
   ○ D. the working poor

7. As Mexico City has grown, it has seen increases in all of the following **except**
   ○ A. crime rates.
   ○ B. air pollution.
   ○ C. average family size.
   ○ D. poor slum neighborhoods.

8. Which of these conclusions is **best** supported by the information on the graph below?

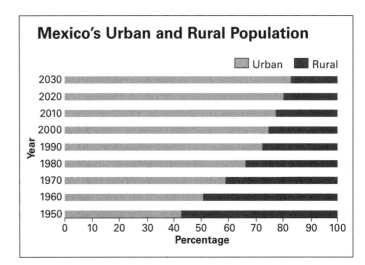

Mexico's Urban and Rural Population

   ○ A. Mexico was more rural than urban until the 1960s.
   ○ B. Since 1950, Mexico has become more rural than urban.
   ○ C. Mexico will not become an urban country until the 2020s.
   ○ D. In 2000, about half of all Mexicans lived in rural areas.

Assessment | 9

Applying Geography Skills: Comparing Maps

Use the maps and your knowledge of geography to complete the tasks below.

Mexico City in 1950

Mexico City in 1980

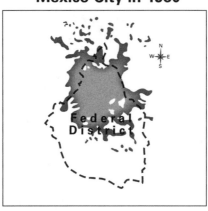

Mexico City in 2000

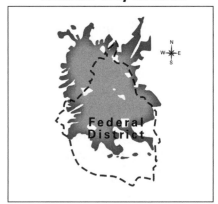

The gray areas on these maps show the size of Mexico City in three different years. The dashed lines show the boundaries of Mexico's Federal District during that period.

1. Identify the period of time covered by the three maps.

2. Compare the boundaries of the Federal District in the three maps. Describe the changes, if any, you see in the Federal District's size over that period.

3. Compare the boundaries of Mexico City in the three maps. Describe the changes, if any, you see in the city's size over that period.

Test Terms Glossary
To **identify** means to tell what something is.

To **compare** means to consider how two things are similar or different.

To **describe** means to provide details about something.

Exploring the Essential Question

Why does spatial inequality exist in urban areas?

In Chapter 9, you explored why Mexico City has spatial inequality. Now you will use what you learned to complete the task below.

Data on Two Mexico City Neighborhoods

Type of Data	Benito Juárez	Milpa Alta
Population density (people per square mile)	25,000–35,000	under 15,000
People over age 15 with more than a primary school education	over 75%	under 55%
Homes built with good materials	over 85%	under 65%
Homes with running water	over 75%	25%–50%
Number of police officers	1,000–1,500	under 500
Green space per person	30–60 square feet	60–100 square feet

The Task: Analyzing Inequality in Two Mexico City Neighborhoods

The table shows data about two Mexico City neighborhoods. One is Benito Juárez, and the other is Milpa Alta. Use the data to create a picture in your mind of each neighborhood. Your task is to write a postcard to a friend about these two neighborhoods.

Step 1: Examine the data for **Benito Juárez**. Determine whether more "haves" or "have nots" may live in this neighborhood. Also determine whether this neighborhood is in the heart of the city or at the outskirts. Circle at least two pieces of data that support your conclusions.

Step 2: Examine the data for **Milpa Alta**. Determine whether more "haves" or "have nots" may live in this neighborhood. Also determine whether this neighborhood is in the heart of the city or at the outskirts. Circle at least two pieces of data that support your conclusions.

Step 3: Write a postcard to a friend about a "visit" to these two neighborhoods. Use correct letter form and complete sentences. Make sure your postcard has these things:
A. today's date
B. a greeting, such as "Dear friend," followed by a comma
C. an opening that identifies the two neighborhoods as parts of Mexico City
D. a brief comparison of the two neighborhoods. Use your knowledge of Mexico City to add colorful details to this part of your postcard.
E. a conclusion telling which neighborhood you liked better and why
F. a closing such as "Sincerely" and your signature

> **Writing Tips: Postcard Basics**
> Postcards are short letters. Remember to use all the parts of a letter when you write a postcard. These include the date, a greeting (salutation), the body (details about what you have seen), a closing, and your signature.

Assessment   9

Applying Geography Skills: Sample Responses

1. The maps cover the period from 1950 to 2000.
2. The Federal District did not change in size during this period.
3. Mexico City more than doubled in area between 1950 and 1980 and then almost doubled again between 1980 and 2000.

Exploring the Essential Question: Sample Response

Step 1: Benito Juárez probably has more "haves" than "have nots." Data supporting this determination: large percentages of homes built with good materials and homes with running water, as well as high education levels. It is also likely to be in the heart of the city. Its high population density and limited green space indicate that it is an urban environment.

Step 2: Milpa Alta probably has more "have nots" than "haves." Data supporting this determination: smaller percentages of homes built with good materials and homes with running water, as well as lower education levels. It is also likely to be on the outskirts of the city. Its lower population density and larger amount of green space indicate that it is a more suburban environment.

Step 3: The postcard should include the elements listed in the prompt. These elements are identified by letter in the response below.

A. June 28, 2006

B. Dear friend,

C. While in Mexico City, I visited the two neighborhoods known as Benito Juárez and Milpa Alta.

D. Benito Juárez is a crowded neighborhood in the heart of the city. It has many nice homes. Most of the people there are well educated and have a high standard of living. Judging by all the police, they might also have a lot of crime to worry about. Milpa Alta is located on the outskirts of the city. Most homes there lack running water. Many people lack education as well. This may be why they have a lower standard of living.

E. Still, I liked Milpa Alta best because it had more open space and because its people are so friendly.

F. Sincerely,
Your friend

Mastering the Content Answer Key

1. D	2. D	3. D	4. C
5. C	6. A	7. C	8. A

Applying Geography Skills Scoring Rubric

Score	General Description
2	Student responds to all parts of the task. Response is correct and clear.
1	Student responds to some parts of the task. Response is mostly correct.
0	Response does not match the task or is incorrect.

Exploring the Essential Question Scoring Rubric

Score	General Description
3	Student responds to all parts of the task. Response is correct, clear, and supported by details.
2	Student responds to most or all parts of the task. Response is generally correct but may lack details.
1	Student responds to at least one part of the task. Response may contain errors and lack details.
0	Response does not match the task or is incorrect.

Use these maps to help you complete Part 3 of your Reading Notes.

Population Density of the Federal District

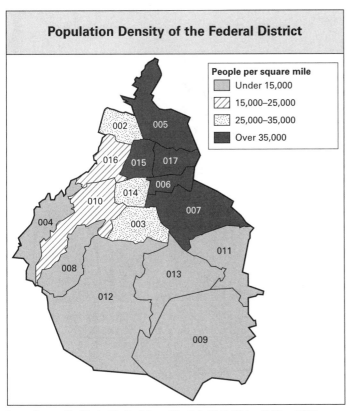

People per square mile
- Under 15,000
- 15,000–25,000
- 25,000–35,000
- Over 35,000

Source: *Demographia*, "Mexico City Population and Density by District (Delegación) from 1960," www.demographia.com.

Homes Built with Good Materials in the Federal District

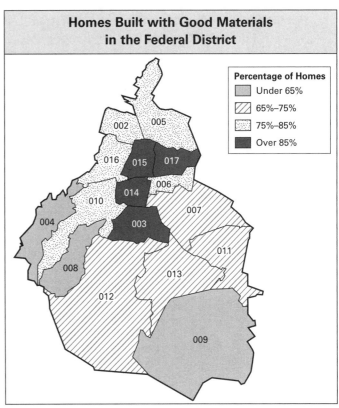

Percentage of Homes
- Under 65%
- 65%–75%
- 75%–85%
- Over 85%

Source: Sigeco: *Sistema de Información Geoeconómica*, "Viviendas Particulares Construidas con Materiales Adecuados," www.df.gob.mx.

Green Space per Person in the Federal District

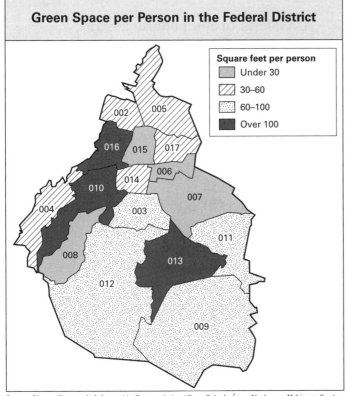

Square feet per person
- Under 30
- 30–60
- 60–100
- Over 100

Source: Sigeco: *Sistema de Información Geoeconómica*, "Superficie de Áreas Verdes por Habitante Según Delegación," www.df.gob.mx.

Divisions of the Federal District
002 Azcapotzalco
003 Coyoacán
004 Cuajimapla
005 Gustavo A. Madero
006 Iztacalco
007 Itzapalapa
008 Magdalena Contreras
009 Milpa Alta
010 Alvaro Obregón
011 Tláhuac
012 Tlalpan
013 Xochimilco
014 Benito Juárez
015 Cuauhtémoc
016 Miguel Hidalgo
017 Venustiano Carranza

Population over Age 15 in the Federal District with Education Beyond Primary School

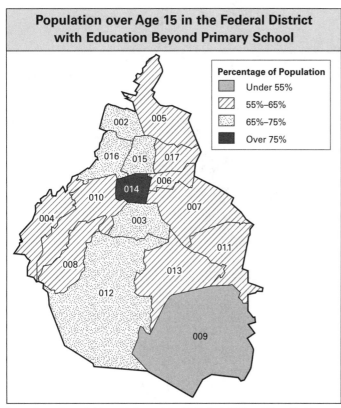

Percentage of Population
- Under 55%
- 55%–65%
- 65%–75%
- Over 75%

Source: *Sigeco: Sistema de Información Geoeconómica*, "Población de 15 Años y Más por Nivel de Instrucción Según Delegación," www.df.gob.mx.

Police Officers in the Federal District

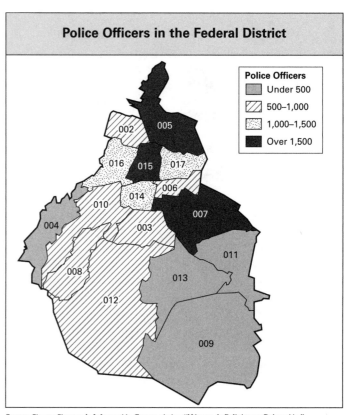

Police Officers
- Under 500
- 500–1,000
- 1,000–1,500
- Over 1,500

Source: *Sigeco: Sistema de Información Geoeconómica*, "Número de Policías por Delegación," www.df.gob.mx.

Homes with In-House Water Supply in the Federal District

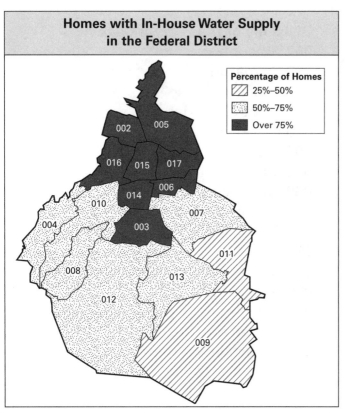

Percentage of Homes
- 25%–50%
- 50%–75%
- Over 75%

Source: Instituto Nacional de Estadístico Geografia e Informática (INEGI), *Anuorio Estadistica de Distrito Federal*, 2000.

Divisions of the Federal District

002 Azcapotzalco
003 Coyoacán
004 Cuajimapla
005 Gustavo A. Madero
006 Iztacalco
007 Itzapalapa
008 Magdalena Contreras
009 Milpa Alta
010 Alvaro Obregón
011 Tláhuac
012 Tlalpan
013 Xochimilco
014 Benito Juárez
015 Cuauhtémoc
016 Miguel Hidalgo
017 Venustiano Carranza

Write an Article About Life in Mexico City

As part of your exchange program with a university in Mexico City, you will write an article for your own school's newspaper. In the article, you will describe life in Mexico City. Draw on what you learned from your readings, your neighborhood visits, your surveys, and your discussions at the cafe.

Your article must include

- an appropriate and appealing title.
- an introduction with background information about Mexico City. Include geographic and historical details.
- two or three paragraphs describing life in Mexico City. Use at least three of these terms: *rural decline, spatial inequality, standard of living, urbanization*. Also, share the survey results from at least two of your neighborhood visits.
- a conclusion with some of your thoughts about your experiences in Mexico City.
- two "photographs" from your visits. These can be drawings you make or copies of photographs from a book or the Internet. Make sure they show something you wrote about in the article. Write a brief caption for each.
- writing that is free of grammar and spelling mistakes.
- clever and creative touches that will make your article more realistic.

Neighborhood Visit 1

Part 1: Read Section 9.3. Then answer these questions:

What challenges do farmers face in Mexico's countryside? *Only 15% of Mexico's land is good for farming. Most of the best land is held by a few wealthy owners. Small farmers can't buy seeds, fertilizer, and machinery to compete with large farms. Many end up selling their land.*

Why do many farmers decide to migrate to the city? *Farmers migrate to the city to try to find a better life. They hope to get jobs that pay a decent wage, to enjoy a higher standard of living, and to get their children into better schools.*

Part 2: Listen carefully to the interview. Then complete as much of the survey as you can.

Neighborhood Survey	
Population density	Answer not given.
Green space per person	18 square feet
Percentage of homes built with good materials	Answer not given.
Percentage of people over age 15 with education beyond primary school	57%
Percentage of homes with water	55%
Number of police officers	Answer not given.

Part 3: Color the area on the map where you think this neighborhood is located. Then complete the sentence. Include three details that support your answer. Use your Reading Notes, your survey, or the maps on Student Handout 9 to help you.

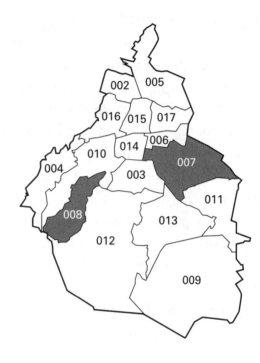

I think we visited a neighborhood in *Possible answers: Itzapalapa, Magdalena Contreras* because…

Possible supporting statements:

- *The survey revealed that there is 18 square feet of green space per person, and the map shows that this area has less than 30 square feet.*
- *The survey revealed that 57% of the population over age 15 has an education beyond primary school, and the map shows that this area has between 55% and 65%.*
- *The survey revealed that 55% of homes have an in-house water supply, and the map shows that this area has between 50% and 75%.*

Neighborhood Visit 2

Part 1: Read Section 9.4. Then answer these questions:

In what ways is Mexico City still growing?
Mexico City is spreading up the sides of the Valley of
Mexico and filling in areas that were once covered
by the valley's lakes.

What problems is Mexico City experiencing as a
result of its rapid growth? There is not enough land,
housing, or clean water for the city's population.
Roads are clogged with traffic. Buses and subways
are packed. One of the city's worst problems is air
pollution. There are not enough jobs for everyone.
Poverty and crime have increased.

Part 2: Listen carefully to the interview. Then
complete as much of the survey as you can.

Neighborhood Survey	
Population density	34,000 people per square mile
Green space per person	Answer not given.
Percentage of homes built with good materials	Answer not given.
Percentage of people over age 15 with education beyond primary school	66%
Percentage of homes with water	Answer not given.
Number of police officers	800

Part 3: Color the area on the map where you
think this neighborhood is located. Then complete the sentence. Include three details that
support your answer. Use your Reading Notes,
your survey, or the maps on Student Handout 9
to help you.

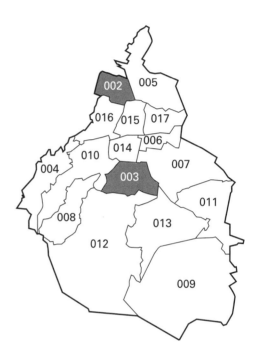

I think we visited a neighborhood in
Possible answers: Azcapotzalco, Coyoacán
because...

Possible supporting statements:
- The survey revealed that the population
  density is 34,000 people per square mile, and
  the map shows that this area has between
  25,000 and 35,000.
- The survey revealed that 66% of the population over age 15 has an education beyond
  primary school, and the map shows that this
  area has between 65% and 75%.
- The survey revealed that there are
  800 police officers, and the map shows
  that this area has between 500 and 1,000.

Neighborhood Visit 3

Part 1: Read the introduction to Section 9.5 and the subsection "The 'Have Nots' Struggle to Survive." Then answer these questions:

What are the living conditions for Mexico City's recent migrants? *They often live in slums on the edge of the city in one-room shacks made of cardboard and junk. Many of these houses lack electricity and water. The dirt streets are often littered with trash. Many of these people have little or no work.*

What are the living conditions for Mexico City's working poor? *They live in neighborhoods that are usually closer to the center of the city than the slums are. Some live in cinder-block homes with metal or tar-covered roofs. Others live in rundown apartment buildings. They usually have electricity but not always running water. The streets are usually paved.*

Part 2: Listen carefully to the interview. Then complete as much of the survey as you can.

Neighborhood Survey	
Population density	*Answer not given.*
Green space per person	*22 square feet*
Percentage of homes built with good materials	*78%*
Percentage of people over age 15 with education beyond primary school	*Answer not given.*
Percentage of homes with water	*more than 75%*
Number of police officers	*Answer not given.*

Part 3: Color the area on the map where you think this neighborhood is located. Then complete the sentence. Include three details that support your answer. Use your Reading Notes, your survey, or the maps on Student Handout 9 to help you.

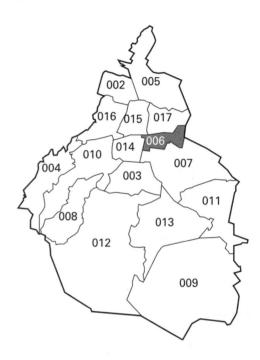

I think we visited a neighborhood in

Iztacalco

because…

Possible supporting statements:

- *The survey revealed that there are 22 square feet of green space per person, and the map shows that this area has less than 30.*
- *The survey revealed that 78% of the homes were built with good materials, and the map shows that this area has between 75% and 85%.*
- *The survey revealed that over 75% of the homes have an in-house water supply, and the map shows that this area has over 75%.*

Neighborhood Visit 4

Part 1: Read the subsection of Section 9.5 called "The 'Haves' Live Well." Then answer these questions:

What types of jobs do the middle class of Mexico City have? How does this affect their lifestyle? Many of the middle class work in business, education, or government. They live in houses or apartment buildings near the center of the city or in modern suburbs farther away. They can usually afford some luxuries, such as a telephone.

Who belongs to Mexico City's upper class? What type of lifestyle do they have? Very wealthy people who are large landowners or business or government leaders belong to the upper class. They have a luxurious lifestyle. They live on large estates with high walls and security systems. They often hire the working poor as maids, gardeners, and drivers.

Part 2: Listen carefully to the interview. Then complete as much of the survey as you can.

Neighborhood Survey	
Population density	34,000 people per square mile
Green space per person	Answer not given.
Percentage of homes built with good materials	94%
Percentage of people over age 15 with education beyond primary school	Answer not given.
Percentage of homes with water	Answer not given.
Number of police officers	1,300

Part 3: Color the area on the map where you think this neighborhood is located. Then complete the sentence. Include three details that support your answer. Use your Reading Notes, your survey, or the maps on Student Handout 9 to help you.

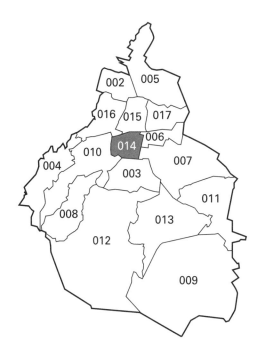

I think we visited a neighborhood in Benito Juárez because…

Possible supporting statements:

- The survey revealed that the population density is 34,000 people per square mile, and the map shows that this area has between 25,000 and 35,000.
- The survey revealed that 94% of the homes were built with good materials, and the map shows that this area has over 85%.
- The survey revealed that there were 1,300 police officers, and the map shows that this area has between 1,000 and 1,500.

Indigenous Cultures: The Survival of the Maya of Mesoamerica

Overview

In this lesson, students learn how the Maya of the Guatemalan highlands and the Chiapas region of Mexico have preserved their traditional ways of life while adapting to modern society. In a **Problem Solving Groupwork** activity, students create and perform dramatizations about five aspects of life in a highland Maya village. They then discuss the ways in which the highland Maya have both preserved and adapted their culture and apply what they've learned through annotated illustrations.

Objectives

Students will

- define and explain the importance of these key geographic terms: *adaptation, indigenous peoples, traditional culture, subsistence farming*.

- create interactive dramatizations that demonstrate the ways that indigenous peoples in the highlands of Guatemala and Chiapas have preserved their traditional Mayan culture and have also adapted to modern life.

- identify the successes and challenges of indigenous peoples around the world in maintaining their traditional cultures in the modern world.

Materials

- *Geography Alive! Regions and People*
- Interactive Student Notebooks
- Transparencies 10A–10H
- Student Handouts 10A–10E (1 version per group of 4)
- CD Tracks 11 and 12

Preview

1 Project *Transparency 10F: Mayan Family at Home.*
Have students work in pairs to complete Preview 10 in their
Interactive Student Notebooks.

2 Have students share their answers. Encourage them to
discuss their varying responses to the last question.

**3 Explain the connection between the Preview and the
upcoming activity.** Tell students that it is understandable that
they would have differing opinions on whether this indigenous
family is more traditional or more modern. Some details, like
the altar and the woman's clothing, represent centuries-old
Mayan traditions. Others, like the television and the man's
clothing, are recent adaptations to Mayan culture. In this activity,
students will learn about five aspects of life in a highland Maya
village. They will create interactive dramatizations that show
the traditional culture that the highland Maya have preserved
as well as the modern adaptations they have made.

Transparency 10F

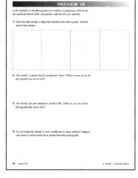
Preview 10

Essential Question and Geoterms

1 Introduce Chapter 10 in *Geography Alive! Regions and
People*. Explain that in this chapter, students will learn about the
highland Maya as an example of an indigenous people. Have
them read Section 10.1. Afterward, ask them to identify at least
four details in the photograph of the Mayan family at home that
reflect ideas in the text they just read.

**2 Introduce the Graphic Organizer and the Essential
Question.** Ask students to examine the illustrated map. Ask,

- What do you see?
- What are the relationships between the parts of the map?
- Where do the highland Maya live?
- What does the photograph in the circle show?
- What aspects of highland Maya life might we learn about
  in and around a village like this one?
- How might life in a highland Maya village be similar to
  the way it was hundreds of years ago? How might life
  have changed?

Have students read the caption. Make sure they understand the
Essential Question, *How do indigenous peoples preserve their
traditional culture while adapting to modern life?* You may
want to post the Essential Question in the classroom or write
it on the board for the duration of the activity.

3 **Have students read Section 10.2.** Then have them work individually or in pairs to complete Geoterms 10 in their Interactive Student Notebooks. Have them share their answers with another student, or have volunteers share their answers with the class.

Problem Solving Groupwork

1 **Put students in mixed-ability groups of four.** You may want to create a transparency that shows them who is in their group and where to sit.

2 **Introduce the activity.** Explain that in this activity, groups will become experts on one aspect of life in a highland Maya village. They will work together to create an interactive dramatization that brings to life a typical scene from that aspect of Mayan life. The dramatizations will have props and costumes and involve members of the audience.

3 **Assign one of five aspects of life in a highland Maya village to each group of students.** Assign each of these aspects of life—community, home and family, work, market day, and traditions—to a group of students. In larger classes, you will need to assign a topic to more than one group.

4 **Distribute materials.** Pass out *Transparencies 10A–10E: Images of Mayan Life* and a corresponding copy of *Student Handouts 10A–10E: Preparing an Interactive Dramatization* to each group according to their assigned topic. Briefly review the steps for creating an interactive dramatization. Encourage students to sound out the Spanish and Quiché greetings as best they can.

5 **Monitor groups as they create their dramatizations.** Allow adequate time—at least two class periods—for preparation. Initial the handout as groups complete each step. Pay particular attention to Step 3 on the handout, making sure each group incorporates all eight items into their dramatization. The group preparing for the topic "market day" will need access to CD Track 11, "Market Day Sound Effects." The group preparing for the topic "traditions" will need access to CD Track 12, "Marimba Music," and *Transparency 10G: Mayan Boy in Traditional Clothing*.

6 **Arrange the classroom for presentations.** When students are ready, create a stage area in the front of the room with the projector centrally located. Set up the CD player for groups to play their sound effects and music.

Geoterms 10

Transparencies 10A–10E and 10G

Student Handouts 10A–10E

7 Have one group set up as the rest of the class reads the corresponding section of *Geography Alive! Regions and People*. Project the transparency depicting the first group's topic. As that group prepares to present, have the remaining students read the corresponding section of their books and complete the appropriate section of Reading Notes 10. This will provide them with background information about that aspect of Mayan life.

8 Have the first group select four participants from the audience and perform their dramatization. Remind performers to speak loud enough to be heard clearly. Let the audience know that they will see some new details about the topic that were not in the reading. Encourage all students to be supportive, respectful, and attentive. (**Note:** Consider having each group act as the visitors for another group's dramatization.)

9 Debrief the dramatization, and encourage students to ask questions. Then have students add any new details they learned about in the presentation to the appropriate section of Reading Notes 10. (**Note:** You might also have students reread the section and identify three details they saw in the dramatization and three they did not.)

10 Repeat Steps 7–9 for the remaining dramatizations. (**Note:** The eight items listed in Step 3 on the handout make an easy evaluation checklist for each presentation. Also consider evaluating these three items: that all group members are actively involved, that all actors can be seen and heard clearly, and that costumes and props are creative and appropriate.)

11 Hold a class discussion. Center the discussion on these questions:

- What did you learn about life in a highland Maya village?
- In what ways have the highland Maya preserved their traditional culture?
- In what ways have the highland Maya adapted to modern life?
- How is life in a highland Maya village similar to life in your community? How is it different?
- What successes and challenges do you predict for the highland Maya in preserving their traditional culture in the modern world?

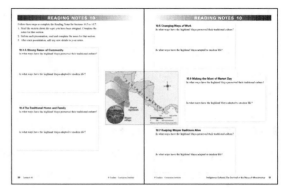

Reading Notes 10

Global Connections

1 Introduce the Global Connections. Have students read Section 10.8. Then explain that they will see how some of the issues they encountered in the activity exist in other areas of the world.

2 Project *Transparency 10H: Global Connections.* Reveal only the world map. Have students analyze the map by discussing and sharing their answers to these questions. Use the additional information given to enrich the discussion.

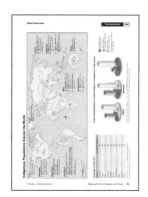

Transparency 10H

• **What interesting details do you see on the map?**

• **What do the shaded areas and numbers represent?**

• **What statements can you make about the locations of indigenous peoples?**
Indigenous peoples are located in all parts of the world. In some places, like South America, many groups live in one area. It is estimated that some 200 indigenous groups live in Brazil. The Bureau of Indian Affairs recognizes more than 560 native tribes in North America. There may be more than 250 million indigenous peoples in over 70 countries. It is estimated that they make up 4% of the world's population.

In most countries, indigenous peoples represent a minority. In Australia, they constitute about 1% of the population; in Greenland, about 90%. Asia has the largest number of indigenous peoples. Even though they make up only 7% of their country's population, indigenous peoples number more than 80 million in China.

• **Why might indigenous groups live in areas that span national borders?**
In most cases, country borders were not determined by indigenous peoples. For example, the Tuareg, who live in several countries in Africa, and their ancestors have been around for thousands of years. Herodotus (c. 484–430 B.C.E.), the ancient Greek historian, recorded details about a nomadic group of people known as the Garamanta living in Libya; the Tuareg are descended from them. Since Herodotus's time, the region of Africa where the Tuareg live has passed through many hands. Many of the present-day national borders were created in the 1960s. They were not determined by the location of the Tuareg, causing the Tuareg to span the borders of Niger, Mali, Algeria, Burkina Faso, and Libya.

3 Have students read Section 10.9 and examine the rest of the information in the section. Then lead a discussion of these questions:

- **What do indigenous peoples gain by adapting to modern life?**

  They are generally poorer than most people in their countries. According to the International Fund for Agricultural Development at the United Nations, one third of the 900 million extremely poor rural people in the world are indigenous.

  One explanation for this poverty is that indigenous peoples have been pushed onto the least fertile and most fragile lands; it is challenging to grow enough food to eat and to make a living. These environments may be isolated, making access to education, new skills, and medical care difficult.

  Another explanation is the traditions that have supported indigenous peoples. The Inuit traditionally hunted fish, seals, caribou, and other game. Some still hunt, but hunting no longer provides a steady source of income.

  Some Inuit have found work in construction or in selling their traditional craftwork. Others have had to rely on government assistance. Indigenous peoples may benefit from adopting the language and customs of the majority population by gaining access to better jobs, health care, and schools.

- **What is most often lost when indigenous peoples adapt to modern life?**

  Indigenous peoples often lose their language, history, and customs. They forget the things that make their culture special. As a result, they may lose their sense of identity, and the world loses some of its cultural diversity.

  It is difficult to identify exactly how many languages exist in the world today; estimates say around 6,800. Most experts agree that half of the world's languages are endangered, or headed for extinction. Many have only a few or even just one speaker. When those individuals die, the language dies too.

  Language is an important way of maintaining traditional culture and the most efficient way of transmitting a culture. Sometimes governments or societies actively discourage minority languages to be spoken, and sometimes speaking the majority language provides a better chance of success. People of all cultures lose something when a language becomes extinct.

- **Can indigenous peoples preserve their traditional culture while adapting to modern life?**

Processing

Have students complete Processing 10 in their Interactive Student Notebooks. You may want to project *Transparency 10F: Mayan Family at Home* as students complete their assignments.

Online Resources

For more information on indigenous peoples, refer students to Online Resources for *Geography Alive! Regions and People* at www.teachtci.com.

Assessment

Masters for assessment appear on the next three pages followed by answers and scoring rubrics.

Processing 10

Transparency 10F

Assessment 10

Mastering the Content

Shade the oval by the letter of the best answer for each question.

1. Mayan judges often require a person who does something wrong to another person to
   - A. go to jail.
   - B. visit a healer.
   - C. pay restitution.
   - D. leave the community.

2. Which term describes a group that has lived in an area since before it was taken over by outsiders?
   - A. indigenous people
   - B. foreign immigrants
   - C. plural society
   - D. political refugees

3. A traditional culture is based **mainly** on which of the following?
   - A. ancestors' ways of life
   - B. speaking two languages
   - C. slash-and-burn agriculture
   - D. adapting to modern society

4. Look at the elevation diagram of the Mayan highlands below. Choose the letter where you would **most likely** find a cloud forest.
   - A. A
   - B. B
   - C. C
   - D. D

5. How do **most** Mayan children learn traditional skills such as farming and weaving?
   - A. in village schools
   - B. from their parents
   - C. in municipal councils
   - D. from religious brotherhoods

6. Which group is **most likely** to use the slash-and-burn method of clearing land?
   - A. commercial growers
   - B. migrant workers
   - C. plantation owners
   - D. subsistence farmers

7. How have Mayan markets adapted to the modern world?
   - A. Food stalls are all together.
   - B. Markets are on Sunday.
   - C. Weavers offer old designs.
   - D. Money has replaced barter.

8. What has happened to the traditional Mayan religious beliefs in Guatemala?
   - A. They have disappeared.
   - B. They are followed in secret.
   - C. They have blended with Catholicism.
   - D. They have replaced the Catholic faith.

**Elevation
Feet**
Over 9,000
6,000–9,000
3,000–6,000
0–3,000

Applying Geography Skills:
Analyzing a Complex Graph

Use the graphs and your knowledge of geography to complete the tasks below.

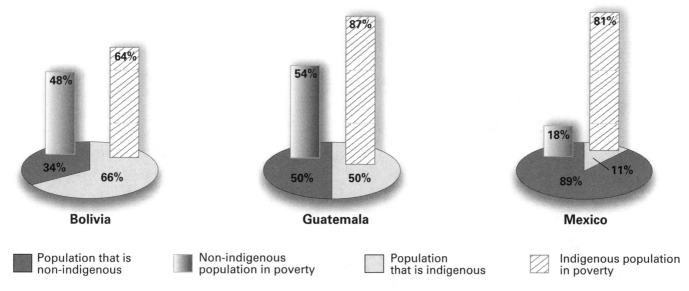

1. Complete this table using data from the graphs. Part of the table has been filled in for you.

	Non-indigenous Population	Non-indigenous Population in Poverty	Indigenous Population	Indigenous Population in Poverty
Bolivia				
Guatemala			50%	
Mexico		18%		

2. Use the information in your table to make a generalization about indigenous peoples in Latin America. Use the sentence starter below to begin your generalization.

In general, indigenous peoples in Latin America...

Test Terms Glossary
A **generalization** is a conclusion that is based on a number of cases.

Exploring the Essential Question

How do indigenous peoples preserve their traditional culture while adapting to modern life?

In Chapter 10, you explored how the Mayan people preserve their traditional culture while adapting to the modern world. Now you will use what you learned. Use the illustration below and your knowledge of geography to complete this task.

The Task: Describing Old and New in a Mayan Village

This drawing shows a busy plaza in a Mayan village in Guatemala. Your task is to write a paragraph describing the mix of old and new in this village. Your paragraph should show how Mayan life has both changed and stayed the same since the Spanish came to Guatemala.

Step 1: Find two places in the plaza that show aspects of traditional Mayan culture. Label them 1 and 2.

Step 2: Find two places in the plaza that show adaptations to modern life. Label them 3 and 4.

Step 3: On a separate piece of paper, write a paragraph about the blending of old and new in a Mayan village. Your paragraph should have these things:

A. a title

B. a topic sentence that states what you plan to show

C. at least one sentence about ways Maya have preserved their traditional culture. Use the items you marked 1 and 2 as examples.

D. at least one sentence about ways Maya have adapted to modern life. Use the items you marked 3 and 4 as examples.

E. a concluding sentence that summarizes your paragraph

Writing Tips: Providing Examples

A good paragraph includes information that supports the topic sentence. Often that information takes the form of examples. Writers use examples to show three things: (1) what they mean, (2) that something is true, or (3) what something is like.

Suppose your topic sentence is, *Mayans have preserved some of their old ways while adapting to modern life.*

Give examples to show what you mean by "old ways" and "modern life."

Applying Geography Skills: Sample Responses

1.

	Non-indige-nous Population	Non-indigenous Population in Poverty	Indigenous Population	Indigenous Population in Poverty
Bolivia	34%	48%	66%	64%
Guatemala	50%	54%	50%	87%
Mexico	89%	18%	11%	81%

2. In general, indigenous peoples in Latin America are far more likely to live in poverty than non-indigenous peoples.

Exploring the Essential Question: Sample Response

Step 1: Details identified as showing traditional culture may include traditional clothing, baskets, and foods; the ancestral shrine; and the sacred tree.

Step 2: Details identified as showing modern culture may include modern clothing, metal containers, architectural details, and the church.

Step 3: The paragraph should include the information asked for in the prompt.

Old and New in a Mayan Village

The Maya have preserved some of their old ways while adapting to modern life. Some villagers still dress in traditional clothes and produce old-style crafts. They may also follow rituals based on Mayan beliefs. At the same time, Maya often wear modern clothes. They may use modern inventions such as radios and telephones. Most Maya have converted to the Catholic religion. They have learned how to use money along with barter. Their village councils enforce modern laws along with traditional values. Blending old and new in this way must be difficult, but the Maya are doing it every day.

**Mastering the Content
Answer Key**

1. C	2. A	3. A	4. B
5. B	6. D	7. D	8. C

**Applying Geography Skills
Scoring Rubric**

Score	General Description
2	Student responds to all parts of the task. Response is correct and clear.
1	Student responds to some parts of the task. Response is mostly correct.
0	Response does not match the task or is incorrect.

**Exploring the Essential
Question Scoring Rubric**

Score	General Description
3	Student responds to all parts of the task. Response is correct, clear, and supported by details.
2	Student responds to most or all parts of the task. Response is generally correct but may lack details.
1	Student responds to at least one part of the task. Response may contain errors and lack details.
0	Response does not match the task or is incorrect.

Prepare a Dramatization About the Mayan Community

Work with your group to create an interactive dramatization about the Mayan community. Have your teacher initial each step as you complete it.

_____ **Step 1: Assign roles.** Everyone will participate in the dramatization. Review the roles below, and divide them among the members of your group. Make sure everyone understands his or her responsibilities.

Geographer You will lead the group during Step 2. Make sure everyone understands and uses key geographic information about the Mayan community in the dramatization.

Director You will lead the group during Step 3. Make sure the dramatization includes all required elements and that everyone is involved.

Props Master You will lead the group during Step 4 as it organizes and gathers costumes and props. Make sure the dramatization is as realistic as possible.

Host You will lead the group during Step 5 as it rehearses its dramatization. During the presentation, you will invite audience members to participate. You will also answer any questions they have.

_____ **Step 2: Learn about the Mayan community.** Carefully examine *Transparency 10A: Mayan Community Officials* to see what the image reveals about the Mayan community. Then take turns reading aloud from Section 10.3, "A Strong Sense of Community." Finally, read these facts:

- A *vara* (wand of office) is a symbol of someone who holds a high position in the Mayan community. Often it is a silver-knobbed cane decorated with ribbons.
- The municipal council has many responsibilities. During festivals and market days, the council members sit outside the town hall in the plaza. They make decisions and listen to the people.
- Members of the *cofradia (cargo)* guard images of Catholic saints in their homes. People come to leave offerings for the saints.

Now have the Geographer lead a discussion of the questions below. Use this information to help you complete the corresponding section of Reading Notes 10 in your Interactive Student Notebook.

- What types of government officials do the highland Maya have?
- What are the traditional duties of the *cofradias*, or *cargos*?
- Why is the tradition of restitution necessary for the Mayan community?
- How have the Maya adapted to challenges faced by their communities?
- What are some features of a traditional Mayan village?

_____ **Step 3: Plan your interactive dramatization.** You must present a five-minute interactive dramatization about the Mayan community that involves four members of the audience. The goal is to show the cultural traditions and adaptations among the highland Maya.

Your dramatization must make the audience feel as if they are observing Mayan officials in a highland village discussing important community issues. The Director should make sure everyone is involved in presenting your dramatization. Your dramatization must include these parts:

1. Greet your visitors by saying *sakiric* (good morning) or *xek'ij* (good afternoon) in Quiché. Invite them to join you around the table. Tell them you are part of the municipal council in this highland Maya community.

2. Have your visitors shine the top and add decorative ribbons to a council member's *vara*. Discuss how the council members are traditionally chosen in the Mayan community.

3. Say "We have a strong sense of community in our village," and explain what you mean.

4. Show a piece of evidence from a dispute you are settling. Ask your visitors how they might solve the problem. Then share how you, as council members, will solve it. Explain why you chose to solve it that way.

5. Bring your visitors on a tour of the village center. Point out where you conduct important business on festival and market days.

6. Stop at the home of a member of a *cofradia* (also called a *cargo*). Have one council member show the statue of the saint that is kept there. Invite the visitors to examine the offerings (fruit, money, and flowers) that people have left for the saint.

7. Have a visitor read a letter that one of you received from your son, who is living in the city. Tell them why he left the village. Express your concern that he is losing his traditional culture.

8. Ask if your visitors have any questions, and answer them. Thank them for coming, and say goodbye using the Quiché words *chajij ib la*.

____ **Step 4: Brainstorm ideas for costumes and props.** Make your dramatization as realistic as possible. Before you begin creating costumes and props, the Props Master—using ideas from the group—should complete the boxes below. **Remember:** During your presentation, the transparency will be projected on the screen behind your group.

List costumes you will include in the dramatization.	List materials needed to create costumes.	List group members who will create costumes.

List props you will include in the dramatization.	List materials needed to create props.	List group members who will create props.

____ **Step 5: Rehearse your dramatization.** After you have created your costumes and props, make sure you can present your dramatization in five minutes. As you rehearse, the Host should make sure that

- all group members are actively involved.
- actors speak their lines loudly, clearly, and at the right time.
- actors use their costumes and props appropriately.
- actors know when and how visitors will participate in the dramatization.

Prepare a Dramatization About the Mayan Home and Family

Work with your group to create an interactive dramatization about the Mayan home and family. Have your teacher initial each step as you complete it.

____ **Step 1: Assign roles.** Everyone will participate in the dramatization. Review the roles below, and divide them among the members of your group. Make sure everyone understands his or her responsibilities.

Geographer You will lead the group during Step 2. Make sure everyone understands and uses key geographic information about the Mayan home and family in the dramatization.

Director You will lead the group during Step 3. Make sure the dramatization includes all required elements and that everyone is involved.

Props Master You will lead the group during Step 4 as it organizes and gathers costumes and props. Make sure the dramatization is as realistic as possible.

Host You will lead the group during Step 5 as it rehearses its dramatization. During the presentation, you will invite audience members to participate. You will also answer any questions they have.

____ **Step 2: Learn about the Mayan home and family.** Carefully examine *Transparency 10B: Mayan Women Cooking for Their Families* to see what the image reveals about the Mayan home and family. Then take turns reading aloud from Section 10.4, 'The Traditional Home and Family." Finally, read these facts:

- Mayan women have many responsibilities. After a morning of cooking and cleaning, women carry their laundry in a basket on their heads or backs to a nearby river or other water source. They wash the clothes by hand while enjoying conversation with other women.
- A backstrap loom is used for weaving. The top rod of the loom is attached to a tree or post. The bottom rod is attached to a belt around the weaver's back. The weaver kneels to use the loom.
- Some Mayan women keep small gardens outside their homes. They grow flowers, fruit, and vegetables. The gardens help to feed families and sometimes provide a small income.

Now have the Geographer lead a discussion of the questions below. Use this information to help you complete the corresponding section of Reading Notes 10 in your Interactive Student Notebook.

- What is the traditional role of Mayan men? Women? Children?
- What items are traditional in a highland Maya home? What are modern?
- How are tortillas made? What are the main tools used?
- How has the tradition of weaving changed over time?

____ **Step 3: Plan your interactive dramatization.** You must present a five-minute interactive dramatization about the Mayan home and family that involves four members of the audience. The goal of your dramatization is to show the cultural traditions and adaptations among the highland Maya.

Your dramatization must make the audience feel as if they are observing members of a Mayan family in their highland home. The Director should make sure everyone is involved in presenting your dramatization. Your dramatization must include these parts:

1. Greet your visitors by saying *sakiric* (good morning) or *xek'ij* (good afternoon) in Quiché. Invite them to sit on the floor with you or in one of the two chairs your family owns. Tell them you are the women and children of this family; the men are working in the fields until sundown.

2. Have your visitors watch as one of you, acting as a woman, makes tortillas. While you work, explain the process and tools you use. Invite your visitors to make and eat their own tortillas.

3. Say "Women have many responsibilities," and explain what you mean.

4. One of you, acting as a child, give a tour of the home. Ask your visitors to guess which items are traditional (clay pots, family altar) and which are modern (radio, metal utensils).

5. Show the backstrap loom used for weaving. Explain why some of the children are not in school and how they learn important traditional tasks like weaving. Have your visitors try using the loom.

6. Bring your visitors out to the garden. Invite them to pick some flowers or vegetables.

7. One of you, acting as a woman, walk the visitors down to the river where you wash clothes. Carry a basket of clothes on your head or your back. Invite your visitors to try carrying the basket. Demonstrate how you wash clothes by hand, and have your visitors help you.

8. Ask if your visitors have any questions, and answer them. Thank them for coming, and say goodbye using the Quiché words *chajij ib la*.

_____ **Step 4: Brainstorm ideas for costumes and props.** Make your dramatization as realistic as possible. Before you begin creating costumes and props, the Props Master—using ideas from the group—should complete the boxes below. **Remember:** During your presentation, the transparency will be projected on the screen behind your group.

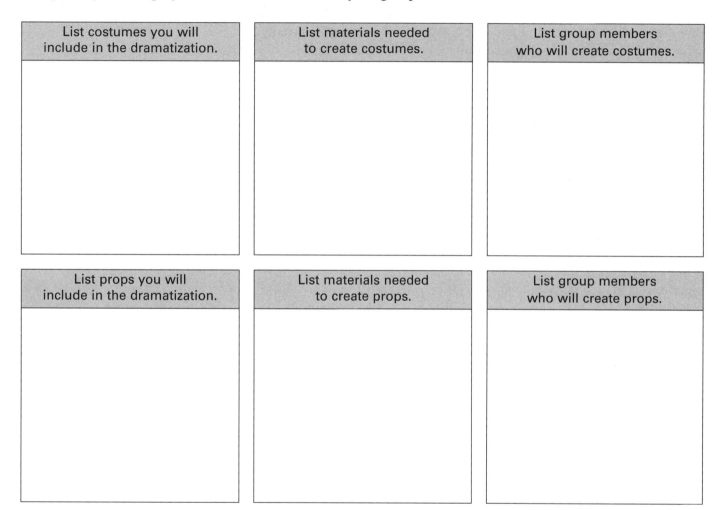

List costumes you will include in the dramatization.	List materials needed to create costumes.	List group members who will create costumes.

List props you will include in the dramatization.	List materials needed to create props.	List group members who will create props.

_____ **Step 5: Rehearse your dramatization.** After you have created your costumes and props, make sure you can present your dramatization in five minutes. As you rehearse, the Host should make sure that

- all group members are actively involved.
- actors speak their lines loudly, clearly, and at the right time.
- actors use their costumes and props appropriately.
- actors know when and how visitors will participate in the dramatization.

Prepare a Dramatization About Mayan Work

Work with your group to create an interactive dramatization about Mayan work. Have your teacher initial each step as you complete it.

_____ **Step 1: Assign roles.** Everyone will participate in the dramatization. Review the roles below, and divide them among the members of your group. Make sure everyone understands his or her responsibilities.

Geographer You will lead the group during Step 2. Make sure everyone understands and uses key geographic information about Mayan work in the dramatization.

Director You will lead the group during Step 3. Make sure the dramatization includes all required elements and that everyone is involved.

Props Master You will lead the group during Step 4 as it organizes and gathers costumes and props. Make sure the dramatization is as realistic as possible.

Host You will lead the group during Step 5 as it rehearses its dramatization. During the presentation, you will invite audience members to participate. You will also answer any questions they have.

_____ **Step 2: Learn about Mayan work.** Carefully examine _Transparency 10C: Mayan Farmers in the Milpa_ to see what the image reveals about Mayan work. Then take turns reading aloud from Section 10.5, "Changing Ways of Work." Finally, read these facts:
- While Mayan farmers burn plants to clear the land, they whistle. Whistling is thought to attract helpful winds.
- Mayan farmers plant corn and beans together as a natural way to fertilize the soil. Corn takes the mineral nitrogen out of the soil. Beans replace it. The corn stalks also provide shade for young bean plants.
- Women and children help with the harvest. Mayan farmers also ask other farmers to help them harvest their crops.

Now have the Geographer lead a discussion of the questions below. Use this information to help you complete the corresponding section of Reading Notes 10 in your Interactive Student Notebook.
- Why is farming important to the Maya?
- How do highland Maya farmers traditionally clear the land?
- Besides corn, what products do they grow?
- How have highland Maya farmers adapted to deal with the challenges they face?

_____ **Step 3: Plan your interactive dramatization.** You must present a five-minute interactive dramatization about Mayan work that involves four members of the audience. The goal of your dramatization is to show cultural traditions and adaptations among the highland Maya.

Your dramatization must make the audience feel as if they are observing Mayan farmers working in their *milpas* in the highlands. The Director should make sure everyone is involved in presenting your dramatization. Your dramatization must include these parts:

1. Greet your visitors by saying *sakiric* (good morning) or *xek'ij* (good afternoon) in Quiché. Invite them to join you in the field. Tell them that you are farmers working to grow your crops.

2. Say "Corn is the giver of life," and explain what you mean.

3. Proudly give your visitors some corn. Tell them how important farming is to your culture. Ask them to share what jobs are in their family traditions.

4. Demonstrate the traditional method of clearing the land. Invite your visitors to use the steel axe and to whistle along with you as you light "fires." Make sure you keep an eye on the "fires" during the rest of your presentation.

5. Point out the crops you have growing right now. Have your visitors pick some ripe vegetables and fruits. If they are up to the challenge, have them try your fresh chilies! For those less daring, some beans might be nice.

6. Have your visitors plant bean seeds between the cornstalks. Tell them that this helps to fertilize the soil. Give examples of other methods farmers use to keep their land fertile.

7. Tell your visitors that sometimes you must do other jobs besides farming, and explain why. Gesture toward the coffee plantations on the coast where you handpick coffee berries to support your families.

8. Ask if your visitors have any questions, and answer them. Thank them for coming. Say goodbye using the Quiché words *chajij ib la*.

____ **Step 4: Brainstorm ideas for costumes and props.** Make your dramatization as realistic as possible. Before you begin creating costumes and props, the Props Master—using ideas from the group—should complete the boxes below. **Remember:** During your presentation, the transparency will be projected on the screen behind your group.

List costumes you will include in the dramatization.	List materials needed to create costumes.	List group members who will create costumes.

List props you will include in the dramatization.	List materials needed to create props.	List group members who will create props.

____ **Step 5: Rehearse your dramatization.** After you have created your costumes and props, make sure you can present your dramatization in five minutes. As you rehearse, the Host should make sure that

- all group members are actively involved.
- actors speak their lines loudly, clearly, and at the right time.
- actors use their costumes and props appropriately.
- actors know when and how visitors will participate in the dramatization.

Prepare a Dramatization About the Mayan Market Day

Work with your group to create an interactive dramatization about the Mayan market day. Have your teacher initial each step as you complete it.

_____ **Step 1: Assign roles.** Everyone will participate in the dramatization. Review the roles below, and divide them among the members of your group. Make sure everyone understands his or her responsibilities.

Geographer You will lead the group during Step 2. Make sure everyone understands and uses key geographic information about the Mayan market day in the dramatization.

Director You will lead the group during Step 3. Make sure the dramatization includes all required elements and that everyone is involved.

Props Master You will lead the group during Step 4 as it organizes and gathers costumes and props. Make sure the dramatization is as realistic as possible.

Host You will lead the group during Step 5 as it rehearses its dramatization. During the presentation, you will invite audience members to participate. You will also answer any questions they have.

_____ **Step 2: Learn about the Mayan market day.** Carefully examine *Transparency 10D: The Market at Chichicastenango* to see what the image reveals about the Mayan market day. Then take turns reading aloud from Section 10.6, "Making the Most of Market Day." Finally, read these facts:

- Besides selling fruits and vegetables in the market, Mayan vendors also sell flowers and spices. As with other products, flowers and spices are found in their own area of the market.
- One service offered is corn milling. For a small fee, a Mayan woman can have corn turned into flour with a motor-operated mill.
- Other products that are available are cloth, clothes, and manufactured goods like radios.

Now have the Geographer lead a discussion of the questions below. Use this information to help you complete the corresponding section of Reading Notes 10 in your Interactive Student Notebook.

- What day of the week is a popular choice for market day?
- How is the market arranged?
- What types of products and services are available?
- How have Mayan markets changed as a result of tourism?

_____ **Step 3: Plan your interactive dramatization.** You must present a five-minute interactive dramatization about the Mayan market day that involves four members of the audience. The goal of your dramatization is to show cultural traditions and adaptations among the highland Maya.

Your dramatization must make the audience feel as if they are observing people shopping and working in a highland Maya marketplace. The Director should make sure everyone is involved in presenting your dramatization. Your dramatization must include these parts:

1. Greet your visitors by saying *buenos dias* (good morning) or *buenas tardes* (good afternoon) in Spanish. Invite them to join you in the marketplace. Tell them that you are people shopping and working in a highland Maya market.

2. Point to the village church and say, "Today is Sunday. The market will become busy now that church services are finished." Explain what you mean. Tell your visitors when the other market day is in your village.

3. Play CD Track 11 while you tour the sections of the market. Tell your visitors why they can hear both Spanish and one of the many Mayan dialects being spoken in the market.

4. Stop to let your visitors get their shoes repaired or to have their photograph taken by one of the street vendors.

5. Show the basket of vegetables you hope to sell and exchange for spices and flowers. Have your visitors help you choose the best products by smelling the spices and fresh flowers.

6. Visit the section where manufactured goods are sold. Have your visitors examine the radios and plastic toys for sale.

7. Ask your visitors if they would like to purchase some homemade tortillas. Because they are visitors, they may use paper money, as most people do. Explain that if they were Maya, they might have bartered for what they wanted. Demonstrate a barter exchange for your visitors after they have made their purchases.

8. Ask if your visitors have any questions, and answer them. Thank them for coming, and say goodbye using the Spanish word *adios*.

____ **Step 4: Brainstorm ideas for costumes and props.** Make your dramatization as realistic as possible. Before you begin creating costumes and props, the Props Master—using ideas from the group—should complete the boxes below. **Remember:** During your presentation, the transparency will be projected on the screen behind your group.

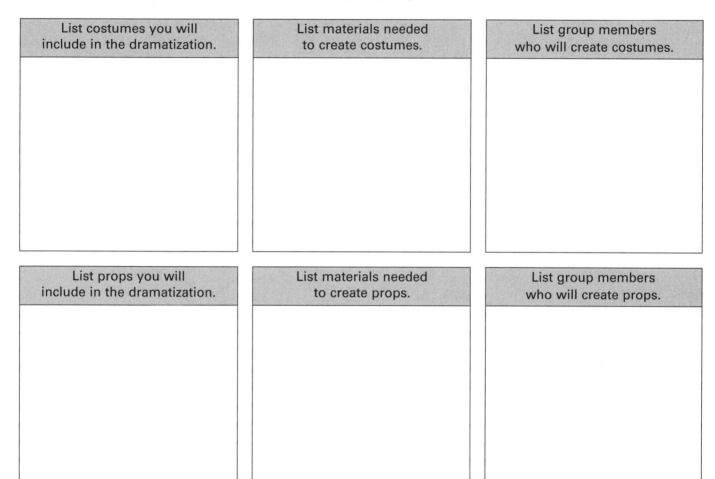

List costumes you will include in the dramatization.	List materials needed to create costumes.	List group members who will create costumes.

List props you will include in the dramatization.	List materials needed to create props.	List group members who will create props.

____ **Step 5: Rehearse your dramatization.** After you have created your costumes and props, make sure you can present your dramatization in five minutes. As you rehearse, the Host should make sure that

- all group members are actively involved.
- actors speak their lines loudly, clearly, and at the right time.
- actors use their costumes and props appropriately.
- actors know when and how visitors will participate in the dramatization.

Prepare a Dramatization About Mayan Traditions

Work with your group to create an interactive dramatization about Mayan traditions. Have your teacher initial each step as you complete it.

_____ **Step 1: Assign roles.** Everyone will participate in the dramatization. Review the roles below, and divide them among the members of your group. Make sure everyone understands his or her responsibilities.

Geographer You will lead the group during Step 2. Make sure everyone understands and uses key geographic information about Mayan traditions in the dramatization.

Director You will lead the group during Step 3. Make sure the dramatization includes all required elements and that everyone is involved.

Props Master You will lead the group during Step 4 as it organizes and gathers costumes and props. Make sure the dramatization is as realistic as possible.

Host You will lead the group during Step 5 as it rehearses its dramatization. During the presentation, you will invite audience members to participate. You will also answer any questions they have.

_____ **Step 2: Learn about Mayan traditions.** Carefully examine _Transparency 10E: Religious Festival in a Mayan Village_ to see what the image reveals about Mayan traditions. Then take turns reading aloud from Section 10.7, "Keeping Mayan Traditions Alive." Finally, read these facts:

- During the Catholic celebration of Easter week, processions reenact the last days of Jesus' life. Participants carry long staffs with crosses on top. Crosses are an important symbol of Catholicism.
- On Easter Day, some Mayan villages cover the street with flower petals and colored wood shavings. Called _alfombras,_ these colorful "carpets" have beautiful designs.
- A healer can be recognized by the pouch he carries. This small bag contains medicinal plants and other objects for healing.

Now have the Geographer lead a discussion of the questions below. Use this information to help you complete the corresponding section of Reading Notes 10 in your Interactive Student Notebook.

- How do traditional Mayan and Catholic beliefs influence modern Mayan religious practices?
- What does a traditional Mayan healer do?
- What is a marimba? What part does music play in traditional Mayan culture?
- When do highland Maya wear traditional clothing? What do the designs in the clothing tell us?

____ **Step 3: Plan your interactive dramatization.** You must present a five-minute interactive dramatization about Mayan traditions that involves four members of the audience. The goal of your dramatization is to show cultural traditions and adaptations among the highland Maya.

Your dramatization must make the audience feel as if they are observing people watching a religious procession in a highland Maya village. The Director should make sure everyone is involved in presenting your dramatization. Your dramatization must include these parts:

1. Greet your visitors by saying *sakiric* (good morning) or *xek'ij* (good afternoon) in Quiché. Invite them to join you in the crowd. Tell them you are watching a religious procession in your village.

2. Show your visitors a long staff with a cross on it. Then show them an incense burner. Ask what religion they think each object represents. Explain how the Mayan religion combines Catholic and traditional beliefs.

3. Have your visitors bend down to touch the flower petals and colored wood shavings of the *alfombra*. Tell them that the village is celebrating Easter Sunday.

4. Say "Healers have an important role in our community," and explain what you mean.

5. Have your visitors pantomime the actions they might take to get well if they felt sick to their stomach. Bring out a healer's pouch, and show them the medicinal plants he would use to help. Explain the ways in which this is similar to and different from the treatment your visitors might seek in their own communities.

6. Pretend to perform a musical piece by playing CD Track 12. Allow your visitors to play a marimba if they are careful.

7. Introduce your visitors to your neighbors by projecting *Transparency 10G: Mayan Boy in Traditional Clothing*. Have your visitors examine the design of his clothing. Explain why all the observers are wearing traditional clothing today.

8. Ask if your visitors have any questions, and answer them. Thank them for coming, and say goodbye using the Quiché words *chajij ib la*.

____ **Step 4: Brainstorm ideas for costumes and props.** Make your dramatization as realistic as possible. Before you begin creating costumes and props, the Props Master—using ideas from the group—should complete the boxes below. **Remember:** During your presentation, the transparency will be projected on the screen behind your group.

List costumes you will include in the dramatization.	List materials needed to create costumes.	List group members who will create costumes.

List props you will include in the dramatization.	List materials needed to create props.	List group members who will create props.

____ **Step 5: Rehearse your dramatization.** After you have created your costumes and props, make sure you can present your dramatization in five minutes. As you rehearse, the Host should make sure that

• all group members are actively involved.

• actors speak their lines loudly, clearly, and at the right time.

• actors use their costumes and props appropriately.

• actors know when and how visitors will participate in the dramatization.

Follow these steps to complete the Reading Notes for Sections 10.3 to 10.7:

1. Read the section about the topic you have been assigned. Complete the notes for that section.

2. Before each presentation, read and complete the notes for that section.

3. After each presentation, add any new details to your notes.

10.3 A Strong Sense of Community

In what ways have the highland Maya preserved their traditional culture?

Possible answer: Mayan towns have municipal councils that follow Mayan customs. Religious brotherhoods guard images of Catholic saints and organize ceremonies and festivals. Mayan judges often use restitution instead of jail terms.

In what ways have the highland Maya adapted to modern life?

Possible answer: Most Mayan towns have a mayor who governs according to national laws. For serious crimes, such as murder, offenders are sent to national courts. Some Maya move to cities to find work or to get an education.

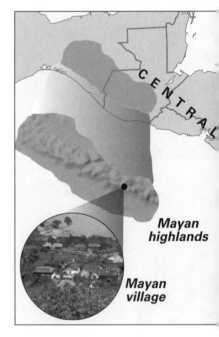

Mayan
highlands

Mayan
village

10.4 The Traditional Home and Family

In what ways have the highland Maya preserved their traditional culture?

Possible answer: A traditional Mayan house has little furniture. There is a family altar for religious worship. There is a clear division of labor: men work in the fields, and women work at home.

In what ways have the highland Maya adapted to modern life?

Possible answer: A Mayan house in a larger town might have electricity, running water, a radio, or a television. Women might use a metal press to make tortillas. Some children listen to popular music and wear jeans, T-shirts, and sneakers instead of traditional Mayan clothing.

10.5 Changing Ways of Work

In what ways have the highland Maya preserved their traditional culture?

Possible answer: Most Maya are subsistence farmers who grow corn and other vegetables on small plots called "milpas." Corn is the most important crop. Some farmers still clear their land using the slash-and-burn method.

In what ways have the highland Maya adapted to modern life?

Possible answer: Some Mayan farmers use tools, such as axes with steel blades, to clear the land. Some use chemical fertilizers. Others spend part of the year working for wages on commercial plantations.

0   150   300 miles

0   150   300 kilometers
Albers Conic Equal-Area projection

10.6 Making the Most of Market Day

In what ways have the highland Maya preserved their traditional culture?

Possible answer: Mayan markets are held one or two days a week. Stalls selling the same type of goods are usually grouped together. Mayan markets feature fruits and vegetables, household goods, food stalls, and stalls that offer services.

In what ways have the highland Maya adapted to modern life?

Possible answer: Some Mayan markets sell items just for tourists. Most trading is done with money instead of barter. Spanish has replaced Mayan languages as the common tongue in the markets.

10.7 Keeping Mayan Traditions Alive

In what ways have the highland Maya preserved their traditional culture?

Possible answer: The Maya listen to traditional music and watch traditional dances to celebrate religious occasions. At festivals, they wear traditional clothing, such as huipiles. Mayan healers are often sought out for treatment of illnesses.

In what ways have the highland Maya adapted to modern life?

Possible answer: Mayan men wear modern clothing for everyday life. Maya will go to modern doctors for major problems.

Dealing with Extreme Weather: Hurricanes in the Caribbean

Overview

In this lesson, students learn about hurricanes as an example of extreme weather and how people in the Caribbean deal with this physical phenomenon. In a **Visual Discovery** activity, students analyze five images that represent key stages in the life of a hurricane: birth, strengthening, tracking, landfall, and aftermath. Students "step into" selected images, using information from their books to bring the images to life. They apply what they have learned by creating a government agency brochure to help citizens plan for and deal with hurricanes in the Caribbean.

Objectives

Students will

- define and explain the importance of these key geographic terms: *El Niño, extreme weather, meteorology, natural disaster, tropical cyclone*.

- describe the weather conditions that cause a hurricane to form and strengthen.

- identify ways in which people deal with hurricanes in the Caribbean.

- analyze the relationship between an El Niño and extreme weather around the world.

Materials

- *Geography Alive! Regions and People*
- Interactive Student Notebooks
- Transparencies 11A–11F
- Student Handout 11A (1 copy, cut apart)
- Student Handout 11B (1 copy, copied in green and cut apart)
- Student Handout 11C (1 copy, copied in blue and cut apart)
- Student Handout 11D (2 or 3 copies, copied in yellow and cut apart)
- Student Handout 11E (3 copies, copied in red and cut apart)
- Student Handout 11F (1 for every 4 students)
- beach ball (optional)
- masking tape

Preview

1 Have students complete Preview 11 in their Interactive Student Notebooks. When they are finished, ask several volunteers to share some of the details they included on their maps.

2 Explain the connection between the Preview and the upcoming lesson. Ask how many students included information about tropical cyclones, or hurricanes, on their maps. Explain that the Caribbean receives an average of six tropical cyclones each year. Tropical cyclones are considered the Earth's most dangerous and violent weather. They have different names depending on where they originate: they are known as *hurricanes* in the Atlantic Ocean, *typhoons* in the Pacific Ocean, and *cyclones* in the Indian Ocean. In this lesson, students will learn how hurricanes form and strengthen, and the ways in which the people of the Caribbean deal with this form of extreme weather.

Preview 11

Essential Question and Geoterms

1 Introduce Chapter 11 in *Geography Alive! Regions and People*. Explain that in this chapter, students will learn about hurricanes as an example of extreme weather and of how people in the Caribbean deal with this physical phenomenon. Have students read Section 11.1. Afterward, ask them to identify at least four details in the photograph of the hurricane that relate to ideas they just read about.

2 Introduce the Graphic Organizer and the Essential Question. Have students examine the map that shows the course of a hurricane. Ask,

- What do you see?
- What does the red symbol represent?
- Where did the hurricane come from? How do you know?
- Why is the hurricane symbol placed at four different points?
- What might be happening with the hurricane at each point?
- In what ways do you think people are affected by the hurricane at each point?

Have students read the accompanying text. Make sure they understand the Essential Question, *What causes extreme weather, and how do people deal with it?* You may want to post the Essential Question in the room or write it on the board for the duration of the activity.

3 Have students read Section 11.2. Then have them work individually or in pairs to complete Geoterms 11 in their Interactive Student Notebooks. Have them share their answers with another student, or have volunteers share their answers with the class.

Geoterms 11

Visual Discovery

1 Arrange students in mixed-ability pairs. You may want to prepare a transparency that shows them with whom they will work and where they will sit.

2 Have students read Section 11.3. This section contains information on weather that will help students to better understand hurricanes.

Phase 1: A Hurricane Is Born

1 Project *Transparency 11A: Satellite Image of the Atlantic Ocean.* Help students analyze the image by asking,

- What do you see?
- What do the green masses represent? What do the white masses represent?
- What differences do you notice between the clouds off the coast of Africa and those in the middle of the Atlantic Ocean?
- The spiraling clouds are forming a hurricane. Where might the hurricane have come from?
- Do you think it began over the ocean or over the land?
- What conditions might exist off the coast of Africa that would have caused this hurricane to form?
- Are there any other places shown here where similar conditions might exist?
- Do you think this image shows the possibility of another hurricane forming? Why or why not?

Transparency 11A

2 Have students read Section 11.4 and complete the corresponding section of Reading Notes. Ask several volunteers to share their responses. Use Guide to Reading Notes 11 to review the main points with them.

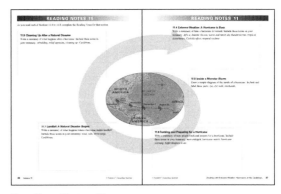

Reading Notes 11

3 Review the key vocabulary and concepts of Section 11.4. Give one label cut from *Student Handout 11A: Labels for the Birth of a Hurricane* to each of four pairs of volunteers. Have pairs tape them to the appropriate place on the projected satellite image. They should place labels as follows:

- *warm, moist tropical air:* in the Atlantic Ocean between the Tropic of Cancer and the Tropic of Capricorn
- *tropical disturbance:* on the clouds off the coast of Africa
- *Coriolis effect:* on or around the hurricane
- *tropical cyclone:* on the hurricane

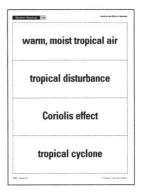

Student Handout 11A

Have students explain why they placed the labels as they did.

Phase 2: Inside a Monster Storm

1 Project *Transparency 11B: Satellite Image of Hurricane Isabel.* Help students analyze the image by asking,

- What do you see?
- What does the brightly colored object represent?
- What do you think the colors in the hurricane represent?
- What other parts appear to make up the hurricane?
- What might the conditions be like inside the hurricane?
- What is the relative location of this hurricane?
- In what direction do you think this hurricane will travel?
- What conditions might cause this hurricane to strengthen as it continues along its path?

Transparency 11B

2 Have students read Section 11.5 and complete the corresponding Reading Notes. Have several volunteers share their diagrams, and use the Guide to Reading Notes to review the main points with them.

3 Have students prepare to bring Hurricane Isabel to life by conducting an act-it-out. Explain that they will now act out the formation of the hurricane. Just like a hurricane, the act-it-out will happen in stages. Follow these steps:

- Move desks and chairs to the edges of the room to create a large open space. Alternatively, use a a field or a gymnasium.
- Assign two pairs of students to role-play a tropical disturbance, two pairs to be a tropical depression, four or five pairs to be a tropical storm, and five or six pairs to be a hurricane. Give each pair an appropriate role card cut from *Student Handouts 11B–11E: Role Cards for "Forming a Hurricane" Act-It-Out.*
- As groups practice their roles, use masking tape to create a floor map. Make an outline of the west coast of Africa on the right side of the room. On the left side of the room, create outlines to represent the Caribbean islands.
- Label the floor map by placing large signs on each of these locations: *Africa, Caribbean islands,* and *Atlantic Ocean.* Also add a sign that displays a compass rose.
- Consider giving students strips of colored crepe paper to help identify their roles: green for tropical disturbance, blue for tropical depression, yellow for tropical storm, and red for hurricane.

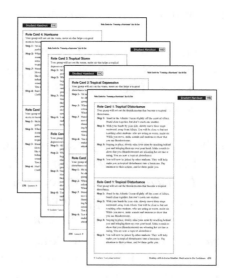

Student Handouts 11B–11E

4 Conduct the act-it-out. Follow these steps:

- Have students take the places indicated on their role cards and then perform their roles. They may need to practice the entire act-it-out a couple of times.

- Once students have successfully formed a hurricane and begun moving it toward the Caribbean islands, stop the act-it-out. Have students identify where the eye, eye wall, and rainbands are. (**Note:** You might have them use a beach ball to represent the eye of the hurricane. You may also want to consider video-taping the act-it-out to allow students to more easily identify these features later.)

- Have the hurricane make landfall by moving over the Caribbean islands.

- To show the weakening of the hurricane over land, have some students fall to the floor.

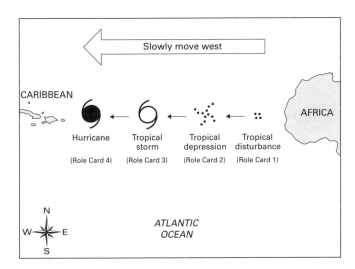

Phase 3: Tracking and Preparing for a Hurricane

1 Project _Transparency 11C: Tracking Hurricane Ivan._ Ask,

- What do you see?

- What do the black line and dots represent?

- Where is the hurricane located at 11 A.M. on Friday?

- Why do you think the potential one- to three-day track area widens as it moves away from the hurricane's current location?

- What do the colors red and orange on the islands represent?

- What might be the difference between a hurricane warning and a hurricane watch?

- Which countries will likely see the most dramatic impact from this hurricane?

- How might a map like this help people in the Caribbean deal with hurricanes?

Transparency 11C

2 **Have students read Section 11.6 and complete the corresponding Reading Notes.** Have a few volunteers share their responses, and use the Guide to Reading Notes to review the main points with them.

Phase 4: Landfall: A Natural Disaster Begins

1 **Project** *Transparency 11D: Hurricane Ivan Approaches Cuba.* Ask,

Transparency 11D

- What do you see?
- What is happening to the trees and telephone pole?
- What force in the hurricane causes them to bend so dramatically?
- How powerful or fast do you think the wind is? *The winds at this time were measured at over 70 mph. Soon after this photograph was taken, winds reached 124 mph with gusts up to 162 mph.*
- What other weather conditions has the approaching hurricane brought to this location?
- What do you think might happen here in the next few hours as the hurricane passes over the island?
- Where do you think these people are going? What might they be thinking or experiencing?

2 **Have students read Section 11.7 and complete the corresponding Reading Notes.** Have volunteers share their responses, and review the main points with the class.

3 **Have students prepare to bring the image to life by conducting an act-it-out.** Have pairs of students join together to form groups of four; you will need six groups in all. Give each group a copy of *Student Handout 11F: Directions for "Approaching Hurricane" Act-It-Out.* Assign each group a character from the list on the handout, and give them several minutes to complete the steps on the handout from that character's perspective.

Student Handout 11F

4 **Conduct the act-it-out.** Choose one actor from each group to stand in front of the image as if joining the two people in the scene. As the reporter, ask the characters some of the questions from the handout. Afterward, have the audience give the actors a round of applause. (**Note:** Consider involving the audience by allowing them to ask appropriate questions. You may need to give audience groups a minute to brainstorm questions.)

Phase 5: Cleaning Up After a Natural Disaster

1 Project *Transparency 11E: The Dominican Republic After Hurricane Georges.* Ask,

- What do you see?
- What has happened to these buildings?
- What about a hurricane might cause such flooding and damage?
- What category do you think this hurricane was? *Hurricane Georges was a Category 3 hurricane when it hit the Dominican Republic on September 22, 1998.*
- What other damage might you expect to see near this location? *Approximately 280 Dominicans were killed and another 300,000 left homeless by Hurricane Georges.*
- How much might it cost to clean up after a hurricane like this? *Hurricane Georges cost the Dominican Republic approximately $2 billion in damage, which was 14% of the country's GDP in the previous year.*
- How might the people of the Caribbean deal with the aftermath of such a hurricane?
- In what ways do you think this hurricane will help the people of the Caribbean deal with hurricanes in the future?

Transparency 11E

2 Have students read Section 11.8 and complete the corresponding Reading Notes. Have volunteers share their responses, and review the main points with the class.

Global Connections

1 Introduce the Global Connections. Have students read Section 11.9. Then explain that they will now examine the impact an El Niño has on extreme weather around the world.

2 Project *Transparency 11F: Global Connections.* Help students begin to analyze the map by asking,

- **What interesting details do you see?**

- **El Niño isn't labeled on this map. Where do you think it is located?**

- **In what regions of the world is an El Niño's influence felt?**

3 Have students turn to Section 11.10. Independently or as a class, have students read the text on the left side and analyze the other information in the section. Then facilitate a class discussion by asking the questions that follow. Use the additional information given to enrich the discussion.

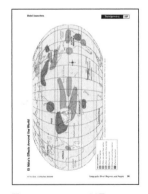

Transparency 11F

- **What parts of the world are most affected by an El Niño?**

The Pacific region shows the most effects from an El Niño. Parts of the western coasts of North and South America are wetter than usual. The coast of California experienced higher than normal precipitation during the El Niño of 1997–1998. The total seasonal rainfall for San Francisco was over 47 inches, or 230% above the norm. Such rainfall can lead to coastal erosion, flooding, and landslides.

In South America, the Andes received unusually warm rainfall instead of the typical snowfall. These rains created flooding as they washed into the lowlands of Bolivia. The western Pacific, in contrast, is very dry. During the 1997–1998 El Niño, a widespread drought affected many countries, such as Indonesia and Malaysia. Springs and streams dried up and crops failed.

Earlier, from 1991 to 1995, Australia experienced a four-year drought related to an El Niño. The costs were devastating. The economy experienced a $5 billion loss, and the government spent $590 million on drought relief.

- **What relationship exists between an El Niño and extreme weather?**

An El Niño can affect weather in ways you might not expect. For example, during an El Niño, there are fewer Atlantic hurricanes. Of those that do develop, they are less likely to become major hurricanes (Categories 3–5 on the Saffir-Simpson scale). The eastern Pacific, on the other hand, experiences a more active hurricane season.

There are other relationships between an El Niño and extreme weather in the United States. During an El Niño, California and the southern U.S. suffer an unusually stormy winter with increased rainfall. The northern U.S., however, sees warmer temperatures and less stormy conditions. The potential for extreme weather, such as blizzards, is less for this region during an El Niño.

- **How can understanding an El Niño's effects help meteorologists to predict extreme weather?**

Scientists have made great progress in predicting when an El Niño will occur. That means they may also be able to predict extreme weather more accurately. Extreme weather can cost billions of dollars. Better predictions will help agencies plan for damage to water resources and supply lines caused by flooding and drought. Transportation officials can prepare for disruption of land travel and sea navigation. And farmers can make plans to avoid potential crop and livestock damage.

Processing

Have students complete Processing 11 in their Interactive Student Notebooks.

Online Resources

For more information on extreme weather, refer students to Online Resources for *Geography Alive! Regions and People* at www.teachtci.com.

Assessment

Masters for assessment appear on the next three pages followed by answers and scoring rubrics.

Processing 11

Mastering the Content

Shade the oval by the letter of the best answer for each question.

1. Hurricanes, tornadoes, and blizzards are all examples of
   ◯ A. heat transfer.
   ◯ B. climate zones.
   ◯ C. tropical storms.
   ◯ D. extreme weather.

2. What is the scientific study of climate and weather called?
   ◯ A. geology
   ◯ B. meteorology
   ◯ C. human geography
   ◯ D. physical geography

3. Which of these is **most likely** to cause a natural disaster?
   ◯ A. a tropical cyclone
   ◯ B. an El Niño event
   ◯ C. a prevailing wind
   ◯ D. the Coriolis effect

4. Which of these is the **best** definition of an El Niño?
   ◯ A. a natural disaster
   ◯ B. a tropical cyclone
   ◯ C. a warm ocean current
   ◯ D. a strong prevailing wind

5. What causes the Coriolis effect?
   ◯ A. the rotation of Earth
   ◯ B. warm ocean temperatures
   ◯ C. the tilt of Earth on its axis
   ◯ D. extreme weather conditions

6. What is the **best** title for Part 4 of this diagram?

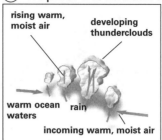 ① Tropical Disturbance

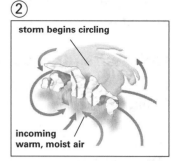 ②

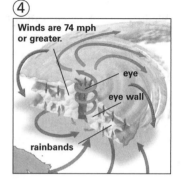

   ◯ A. Tropical Cyclone
   ◯ B. Tropical Downpour
   ◯ C. Tropical Depression
   ◯ D. Tropical Thunderstorm

7. Which aspect of a hurricane creates the **most** damage once the storm reaches land?
   ◯ A. high winds
   ◯ B. storm surge
   ◯ C. heavy rainfall
   ◯ D. lightning strikes

8. What happens when a hurricane moves over a large landmass?
   ◯ A. It stops raining.
   ◯ B. It grows in size.
   ◯ C. It loses strength.
   ◯ D. It picks up speed.

Applying Geography Skills: Using the Saffir-Simpson Scale

Use the diagram of the Saffir-Simpson scale and your knowledge of geography to complete the tasks below.

Saffir-Simpson Scale

Category 1 hurricane
wind speed: 74–95 mph
storm surge: 4–5 feet

Category 2 hurricane
wind speed: 96–110 mph
storm surge: 6–8 feet

Category 3 hurricane
wind speed: 111–130 mph
storm surge: 9–12 feet

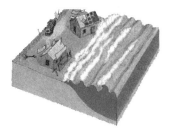

Category 4 hurricane
wind speed: 131–155 mph
storm surge: 13–18 feet

Category 5 hurricane
wind speed: over 156 mph
storm surge: over 19 feet

1. Briefly state what the Saffir-Simpson scale is used for.

2. On July 6, 2005, Hurricane Dennis reached the island of Hispañiola in the Caribbean. At that time, it was ranked as a Category 1 storm on the Saffir-Simpson scale. Tell how high the storm surge of Dennis was at this point.

3. On July 8, Dennis slammed into Cuba with wind speeds of up to 150 miles per hour. Rank Dennis on the Saffir-Simpson scale at this point.

4. On July 10, Dennis reached Florida. By then its wind speeds had dropped to between 115 and 120 miles per hour. Rank the storm at this point.

Test Terms Glossary
To **state** means to briefly tell in words.

To **rank** means to decide the position of people or things on a list or scale.

Exploring the Essential Question

What causes extreme weather, and how do people deal with it?

In Chapter 11, you explored the causes of extreme weather and how people deal with it. Now you will use what you learned. Use the map below and your knowledge of geography to complete this task.

The Task: Writing an Extreme Weather Warning

The map shows the predicted path of an Atlantic hurricane. The advisory contains information on this storm as of September 10, 2004. Your task is to use this information to write an extreme weather warning for the Cayman Islands.

Step 1: Circle the following information about the storm on the map or in the advisory:

- its name
- its location on Friday morning
- its rate of travel and expected arrival time in the Cayman Islands
- its maximum wind speed and expected storm surge

Step 2: Use the Saffir-Simpson scale on the "Applying Geography Skills" page of this assessment to rank the storm. (Skip this step if you do not have the scale.)

Step 3: Write an extreme weather warning for the Cayman Islands to be issued the morning of September 10. Your warning should cover the five "Ws" of good news reporting: who, what, when, where, and why. Be sure to include these things:

A. the name of the storm (who)
B. its strength and Saffir-Simpson rating (what)
C. its current location (where)
D. its travel speed and expected arrival time in the Cayman Islands (when)
E. reasons Cayman Islanders should prepare for this storm and what they should do to get ready (why)

The Path of Hurricane Ivan

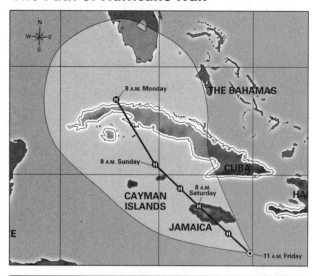

Hurricane Ivan Advisory
11:00 A.M., Friday, September 10, 2004
Maximum wind speed: 145 mph
Expected storm surge: 13–18 feet
Rate of travel: 12 mph

- ● Current hurricane location
- Ⓗ Forecasted hurricane positions
- ◔ Potential 1–3 day track area
- ▬ Hurricane warning
- ▭ Hurricane watch

Writing Tips: Who, What, Where, When, and Why
Reporters know that many people will read or hear only the first part of a news story. For this reason, they put the most important information first. Usually this is who, what, when, where, and why. Less important details are included later in the story.

Applying Geography Skills: Sample Responses

1. The Saffir-Simpson scale is used to rate hurricane strength.
2. On July 6, 2005, the storm surge of Dennis was 4 to 5 feet high.
3. By July 8, Dennis had become a Category 4 hurricane.
4. By July 10, Dennis had weakened to a Category 3 hurricane.

Exploring the Essential Question: Sample Response

Step 1: Students should have circled these items: the words *Hurricane Ivan,* the circle with the black dot on the map, 12 mph, 8 A.M. Sunday, 145 mph, 13–18 feet

Step 2: Students should rank Ivan as a Category 4 hurricane.

Step 3: The extreme weather warning should include the elements identified in the prompt.

Extreme Weather Warning for the Cayman Islands

Hurricane Ivan has reached the Caribbean. Ivan is a very strong Category 4 hurricane. Its current location is southeast of Jamaica. Ivan is traveling in a northwest direction at about 12 miles per hour. It is expected to reach the Cayman Islands early Sunday morning. Ivan is an extremely dangerous storm. Its 145 mph winds are likely to cause severe damage once it hits land. Cayman Islanders should prepare by tying down loose objects and boarding up their windows. People living close to the coast should move inland to higher ground to escape flooding. Once the hurricane arrives, stay indoors until the storm has moved on and all danger has passed.

Mastering the Content Answer Key

1. D	2. B	3. A	4. C
5. A	6. A	7. B	8. C

Applying Geography Skills Scoring Rubric

Score	General Description
2	Student responds to all parts of the task. Response is correct and clear.
1	Student responds to some parts of the task. Response is mostly correct.
0	Response does not match the task or is incorrect.

Exploring the Essential Question Scoring Rubric

Score	General Description
3	Student responds to all parts of the task. Response is correct, clear, and supported by details.
2	Student responds to most or all parts of the task. Response is generally correct but may lack details.
1	Student responds to at least one part of the task. Response may contain errors and lack details.
0	Response does not match the task or is incorrect.

warm, moist tropical air

tropical disturbance

Coriolis effect

tropical cyclone

Role Card 1: Tropical Disturbance

Your group will act out the thunderstorms that become a tropical disturbance.

Step 1: Stand in the Atlantic Ocean slightly off the coast of Africa. Stand close together, but don't touch one another.

Step 2: With your hands by your side, slowly move three steps westward, away from Africa. You will be close to but not touching other students, who are acting as warm, moist air. While you move, make sounds and motions to show that you are thunderstorms.

Step 3: Staying in place, slowly raise your arms by reaching behind you and bringing them up over your head. Make sounds to show that you (thunderstorms) are releasing hot air that is rising. You are now a *tropical disturbance*.

Step 4: You will now be joined by other students. They will help make you (a tropical disturbance) into a hurricane. Pay attention to their actions, and let them guide you.

Role Card 1: Tropical Disturbance

Your group will act out the thunderstorms that become a tropical disturbance.

Step 1: Stand in the Atlantic Ocean slightly off the coast of Africa. Stand close together, but don't touch one another.

Step 2: With your hands by your side, slowly move three steps westward, away from Africa. You will be close to but not touching other students, who are acting as warm, moist air. While you move, make sounds and motions to show that you are thunderstorms.

Step 3: Staying in place, slowly raise your arms by reaching behind you and bringing them up over your head. Make sounds to show that you (thunderstorms) are releasing hot air that is rising. You are now a *tropical disturbance*.

Step 4: You will now be joined by other students. They will help make you (a tropical disturbance) into a hurricane. Pay attention to their actions, and let them guide you.

Role Card 2: Tropical Depression

Your group will act out the warm, moist air that helps a tropical disturbance to become a tropical depression.

Step 1: Sit in the Atlantic Ocean off the coast of Africa. You should be about four steps west of the thunderstorms (another group of students).

Step 2: When the thunderstorms reach you, watch for hot air to be released (the students will lift their arms to the ceiling). When they do, rush toward them, staying close to the floor.

Step 3: Stand up and form a circle with the thunderstorms. Begin moving the circle slowly counterclockwise. Just as the thunderstorms did earlier, slowly raise your arms by reaching behind you and bringing them up over your head. Make sounds to show that you are releasing hot air that is rising. You are now a *tropical depression*.

Step 4: You will now be joined by other students. They will help make you (a tropical depression) into a tropical storm. Pay attention to their actions, and let them guide you.

Role Card 2: Tropical Depression

Your group will act out the warm, moist air that helps a tropical disturbance to become a tropical depression.

Step 1: Sit in the Atlantic Ocean off the coast of Africa. You should be about four steps west of the thunderstorms (another group of students).

Step 2: When the thunderstorms reach you, watch for hot air to be released (the students will lift their arms to the ceiling). When they do, rush toward them, staying close to the floor.

Step 3: Stand up and form a circle with the thunderstorms. Begin moving the circle slowly counterclockwise. Just as the thunderstorms did earlier, slowly raise your arms by reaching behind you and bringing them up over your head. Make sounds to show that you are releasing hot air that is rising. You are now a *tropical depression*.

Step 4: You will now be joined by other students. They will help make you (a tropical depression) into a tropical storm. Pay attention to their actions, and let them guide you.

Role Card 3: Tropical Storm

Your group will act out the warm, moist air that helps a tropical depression to become a tropical storm.

Step 1: Sit in the Atlantic Ocean, all around the edges of the performance area.

Step 2: When you see a group of students (a tropical depression) begin to move in a circle, watch for hot air to be released (they will lift their arms to the ceiling). When this happens, rush toward the tropical depression, staying close to the ground.

Step 3: Stand up and form a circle around the tropical depression. Move counterclockwise with them, but a little faster. Just as they did earlier, slowly raise your arms by reaching behind you and bringing them up over your head. Make sounds to show that you are releasing hot air that is rising. You are now a *tropical storm*.

Step 4: You will now be joined by other students. They will help to make you (a tropical storm) into a hurricane. Pay attention to their actions, and let them guide you.

Role Card 3: Tropical Storm

Your group will act out the warm, moist air that helps a tropical depression to become a tropical storm.

Step 1: Sit in the Atlantic Ocean, all around the edges of the performance area.

Step 2: When you see a group of students (a tropical depression) begin to move in a circle, watch for hot air to be released (they will lift their arms to the ceiling). When this happens, rush toward the tropical depression, staying close to the ground.

Step 3: Stand up and form a circle around the tropical depression. Move counterclockwise with them, but a little faster. Just as they did earlier, slowly raise your arms by reaching behind you and bringing them up over your head. Make sounds to show that you are releasing hot air that is rising. You are now a *tropical storm*.

Step 4: You will now be joined by other students. They will help to make you (a tropical storm) into a hurricane. Pay attention to their actions, and let them guide you.

Role Card 4: Hurricane

Your group will act out the warm, moist air that helps a tropical storm to become a hurricane.

Step 1: Sit in the Atlantic Ocean, all around the edges of the performance area.

Step 2: When you see the students form a second circle (a tropical storm), watch for hot air to be released (they will lift their arms to the ceiling). When this happens, rush toward the tropical storm, staying close to the ground.

Step 3: Stand up and form a circle around the tropical storm. Move counterclockwise with them, but a little faster. Just as they did earlier, slowly raise your arms by reaching behind you and bringing them up over your head. Make sounds to show that you are releasing hot air that is rising. You are now a *hurricane*.

Step 4: Start to move the hurricane westward toward the Caribbean islands.

Role Card 4: Hurricane

Your group will act out the warm, moist air that helps a tropical storm to become a hurricane.

Step 1: Sit in the Atlantic Ocean, all around the edges of the performance area.

Step 2: When you see the students form a second circle (a tropical storm), watch for hot air to be released (they will lift their arms to the ceiling). When this happens, rush toward the tropical storm, staying close to the ground.

Step 3: Stand up and form a circle around the tropical storm. Move counterclockwise with them, but a little faster. Just as they did earlier, slowly raise your arms by reaching behind you and bringing them up over your head. Make sounds to show that you are releasing hot air that is rising. You are now a *hurricane*.

Step 4: Start to move the hurricane westward toward the Caribbean islands.

Prepare Your Character for the Act-It-Out

You will work with your group to bring to life a character in western Cuba as Hurricane Ivan approaches.

Step 1: Circle the character your teacher assigns to your group.

- a mother of six children who lives in a small wooden house with a tin roof
- a laborer who works on a small tobacco plantation
- a fisherman who fishes on the Caribbean coast
- a government official who works in the Department of Disaster Management
- a doctor who works in a local hospital
- a meteorologist who reports for the national radio station

Step 2: Pretend you are the character that your teacher has assigned to your group. Discuss these questions with your group:

- Who are you?
- What are you doing?
- What are your concerns as the hurricane approaches?
- What do you expect to happen during the hurricane?
- In what ways do you think your life might change as a result of the hurricane hitting your country?

Make sure everyone in your group can answer the questions.

Step 3: Brainstorm ideas on how the actor can make the character as realistic as possible. For example, the actor might use certain body postures, facial expressions, and simple props.

As you read each of Sections 11.4 to 11.8, complete the Reading Notes for that section.

11.8 Cleaning Up After a Natural Disaster

Write a summary of what happens after a hurricane. Include these terms in your summary: *rebuilding, relief agencies, cleaning up, Caribbean.*

Possible answer: Once a hurricane has passed, people face the task of <u>rebuilding</u>. A hurricane may destroy homes and damage schools, hospitals, roads, bridges, and power lines. <u>Relief agencies</u> are set up to find and treat the injured and to supply food, water, shelter, and clothing. The next task is <u>cleaning up</u>. This includes draining floodwaters, clearing roads, and knocking down damaged buildings. Because this work requires time and money, it may take months or even years for a <u>Caribbean</u> island to recover from a hurricane.

11.7 Landfall: A Natural Disaster Begins

Write a summary of what happens when a hurricane makes landfall. Include these terms in your summary: *wind, rain, storm surge, Caribbean.*

Possible answer: When a hurricane makes landfall, it lashes everything in its path with <u>wind</u> and <u>rain</u>. Fierce winds can uproot trees, shatter windows, blow off roofs, and flip over cars. Heavy rains often cause terrible flooding and sometimes deadly mudslides. A hurricane's most destructive feature is the <u>storm surge</u>. In 1999, a Category 4 storm hit several <u>Caribbean</u> islands. Its 15-foot storm surge caused lots of destruction.

11.4 Extreme Weather: A Hurricane Is Born

Write a summary of how a hurricane is formed. Include these terms in your summary: *Africa, Atlantic Ocean, warm and moist air, thunderstorms, tropical disturbance, Coriolis effect, tropical cyclone.*

Possible answer: Hurricanes in the <u>Atlantic Ocean</u> usually start off the coast of <u>Africa</u>. In the summer, <u>warm and moist air</u> rises from the ocean to form <u>thunderstorms</u>. Several thunderstorms come together to create a <u>tropical disturbance</u>. As the tropical disturbance grows, more warm and moist air rises from the ocean. This air begins to circle in a counterclockwise direction due to the <u>Coriolis effect</u>. Once wind speeds reach 74 miles per hour, the storm becomes a <u>tropical cyclone</u> (a hurricane).

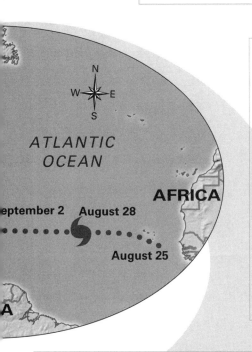

11.5 Inside a Monster Storm

Draw a simple diagram of the inside of a hurricane. Include and label these parts: *eye, eye wall, rainbands.*

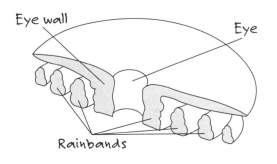

11.6 Tracking and Preparing for a Hurricane

Write a summary of how people track and prepare for a hurricane. Include these terms in your summary: *meteorologist, hurricane watch, hurricane warning, Saffir-Simpson scale.*

Possible answer: <u>Meteorologists</u> track a hurricane and then warn people in the storm's path. When a storm might hit land within 24 to 36 hours, they issue a <u>hurricane watch</u>. When it is less than 24 hours away, they issue a <u>hurricane warning</u>. Meteorologists use the <u>Saffir-Simpson</u> scale to rate a hurricane's strength from 1 to 5. These things give people a chance to prepare for the storm.

Land Use Conflict in the Amazon Rainforest

Overview

In this lesson, students learn about six groups that have competing interests in how to preserve and use the resources of the Amazon rainforest. In a **Response Group** activity, they create and present short news reports about these groups. Students discuss a series of questions that force them to evaluate each group's ideas and then propose their own ideas for how to reconcile those competing interests.

Objectives

Students will

- define and explain the importance of these key geographic terms: *biodiversity, carbon-oxygen cycle, deforestation, sustainable development, tropical rainforest.*
- teach the class about one of the groups that has an interest in the preservation or use of the resources of the Amazon rainforest.
- analyze and discuss a series of questions to help them understand the competing viewpoints of these various groups.
- investigate ideas from around the world about how to address land use conflict in the rainforest and determine which would be most applicable to the Amazon region.

Materials

- *Geography Alive! Regions and People*
- Interactive Student Notebooks
- Transparencies 12A and 12B
- Information Master 12 (1 transparency)
- Student Handout 12A (1 copy for every 4 students)
- Student Handout 12B (1 copy for every 8 students)
- scissors

Preview

1 **Have students complete Preview 12 in their Interactive Student Notebooks.** After they have finished their sketches, ask several volunteers to share their proposals and explanations.

2 **Project the top image on *Transparency 12A: Two Landsat Images*.** (**Note:** The two images on the transparency are satellite pictures of the same area of the Amazon rainforest, in the Brazilian state of Rondonia. The first was taken in 1975, the second in 2001.) Help students analyze the image by asking,

- What features do you see in this image?
- What patterns do you see on the landscape?
- From where do you think this image was taken?
- What do you think this is a picture of? What details support your hypothesis?
- This image was taken in 1975. How might the landscape have changed since then?

3 **Project the second image, and have students analyze both pictures.** Tell students that this is an image of the same location in the Amazon rainforest taken some time later. Ask,

- Compare the two images. What features are the same? What features have changed?
- How much time do you think has passed between the first image and the second? *Twenty-six years have passed between the two images.*
- What are possible explanations for the differences between the two images? *In this area of the Amazon, there has been significant deforestation since 1975 due to logging and the clearing of land for farming.*
- What might be some of the reasons the Amazon rainforest is being cut down?
- What might be some ideas people have about how the resources of the rainforest should be used or preserved?

4 **Make a connection between the Preview and the upcoming activity.** Explain to students that just as they had different ideas about how to best use the new land for their community, groups who live and work in the Amazon rainforest have different ideas about how to best use its land and resources. These differing ideas often lead to conflict among the groups. Explain that in this activity, students will learn about the different groups, how they want to use or preserve the rainforest's resources, and why they believe their ideas are justified. They will also investigate and propose possible solutions to land use conflict in the Amazon rainforest.

Preview 12

Transparency 12A

Essential Question and Geoterms

1 Introduce Chapter 12 in *Geography Alive! Regions and People.* Explain that in this chapter, students will learn about how various groups want to preserve or use the resources of the Amazon rainforest and why. Students will also propose ideas about how to address the needs of these various groups. Have students read Section 12.1. Afterward, ask them to identify at least four details in the two photographs that represent ideas in the text they just read.

2 Introduce the Graphic Organizer and the Essential Question. Have students examine the illustration. Ask,

- What do you see?
- Several groups that have an interest in the rainforest are represented in this illustration. What are those groups?
- Based on this illustration, how do you think each of these groups uses the resources of the rainforest?

Have students read the accompanying text. Make sure they understand the Essential Question, *How should the resources of rainforests be used and preserved?* You may want to post the Essential Question in the room or write it on the board for the duration of the activity.

3 Have students read Section 12.2. Then have them work individually or in pairs to complete Geoterms 12 in their Interactive Student Notebooks. Ask them to share their answers with another student, or have volunteers share their answers with the class.

Geoterms 12

Response Group

Phase 1: Preparing and Presenting Amazon Rainforest News Reports

1 Arrange students in mixed-ability groups of four. You may want to prepare a transparency that shows them with whom they will work and where they will sit. (**Note:** You will need at least six groups in all to represent the six rainforest interest groups. If you have a smaller class size, you may want to create groups of three.)

2 Explain Phase 1 of the activity. Tell students that in this first phase of the activity, each group will create a short news report to teach the rest of the class about a particular group with an interest in preserving or using the resources of the Amazon rainforest.

3 **Assign one rainforest group—native Amazonians, rubber tappers, loggers, settlers, cattle ranchers, or environmental groups—to each group of students.** Have groups read the section of the chapter (Sections 12.3 to 12.8) about their assigned group and complete the corresponding section of Reading Notes 12.

4 **Project** *Information Master 12: Preparing a News Report.* Review the directions with students. Give groups adequate time to prepare and rehearse their news reports. Circulate as they work, reminding them that their reports must

- involve all group members.
- include key information from Reading Notes 12.
- incorporate simple props or costumes.
- be one to two minutes long.

5 **Have the first group perform their news report.** Clear a space at the front of the room where the first group can perform their news report. While the group is preparing to present its report, have the rest of the class read the section of Chapter 12 that corresponds to that group. Remind actors to speak loudly, clearly, and slowly enough for everyone to hear.

6 **Have the rest of the class complete the corresponding section of Reading Notes 12.** After the news report, ask the rest of the class to complete the related Reading Notes. Then ask several volunteers to share their answers. Use Guide to Reading Notes 12 to check for accuracy. (**Note:** You may want to record the answers on a transparency of the Reading Notes.)

7 **Repeat Steps 5 and 6 until all groups have presented their reports and students have completed Sections 12.3 to 12.8 of the Reading Notes.** (**Note:** For middle school students, you may want to do Steps 8 and 9 after the first three news reports and then again after the last three news reports, rather than waiting until all the reports have been given.)

8 **Give a copy of** *Student Handout 12A: Statements of Amazon Rainforest Interest Groups* **to each group.** Explain that the top half lists statements that each rainforest group might make and the bottom half lists statements that might be directed toward each interest group. Give groups several minutes to discuss which two statements—one from each set—best match each of the six rainforest groups. They must be prepared to explain their choices. (**Note:** While some statements logically relate to one rainforest group more than another, the goal is not so much for students to find the "right" answers as to use what they've learned about each group to make reasonable arguments.)

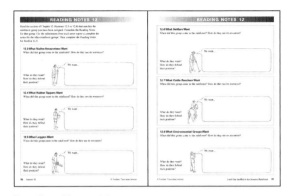

Reading Notes 12

Information Master 12

Student Handout 12A

9 Facilitate a class discussion. Follow these steps:

- Have each group select a Presenter.
- Have a Presenter from one group, such as cattle ranchers, stand and share which two statements that group thinks relate to cattle ranchers and why.
- Have the Presenter ask for a show of hands of which groups disagree with those choices and then call on another group to share their ideas.
- Continue until most or all of the different ideas are shared.
- Select a Presenter from another rainforest group (such as rubber tappers), and repeat the process.

Note: Depending on the time available, conduct a short discussion for each of the six rainforest groups or for just a few.

Phase 2: Ranking the Amazon Rainforest Groups

1 Explain Phase 2 of the activity. Tell groups that in this phase of the activity, they will discuss a series of questions. For each question, their job is to rank the rainforest groups based on which they think makes the strongest case down to which makes the weakest case. Explain that their rankings may change depending on the question. Students need to be prepared to explain why they believe that the top two groups in their rankings make the strongest case and why the bottom group makes the weakest case. (**Note:** Some students may want to defend the perspective of the group from their news report. Emphasize that instead they need to objectively analyze the perspectives of *all* groups as they discuss the questions.)

2 Pass out a set of six interest groups cut from *Student Handout 12B: Amazon Rainforest Interest Groups* to each group. Have groups cut along the dashed lines to create a slip for each interest group.

3 Give students Question 1 (below) and have them rank the Amazon rainforest interest groups. Read students the first question:

- *Question 1:* Which group has the most legitimate claim to decide what should be done to preserve or use the resources of the Amazon rainforest?

Give groups several minutes to discuss the question, rank each rainforest group by putting the slips of paper in order from strongest case to weakest case, and prepare their explanations of why the top two groups have the strongest cases and the bottom group has the weakest.

Student Handout 12B

4 Facilitate a discussion of Question 1. Follow this procedure:

- Have each group select a Presenter.
- Call on one Presenter to stand and share that group's rankings and explanations.
- Encourage a student-centered discussion by having that Presenter ask for a show of hands of which groups disagree with their choices and call on the next Presenter from a group with different rankings.

5 Repeat Steps 3 and 4 for Questions 2–4. Have groups rotate the role of Presenter with each new question.

- *Question 2:* Which group wants to use or preserve the resources of the rainforest in ways that will be most helpful to the country and people of Brazil?
- *Question 3:* Which group wants to use or preserve the resources of the rainforest in ways that will be most helpful to people around the world (the global community)?
- *Question 4:* Considering all the factors from the previous questions, which group makes the strongest case for how to use or preserve the resources of the Amazon rainforest?

6 Have students carefully read Section 12.9. Then ask groups to imagine that it is their job to recommend *two ideas,* from those described in this section or other ideas of their own, that should be implemented to address land use conflict in the Amazon rainforest. In their groups, have students discuss the following two questions and then write their answers in Section 12.9 of their Reading Notes:

- Which two ideas would you recommend?
- Which rainforest groups' needs would be met by these ideas, and how?

Suggest that the ideas with the best chance of success might be those that address the needs and wants of as many of the rainforest interest groups as possible.

7 Facilitate a class discussion of ideas. Call on a new Presenter to share the two ideas their groups would recommend and to explain which rainforest groups' needs would be met by them and how. Have each Presenter select the following Presenter from a group with ideas or proposals different from their own. Encourage students to note ideas that they think are particularly good and practical, as they will be able to refer to them in the Processing assignment.

Global Connections

1 **Introduce the Global Connections.** Have students read Section 12.10. Explain that they will now see how some of the issues from the activity exist in other areas of the world.

2 Project *Transparency 12B: Global Connections*. Have students analyze the map by discussing their answers to the following questions. Use the additional information given to enrich the discussion.

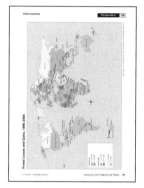

Transparency 12B

- **What interesting details do you see on this map?**

- **What do the various colors of the countries represent?**
  They represent the levels of deforestation and reforestation around the world. Brown indicates a country in which 2.5% or more of the forests have been lost (for example, Nicaragua). Orange indicates a country that has lost between 0.1% and 2.4% of its forests (Ecuador). Light green indicates a country with between 0.1% and 2.4% reforestation (Cuba); dark green shows countries with over 2.5% reforestation (Uruguay). Yellow indicates no change (Suriname).

- **Which countries are experiencing the greatest loss of forests? Why might this be so?**
  In Latin America, the countries of El Salvador, Nicaragua, and Haiti are experiencing the highest percentage of deforestation; in Africa, Mauritania, Niger, Nigeria, Togo, Cote D'Ivoire, Sierra Leone, Rwanda, and Burundi.

  These countries might be experiencing a large increase in population, putting pressure on valuable resources like trees. In addition, the income level, or per capita GDP, of people in these countries might be low, forcing them to look for cheap sources of fuel for cooking and heating.

- **Which countries are experiencing the greatest amount of reforestation? Why might this be so?**
  Diverse countries such as Uruguay in South America, Egypt in Africa, Ireland and Belarus in Europe, and Kyrgyzstan, Oman, and United Arab Emirates in Asia have the highest percentages of reforestation.

  The West African nation of Gabon has experienced no change in its natural forest. This is likely to continue because unlike many of its neighbors, Gabon has recently set aside 10,000 square miles of tropical rainforest, roughly 10% of the entire country, for a series of 13 national parks. Logging and other kinds of development will be banned inside the borders. Once completed, this will be largest park system in the world.

3 Have students read Section 12.11 and examine the rest of the information in the section. Then lead a discussion of these questions:

• **What does each graph represent?**

• **The eight countries that are labeled in red on the map are also represented in the graphs. What relationships do you see between the information on the map and the data in the graphs?**

• **What hypotheses might explain the relationships you identified between the graphs and the map?**

Processing

Have students complete Processing 12 in their Interactive Student Notebooks. Remind them that they can use any ideas or proposals from Section 12.9 of their Reading Notes to help them complete this assignment. (**Note:** Consider getting the address of the Brazilian Embassy or the nearest Brazilian consulate and have students actually send their letters there.)

Online Resources

For more information on land use conflicts, refer students to Online Resources for *Geography Alive! Regions and People* at www.teachtci.com.

Assessment

Masters for assessment appear on the next three pages followed by answers and scoring rubrics.

Processing 12

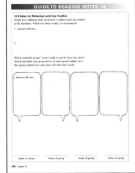

Reading Notes 12

Mastering the Content

Shade the oval by the letter of the best answer for each question.

1. In which region of South America is the Amazon rainforest located?

    ◯ A. region A

    ◯ B. region B

    ◯ C. region C

    ◯ D. region D

South America

PACIFIC OCEAN

ATLANTIC OCEAN

2. Rainforests are called the "lungs of the Earth" because of their role in the

    ◯ A. food web.

    ◯ B. Coriolis effect.

    ◯ C. El Niño current.

    ◯ D. carbon-oxygen cycle.

3. What is the **main** cause of land use conflict in the Amazon rainforest?

    ◯ A. opposition by the government to the movement of farmers to the rainforest

    ◯ B. differences among many different groups over how best to use the rainforest

    ◯ C. conflicts between ranchers and farmers over how much land to clear in the rainforest

    ◯ D. arguments among environmental groups over how to preserve biodiversity in the rainforest

4. Which of the following would groups who want sustainable development in the Amazon rainforest **most likely** support?

    ◯ A. the building of more roads into the rainforest

    ◯ B. the harvesting of rainforest trees to create more jobs

    ◯ C. the clearing of rainforest to create farms and ranches

    ◯ D. the use of rainforest resources without destroying them

5. Which of these groups is **most** responsible for deforestation of the rainforest?

    ◯ A. rubber tappers

    ◯ B. native peoples

    ◯ C. logging companies

    ◯ D. environmental groups

6. Which of these do environmental groups in the Amazon rainforest **most** want to protect?

    ◯ A. biodiversity

    ◯ B. ecotourism

    ◯ C. deforestation

    ◯ D. wetlands

7. What can settlers in the Amazon basin do to promote sustainable development of the rainforest?

    ◯ A. clear more land to make larger farms

    ◯ B. use cleared land to raise cattle instead of crops

    ◯ C. plant crops that grow under the rainforest canopy

    ◯ D. encourage more poor farmers to migrate to the rainforest

8. Which statement is **best** supported by the graph?

Loss of Tropical Rainforest Worldwide

Current area of tropical rainforest

Original area of tropical rainforest

| 0 | 1 million | 2 million | 3 million | 4 million | 5 million | 6 million |

Area (square miles)

    ◯ A. Rainforest loss has increased in the last 10 years.

    ◯ B. About half of the world's rainforests have been lost.

    ◯ C. Rainforest once covered about 3 million square miles.

    ◯ D. Two thirds of the world's rainforests have disappeared.

Assessment | **12**

Applying Geography Skills:
Reading a Biodiversity Diagram

Use the rainforest biodiversity diagram and your knowledge of geography to complete the tasks below. Write your answers in complete sentences.

Biodiversity in the Amazon Rainforest

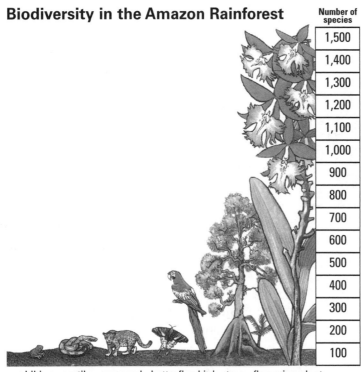

Number of species
1,500
1,400
1,300
1,200
1,100
1,000
900
800
700
600
500
400
300
200
100

amphibian reptile mammal butterfly bird tree flowering plant

1. Circle the smallest group of species on the diagram. (Species are a kind or variety of something.) Identify the group. Estimate its number of species in the Amazon rainforest.

2. Explain why flowering plants are drawn larger than birds on the diagram.

3. Predict what is likely to happen to biodiversity in the Amazon basin if deforestation continues. Explain why you think this will happen.

Test Terms Glossary

To **estimate** means to make a rough calculation of something.

To **predict** means to say what is likely to happen in the future based on what you already know.

Exploring the Essential Question

How should the resources of rainforests be used and preserved?

In Chapter 12, you explored how different groups of people use the resources of the rainforest. Now you will use what you learned. Use the information on the diagram below and your knowledge of geography to complete this task.

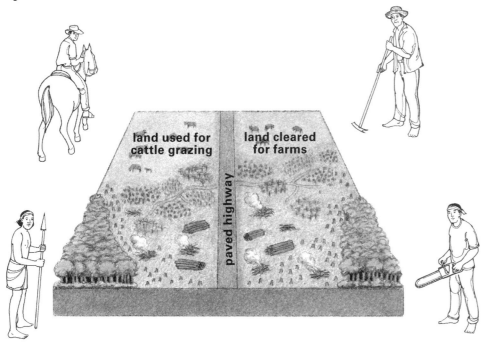

The Task: Creating a "What We Want in the Rainforest" Poster

This diagram shows different ways land is used in the rainforest. Each figure around the diagram represents a group with an interest in the rainforest. Your task is to create a poster that shows the ideas of one of these groups.

Step 1: Identify the group you will create a poster for. Circle the figure above that represents that group.

Step 2: Identify the way of using land that your group thinks is best. Draw a line from your group to the part of the rainforest where that group is most likely to be found.

Step 3: On a large sheet of paper, create a poster representing the views of your group. Make sure it has the following:
A. a title. You may use "What We Want in the Rainforest" or create your own title.
B. the name or a symbol of the group your poster represents
C. a few words or images that show what your group wants and why its views on land use in the rainforest are important

Applying Geography Skills: Sample Responses

1. Students should circle *amphibian* on the diagram. There are about 60 species of amphibians in the Amazon rainforest. Accept any estimate under 100.
2. Flowering plants are drawn larger than birds on the diagram because the number of species of such plants is more than three times the number of bird species.
3. If deforestation of the Amazon basin continues, the biodiversity of the rainforest is likely to decline. This will happen because cleared land used for farming and raising cattle cannot support most of the species that live in forested areas.

Exploring the Essential Question: Sample Response

Steps 1 and 2: Responses will depend on the group each student has chosen to represent.

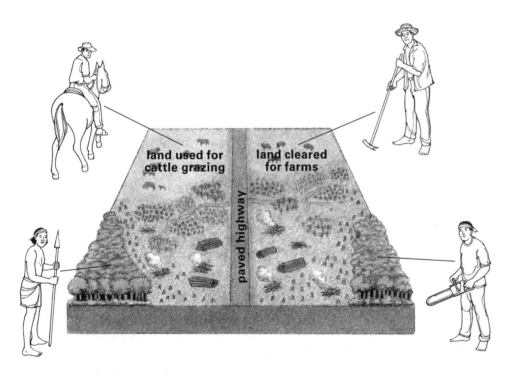

land used for cattle grazing

land cleared for farms

paved highway

Step 3: Posters should have these three elements:
A. a title
B. the name or a symbol of the group represented
C. a clear statement of what that group wants and why its views on land use in the rainforest are important

Mastering the Content Answer Key

1. A	2. D	3. B	4. D
5. C	6. A	7. C	8. B

Applying Geography Skills Scoring Rubric

Score	General Description
2	Student responds to all parts of the task. Response is correct and clear.
1	Student responds to some parts of the task. Response is mostly correct.
0	Response does not match the task or is incorrect.

Exploring the Essential Question Scoring Rubric

Score	General Description
3	Student responds to all parts of the task. Response is correct, clear, and supported by details.
2	Student responds to most or all parts of the task. Response is generally correct but may lack details.
1	Student responds to at least one part of the task. Response may contain errors and lack details.
0	Response does not match the task or is incorrect.

Create an Amazon Rainforest News Report

Work with your group to create a news report about the rainforest group you have been assigned. Follow these steps:

Step 1: Review the roles. Assign one of these roles to each member of your group. Make sure everyone understands his or her responsibilities.

- **News Anchorperson:** This person gives a brief history of when your group came to the rainforest. He or she also explains how your group uses the resources of the rainforest.

- **Reporter:** This person interviews two people from the rainforest group.

- **Interviewee 1:** This person is a member of the rainforest group who is interviewed by the Reporter. He or she explains one or more ideas about *what* this group wants to do to preserve or use the rainforest's resources.

- **Interviewee 2:** This person is a member of the rainforest group who is interviewed by the Reporter. He or she explains *why* the group's ideas for preserving or using the rainforest's resources are justified, or good.

Step 2: Create your news report. You must design a news report about your rainforest group. The report should be one to two minutes long. Also, you must create at least one simple, appropriate prop or costume piece for each person to be interviewed.

Step 3: Rehearse your news report. Make sure everyone speaks loudly and clearly enough to be heard by the audience.

Matching Statements with Rainforest Interest Groups

Which group would make each of these statements?

Statement 1: We've been here longer than anyone. Our land and way of life should be protected.

Statement 2: Land that has been opened to us in the rainforest finally gives us a chance to provide food for our families. You can't take that away.

Statement 3: What we do to earn a living doesn't hurt the rainforest. Because of that, we should have land of our own in the rainforest.

Statement 4: We're taking land that has already been cleared and making it productive. Besides, we provide a valuable product to hungry people all around the world.

Statement 5: People in other countries use the valuable resources of their land to provide jobs for people and improve the economic situation of their country. Why can't we do the same?

Statement 6: We must stop much of what is happening to the rainforest, or eventually people all over the Earth will suffer.

Which group is each of these statements directed toward?

Statement 1: Unless you change the way you do things, the valuable resource you take from the rainforest won't be around much longer. Then what will you do?

Statement 2: You are such a small group, your interests shouldn't outweigh the needs of an entire country. Besides, the way you live just doesn't fit with modern times.

Statement 3: The way you use the rainforest's land turns the forest into grasslands. Grassland may benefit you, but it hurts lots of other people, both here in the Amazon basin and around the world.

Statement 4: Why can't you be given land somewhere else? Besides, rainforest land isn't even good for how you want to use it.

Statement 5: It's easy for you to tell the rest of us what should be done with the rainforest. But you don't rely on the rainforest's land and resources to live, like we do.

Statement 6: The way you make your living in the rainforest is old-fashioned. You are keeping others from using that land more productively.

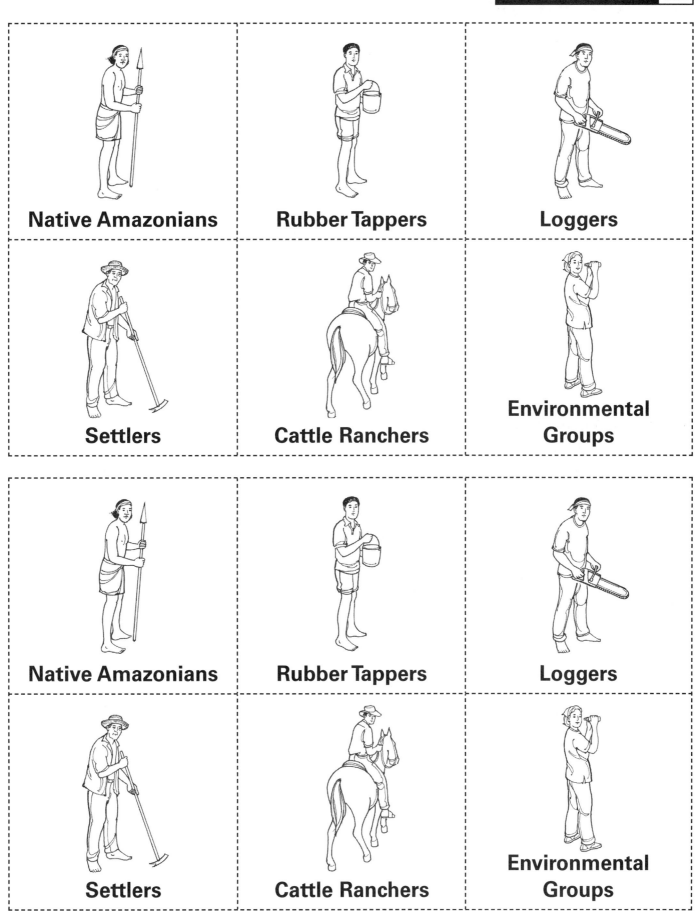

Native Amazonians

Rubber Tappers

Loggers

Settlers

Cattle Ranchers

Environmental Groups

Native Amazonians

Rubber Tappers

Loggers

Settlers

Cattle Ranchers

Environmental Groups

Read the section of Chapter 12 (Sections 12.3 to 12.8) that matches the rainforest group you have been assigned. Complete the Reading Notes for that group. Use the information from each news report to complete the notes for the other rainforest groups. Then complete the Reading Notes for Section 12.9.

12.3 What Native Amazonians Want

When did this group come to the rainforest? How do they use its resources? Native Amazonians have lived in the rainforest for about 12,000 years. They hunt, fish, and grow crops on small plots of land they clear. When a field is no longer fertile, they clear a new one and leave the old one to be covered by the forest.

What do they want? How do they defend their position?

> We want... the government to make us the legal owners of our homelands so we can live where we belong, on our own land. Our people have lived in these forests for 12,000 years, and our use of the land and its resources is sustainable.

12.4 What Rubber Tappers Want

When did this group come to the rainforest? How do they use its resources? Rubber tappers first came to the Amazon in the 1870s to work on rubber tree plantations. Tappers remove sap from rubber trees by making cuts in the bark, which does not harm the trees.

What do they want? How do they defend their position?

> We want... to continue to make a living by tapping rubber. To do this, the practice of clearing all trees from the rainforest must stop. We want the government to set up protected areas where we can continue rubber tapping. We have lived and worked in the rainforest for generations, and we use its resources, particularly rubber trees, in a sustainable way.

12.5 What Loggers Want

When did this group come to the rainforest? How do they use its resources? Loggers began moving into the Amazon basin in the 1960s. They harvest trees for a variety of uses. Valuable hardwoods like mahogany and rosewood are used to make furniture. Other trees are used for lumber and to make paper.

What do they want? How do they defend their position?

> We want... to continue clear-cutting in the rainforest, which is the most economical way to harvest trees. Our logging companies provide jobs for thousands in Brazil. The trees we harvest provide wood for furniture factories and paper mills, and Brazil exported more than $5 billion of wood in 2004. This helps its economy and all the people of Brazil, not just a small group.

12.6 What Settlers Want

When did this group come to the rainforest? How do they use its resources? In the 1960s, the Brazilian government began encouraging poor people to move to the Amazon rainforest. These settlers cleared the land the government gave them and used it for farming.

What do they want?
How do they defend their position?

We want... rainforest land to farm so we can feed our families. Farming on rainforest land is difficult, but the best farmland in our country is already owned by others. The government gave us this land and encouraged us to move here. There is no land for us in other parts of the country, so we must use this land to survive.

12.7 What Cattle Ranchers Want

When did this group come to the rainforest? How do they use its resources? Cattle ranchers came to parts of the Amazon basin starting in the 1960s. They clear land, or use land already cleared by loggers and farmers, for grazing their cattle. Cattle eat the grass in an area down to the dirt and are then moved to a new area.

What do they want?
How do they defend their position?

We want... large tracts of rainforest land so we can go on cattle ranching in this area. While some argue we don't belong in the rainforest, we are making good use of the land. The cattle we raise help feed people here in Brazil. We also export over $1 billion of beef per year to other countries, like the United States. That helps the Brazilian economy and all the people of Brazil, not just certain groups.

12.8 What Environmental Groups Want

When did this group come to the rainforest? How do they use its resources? Scientists and environmentalists started coming to the rainforest in the 1970s. Some study rainforest plants, hoping to find cures for diseases. Some study wildlife, and others work with native peoples.

What do they want?
How do they defend their position?

We want... to protect the biodiversity of the rainforest by slowing down deforestation and development. 2.5 acres of rainforest contain 750 kind of trees, 1,500 kinds of plants, 125 types of mammals, and 400 types of birds. Deforestation and development must be slowed so we can protect these rainforest species and study them. Once they are gone, they are lost forever.

12.9 Ideas for Reducing Land Use Conflict

People have different ideas about how to address land use conflict in the rainforest. Which two ideas would you recommend?

1. Answers will vary.

2.

Which rainforest groups' needs would be met by these two ideas? Sketch and label each group below. In each speech bubble, have that group explain how your ideas will meet their needs.

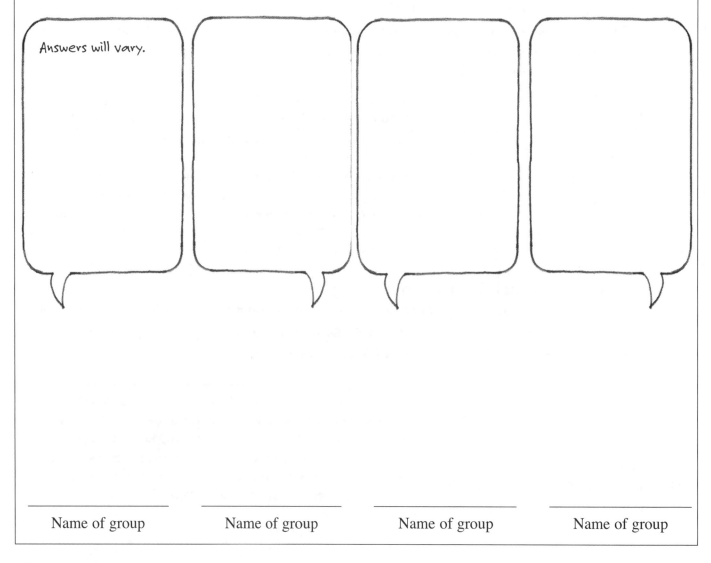

Answers will vary.

| Name of group | Name of group | Name of group | Name of group |

Life in the Central Andes: Adapting to a Mountainous Region

Overview

In this lesson, students learn how people have adapted to the varied environments of the Andes Mountains. In a **Social Studies Skill Builder,** they assume the role of magazine editors organizing a feature article on life in the central Andes. They read about the physical characteristics of four elevation zones—*tierra caliente, tierra templada, tierra fría,* and *tierra helada*—and categorize photographs and other geographic information on how people have adapted to life in each zone. Afterward, they extend their learning by researching how people have adapted to living in other mountainous regions around the world.

Objectives

Students will

- define and explain the importance of these key geographic terms: *altitudinal zonation, snow line, terracing, tree line, vertical trade*.

- describe the physical characteristics of four elevation zones: tierra caliente, tierra templada, tierra fría, and tierra helada.

- identify ways in which people of the central Andes have adapted to life in each of the four elevation zones.

- analyze the impact of retreating mountain glaciers on people living in mountainous regions around the world.

Materials

- *Geography Alive! Regions and People*
- Interactive Student Notebooks
- Transparencies 13A and 13B
- Placards 13A–13C (3 sets)
- Information Master 13 (1 transparency)
- Student Handout 13 (cut apart)

Preview

1 **Have students complete Part 1 of Preview 13 in their Interactive Student Notebooks.** Ask several volunteers to share their responses.

2 Project *Transparency 13A: A Village in the Andes Mountains.* On the elevation profile, point out the approximate elevation of this location, the town of Chinchero, Peru. Then have students complete Part 2 of Preview 13 and share their ideas.

3 **Explain the connection between the Preview and the upcoming activity.** Tell students that our physical environment is one influence on how we live. For example, people in a desert might live very differently from people in a tropical rainforest because the physical environments are so different. Students may have noted that they would likely have different routines and activities if they lived in the Andes. In this lesson, they will learn about the physical characteristics of the central Andes and how people have adapted to the varied environments in this mountainous region.

Essential Question and Geoterms

1 **Introduce Chapter 13 in** *Geography Alive! Regions and People.* Explain that in this chapter, students will learn about ways in which people of the central Andes have adapted to living in a mountainous region. Have students read Section 13.1. Afterward, ask them to identify at least four details in the photograph of the Andes Mountains that reflect ideas in the text they just read.

2 **Introduce the Graphic Organizer and the Essential Question.** Ask students to examine the diagram of elevation zones in the Andes Mountains. Ask,

- What do you see?
- What landform is represented in this diagram?
- How is the mountain divided? How do these four zones differ from one another?
- What might life be like for people living in each of these elevation zones?

Have students read the accompanying text. Make sure they understand the Essential Question, *How do people adapt to living in a mountainous region?* You may want to post the Essential Question in the room or write it on the board for the duration of the activity.

3 **Have students read Section 13.2.** Then have them work individually or in pairs to complete Geoterms 13 in their Interactive Student Notebooks. Have them share their answers in pairs, or have volunteers share their answers with the class.

Preview 13

Transparency 13A

Geoterms 13

Social Studies Skill Builder

1 Arrange the classroom and prepare materials.

- Create a "magazine publishing company" by setting up three identical sets of graphics stations: three stations on one side of the room, three on the other, and three in the back. Place two desks together to create each station.
- Place graphics at each station. Place *Placard 13A* at each Station 1, *Placard 13B* at each Station 2, and *Placard 13C* at each Station 3.
- Cut the cards from a copy of *Student Handout 13: Zone Cards.*

2 Place students in mixed-ability pairs. You may want to prepare a transparency that shows students with whom they will work and where they will sit.

3 Introduce the activity.

- Explain that students are about to take on the role of magazine editors. The class will now be the publishing company where they work.
- Explain that the magazine is preparing a feature article on life in the central Andes, but the graphics for the article have been accidentally scattered about the room. It is the editors' job to label and organize the graphics for the article. First they will read and take notes about the physical characteristics of one of four elevation zones of the central Andes and the ways in which people have adapted to living in that zone. They will then examine the graphics—photographs and other geographic information—and determine which belong in that section of the feature article.
- Assign one third of the pairs to use the stations in each part of the room.

4 Project a transparency of *Information Master 13: Creating a Feature Article Layout.* Review the directions with students.

5 Give each pair their first Zone Card from Student Handout 13, and have them begin. Allow ample time (about two class periods) for completing the activity. Remind pairs to have you check their completed "feature article layout" (Reading Notes) for each zone before they begin work on another. Alternatively, circulate around the room to check students' work.

6 After the activity, review the entire set of Reading Notes as a class. Use Guide to Reading Notes 13 to check that students categorized the graphics correctly.

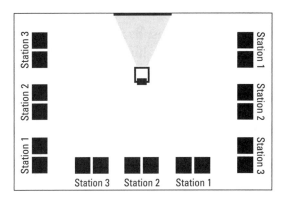

Placards 13A–13C

Student Handout 13   **Information Master 13**

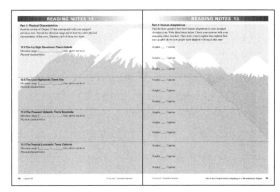

Reading Notes 13

7 Wrap up the activity. Ask students to rank the four elevation zones according to where they would most want to live, using 1 for the most desirable and 4 for the least desirable. Encourage them to think about the types of adaptations people have made in each zone. Ask several volunteers to share their ranking and the reasoning behind it.

Global Connections

1 Introduce the Global Connections. Have students read Section 13.7. Then explain that they will now examine the role of glaciers in the lives of people living in mountainous regions around the world.

2 Project *Transparency 13B: Global Connections.* Reveal only the map, and ask,

- **What interesting details do you see?**

- **Where are glaciers located around the world?**

- **Besides the Andes, in what mountain ranges will you find glaciers?**

3 Reveal the satellite image of the Gangotri Glacier. Help students to analyze the image by asking,

Transparency 13B

- **In what mountain range is the Gangotri Glacier located?**

- **What happened to the glacier between 1780 and 2001?**

- **About how many miles did the glacier retreat in those years?**

4 Have students read Section 13.8 and examine the rest of the information in the section. Then lead a discussion of the questions that follow. Use the additional information given to enrich the discussion.

- **What is happening to mountain glaciers around the world?**
  Most of the world's mountain glaciers are retreating. According to NASA's National Snow and Ice Data Center, Glacier National Park in Montana has lost 110 of its glaciers over the past 150 years. In the next 25 years, scientists predict the park will lose the remaining 37. A similar phenomenon is happening in the Canadian Rockies and the mountains of Alaska.

  Retreating mountain glaciers are not unique to North America. In the past 30 years, Peru's mountain glaciers have lost nearly 25% of their area. The glacial area in the Ruwenzori Mountains of Uganda has decreased by 75% since the 1990s.

Not all mountain glaciers are retreating. Visitors to the Moreno Glacier in Argentina are awed by the sight of blocks of ice dropping into the lake below the advancing glacier, which moves at a rate of 30 centimeters per day.

- **Why are some mountain glaciers retreating?**
  Most scientists blame climate change for this phenomenon. Glaciers are particularly sensitive to changes in temperature and precipitation. During warmer, drier seasons, glaciers melt more rapidly. During colder, rainy seasons, they melt more slowly. Scientists track these changes by measuring individual glaciers and comparing their size over time. For a variety of reasons, climate records show that the Earth's climate is slowly warming. Many scientists believe that this trend is responsible for the increased rate at which glaciers are retreating.

- **What impact do retreating glaciers have on people in mountainous regions?**
  People in these regions are dependent on glaciers as a water source. Up to 95% of the water in the river systems of dry countries is supplied by glaciers. Even Germany, with a more temperate climate, derives 40% of its natural water supply from mountain glaciers.

  Scientists are also concerned that melting mountain glaciers have the potential to cause devastating natural disasters. Glaciers typically store large amounts of water; when this water is released suddenly, it can cause flooding, landslides, and avalanches. In 1941, a chunk of the glacier overlooking Lake Palcacocha in the city of Huaraz, Peru, fell into the lake, triggering a massive flood that killed 5,000 to 7,000 people and destroyed one third of the city.

Processing

Have students complete Processing 13 in their Interactive Student Notebooks.

Online Resources

For more information on life in the central Andes, refer students to Online Resources for *Geography Alive! Regions and People* at www.teachtci.com.

Assessment

Masters for assessment appear on the next three pages followed by answers and scoring rubrics.

Processing 13

Assessment `13`

Mastering the Content

Shade the oval by the letter of the best answer for each question.

1. The Andes Mountains line the west coast of
   ○ A. Canada.
   ○ B. Mexico.
   ○ C. South America.
   ○ D. Central America.

2. Vertical trade is the trading of goods between
   ○ A. poor and wealthy areas.
   ○ B. farming and urban areas.
   ○ C. northern and southern areas.
   ○ D. lowland and highland areas.

3. Which factor explains why low elevations have denser air than high elevations?
   ○ A. condensation
   ○ B. evaporation
   ○ C. gravity
   ○ D. latitude

4. Quito, the capital of Ecuador, is located at 9,250 feet above sea level. According to the diagram below, Quito is in which elevation zone?

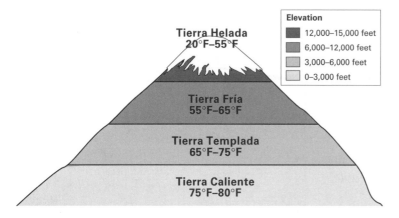

Elevation	
■	12,000–15,000 feet
▨	6,000–12,000 feet
▨	3,000–6,000 feet
□	0–3,000 feet

Tierra Helada
20°F–55°F

Tierra Fría
55°F–65°F

Tierra Templada
65°F–75°F

Tierra Caliente
75°F–80°F

   ○ A. tierra fría
   ○ B. tierra helada
   ○ C. tierra caliente
   ○ D. tierra templada

5. What is the main commercial crop grown in the tierra templada?
   ○ A. bananas
   ○ B. coffee
   ○ C. tomatoes
   ○ D. wheat

6. At which of these elevation zones is the tree line found in the Andes?
   ○ A. tierra fría
   ○ B. tierra helada
   ○ C. tierra caliente
   ○ D. tierra templada

7. Terracing is a farming method that makes it possible to raise crops
   ○ A. above the snow line.
   ○ B. on steep hillsides.
   ○ C. in tropical lowlands.
   ○ D. below forest canopies.

8. Which of these elevation zones lies mostly above the tree line?
   ○ A. tierra fría
   ○ B. tierra helada
   ○ C. tierra caliente
   ○ D. tierra templada

Applying Geography Skills:
Analyzing a Circle Graph and a Climate Map

Use the circle graph, climate map, and your knowledge of geography to complete the tasks below.

World Banana Production

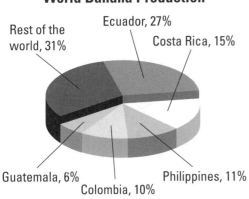

World Banana Production

Ecuador, 27%

Costa Rica, 15%

Rest of the world, 31%

Guatemala, 6%

Colombia, 10%

Philippines, 11%

Climate Zones of Latin America

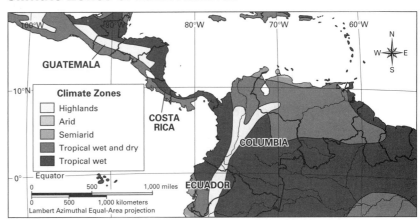

1. Calculate the percentage of the world's bananas that comes from the four Latin American countries of Ecuador, Costa Rica, Columbia, and Guatemala.

2. Identify the two climate zones that are found in all four of these Latin American countries.

3. Describe the climate that seems best suited for growing bananas.

Test Terms Glossary

To **calculate** means to figure out or estimate a figure using math.

To **identify** means to tell what something is.

To **describe** means to provide details about something.

Exploring the Essential Question

How do people adapt to living in a mountainous region?

In Chapter 13, you explored how people live in the four elevation zones of the Andes Mountains. Now you will use what you learned. Use the information on the diagram and your knowledge of geography to complete this task.

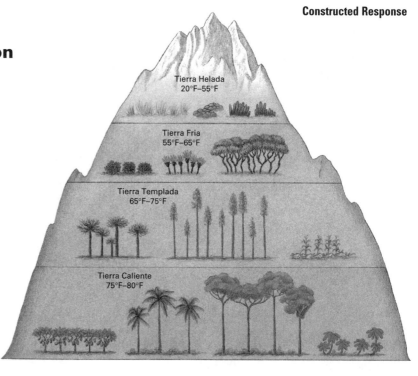

Tierra Helada
20°F–55°F

Tierra Fria
55°F–65°F

Tierra Templada
65°F–75°F

Tierra Caliente
75°F–80°F

The Task: Writing a Letter About Where to Live in the Andes

This diagram shows the four elevation zones of the Andes Mountains. Your task is to decide which zone you would **most** recommend to a friend who is moving to Ecuador.

Step 1: Look at the climate data and vegetation in each elevation zone on the diagram. Circle the zone that you think would be best to live in.

Step 2: On another sheet of paper, write a letter to a friend with your thoughts about the best place to live in Ecuador. Make sure your letter has these things:

A. a greeting, such as "Dear friend," followed by a comma

B. an opening that states which zone you think your friend should move to

C. several supporting sentences that justify your choice. Your supporting sentences should contain details about

  • the climate of the zone you chose.

  • the clothing your friend should pack to live in that zone.

  • the vegetation and crops that grow in that zone.

  You may also add other details to justify your choice.

D. a conclusion that restates what elevation zone you are recommending to your friend

E. a closing such as "Sincerely," or "Regards," and your signature

Writing Tips: Using Transition Words
Transition words help you move smoothly from one supporting sentence to the next. As you add each new piece of information to support your choice, use transition words such as *additionally, for example, also, next,* and *finally.*
For example,

In addition, the vegetation of this zone is lush and tropical.

Test Terms Glossary
To **justify** means to tell why a position or point of view is right.

Applying Geography Skills: Sample Responses

1. 58%
2. tropical wet and tropical wet and dry
3. Bananas are best grown in a hot and humid climate. They like a lot of sunlight and rain.

Exploring the Essential Question: Sample Response

Step 1: One elevation zone should be circled.

Step 2: The letter should include the elements listed in the prompt. These elements are identified by letter in the response below. Note the transition words in this response.

A. Dear friend,

B. When you move to Ecuador, you should live in the tierra fría.

C. **To begin with,** you won't have to worry about getting too hot even though you will be living on the equator. Temperatures in the tierra fría average between 55 and 65 degrees. Just be sure to bring winter clothes with you. This area also has a good mix of vegetation. You will find both forests and mountain meadows. **In addition,** farmers there raise foods that you like, including potatoes, apples, and corn. **Finally,** I think you will like living where the Incas used to live. You will have fun visiting Inca ruins.

D. **In closing,** I think the terra fría will be the coolest, prettiest, and most historic place you could choose in Ecuador.

E. Your friend,

Mastering the Content Answer Key

1. C	2. D	3. C	4. A
5. B	6. A	7. B	8. B

Applying Geography Skills Scoring Rubric

Score	General Description
2	Student responds to all parts of the task. Response is correct and clear.
1	Student responds to some parts of the task. Response is mostly correct.
0	Response does not match the task or is incorrect.

Exploring the Essential Question Scoring Rubric

Score	General Description
3	Student responds to all parts of the task. Response is correct, clear, and supported by details.
2	Student responds to most or all parts of the task. Response is generally correct but may lack details.
1	Student responds to at least one part of the task. Response may contain errors and lack details.
0	Response does not match the task or is incorrect.

tierra caliente	**tierra templada**	**tierra fría**	**tierra helada**
tierra caliente	**tierra templada**	**tierra fría**	**tierra helada**
tierra caliente	**tierra templada**	**tierra fría**	**tierra helada**
tierra caliente	**tierra templada**	**tierra fría**	**tierra helada**

Prepare a Feature Article on Life in the Central Andes

Step 1: Get a Zone Card—for tierra caliente, tierra templada, tierra fría, or tierra helada—from the "managing editor" (your teacher). Read the section of Chapter 13 that matches the card.

Step 2: Turn to Reading Notes 13 in your Interactive Student Notebook. Complete Part 1 of the Reading Notes for that elevation zone.

Step 3: Visit the three graphics stations on your side of the magazine publishing company. Use the information in your Reading Notes and your book to identify *one graphic* at each station that corresponds to the elevation zone you read about. Write the letter of each graphic you select in Part 2 of your Reading Notes.

Step 4: Complete Part 2 of your Reading Notes for that elevation zone.

Step 5: Have the managing editor check your feature article layout (your Reading Notes) for that elevation zone. Then get a new Zone Card and repeat these steps.

Part 1: Physical Characteristics

Read the section of Chapter 13 that corresponds with your assigned elevation zone. Record the elevation range and at least two other physical characteristics of that zone. Illustrate *each* of those two items.

13.6 The Icy High Elevations: Tierra Helada

Elevation range: 12,000–15,000 feet above sea level

Physical characteristics: Possible answer: Extreme environment; cold, windy climate; often freezes at night; snow falls at the highest elevations; snow line lies at the upper edge of this zone; trees are rare; the most common plants are low-lying shrubs and hardy grasses.

13.5 The Cool Highlands: Tierra Fría

Elevation range: 6,000–12,000 feet above sea level

Physical characteristics: Possible answer: Average temperatures vary from 55°F to 65°F; night temperatures dip below freezing at higher elevations; steep, rugged mountains; flat basins and plateaus lie between the mountains; a high plateau, the Altiplano, lies between Peru and Bolivia and contains Lake Titicaca; pines and other conifers grow where there is enough rain; only shrubs and grasses grow in dry areas.

13.4 The Pleasant Uplands: Tierra Templada

Elevation range: 3,000–6,000 feet above sea level

Physical characteristics: Possible answer: Climate is temperate; temperatures range from 65°F to 75°F; frost is rare; pleasant weather lasts all year; palms, bamboo, and jungle vines are common at lower elevations; broadleaf evergreen forest is typical at higher elevations.

13.3 The Tropical Lowlands: Tierra Caliente

Elevation range: 0–3,000 feet above sea level

Physical characteristics: Possible answer: Climate is generally hot and humid; average temperature ranges from 75°F to 80°F; broadleaf evergreen forests cover the eastern slopes of the Andes; natural vegetation on the western slopes ranges from lush rainforest to tropical grassland; Peru's coast gets little rainfall and is a desert.

Part 2: Human Adaptations

Find the three graphics that show human adaptations in your assigned elevation zone. Write their letters below. Check your answers with your managing editor (teacher). Then write a short caption that explains how each graphic shows how people have adapted to living in this zone.

Graphic D Caption: This shows nutritional information on quinoa. Farmers in the tierra helada plant quinoa because it is one of the few crops that will grow at high elevations.

Graphic G Caption: This shows a herd of llamas. People raise llamas in the tierra helada because they produce thick wool and make good pack animals for carrying heavy loads across the mountains.

Graphic J Caption: This is a copper mine. The high Andes have many mineral deposits, and many mines are located in the tierra helada.

Graphic C Caption: This is a diagram of a potato plant. Farmers in the tierra fría plant potatoes because they grow well at high elevations.

Graphic F Caption: This shows farmers plowing fields. Farmers in the tierra fría use terracing to carve fields out of the steep hillsides.

Graphic I Caption: This is an adobe house. People in the tierra fría build thick-walled homes out of stone or adobe brick.

Graphic B Caption: This shows information on Ecuador's flower exports. Farmers in the tierra templada grow carnations, daisies, and roses in Ecuador because the weather is mild.

Graphic E Caption: This is a coffee plantation. Farmers in the tierra templada raise this crop because the conditions are ideal for growing high-quality coffee.

Graphic L Caption: This is a hacienda, which is a large estate. People in the tierra templada build solid homes made of concrete brick or plaster and covered with tile roofs.

Graphic A Caption: This shows information on banana production. Farmers in the tierra caliente plant bananas because they do well in the heat.

Graphic H Caption: This is a sugarcane field. Farmers in the tierra caliente plant sugarcane because it does well in the heat.

Graphic K Caption: This is a bamboo house. People in the tierra caliente live in open-air houses; some are raised on stilts to protect against flooding.

Europe and Russia

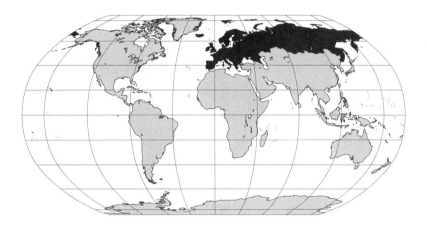

Supranational Cooperation in the European Union

Overview

In this lesson, students learn about the forces that work for and against supranational cooperation in the European Union. They begin by analyzing a population cartogram of European countries in an **Experiential Exercise**. Students then use the cartogram as a map as they experience travel in Europe before and after the formation of the EU. Finally, students read about the unique economic, political, and cultural cooperation within the European Union as well as about other examples of international cooperation.

Objectives

Students will

- define and explain the importance of these key geographic terms: *centrifugal force, centripetal force, common market, supranational cooperation.*

- analyze a population cartogram of selected European countries.

- experience the forces that unite and divide members of the European Union.

- examine other examples of international cooperation.

Materials

- *Geography Alive! Regions and People*
- Interactive Student Notebooks
- Transparencies 14A and 14B
- Information Masters 14A and 14B (1 transparency of each)
- Student Handout 14A (2 copies, cut apart)
- Student Handout 14B (1 per student)
- Student Handout 14C (12 copies, cut apart)
- Student Handout 14D (1 copy, cut apart)
- Student Handout 14E (8 copies, cut apart)
- Student Handout 14F (16 copies, cut apart)
- CD Track 13
- masking tape
- scissors

Preview

Have students complete Preview 14 in their Interactive Student Notebooks. Allow several to share their answers. Afterward, tell students that in this lesson they will learn about the "neighborhood" of the European Union. They will discover what forces have caused European countries to cooperate and what forces have led to division.

Preview 14

Essential Question and Geoterms

1 Introduce Chapter 14 in *Geography Alive! Regions and People.* Direct students' attention to the photograph of the EU flag. Ask,

- What do you see?
- What in this photograph might represent "old" Europe? "New" Europe?
- What might European countries gain by joining together? What might they lose?

2 Have students read Section 14.1. Explain that in this chapter, they will learn how the countries of Europe are cooperating with one another in the European Union. After students have read the section, ask them to point out details in the photograph that reflect Europe as a group of separate countries and others that represent supranational cooperation in the European Union.

3 Introduce the Graphic Organizer and the Essential Question. Have students examine the two maps with arrows. Ask,

- What do you see?
- How are the two maps similar? How are they different?
- Which map shows forces leading to cooperation within the European Union? What might be some of these forces?
- What forces might be represented by the second map?

Have students read the accompanying text. Make sure they understand the Essential Question, *What forces work for and against supranational cooperation among nations?* You may want to post the Essential Question in the classroom or write it on the board for the duration of this activity.

4 Have students read Section 14.2. Then have them work individually or in pairs to complete Geoterms 14 in their Interactive Student Notebooks. Ask volunteers to share their answers with the class.

Geoterms 14

Experiential Exercise

1 Before class, prepare a large population cartogram on the floor. Students will analyze the cartogram in Phase 1. In Phases 2 and 3, they will use it to "travel" through Europe.

- Following the diagram below, use masking tape to create the floor cartogram.
- Set up eight groups of desks around the periphery of the cartogram.
- Place the projector between Spain and Italy.

(**Note:** A cartogram is a specialty map, usually drawn with straight lines, in which countries are sized based on such data as population figures rather than land mass. The eight EU countries on this cartogram were chosen based on proximity to other EU nations, population, use of the euro, and length of EU membership.)

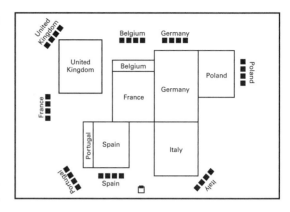

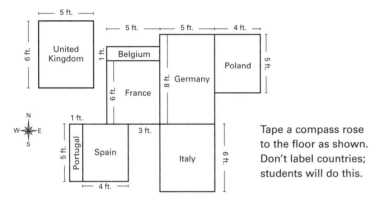

Tape a compass rose to the floor as shown. Don't label countries; students will do this.

2 Introduce the activity. Tell students that in this activity they will "travel" through Europe before and after the formation of the European Union.

Phase 1: Analyzing the European Population Cartogram

1 Divide students into eight roughly equal-size groups. Have them sit in the eight groups of desks around the periphery of the cartogram. (**Note:** To more accurately represent the relative populations of the countries, have slightly larger groups sit at the desks for Germany, the UK, Italy, and France, without revealing to students which groups represent which countries.) Explain that they will begin their travels by analyzing the map you've created on the floor.

2 Have students analyze the cartogram. Ask,

- What do you see?
- How is this similar to other maps you have seen? How is it different?
- What type of map is this? *a cartogram*
- On what kind of data might this cartogram be based? *It's based on population data. Each square foot represents approximately 2 million people.*

3 **Label the countries on the cartogram.**

- Distribute one country label cut from *Student Handout 14A: Cartogram Labels* to each group. Give groups one minute to discuss where they think the labels belong.

- Have all groups send a student to place their labels on the cartogram. Discuss the label placements with the class as you correct any placements, if necessary.

- Tape the labels to the cartogram. Tape a second copy of each label to a set of desks as shown in the diagram.

- Display *Transparency 14A: The European Union.* Discuss similarities and differences between the floor cartogram and the political map. (**Note:** Students can also refer to the map in Section 14.2 of their books.)

4 **Debrief the experience.** Ask,

- Which countries have the largest populations? The smallest?

- For countries with larger populations, what might be the advantages of European cooperation? The disadvantages?

- For countries with smaller populations, what might be the advantages of European cooperation? The disadvantages?

Phase 2: Experiencing Business and Travel Before the European Union

1 **Prepare materials.**

- Each student will need a copy of *Student Handout 14B: Tourist Pocketbook.*

- Each country will need 14 of its currency cut from *Student Handout 14C: European Currency,* a corresponding chart cut from *Student Handout 14D: Currency Conversion Charts,* 16 of its bumper stickers cut from *Student Handout 14E: Bumper Stickers for Phase 2,* a pencil, and a pair of scissors.

2 **Have students sit in their groups of desks from Phase 1.** Tell students they are "citizens" of the countries they are sitting by. They will now see what travel in Europe was like for custom agents, currency exchangers, merchants, and tourists before the EU.

3 **Project a transparency of** *Information Master 14A: Experiencing Travel Before the European Union.* Guide students through Phase 2 by revealing one step at a time. These tips will help the activity unfold smoothly:

- **Step 1:** Explain that Belgium has three official languages, Dutch, French, and German. French will be used in this activity.

- **Step 2:** Assign roles. If a country has only three students, assign one student the roles of both Customs Agent and Currency Exchanger. Have Customs Agents and Currency

Student Handout 14A   **Transparency 14A**

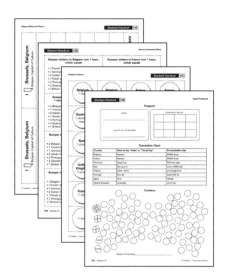

Student Handouts 14B–14E

Information Master 14A

Exchangers sit at their countries' desks with a pencil, a pair of scissors, the conversion chart, and currency. Have Merchants sit in their countries with their bumper stickers. Have Tourists stand in their countries with their Tourist Pocketbooks. Explain the roles, using students to model them:

Customs Agents will check passports of tourists who enter their country, making sure each says "hello" correctly in the country's language and initialing one check box on each passport.

Currency Exchangers will exchange money for tourists by consulting the conversion chart to determine how many coins are needed for each exchange, cutting the proper number of coins from the tourist's pocketbook (coins do not need to be cut out individually), and giving the tourist one of their country's currency. (**Note:** It is essential to model how to use the conversion charts. Using Belgium's chart, act out exchanges with French, Italian, and Portuguese tourists. Point out that each tourist's currency includes $\frac{1}{2}$, $\frac{1}{4}$, and $\frac{1}{8}$ coins. The conversions are representative of the actual exchange rates.)

Merchants will sell bumper stickers. Each sticker costs one of their country's currency. They must check that Tourists give them the right kind of currency.

Tourists, using the chart on the transparency, will fill in the name of their countries' currency in their pocketbooks and then travel through Europe buying bumper stickers. They will say "hello" to the Customs Agent in his or her language and have their passports checked. They will exchange the correct number of coins from their pocketbooks for one of the local currency and use the local currency to purchase one bumper sticker from the Merchant.

Explain that Tourists will have five minutes to experience travel in Europe before the EU. Those who have bought one bumper sticker from every country may use any remaining time to try to buy a second one from any country. (**Note:** The materials allow Tourists to buy no more than two stickers from each country.)

- **Step 3:** Tell Tourists they will begin by buying a bumper sticker from their home country's Merchant. Then have Tourists travel through Europe visiting Customs Agents, Currency Exchangers, and Merchants. Stop travel after five minutes.

- **Step 4:** As students respond to these questions, collect all currency, conversion charts, and bumper stickers (these will not be used in Phase 3). Allow students to propose various ideas, but ultimately guide them to these methods for simplifying travel in Europe: (1) eliminate passport checks, (2) allow any language to be spoken, and (3) use a common currency.

Phase 3: Experiencing Business and Travel Under the European Union

1 Prepare materials. Belgium, France, Germany, Italy, Portugal, and Spain will each need 8 euros; Poland and the United Kingdom will both need 24 of their currency (all cut from *Student Handout 14C: European Currency*). Each country will also need 32 of its bumper stickers cut from *Student Handout 14F: Bumper Stickers for Phase 3*.

2 Have students return to their countries' desks. Explain that during Phase 3, they will see how travel in Europe changed under the EU.

 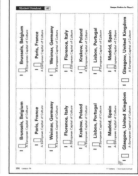

Student Handout 14C   **Student Handout 14F**

3 Project a transparency of *Information Master 14B: Experiencing Travel Under the European Union.* Guide students through Phase 3 by revealing one step at a time. Follow these guidelines to help the activity unfold smoothly:

- **Step 1:** Explain that most EU countries use a common currency, the euro. The United Kingdom chose not to adopt the euro; it still uses the pound. Poland has not yet been allowed to adopt the euro because the EU has not considered its economy stable enough; it still uses the zloty.

Information Master 14B

- **Step 2:** Have students switch roles: Customs Agents and Currency Exchangers will now be Tourists, Merchants will now be Currency Exchangers, and Tourists will now be Merchants. Remind students that there are no Customs Agents, as the class agreed to eliminate passport checks. Have the new Currency Exchangers sit at their countries' desks with a pencil, a pair of scissors, and currency. Have Merchants sit in their countries with scissors and their bumper stickers. Have Tourists stand in their countries with their Tourist Pocketbooks. Review the roles, using students to model them:

  Currency Exchangers will exchange currency for Tourists from Poland and the United Kingdom. (**Note:** An even exchange rate is used for simplicity.)

  Merchants will sell Tourists a bumper sticker for one of their countries' currency. For Tourists who have the local currency in their pocketbooks, Merchants will cut out just one coin for the purchase.

  Tourists, using the transparency chart, will fill in the name of their countries' currency in their pocketbooks and then travel through Europe buying bumper stickers. They don't need their passport checked, they may speak in any language they choose, and they must stop at the Currency Exchanger only if someone in the transaction is from Poland or the UK.

Tell the class that Tourists will have five minutes to experience travel in the European Union. Those who have bought one bumper sticker from every country may use any remaining time to try to buy a second from each country. (**Note:** The materials allow Tourists to buy no more than two from each country.) Have students predict whether this second group of Tourists will be able to purchase more or fewer stickers than the first group.

- **Step 3:** While students travel, play CD Track 13, "European Anthem." Stop travel after five minutes or when most tourists have purchased two stickers from each country.

- **Step 4:** Explain that the music was the final movement of Ludwig van Beethoven's "Ode to Joy," which is the European Anthem. Answers to the questions could include these: *Question B,* "a lessening of borders and a common currency made trading easier." *Question C,* "countries' borders became less distinct; all the countries were part of one supranational region." *Question D,* "people could speak any language, and each country still highlighted its capital of culture." *Question E,* "countries lost their individual currency and had to call their cities *European* capitals of culture."

4 **Have students turn to Reading Notes 14.** For Section 14.3, encourage them to predict what they will read. Ask, *What are some examples of economic cooperation from your experience in the classroom?* Then have them read the section and complete the corresponding Reading Notes. Use Guide to Reading Notes 14 to review the information and its connections to the experience. Repeat for Sections 14.4 and 14.5. Finally, have them read Section 14.6 as a transition into the Global Connections.

Reading Notes 14

Global Connections

1 **Introduce the Global Connections.** Tell students that the European Union is not the only example of international cooperation. As they look at other examples, ask them to think about what forces work for and against such cooperation.

2 **Project** *Transparency 14B: Global Connections.* Help students analyze the map by asking the questions below. Use the additional information given to enrich the discussion.

- **What can we learn from this map?**

- **How are different types of international cooperation represented?**

  Various colors and symbols are used to show economic cooperation, political cooperation, and cultural cooperation.

Transparency 14B

Supranational Cooperation in the European Union 321

- **Why do some countries have more than one symbol?**

  These countries belong to more than one international organization. For example, Brazil is shaded dark green for its membership in the Free Trade Area of the Americas and has a green square for its membership in the Southern Cone Common Market.

- **Which type of international cooperation is most common?**

  According to the map, economic cooperation is most prevalent. This allows countries to combine their goods so that together they can have a larger impact on the global market. It also creates common markets, which lessens trade restrictions. At the same time, it allows countries independent control over their political and cultural affairs.

3 Have students read Section 14.7. You may want to read this section as a class so you can more easily facilitate a discussion of these questions:

- **Why do countries join more than one international organization?**

  Each organization has a different purpose, and more than one may serve a country's interests. For example, three of the organizations the United States is involved with are the Free Trade Area of the Americas, the Organization of Economic Cooperation and Development, and the North Atlantic Treaty Organization. FTAA allows the U.S. to expand trade with fewer barriers to many countries in the Western Hemisphere; the OECD gives the U.S. the opportunity to meet with other countries to discuss economic growth; and NATO provides the U.S. with political and military alliances with many European nations.

- **Are all international organizations like the EU?**

  The EU is the best example of a true international organization. Almost all international organizations require nations to give up some individual control, but few have the integrated economic, political, and cultural cooperation of the EU. For example, although the members of the Organization of the Petroleum Exporting Countries cooperate economically in an effort to control the world oil market, they agree on little else. OPEC does not make official political or cultural decisions for its members. The diversity of its countries' views on non-economic matters can be seen by the variety of the other international organizations to which its members belong.

- **What forces might work for and against supranational cooperation in the United Nations?**

   According to the UN charter, its member countries cooperate "to maintain international peace and security." World peace is the dominant centripetal force of the UN. Additionally, the UN provides avenues for international economic, political, and cultural cooperation. The UN's strongest centrifugal force is the diversity of its 191 member nations. Different political objectives and cultural norms make consensus difficult to achieve on many issues.

Processing

Have students complete Processing 14. Here are some examples of details students might add to the drawing:

- An orange tree, an apple tree, and two stick figures: *Neighbors trading oranges for apples without adding a fee is like trade under the **common market** of the European Union.*

- An Eiffel Tower climber and a Leaning Tower of Pisa water slide: *The different equipment in the backyards is a **centrifugal force** like the unique cultural symbols within the EU.*

- A fence section lying on the ground: *The removal of backyard fences is a **centripetal force** like the lessening of border checks within the EU.*

- A "Neighborhood Watch" sign with the stars of the EU flag along the border: *A neighborhood watch program is like the **supranational cooperation** of the EU.*

Processing 14

Online Resources

For more information on the European Union, refer students to Online Resources for *Geography Alive! Regions and People* at www.teachtci.com.

Assessment

Masters for assessment appear on the next three pages followed by answers and scoring rubrics.

Mastering the Content

Shade in the oval by the letter of the best answer for each question.

1. Sometimes countries give up some control of their own affairs to work together on goals they all share. This is a form of
   ○ A. spatial inequality.
   ○ B. economic activity.
   ○ C. sustainable development.
   ○ D. supranational cooperation.

2. Which of these is the **best** definition of centripetal forces?
   ○ A. forces that pull people together
   ○ B. forces that promote urbanization
   ○ C. forces that reduce land use conflict
   ○ D. forces that improve living standards

3. The European Union began with the development of a
   ○ A. plural society.
   ○ B. consumer class.
   ○ C. common market.
   ○ D. defense organization.

4. What happens when a member country does not agree with a decision made by the EU government?
   ○ A. The country may refuse to obey the decision.
   ○ B. The country must carry out the decision anyway.
   ○ C. The decision does not go into effect anywhere in the EU.
   ○ D. The decision goes into effect only in countries that support it.

5. How has the EU promoted economic cooperation across Europe?
   ○ A. It has reduced trade barriers.
   ○ B. It has banned foreign imports.
   ○ C. It has raised workers' salaries.
   ○ D. It has ended business competition.

6. Which of these is **most likely** to be a centrifugal force within the EU in the future?
   ○ A. trade barriers
   ○ B. closed borders
   ○ C. pollution problems
   ○ D. cultural differences

7. Which of these statements is **best** supported by the information in the graph below?

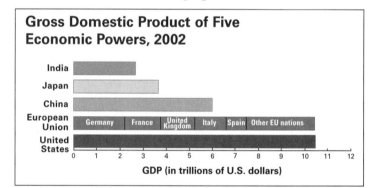

Gross Domestic Product of Five Economic Powers, 2002

   ○ A. The EU produces fewer goods and services than China.
   ○ B. The EU trades more with the United States than with India.
   ○ C. The EU has about the same economic power as the United States.
   ○ D. The EU has a higher GDP than India, Japan, and China combined.

8. Which of these was **not** created to promote a European cultural identity?
   ○ A. the EU flag
   ○ B. Europe Day
   ○ C. the EU pledge
   ○ D. European citizenship

Applying Geography Skills: Analyzing a Cartogram

Use the cartogram and your knowledge of geography to complete the tasks below.

Representation in the European Parliament, 2005

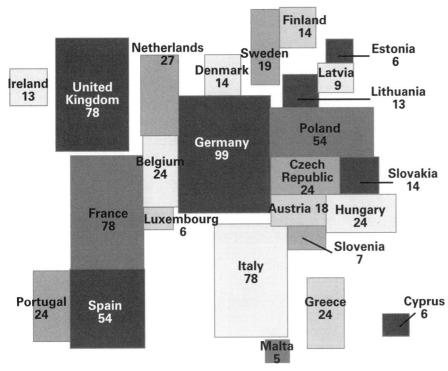

1. Identify the four countries with the most representatives in the European Parliament in 2005. Calculate how many representatives these EU members had altogether.

2. Identify the six smallest countries in the EU in 2005. Calculate how many representatives these EU countries had altogether.

3. Write a sentence contrasting the voting power of the four largest countries with the six smallest ones.

4. State whether you think the results you found are likely to unite or divide the EU. Briefly explain why.

Test Terms Glossary

To **calculate** means to figure out using math.

To **contrast** means to show how two things are different.

To **explain** means to give reasons for something.

Exploring the Essential Question

What forces work for and against supranational cooperation among nations?

In Chapter 14, you explored supranational cooperation in Europe. Now you will use what you learned. Use the cartoon, the table, and your knowledge of geography to complete this task.

The Task: Analyzing a Political Cartoon

Not all EU members were in the euro zone by 2005. Some chose not to adopt the common currency. Others were not allowed to use the euro until their economies improved. Both groups are listed in the table. Use this information to help you decide what the cartoonist wanted to show about the impact of the euro. Is the euro uniting the EU countries? Or is the euro dividing the EU countries?

EU Countries, 2005

Inside the Euro Zone	Outside the Euro Zone
Belgium	Cyprus
Germany	Czech Republic
Greece	Denmark*
Spain	Estonia
France	Hungary
Ireland	Latvia
Italy	Lithuania
Luxembourg	Malta
Netherlands	Poland
Austria	Slovakia
Portugal	Slovenia
Finland	Sweden*
	United Kingdom*

*Countries that chose not to adopt the euro

Step 1: Circle the countries in the cartoon whose borders have been partly erased. Circle these same countries in the table. Describe the pattern you see.

Step 2: Contrast the number of countries in the euro zone and outside the euro zone as of 2005.

Step 3: On a separate sheet of paper, write a paragraph about the cartoon. Your paragraph should

A. describe what the cartoon shows.

B. state what you think the cartoonist wanted to show about the impact of the euro on Europe.

C. use details from the cartoon to support your position.

Applying Geography Skills: Sample Responses

1. The four largest countries are the United Kingdom, Germany, France, and Italy. They have 333 representatives together.
2. The six smallest countries are Estonia, Latvia, Luxembourg, Malta, Cyprus, and Slovenia. Together they have 39 representatives.
3. The four countries with the most representatives in the European Parliament have far more voting power than the six smallest countries.
4. Answers will vary. Accept either unite or divide if student provides an explanation for that point of view.

Exploring the Essential Question: Sample Responses

Step 1: Countries with erased borders: Germany, France, Belgium, Netherlands, Luxembourg, Italy, Spain, Portugal, and Austria. All of these countries were in the euro zone in 2005.

Step 2: The numbers of countries inside and outside the euro zone were almost equal as of 2005.

Step 3: The paragraph should include the information listed in the prompt.

Sample response 1: The cartoon shows a map of Europe with some borders as dashed lines. The cartoonist drew the cartoon to show that the euro is uniting the EU countries. The cartoonist pictures the euro as an eraser that helps borders disappear. This makes trade and travel easier among these countries. As more countries enter this zone, the euro's power to unite people will increase.

Sample response 2: The cartoon shows a map of Europe with some borders as dashed lines. The cartoonist drew the cartoon to show that the euro is dividing the EU countries. The cartoonist pictures Europe as split between countries inside and outside the euro zone. Countries inside the zone may feel more united. But countries outside the zone may resent being left out. Their economies may suffer as well. This may turn their people against the EU.

Mastering the Content
Answer Key

1. D	2. A	3. C	4. B
5. A	6. D	7. C	8. C

Applying Geography Skills Scoring Rubric

Score	General Description
2	Student responds to all parts of the task. Response is correct and clear.
1	Student responds to some parts of the task. Response is mostly correct.
0	Response does not match the task or is incorrect.

Exploring the Essential Question Scoring Rubric

Score	General Description
3	Student responds to all parts of the task. Response is correct, clear, and supported by details.
2	Student responds to most or all parts of the task. Response is generally correct but may lack details.
1	Student responds to at least one part of the task. Response may contain errors and lack details.
0	Response does not match the task or is incorrect.

Tourist Map of Europe

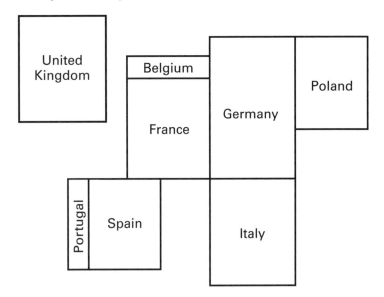

European Currencies

Country	Currency
Belgium	franc
France	franc
Germany	deutsche mark
Italy	lira
Poland	zloty
Portugal	escudo
Spain	peseta
United Kingdom	pound

Follow these steps to experience travel before the European Union:

Step 1: Prepare for travel.

- Fill in your name and country on your passport.
- With your group, learn how to say "hello" or "good day" in your European language.

Step 2: Listen as your teacher assigns and explains the four roles.

- *Customs Agents* will check the passport of each person who enters the country.
- *Currency Exchangers* will exchange money for the local currency using a conversion chart.
- *Merchants* will sell bumper stickers to Tourists who visit the country.
- *Tourists* will travel to different countries, speaking the language of and buying a bumper sticker in each.

Step 3: Experience business and travel in Europe before the EU.

Step 4: Respond to these questions:

A. Tourists, what was the best part of your travels? What made your travels difficult?

B. Customs Agents, based on what you observed, what could be done to make travel easier in Europe?

C. Currency Exchangers, based on what you observed, what could be done to make travel easier in Europe?

D. Merchants, do you have any other suggestions for improving travel in Europe?

Tourist Map of European Union

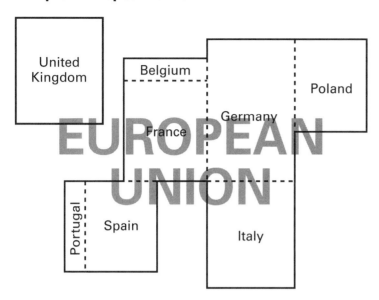

European Currencies

Country	Currency
Belgium	euro
France	euro
Germany	euro
Italy	euro
Poland	zloty
Portugal	euro
Spain	euro
United Kingdom	pound

Follow these steps to experience travel under the European Union:

Step 1: Prepare for travel.

• Change your passport to an EU passport by writing "EU CITIZEN" in large letters over your passport.

• Use the table on this page to fill in the name of your country's currency.

Step 2: Listen as your teacher assigns and explains the three roles.

• *Currency Exchangers* will need to exchange money only when currency from the Poland or the United Kingdom is involved. One euro can be exchanged for one Polish zloty or one British (United Kingdom) pound.

• *Merchants* will sell bumper stickers to Tourists who visit the country.

• *Tourists* travel to different countries, buying a bumper sticker in each.

Step 3: Experience business and travel in Europe under the EU.

Step 4: Respond to these questions:

A. How did the second group of tourists' travels compare with the first?

B. The second group of tourists should have been able to buy more bumper stickers than the first. How did cooperation among European nations create more trade in the region?

C. Under the EU, what changed about the nations' political borders?

D. Under the EU, in what ways were countries able to express their various cultures?

E. Under the EU, how did the countries lose some of their individual uniqueness?

United Kingdom

France

Belgium

Portugal

Spain

Italy

Germany

Poland

Passport

NAME

_____

NATION OF CITIZENSHIP

_____

PASSPORT CHECKS

Translation Chart

Country	How to Say "Hello" or "Good Day"	Pronunciation Key
Belgium	Bonjour	bohn-zhour
France	Bonjour	bohn-zhour
Germany	Guten Tag	GOO-ten taak
Italy	Bon giorno	bwon JOHR-noh
Poland	Dzien' dobry	jen-dough-bree
Portugal	Bon dia	bohn DEE-ah
Spain	Hola	OH-lah
United Kingdom	Good day	Good day

Currency

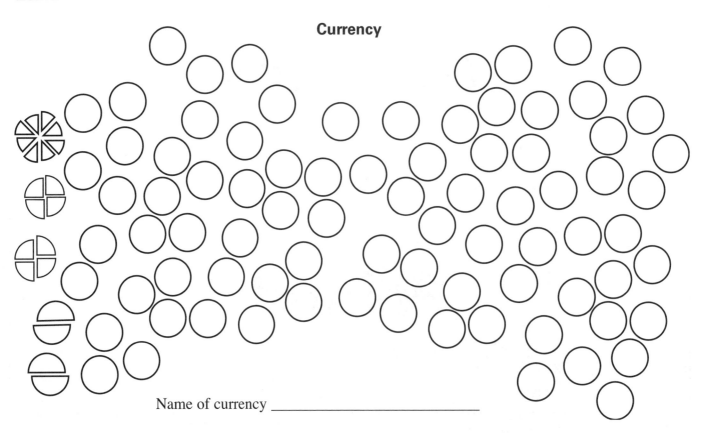

Name of currency _____

Belgium 1 franc	**Belgium** 1 franc	**France** 1 franc	**France** 1 franc
Germany 1 deutsche mark	**Germany** 1 deutsche mark	**Italy** 1 lira	**Italy** 1 lira
Spain 1 peseta	**Spain** 1 peseta	**Portugal** 1 escudo	**Portugal** 1 escudo
United Kingdom 1 pound	**United Kingdom** 1 pound	**United Kingdom** 1 pound	**United Kingdom** 1 pound
Poland 1 zloty	**Poland** 1 zloty	**Poland** 1 zloty	**Poland** 1 zloty
1 euro	1 euro	1 euro	1 euro

Bumper stickers in Belgium cost 1 franc, which equals

- $\frac{1}{2}$ French franc.
- $\frac{1}{2}$ German deutsche mark.
- 4 Italian liras.
- $\frac{1}{2}$ Polish zloty.
- 2 Portuguese escudos.
- 2 Spanish pesetas.
- $\frac{1}{2}$ British (United Kingdom) pound.

Bumper stickers in France cost 1 franc, which equals

- 2 Belgian francs.
- 1 German deutsche mark.
- 8 Italian liras.
- 1 Polish zloty.
- 4 Portuguese escudos.
- 4 Spanish pesetas.
- 1 British (United Kingdom) pound.

Bumper stickers in Germany cost 1 deutsche mark, which equals

- 2 Belgian francs.
- 1 French franc.
- 8 Italian liras.
- 1 Polish zloty.
- 4 Portuguese escudos.
- 4 Spanish pesetas.
- 1 British (United Kingdom) pound.

Bumper stickers in Italy cost 1 lira, which equals

- $\frac{1}{4}$ Belgian franc.
- $\frac{1}{8}$ French franc.
- $\frac{1}{8}$ German deutsche mark.
- $\frac{1}{8}$ Polish zloty.
- $\frac{1}{2}$ Portuguese escudo.
- $\frac{1}{2}$ Spanish peseta.
- $\frac{1}{8}$ British (United Kingdom) pound.

Bumper stickers in Poland cost 1 zloty, which equals

- 2 Belgian francs.
- 1 French franc.
- 1 German deutsche mark.
- 8 Italian liras.
- 4 Portuguese escudos.
- 4 Spanish pesetas.
- 1 British (United Kingdom) pound.

Bumper stickers in Portugal cost 1 escudo, which equals

- $\frac{1}{2}$ Belgian franc.
- $\frac{1}{4}$ French franc.
- $\frac{1}{4}$ German deutsche mark.
- 2 Italian liras.
- $\frac{1}{4}$ Polish zloty.
- 1 Spanish peseta.
- $\frac{1}{4}$ British (United Kingdom) pound.

Bumper stickers in Spain cost 1 peseta, which equals

- $\frac{1}{2}$ Belgian franc
- $\frac{1}{4}$ French franc.
- $\frac{1}{4}$ German deutsche mark.
- 2 Italian liras.
- $\frac{1}{4}$ Polish zloty.
- 1 Portuguese escudo.
- $\frac{1}{4}$ British (United Kingdom) pound.

Bumper stickers in the United Kingdom cost 1 pound, which equals

- 2 Belgian francs.
- 1 French franc.
- 1 German deutsche mark.
- 8 Italian liras.
- 1 Polish zloty.
- 4 Portuguese escudos.
- 4 Spanish pesetas.

I ♥ **Brussels, Belgium**
A Belgian Capital of Culture

I ♥ **Paris, France**
A French Capital of Culture

I ♥ **Weimar, Germany**
A German Capital of Culture

I ♥ **Florence, Italy**
An Italian Capital of Culture

I ♥ **Krakow, Poland**
A Polish Capital of Culture

I ♥ **Lisbon, Portugal**
A Portuguese Capital of Culture

I ♥ **Madrid, Spain**
A Spanish Capital of Culture

I ♥ **Glasgow, United Kingdom**
A British Capital of Culture

I ♥ **Brussels, Belgium**
A Belgian Capital of Culture

I ♥ **Paris, France**
A French Capital of Culture

I ♥ **Weimar, Germany**
A German Capital of Culture

I ♥ **Florence, Italy**
An Italian Capital of Culture

I ♥ **Krakow, Poland**
A Polish Capital of Culture

I ♥ **Lisbon, Portugal**
A Portuguese Capital of Culture

I ♥ **Madrid, Spain**
A Spanish Capital of Culture

I ♥ **Glasgow, United Kingdom**
A British Capital of Culture

I ♥ **Brussels, Belgium**
A European Capital of Culture

I ♥ **Paris, France**
A European Capital of Culture

I ♥ **Weimar, Germany**
A European Capital of Culture

I ♥ **Florence, Italy**
A European Capital of Culture

I ♥ **Krakow, Poland**
A European Capital of Culture

I ♥ **Lisbon, Portugal**
A European Capital of Culture

I ♥ **Madrid, Spain**
A European Capital of Culture

I ♥ **Glasgow, United Kingdom**
A European Capital of Culture

I ♥ **Brussels, Belgium**
A European Capital of Culture

I ♥ **Paris, France**
A European Capital of Culture

I ♥ **Weimar, Germany**
A European Capital of Culture

I ♥ **Florence, Italy**
A European Capital of Culture

I ♥ **Krakow, Poland**
A European Capital of Culture

I ♥ **Lisbon, Portugal**
A European Capital of Culture

I ♥ **Madrid, Spain**
A European Capital of Culture

I ♥ **Glasgow, United Kingdom**
A European Capital of Culture

Read each of Sections 14.3, 14.4, and 14.5. Answer the questions in the arrows
for that section. Then compare what you read to what you experienced in class.

14.3 Economic Cooperation in the EU

Centripetal
Forces

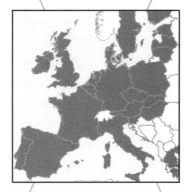

How does a common market
unite Europe?
The common market unites
Europe by allowing goods and
workers to travel more freely
across borders.

How does creation of an EU trading
bloc unite Europe?
The creation of an EU trading bloc
unites Europe by allowing EU countries
to have more power in the global
economy than they would have
individually.

Centrifugal
Forces

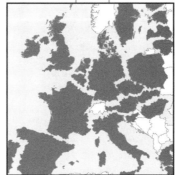

How do the differences between
western and eastern nations
divide the EU?
These differences divide the
EU because wealthier Western
European countries are concerned
that so much money is being spent
in Central and Eastern Europe.
Some Western Europeans also
worry about losing jobs to other
EU workers who are willing to
work for less money.

What divisions are created
by the use of the euro?
Divisions occur when some
European nations refuse to
adopt the euro. Also, the euro
divides the EU into two groups:
countries with economies stable
enough to be allowed to adopt
the euro and countries with less
stable economies.

What economic centripetal or centrifugal forces did the class experience as
it traveled through Europe?
One economic centripetal force the class experienced was that the use of a
common currency made purchasing goods much easier. One economic centrifugal force the class experienced was that, because all of the countries did not
use the euro, some currency exchanges still had to be made.

14.4 Political Cooperation in the EU

Centripetal Forces

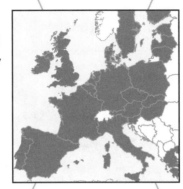

How does the development of a supranational level of government unite Europe?

The development of a supranational level of government unites Europe by allowing it to work on issues that all Europeans share, like pollution. Also, the EU government strengthens Europe's voice in world affairs.

How does the development of a European citizenship unite Europe?

With European citizenship, citizens of member nations can live and work anywhere in the EU and vote in all EU elections.

Centrifugal Forces

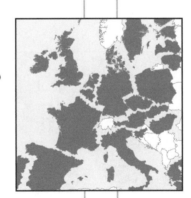

How does the desire of European countries to keep their independence divide Europe?

Some European countries want to make their own decisions in areas like defense and foreign affairs, especially when they disagree with EU decisions.

How can the expansion of EU membership cause division?

EU expansion can cause division because cooperation becomes more difficult with more countries and cultures.

What political centripetal or centrifugal forces did the class experience as it traveled through Europe?

One centripetal force the class experienced was that, as "citizens of Europe," students no longer needed to show their passports to enter other EU countries. One centrifugal force the class experienced was that the United Kingdom did not want to give up power, so it kept the pound instead of adopting the euro.

14.5 Cultural Cooperation in the EU

Centripetal Forces

How has the European Union united Europe by promoting a common culture?
The EU has united Europe by promoting a European cultural identity. This European identity is associated with cultural symbols such as the EU flag, the EU anthem, and Europe Day.

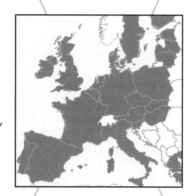

How does increased travel unite Europe?
Increased travel unites Europe by allowing Europeans to begin to view Europe as one united region.

Centrifugal Forces

Why do languages divide the European Union?
They divide the EU because with more than 20 languages, communication can be difficult.

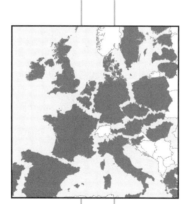

What are some other forces that contribute to divisions among European countries?
National pride and cultural traditions are two other forces that contribute to divisions among European countries.

What cultural centripetal or centrifugal forces did the class experience as it traveled through Europe?
Two cultural centripetal forces the class experienced were that students heard the EU anthem as they traveled and that the bumper stickers highlighted a European cultural identity. One cultural centrifugal force the class experienced was that the many languages of Europe made communicating difficult.

Population Dilemmas in Europe

Overview

In this lesson, students explore the effects of population trends in a **Response Group** activity. After learning how to analyze population pyramids, they reinforce their new knowledge by creating pyramids for three countries at different levels of growth. They apply what they've learned by using population pyramids of European countries to explore three dilemmas: negative population growth, aging population, and declining workforce.

Objectives

Students will

- define and explain the importance of these key geographic terms: *demography, dependency ratio, life expectancy, replacement rate, total fertility rate.*

- analyze population pyramids to examine population trends.

- explore three population dilemmas in Europe: negative population growth, aging population, and declining workforce.

- investigate the relationship between population growth rates and development levels throughout the world.

Materials

- *Geography Alive! Regions and People*
- Interactive Student Notebooks
- Transparencies 15A–15G
- Student Handout 15A (1 set for every 3 students)
- Student Handout 15B (1 set per student, copied onto cardstock)
- blue and red markers
- yellow and orange highlighters
- scissors

Preview

1 Teach students the key elements of a population pyramid.
Project *Transparency 15A: United States, 2000*. Help students
analyze the population pyramid and discover its key elements by
pointing to appropriate features and asking such questions as,

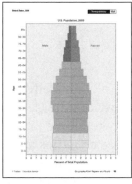

Transparency 15A

- What does the vertical, or up-and-down, axis represent?
- How many years does each age band represent?
- Which age band represents the most years? Why do you
  think this is so?
- In which age band are you? Your siblings? Your mother or
  father? Your grandparents?
- What does the horizontal, or side-to-side, axis represent?
- What percent of the total U.S. population is represented by
  each mark on the horizontal axis?
- Find the bar that represents your age and sex. What percent
  of the total U.S. population is in the same category as you?

2 Identify the diagram as a population pyramid. Have students
discuss these questions, first with a partner and then as a class:

- What can a population pyramid tell us about a country's
  population?
- Why might the information on a population pyramid be
  important, especially to the leaders of a country?

**3 Give students additional information about population
pyramids.** Share these ideas with them:

- A population pyramid is really just a series of bar graphs that
  graphically shows the age groups by sex of a population.
- Population pyramids always have age along the vertical axis
  and population along the horizontal axis, but the data on
  these axes may be divided differently. For example, the
  vertical axis can have wider age bands such as 0–14, 15–64,
  and 65+, or narrower bands like those on the transparency.
  The horizontal axis can represent actual population numbers
  rather than percentage of total population.
- People use population pyramids to get a "picture" of a population's structure. These pyramids make it easy to see which
  parts of a population are larger and which are smaller, and
  how a population as a whole is growing.
- Leaders use information from population pyramids when
  deciding how to best use government funds to serve their
  people. For example, in a country with relatively long 0–4
  and 5–9 age bands, funds might be devoted to building more
  schools. In a country with relatively long 65–69 and above age
  bands, funds might go toward health care for elderly citizens.

4 Have students complete Preview 15 in their Interactive Student Notebooks. Introduce the assignment by asking, *Do you think the population pyramids for all American cities would look the same as this U.S. population pyramid? Why or why not?* Have several volunteers respond. Then project *Transparency 15B: Preview Photographs* and have students complete Preview 15.

5 Have students share their answers. Ask students to point out the unique features of each population pyramid and photograph that helped them make their matches. Make sure these correct answers (and the reasoning behind them) are shared:

 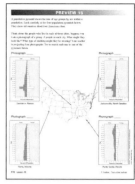

Transparency 15B   **Preview 15**

- *Photograph A:* Punta Gorda, Florida, ranked first in "Percent over 65" in the 2000 Census, a fact that is reflected in the relatively long 60–64, 65–69, 70–74, 75–79, 80–84, and 85+ age bands in its population pyramid.

- *Photograph B:* Lawrence, Kansas, is home to the University of Kansas. Its population pyramid shows relatively long 15–19 and 20–24 age bands for both males and females.

- *Photograph C:* Jacksonville, North Carolina, is home to Marine Corps Base Camp Lejeune and Marine Corps Air Station New River. Its population pyramid shows a long 20–24 age band for males.

- *Photograph D:* Yuma, Arizona, ranked third highest in "Rate of Population Growth, 1990–2000" in the 2000 Census, a fact that is reflected in relatively long 0–4, 5–9, and 10–14 age bands in the population pyramid.

6 Explain the connection between the Preview and the upcoming activity. Tell students that just as they could compare U.S. cities by looking at their population pyramids, countries of the world can be compared using population pyramids. In this activity, they will first create and compare population pyramids for countries growing at different rates around the world. Then they will more closely examine population pyramids of European countries and try to plan for the population dilemmas Europe faces.

Essential Question and Geoterms

1 Introduce Chapter 15 in *Geography Alive! Regions and People*. Explain that in this chapter, students will learn what happens as a country's population changes. Have students read Section 15.1. Afterward, ask them to identify how the photograph taken in the small town of Dolceacqua, Italy, reflects the population trends they just read about.

2 Introduce the Graphic Organizer and the Essential Question. Have students examine the three population pyramids. Then ask,

- What do you see?
- How are the three population pyramids similar? How are they different?
- What can these pyramids teach us about the countries they represent?
- How could these pyramids help us to predict a country's future?

Have students read the accompanying text. Make sure they understand the Essential Question, *How do population trends affect a country's future?* You may want to post the Essential Question in the room or write it on the board for the duration of the activity.

3 Have students read Section 15.2. Then have them work individually or in pairs to complete Geoterms 15 in their Interactive Student Notebooks. Have them share their answers with another student, or have volunteers share their answers with the class.

Response Group

Phase 1: Analyzing World Population Trends

1 Prepare materials.

- Use sticky notes to cover the bottom half of *Transparency 15C: World Population Trends,* including all six country names and the 2025 projected population pyramids.
- For every three students, prepare one copy of all three pages of *Student Handout 15A: Building Population Pyramids,* three blue markers, and three red markers.

2 Prepare students.

- Place students in mixed-ability groups of three. You might prepare a transparency that shows them how to arrange their desks so that students can easily talk among themselves and clearly see the projector screen.
- Tell students that just as U.S. cities have different population pyramids, so do countries in the world. To learn more about population trends, they will build their own population pyramids for three countries that are growing at different rates.

3 Distribute materials and review steps for building population pyramids. Distribute the handouts and markers. Review the directions at the top of Student Handout 15A, and answer

Geoterms 15

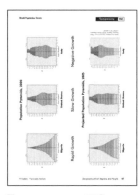

Transparency 15C

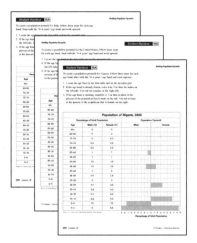

Student Handout 15A

any questions students have. (**Note:** Consider making a transparency of Student Handout 15A and modeling how to begin building a pyramid.)

4 **Monitor student progress.** Each of the three students in a group will build one of the pyramids. Circulate as groups work, assisting as needed. (**Note:** Consider displaying Transparency 15A to give students an actual population pyramid refer to.) As groups finish, encourage them to compare and contrast the pyramids within their groups.

5 **Have students begin to examine their population pyramids using the Geoterms.** When all groups have created all three pyramids, project Transparency 15C, revealing only the top row of pyramids. Keep the country names hidden. Have groups match each pyramid they created to the corresponding pyramid on the transparency. Teach students to begin analyzing the pyramids by comparing their bottoms, tops, and any unique bulges in their age bands. Then have them use their pyramids and the Geoterms to answer these questions:

- What is *demography*? How might demographers use population pyramids?
- What are *total fertility rate* and *replacement rate*? Why would the bottom of the pyramids be the best place to apply these terms? Which pyramids represent countries at or about replacement level? Which pyramids represent countries below replacement level?
- What is *life expectancy*? Why would the top of the pyramids be the best place to apply this term? Which pyramids represent countries with higher life expectancy? Lower life expectancy?
- What is *dependency ratio*? How might the three shades of color (light, medium, and dark) on the pyramids help you figure out dependency ratios?

6 **Have students analyze world population trends using the population pyramids.** Use a transparency marker to outline the general shape of each population pyramid on the upper half of Transparency 15C. Then ask,

- Which pyramid do you think represents a country with rapid population growth? Why?
- Which pyramid shows negative population growth? Why?
- Which pyramid shows slow population growth? Why?
- What country or area of the world might each pyramid represent? Why do you think so?

Reveal the country names underneath the pyramids on Transparency 15C: Nigeria, the United States, and Italy.

7 Introduce students to projected population pyramids.
Reveal the three projected population pyramids on the
bottom of Transparency 15C. Help students analyze them
by asking,

- How are the 2025 pyramids similar to the 2000 pyramids?
  How are they different?

- How does each pair of pyramids help make it easier to get a
  sense of each country's population growth rate?

- The three pyramids for 2025 are called *projected population
  pyramids*. How might they be useful to a country's leaders?

Explain that demographers use projected population pyramids
to help predict future populations. Have students recall the
factors of population change: births, deaths, and migration
(immigration and emigration). Then share this information:

- Demographers begin building projected population pyramids
  by moving the current bands for each age group up the pyramid according to the number of years into the future the
  projection will be. For example, for a pyramid with 5-year
  age bands and a projection 10 years into the future, current
  bands would move two age groups up the pyramid.

- Demographers then predict how many new births should be
  added to the bottom of the pyramid. Second, they predict
  how many people in each age group—particularly in the
  older age bands—will die and not be included in the projected population pyramid. Third, they predict how many people
  in each age group will migrate into or out of the country.

- Demographers do not always predict correctly. For example,
  in the 1980s they did not anticipate how deadly AIDS would
  be or how quickly it would spread. As a result, they over-
  predicted Africa's population for 2000.

- Leaders use projected population pyramids to plan how to
  best prepare their countries for future population issues.

(**Note:** You may want to point out that, as with other kinds of
graphs, the shape of a population pyramid is affected by the scales
used on the axes.)

8 Have students read about population change in Europe.
Explain that Europe has experienced all of the population
growth trends shown on Transparency 15C. Have students
read Section 15.3 as a class. Afterward, have them match the
population pyramids on the transparency to the corresponding
stages on the demographic transition model.

Phase 2: Exploring European Population Dilemmas

Keep students in their groups from Phase 1. Tell them they will now take on the role of European demographic consultants and government officials facing three population dilemmas.

1 Project the 2000 population pyramid on *Transparency 15D: Dilemma One: A Shrinking Population.* Cover Dilemma 1, the 2025 pyramid, and Critical Thinking Question 1. Tell students that for this first dilemma they will focus on Italy. Ask groups to analyze the 2000 population pyramid, noting at least three details the Italian government should be aware of. Allow each group to share one important detail, and then ask, *What type of population growth rate is Italy experiencing?* Finally, reveal Dilemma 1: What causes negative population growth?

2 Have students turn to Reading Notes 15 in their Interactive Student Notebooks. Review the directions with them. Give groups a few minutes to brainstorm causes, and then have them share their ideas as a class. Then have students read Section 15.4. Afterward, use Guide to Reading Notes 15 to review the main causes of negative population growth with the class.

3 Reveal the projected 2025 population pyramid on Transparency 15D. Ask, *How is population in Italy projected to change by 2025?* (**Note:** You may want to point out that by 2025, Italy is projected to have more males than females in every age band up to 60–64, when males and females are almost equal. The higher projection for Italy's male population under 60 can be attributed to males having a slightly higher birth rate and to more males than females migrating to Italy for jobs.) Then reveal Critical Thinking Question 1.

4 Have groups discuss Critical Thinking Question 1 and record their ideas. Tell students they are now Italian government officials who must deal with this population dilemma. Remind groups to discuss the consequences of all of the options before ranking them and to be prepared to justify their rankings.

5 Appoint a Presenter for each group and hold a class discussion. Ask Presenters to begin by sharing their group's top and bottom rankings. Encourage them to cite supporting details from the reading. Encourage a student-centered discussion by having each Presenter select the following Presenter.

6 Ask students to read Section 15.5. Have them reflect on the reading by answering Question 5 in the Reading Notes.

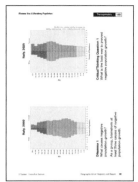

Transparency 15D   **Reading Notes 15**

7 Repeat Steps 1–6 for Dilemma 2: *What causes a population to age?* Make these modifications:

- Begin by projecting the 2000 population pyramid on *Transparency 15E: Dilemma Two: An Aging Population.* Tell students that they will focus on Spain for this second dilemma. Have them analyze and share details about the 2000 population pyramid. Then ask, *Why might Spain be described as having an aging population?* Then reveal Dilemma 2.

- When groups present their rankings, rotate the role of Presenter to a new student.

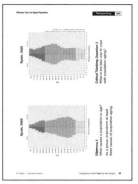
Transparency 15E

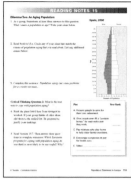
Reading Notes 15

8 Repeat Steps 1–6 for Dilemma 3: *What causes a workforce to decline?* Make these modifications:

- Begin by projecting *Transparency 15F: Dilemma Three: A Declining Workforce.* Display the 2000 and 2025 population pyramids, leaving the text at the bottom of the transparency covered. Tell students that they will focus on Germany for this third dilemma. Have groups compare the pyramids. Then ask, *What are at least three population trends you think the German government needs to be aware of?* Then reveal Dilemma 3.

- When groups present their rankings, rotate the role of Presenter to a new student.

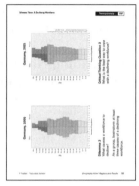
Transparency 15F

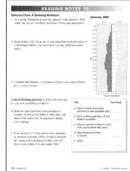
Reading Notes 15

Global Connections

1 **Introduce the Global Connections.** Have students read Section 15.10. Then ask, *How are the population trends of developing countries different from those of Europe?* Explain that students now will compare population pyramids of the developing world with those of the developed world.

2 Project *Transparency 15G: Global Connections.* Help students analyze the information by asking,

- **What can we learn from this map?**

- **Where are most of the developed countries located?**

- **Where are most of the developing countries located?**

- **What seems to be the relationship between the shapes of the population pyramids and development levels?**

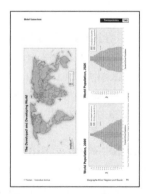
Transparency 15G

3 Have students read Section 15.11, independently or as a class, and examine the rest of the information in the section.

Then lead a discussion of the questions below. Use the additional information given to enrich the discussion.

- **Why are there fewer births in developed countries?**

- **Why are there more births in developing countries?**

- **How might population growth rates affect a country's future?**

  Population growth rates can affect countries' futures in many ways. For developed countries in Europe, a negative growth rate could lead to a loss of economic or military power as there are fewer young people to fuel the economy and military. It may force some countries to reconsider their restrictive immigration policies.

  For developing countries, such as in Africa, a rapid population growth can affect their power in the future. It can be difficult to move funds into economic development when there are so many children to take care of. Finally, the future of countries with slow growth will be dependent on maintaining their slow growth. A population trend change in either direction could have a dramatic effect on these nations.

Processing

Tell students that they will now create flipbooks to analyze population dilemmas of the United States. Pass out *Student Handout 15B: Creating a Flipbook of U.S. Population Pyramids* to each student, and review the directions with them. Once students have created their flipbooks, have them complete Processing 15 in their Interactive Student Notebooks.

Online Resources

For more information on population dilemmas in Europe, refer students to Online Resources for *Geography Alive! Regions and People* at www.teachtci.com.

Assessment

Masters for assessment appear on the next three pages followed by answers and scoring rubrics.

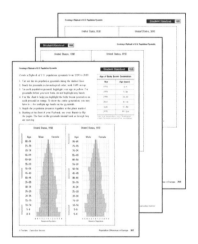

Student Handout 15B

Processing 15

Mastering the Content

Shade in the oval by the letter of the best answer for each question.

1. What do we call the study of human populations and how they change?
   ○ A. biodiversity
   ○ B. demography
   ○ C. life expectancy
   ○ D. human geography

2. Which of these statements is **most likely** true of a European country with a replacement rate under 2.0?
   ○ A. Its population is growing older.
   ○ B. Its population is growing poorer.
   ○ C. Its population is growing very rapidly.
   ○ D. Its population is growing more diverse.

3. Which of these **best** describes population changes in Europe since 2000?
   ○ A. brain drain
   ○ B. rural decline
   ○ C. urban sprawl
   ○ D. negative growth

4. Italy has a total fertility rate of just over 1. Nigeria has a total fertility rate of more than 5. Which of these conclusions can be drawn from these facts?
   ○ A. Italy has a larger population than Nigeria.
   ○ B. Nigeria has a younger population than Italy.
   ○ C. Men in Italy retire later than men in Nigeria.
   ○ D. Women in Nigeria live longer than women in Italy.

5. A country with an aging population is **most likely** to face rapidly rising costs for which of the following?
   ○ A. refugees
   ○ B. pensions
   ○ C. pollution
   ○ D. unemployment

6. According to this graph, in which decade did Germany's labor supply begin to decline?

Changes in Germany's Population and Labor Supply

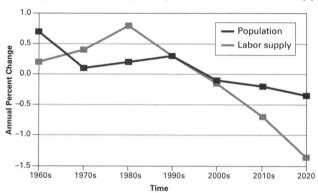

   ○ A. 1960s
   ○ B. 1970s
   ○ C. 1980s
   ○ D. 1990s

7. Life expectancy is a measure of which of the following in a population?
   ○ A. the average age at which people die
   ○ B. the average age at which people retire
   ○ C. the average age at which people become parents
   ○ D. the average age at which people enter the workforce

8. Cash for babies, rising retirement ages, and family-friendly workplace policies are all responses to Europe's declining
   ○ A. birth rates.
   ○ B. living standards.
   ○ C. life expectancies.
   ○ D. migration streams.

Applying Geography Skills:
Analyzing Population Pyramids

Use the population pyramids and your knowledge of geography to complete the tasks below. Write your answers in complete sentences.

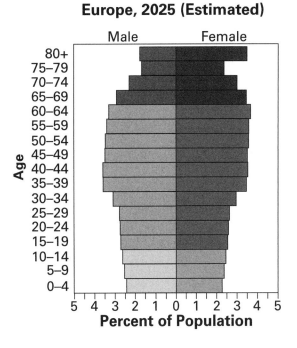

1. Briefly describe what a population pyramid shows.

2. Identify the smallest age group (males and females together) on the 2025 population pyramid.

3. Compare the percentages of 0- to 4-year-olds and 5- to 9-year-olds on the 2000 pyramid. What do these figures show about the birth rate in Europe between 1990 and 2000?

4. Estimate the percentage of men and women at the top of the 2000 pyramid. What do these figures tell you about the life expectancy of each sex in Europe?

Test Terms Glossary
To **describe** means to provide details about something, such as what it is for.

To **estimate** means to make a rough calculation of something.

Exploring the Essential Question

How do population trends affect a country's future?

In Chapter 15, you explored how changes in Europe's population are affecting its future. Now you will use what you learned. Use the information on the population pyramids below and your knowledge of geography to complete this task.

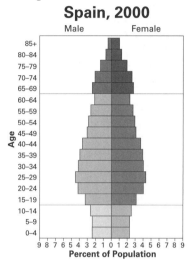

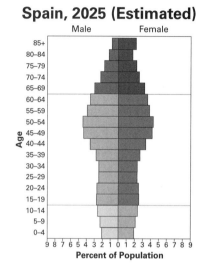

The Task: Planning Ahead for the Aging of Spain

These population pyramids show how Spain's population is likely to change between 2000 and 2025. Your task is to write a business letter to the prime minister of Spain with ideas on how to prepare for these changes. The prime minister is the head of the Spanish government.

Step 1: Circle the baby boom bulge on the 2000 pyramid. (**Hint:** Look for the four widest bars on the graph.) Identify the age groups of the boomers. Tell whether they were most likely in school, in the workforce, or retired as of 2000.

Step 2: Repeat Step 1 for the 2025 pyramid.

Step 3: Write a formal business letter to the prime minister about the challenges Spain faces as the baby boomers begin to retire. Make sure your letter has these elements:

A. your address, today's date, and the address of the person you are writing to: "Office of the Prime Minister, Madrid, Spain"

B. a greeting such as "Dear Prime Minister" followed by a colon

C. an opening paragraph that states the challenges Spain will face as its population ages

D. a body paragraph that explores three things Spain can do now to prepare for the changes ahead

E. a conclusion telling what you believe the prime minister should do first and why

F. a closing, such as "Sincerely," followed by your signature

Writing Tips: Business Letter Basics

A business letter is more formal than a personal letter you might write to a friend. Use complete sentences. State your ideas clearly but briefly. Use proper business form.

Heading: your address and the date

Inside address: the address of the person you are writing to

Salutation: "Dear Ms. (or Mr.) _____:"

Closing: "Sincerely" or "Best regards" and your signature

Test Terms Glossary
To **explore** means to investigate possibilities related to a subject.

Applying Geography Skills: Sample Responses

1. A population pyramid shows the makeup by age group and sex of a population.
2. The smallest age group on the 2025 pyramid is 79–80.
3. The percentage of 0- to 4-year-olds in 2000 was about 2.6 for males and about 2.4 for females. The percentages for 5- to 9-year-olds were about 2.9 for males and about 2.8 for females. These figures show that the birthrate in Europe dropped between 1990 and 2000.
4. The percentage of men at the top of the 2000 pyramid is about 0.8 compared to about 2 for women. These figures show that, in Europe, women have a longer life expectancy than men.

Exploring the Essential Question: Sample Response

Step 1: In 2000, the baby boomers were in the 20-to-39 age groups. Most of the boomers were in the workforce.

Step 2: In 2025, the baby boomers will be in 45-to-64 age groups. Some of the boomers will still be in the workforce; some will be retired.

Step 3: The business letter should include the elements listed in the prompt. These elements are identified by letter in the response below.

B. Dear Prime Minister:

C. Spain's population is aging rapidly. By 2025, many baby boomers will be retired. The retired boomers will need pensions to live on. They will need good health care, too. At the same time, Spain's workforce will be shrinking. This means there will be fewer workers to support Spain's aging population.

D. The Spanish government should prepare for these problems now. First, it should build up Spain's health care system. The government could give scholarships to people who train to be nurses and doctors. It can begin building more hospitals and nursing homes. Second, the government could begin raising more money. It could put a special tax on candy and soft drinks. The money could go into a special account to be used only for pensions. Third, the government could encourage people to work until they are 70 if they are healthy. One way to do this is to give higher pensions to people who work longer.

E. I believe health care is the most important issue for the government to work on now. If people stay healthy as they get older, they won't need expensive medicines and nursing homes. This will be better for old people. It will also be better for Spain.

F. Sincerely,

Mastering the Content Answer Key

1. B	2. A	3. D	4. B
5. B	6. C	7. A	8. A

Applying Geography Skills Scoring Rubric

Score	General Description
2	Student responds to all parts of the task. Response is correct and clear.
1	Student responds to some parts of the task. Response is mostly correct.
0	Response does not match the task or is incorrect.

Exploring the Essential Question Scoring Rubric

Score	General Description
3	Student responds to all parts of the task. Response is correct, clear, and supported by details.
2	Student responds to most or all parts of the task. Response is generally correct but may lack details.
1	Student responds to at least one part of the task. Response may contain errors and lack details.
0	Response does not match the task or is incorrect.

To create a population pyramid for Nigeria, follow these steps for each age band. Start with the "0–4 years" age band and work upward.

1. Locate the age band in the data table and on the pyramid grid.
2. If the age band is already drawn, color it in. Use blue for males on the left side. Use red for females on the right side.
3. If the age band is missing, complete it. Use blue to draw in the percent of the population that is male on the left. Use red to draw in the percent of the population that is female on the right.

Population of Nigeria, 2000

	Percentage of Total Population		Population Pyramid	
Age	**Male (%)**	**Female (%)**	**Male**	**Female**
85+	0	0		
80–84	0	0		
75–79	0	0.5		
70–74	0.5	0.5		
65–69	0.5	0.5		
60–64	1	1		
55–59	1	1		
50–54	1.5	1.5		
45–49	1.5	1.5		
40–44	2	2		
35–39	2.5	2.5		
30–34	3	3		
25–29	3.5	3.5		
20–24	4.5	4.5		
15–19	5.5	5.5		
10–14	6.5	6.5		
5–9	7.5	7.5		
0–4	9	8.5		

Source: *U.S. Census Bureau,* "International Data Base," www.census.gov.

9 8 7 6 5 4 3 2 1 0 1 2 3 4 5 6 7 8 9

Percentage of Total Population

To create a population pyramid for the United States, follow these steps for each age band. Start with the "0–4 years" age band and work upward.

1. Locate the age band in the data table and on the pyramid grid.
2. If the age band is already drawn, color it in. Use blue for males on the left side. Use red for females on the right side.
3. If the age band is missing, complete it. Use blue to draw in the percent of the population that is male on the left. Use red to draw in the percent of the population that is female on the right.

Population of the United States, 2000

Percentage of Total Population			Population Pyramid	
Age	**Male (%)**	**Female (%)**	**Male**	**Female**
85+	0.5	1		
80–84	0.5	1		
75–79	1	1.5		
70–74	1.5	1.5		
65–69	1.5	2		
60–64	2	2		
55–59	2.5	2.5		
50–54	3	3		
45–49	3.5	3.5		
40–44	4	4		
35–39	4	4		
30–34	3.5	3.5		
25–29	3.5	3.5		
20–24	3.5	3.5		
15–19	3.5	3.5		
10–14	3.5	3.5		
5–9	3.5	3.5		
0–4	3.5	3.5		

9 8 7 6 5 4 3 2 1 0 1 2 3 4 5 6 7 8 9

Percentage of Total Population

Source: *U.S. Census Bureau,* "International Data Base," www.census.gov.
Percentages do not total 100% due to rounding.

To create a population pyramid for Italy, follow these steps for each age band. Start with the "0–4 years" age band and work upward.

1. Locate the age band in the data table and on the pyramid grid.
2. If the age band is already drawn, color it in. Use blue for males on the left side. Use red for females on the right side.
3. If the age band is missing, complete it. Use blue to draw in the percent of the population that is male on the left. Use red to draw in the percent of the population that is female on the right.

Population of Italy, 2000

Percentage of Total Population			Population Pyramid	
Age	Male (%)	Female (%)	Male	Female
85+	0.5	1.5		
80–84	0.5	1		
75–79	1.5	2.5		
70–74	2	2.5		
65–69	2.5	3		
60–64	3	3		
55–59	3	3		
50–54	3.5	3.5		
45–49	3	3		
40–44	3.5	3.5		
35–39	4	4		
30–34	4	4		
25–29	4	4		
20–24	3	3		
15–19	2.5	2.5		
10–14	2.5	2.5		
5–9	2.5	2.5		
0–4	2.5	2		

Source: *U.S. Census Bureau,* "International Data Base," www.census.gov.
Percentages do not total 100% due to rounding.

9 8 7 6 5 4 3 2 1 0 1 2 3 4 5 6 7 8 9

Percentage of Total Population

Create a flipbook of U.S. population pyramids from 1950 to 2050.

1. Cut out the six population pyramids along the dashed lines.

2. Stack the pyramids in chronological order, with 1950 on top.

3. On each population pyramid, highlight your age in yellow. For pyramids before you were born, do not highlight any bands.

4. Use the chart to help you highlight the baby boom generation on each pyramid in orange. To show the entire generation, you may have to color multiple age bands on the pyramids.

5. Staple the population pyramids together on the left side.

6. Starting at the front of your flipbook, use your thumb to flip the pages. The bars on the pyramids should look as though they are moving.

Age of Baby Boom Generation	
Year	Age (years)
1950	0–4
1970	6–24
1990	26–44
2010	46–64
2030	66–84
2050	86–104

Source: *United Nations Population Division*, "World Population Prospects: The 2004 Revision Population Base," esa.un.org/unpp/.

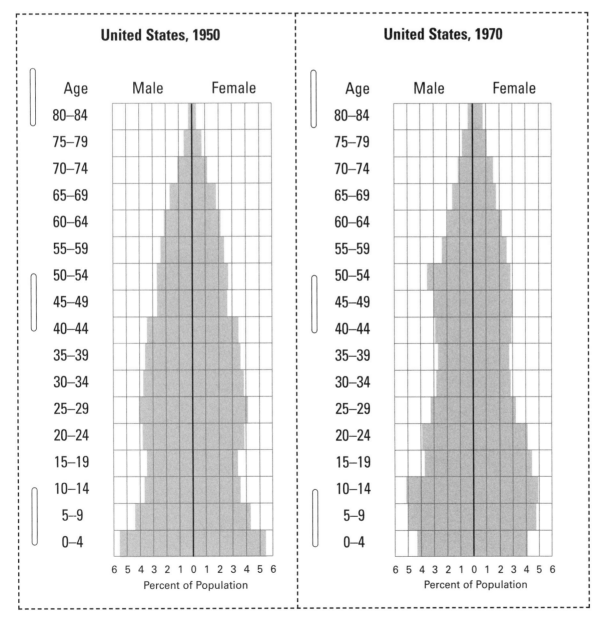

© Teachers' Curriculum Institute

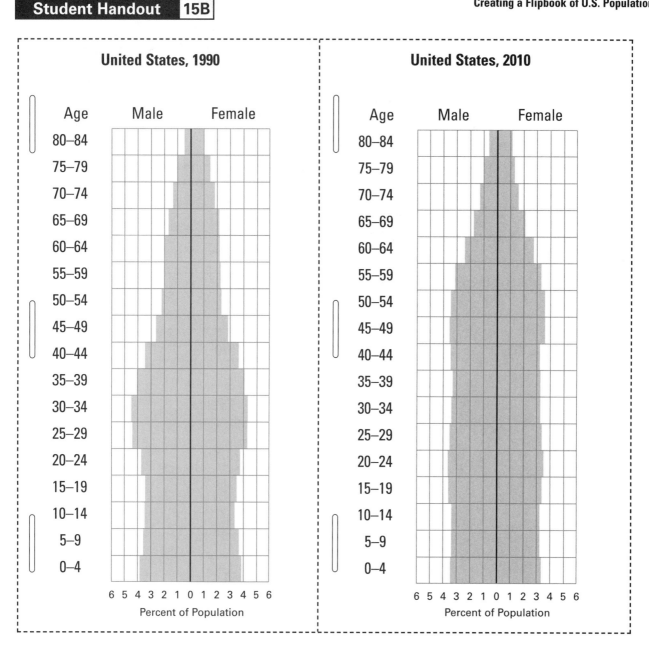

United States, 1990

Age	Male	Female
80–84		
75–79		
70–74		
65–69		
60–64		
55–59		
50–54		
45–49		
40–44		
35–39		
30–34		
25–29		
20–24		
15–19		
10–14		
5–9		
0–4		

6 5 4 3 2 1 0 1 2 3 4 5 6
Percent of Population

United States, 2010

Age   Male   Female

6 5 4 3 2 1 0 1 2 3 4 5 6
Percent of Population

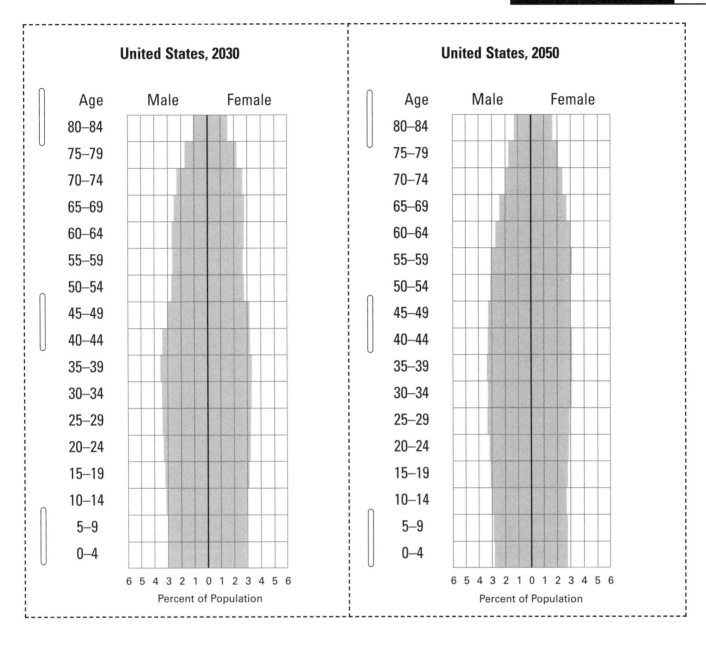

United States, 2030

Age	Male	Female

United States, 2050

Age	Male	Female

Dilemma One: A Shrinking Population

Italy, 2000

1. As a group, brainstorm at least three answers to this question: *What causes negative population growth?* Write your ideas below.

Answers will vary.

2. Read Section 15.4. Circle any of your ideas that match the causes of negative population growth that you read about. List any additional causes below.

Possible answers:
- Women are having fewer children than the 2.1 replacement rate.
- Because it costs a lot of money to raise a child, families are having fewer children.
- Since is difficult to find childcare, families are having fewer children.
- Young women who focus on their education or career tend to have fewer children.

3. Complete this sentence: *Negative population growth can cause problems for a country because...*

it can lead to a loss of economic, military, and political power.

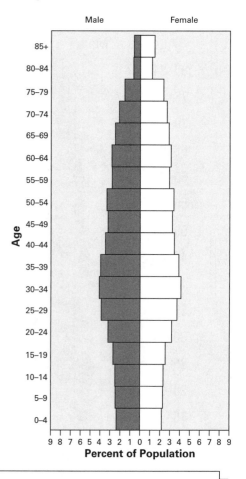

Critical Thinking Question 1: *What is the best way to prevent negative population growth?*

4. Rank the plans listed here from strongest (1) to weakest (5). If your group thinks of other ideas, add them to the ranked list. Be prepared to justify your rankings.

Answers will vary.

5. Read Section 15.5. Then answer these questions in complete sentences: *Which European program for preventing negative population growth do you think is most likely to be successful? Why?*

Answers will vary.

Plan	Your Rank
A. Provide free childcare to working parents.	_____
B. Allow parents to have paid time off when children are born.	_____
C. Encourage parents to have children earlier in their lives.	_____
D. Pay parents a "birth bonus" for each child they have.	_____
E. Other: _____ _____	_____

Dilemma Two: An Aging Population

1. As a group, brainstorm at least three answers to this question: *What causes a population to age?* Write your ideas below.

   Answers will vary.

2. Read Section 15.6. Circle any of your ideas that match the causes of population aging that you read about. List any additional causes below.

   Possible answers:
   - A population ages when there are more old people and fewer young people.
   - A rise in life expectancy causes a population to age.
   - A drop in birth rate causes a population to age.
   - A baby boom after an event such as a war can result in a large generation that then ages.

3. Complete this sentence: *Population aging can cause problems for a country because...*

   it can lead to economic strain on a society as it tries to provide for pensions and health care.

Critical Thinking Question 2: *What is the best way to cope with population aging?*

4. Rank the plans listed here from strongest to weakest. If your group thinks of other ideas, add them to the ranked list. Be prepared to justify your rankings.

   Answers will vary.

5. Read Section 15.7. Then answer these questions in complete sentences: *Which European program for coping with population aging do you think is most likely to be successful? Why?*

   Answers will vary.

Spain, 2000

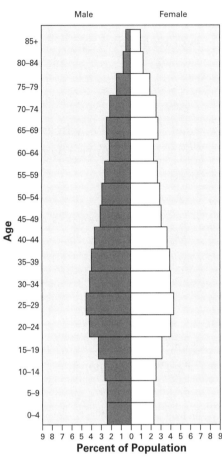

Plan	Your Rank
A. Require people to save for their own retirement.	_____
B. Give people over 65 a "pension bonus" for each extra year they work.	_____
C. Pay relatives who stay home to help older family members.	_____
D. Encourage companies to pay for health care.	_____
E. Other: _____ _____	_____

Dilemma Three: A Declining Workforce

1. As a group, brainstorm at least two answers to this question: *What causes a workforce to decline?* Write your ideas below.

    Answers will vary.

Germany, 2000

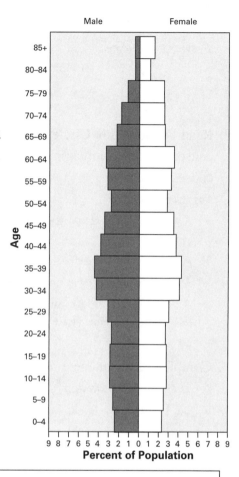

2. Read Section 15.8. Circle any of your ideas that match the causes of a declining workforce you read about. List any additional causes below.

    Possible answers:

    • A workforce declines as the population ages.
    • A workforce declines as the birth rate decreases.

3. Complete this sentence: *A declining workforce can cause problems for a country because...*

    a smaller workforce may be unable to support all of a country's dependents and may hurt businesses.

Critical Thinking Question 3: *What is the best way to cope with a declining workforce?*

4. Rank the plans listed here from strongest to weakest. If your group thinks of other ideas, add them to the ranked list. Be prepared to justify your rankings.

    Answers will vary.

5. Read Section 15.9. Then answer these questions in complete sentences: *Which European program for coping with a declining workforce do you think is most likely to be successful? Why?*

    Answers will vary.

Plan	Your Rank
A. Allow workers from other countries to take available jobs.	_____
B. Give mothers paid time off and flexible schedules.	_____
C. Require current workers to work more years before they retire.	_____
D. Move factories to other countries.	_____
E. Other: _____	
_____	_____

Invisible Borders: Transboundary Pollution in Europe

Overview

In this lesson, students learn how pollution produced in one country can affect other countries both near and far. In a **Visual Discovery** activity, students analyze images and maps to understand the causes and results of radioactive pollution from Chernobyl, acid rain from the "Black Triangle" region, and water pollution in the Tisza and Danube rivers. Afterward, they investigate the sources and spread of one type of global transboundary pollution, acid rain.

Objectives

Students will

- define and explain the importance these key geographic terms: *acid rain, nuclear radiation, river system, transboundary pollution.*
- analyze images and maps to understand the causes, locations, and impact of radioactive pollution, acid rain, and industrial water pollution on Europe.
- investigate the sources and spread of acid rain worldwide.

Materials

- *Geography Alive! Regions and People*
- Interactive Student Notebooks
- Transparencies 16A–16D
- Student Handouts 16A and 16B (1 of each for every 4 students)
- 3 resealable 1-gallon plastic bags filled with confetti
- 4 medium to large pieces of cardboard

Preview

1 **Before class, prepare the classroom and materials.**

- Divide the desks into seven groups as shown below. Allow only a small space between each area so that they are fairly close together. Label the group of desks as *Areas A–F* and *Wind*. The dashed lines show the location of the "wind" desks for the second round of the activity.

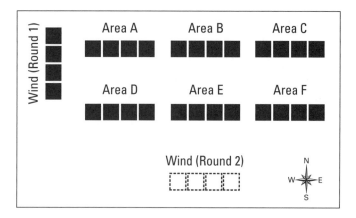

- Fill three 1-gallon plastic bags with confetti. Make the confetti as small and light as possible.
- Place the four pieces of cardboard on the "wind" desks.

2 **Prepare students for the activity.** Tell students that they are about to experience a problem that many European countries face.

- Have four students sit on the "wind" desks. Explain that they will represent the wind. Each time you say "go," they are to wave their pieces of cardboard as they slowly count to 10 and then stop. (**Note:** You may want to join this group during the activity so you can help model how to create a strong, steady wind in the right direction.)
- Choose three students to be "confetti tossers." Give each a bag of confetti. Have them stand in front of "wind" desks, turned sideways so that their bodies will not block the confetti from the wind. Explain that each time you say "go," they are to count to two and then toss five handfuls of confetti into the air in the same direction as the wind is blowing.
- Divide the remaining students into six groups. Place each group in one of Areas A–F. Tell them to watch how the confetti travels each time you say "go." Explain that they also need to note how much confetti falls on their desks each time.

3 Conduct the activity. Explain that you will conduct this activity twice. After each round, you will ask students in Areas A–F how much of the confetti reached them. Follow these directions:

- *Round 1:* The "wind" students are seated directly west of Area A. When you say "go," they should wave their cardboard as they slowly count to 10. The confetti tossers should count to two and then toss five handfuls of confetti into the air, in the direction the wind is blowing.

- *Round 2:* Move the "wind" students southeast of Area A, and conduct the activity again.

4 Debrief the activity. Ask these questions:

- *Students in Areas A–F:* What did you see happen in this experience? Compare the amount of confetti that landed in the six different areas.

- *"Wind" students:* How did the direction of the wind affect the spread of the confetti?

- *Confetti tossers:* Did you feel responsible for what was happening to your classmates? Why or why not?

- *Students in Areas A–F:* How did you feel toward the confetti tossers? Toward the "wind"?

- *All students:* What problems were created by the confetti tossers? What could have been done to prevent those problems?

5 Explain the connection between the Preview and the upcoming activity. Tell students that just as the confetti did not stay near the confetti tossers, pollution also travels away from where it is produced. Have students turn to the political map of Europe and Russia in the atlas at the back of *Geography Alive! Regions and People.* Then ask, *Why is Europe a good place to study pollution that crosses borders, or transboundary pollution?* Explain that students will now examine three case studies of transboundary pollution in Europe.

Essential Question and Geoterms

1 Introduce Chapter 16 in *Geography Alive! Regions and People.* Have students examine the photograph of the destruction of the Chernobyl nuclear power plant. Ask,

- What do you see?
- What might have caused this destruction?
- How might the surrounding town be affected by this destruction?
- How might neighboring countries be affected?

2 **Have students read Section 16.1.** Afterward, explain that in this chapter they will investigate not only the radioactive pollution from Chernobyl, but also the causes and consequences of two other types of transboundary pollution.

3 **Introduce the Graphic Organizer and the Essential Question.** Have students examine the map. Then ask,

- What do you see?
- What seems to be the source of the pollution?
- What do the various shades of the clouds represent?

Have students read the accompanying text. Make sure they understand the Essential Question, *How can one country's pollution become another country's problem?* You may want to post the Essential Question in the room or write it on the board for the duration of the activity.

4 **Have students read Section 16.2.** Then have them work individually or in pairs to complete Geoterms 16 in their Interactive Student Notebooks. Ask them to share their answers with another student, or have volunteers share their answers with the class.

Geoterms 16

Visual Discovery

To introduce this activity, explain that students will analyze photographs and maps, along with reading sections of *Geography Alive! Regions and People,* to learn about transboundary pollution in Europe.

Phase 1: Winds Carry Radiation from Chernobyl

1 **Project the photograph at the top of *Transparency 16A: Transboundary Pollution Problem One* and have students analyze the image.** Cover the maps at the bottom of the transparency. Ask,

- What do you see? (Consider having volunteers come to the screen to point out details.)
- What do you think the man standing outside the car is doing? What might the instrument he is holding be?
- Why is no one in the picture talking?
- Where do you think this picture was taken? What do you think happened to cause this scene?

Transparency 16A   **Reading Notes 16**

2 **Have students read Section 16.3 through "Human Error Creates a Deadly Radiation Leak" and then work with a partner to complete the corresponding portion of Reading Notes 16.** Have a few students share their sentences with the class.

3 Project the maps at the bottom of Transparency 16A and have students analyze them. Ask,

- What do you see?
- What does this series of maps show?
- Where is the source of the pollution? Describe how the pollution spread.
- Which areas seem to be most affected by the pollution? Why might this be so?

4 Have students read the rest of Section 16.3 and work with a partner to complete the corresponding Reading Notes. Continue to project Transparency 16A as they work. Use Guide to Reading Notes 16 to review the answers with the class. Encourage students to add any missing information to their notes. (**Note:** Consider making a transparency of the Guide to Reading Notes to display as the answers are reviewed.)

5 Place students in groups of four to prepare for the first act-it-out. Give each group a copy of *Student Handout 16A: Directions for Act-It-Out 1*. Assign each group one of the characters on the handout. (**Note:** With larger classes, assign the roles of Resident of Belarus and Resident of Lapland to more than one group.) Review the guidelines on the handout, and give groups several minutes to prepare their characters.

6 Conduct the act-it-out. Project the photograph at the top of Transparency 16A again, making it as large as possible. Randomly select one student from each group to "step into" the projected image and take on the various roles. Have the resident(s) of Belarus stand a few feet to the left of the screen and those of Lapland stand across the room. Starting with the characters in the photograph, interview each character using the questions from the handout. After the act-it-out, explain that this photograph was taken in 1990, almost five years after the explosion, at a checkpoint 10 kilometers from the Chernobyl nuclear power plant.

Phase 2: The "Black Triangle" and Acid Rain
1 Project the photograph at the top of *Transparency 16B: Transboundary Pollution Problem Two* and have students analyze the image. Cover the map at the bottom. Ask,

- What do you see?
- What details of the sculpture seem damaged? (Consider having volunteers come to the screen to point out details.)
- What do you think might have caused this damage?

Student Handout 16A

Transparency 16B

2 Have students read Section 16.4 through "Soot from Factories Creates Acid Rain" and then, with a partner, complete the corresponding Reading Notes. Have a few students share their sentences with the class.

Reading Notes 16

3 Project the map at the bottom of Transparency 16B and have students analyze it. Ask,

- What do you see?
- What do the dots on the maps represent? The colors?
- Where are the main sources of the pollution? Describe how the pollution spread.
- Which areas seem to be most affected by the pollution? Why might this be so?

4 Have students read the rest of Section 16.4 and complete the corresponding Reading Notes. Continue to project Transparency 16B as they work. Use the Guide to Reading Notes to review their answers. Encourage students to add any missing information to their notes.

5 Have students reexamine Transparency 16B. Encourage them to use what they learned in Section 16.4 to answer these questions:

- How was this statue damaged?
- What else could be photographed to show the destruction of acid rain?
- What might be done to prevent destruction from acid rain?

Phase 3: The Tisza-Danube Cyanide Spill

1 Project the photograph at the top of *Transparency 16C: Transboundary Pollution Problem Three* and have students analyze the image. Cover the map at the bottom. Ask,

- What do you see?
- What do you think happened to these fish?
- Who are the people? What do you think they are talking about?
- What might have happened to cause this scene?

Transparency 16C **Reading Notes 16**

2 Have students read Section 16.5 through "A Burst Dam Releases Deadly Chemicals" and complete the corresponding Reading Notes with a partner. Have a few students share their sentences with the class.

3 Project the map at the bottom of Transparency 16C and have students analyze it. Ask,

- What do you see?
- What do the various colors represent? What do the shades of the skulls represent?
- Where is the source of the pollution? Describe how the pollution spread.
- Which countries seem to be most affected by the pollution? Why might this be so?

4 Have students read the rest of Section 16.5 and complete the corresponding Reading Notes. Continue to project Transparency 16C as they work. Use the Guide to Reading Notes to review the answers. Encourage students to add any missing information to their notes.

5 Place students in groups of four to prepare for the second act-it-out. Give each group a copy of *Student Handout 16B: Directions for Act-It-Out 2.* Assign each group one of the characters listed on the handout. (**Note:** With larger classes, assign the roles along the river to more than one group.) Review the guidelines, and give groups several minutes to prepare their characters.

6 Conduct the act-it-out. Project the photograph on Transparency 16C again, making it as large as possible. Randomly select one student from each group to "step into" the image and take on the various roles. Have the Worker at the Romanian Gold Mine stand a few feet to the left of the screen, and the Fisherman and Townsperson Along the Danube River stand across the room. Starting with the characters in the photograph, interview each character using the questions from the handout.

Global Connections

1 Introduce the Global Connections. Have students read Section 16.6. Tell them that their groups will now leave Europe to look at transboundary pollution around the world.

2 Project *Transparency 16D: Global Connections.* Help students analyze the images by asking the questions below. Use the additional information given to enrich the discussion.

- **What does the map show?**

- **Where is acid rain already a serious problem?**
  The highest levels of acid rain are in North America and Europe.

Student Handout 16B

Transparency 16D

- **Where are the areas of acid rain potential?**

  In North America, areas of acid rain potential can be found from North Carolina south to Florida, in California, in Washington, and in the southern portion of British Columbia. In Europe, they are located in Portugal, Spain, France, Italy, Greece, and Russia. In Southwest and Central Asia, they are found in Kazakhstan, Turkey, Georgia, Armenia, Azerbaijan, Syria, Iraq, and Iran. In Asia, they are located in India, Nepal, Bangladesh, China, the Philippines, and Indonesia. Australia also includes areas of acid rain potential.

- **What does the diagram show?**

- **Where does most pollution from a source fall?**

  Almost 80 percent of pollution falls close to industrial areas where it is created.

- **What impact do you think upper-level winds have on transboundary pollution?**

  Upper-level winds can carry pollution over far distances, thereby crossing over many countries' borders.

3 **Have students, individually or as a class, read Section 16.7 and examine the rest of the information in the section.** Then lead a discussion of these questions:

- **Why do North America and Europe have the highest acid rain levels?**

  Because North America and Europe have been highly industrialized for hundreds of years, they have the highest acid rain levels. These high levels are due to the large number of factories and vehicles on both continents. Since the late 1900s, governments within these regions, particularly the European Union, have worked to reduce the pollutants that cause acid rain.

- **What changes in Asia are raising acid rain potential there?**

  Industrialization in China, India, and other countries in Asia is raising acid rain potential in the region. As the number of vehicles and factories increase, so do pollution levels. Some environmental experts predict that in East Asia the amount of pollutants that cause acid rain will triple between 1990 and 2020.

- **Why must acid rain be tackled as a global problem?**

  Acid rain must be tackled as a global problem because it is a form of transboundary pollution. As the wind diagram shows, upper-level winds can transport pollutants across oceans. In recent years, the International Consortium for Atmospheric Research on Transport and Transformation has begun to study how pollutants travel globally. ICARTT is particularly interested in the flow of pollution from North America to Europe and from Asia to North America. The consortium includes the United States, Canada, Germany, France, Portugal, and the United Kingdom. It tracks pollutants with everything from aircraft and satellites to ground stations and a research ship.

Processing

Have students complete Processing 16 in their Interactive Student Notebooks. Have a few students share their answers with the class. If time allows, hold a discussion comparing and contrasting transboundary pollution in North America with that in Europe.

Online Resources

For more information on transboundary pollution, refer students to Online Resources for *Geography Alive! Regions and People* at www.teachtci.com.

Processing 16

Assessment

Masters for assessment appear on the next three pages followed by answers and scoring rubrics.

Assessment | 16

Mastering the Content

Shade in the oval by the letter of the best answer for each question.

1. What was the **major** cause of the power plant explosion at Chernobyl?
   - ○ A. brain drain
   - ○ B. human error
   - ○ C. extreme weather
   - ○ D. centrifugal force

2. Which of these was the **main** pollutant released by the Chernobyl power plant explosion?
   - ○ A. cyanide
   - ○ B. nitrogen oxide
   - ○ C. nuclear radiation
   - ○ D. sulfur dioxide

3. The map below **best** illustrates which of the following problems?

Radiation Spread from Chernobyl

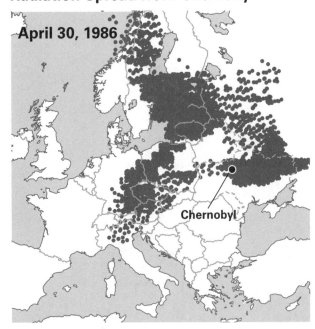

- ○ A. general pollution
- ○ B. non-point-source pollution
- ○ C. toxic-chemical pollution
- ○ D. transboundary pollution

4. Which of these is a **major** cause of acid rain?
   - ○ A. spraying pesticides on crops
   - ○ B. burning fossil fuels for energy
   - ○ C. dumping sewage in river systems
   - ○ D. using uranium to generate electricity

5. Which one of these is **not** a direct result of acid rain?
   - ○ A. damage to monuments
   - ○ B. dying fish
   - ○ C. spread of disease
   - ○ D. weakened trees

6. Power plants and factories in Europe's "Black Triangle" are doing which of these to reduce acid rain?
   - ○ A. switching to coal as a fuel
   - ○ B. building taller smokestacks
   - ○ C. stopping work on windy days
   - ○ D. installing smokestack scrubbers

7. How did the accidental spill of cyanide at a mine in Romania spread to neighboring countries?
   - ○ A. Winds blew cyanide to other countries.
   - ○ B. Rivers carried cyanide to other countries.
   - ○ C. Crops poisoned with cyanide were sold in other countries.
   - ○ D. Storms dropped rain poisoned with cyanide on other countries.

8. The Tisza-Danube cyanide spill is an example of all of the following **except**
   - ○ A. general pollution.
   - ○ B. accidental pollution.
   - ○ C. point-source pollution.
   - ○ D. transboundary pollution.

Applying Geography Skills:
Forming Generalizations from Map Data

Use the map and your knowledge of geography to complete the tasks below.

Cyanide Spread Along the Tisza-Danube River System

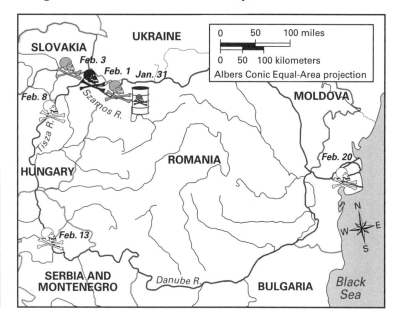

1. Use the map to complete the table. The first row has been filled in for you.

Date	River	Level of Cyanide
Jan. 31	Szamos	medium

2. Use the information above to write a generalization about what happens over time as a toxic spill moves through a river system.

Test Terms Glossary
A **generalization** is a conclusion that is based on a number of cases.

Exploring the Essential Question

How can one country's pollution become another country's problem?

In Chapter 16, you explored how pollution in one country became a problem for other countries. Now you will use what you learned. Use the diagram and your knowledge of geography to complete the task below.

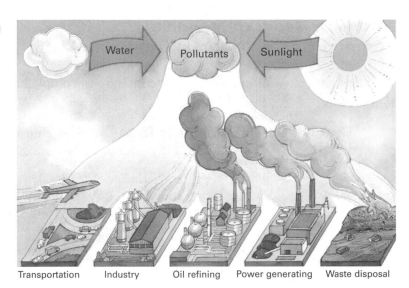

Transportation   Industry   Oil refining   Power generating   Waste disposal

The Task: Creating a Cartoon About Air Pollution

The diagram shows five sources of air pollution. Your task is to create a cartoon about one of them.

Step 1: Think about daily activities that relate to each pollution source listed below. Some ideas are included to help you get started. Add others that you think of.

Transportation	Industry	Oil refining	Power generation	Waste disposal
1. 2.	1. Buy products made with toxic chemicals. 2.	1. Heat home with oil. 2.	1. Leave lights on. 2.	1. Burn trash in fireplace. 2.

Step 2: Circle one activity above to use for your cartoon. List one or two things people can do to reduce air pollution caused by this activity.

Step 3: On another sheet of paper, draw a "before and after" cartoon on air pollution. Your first panel should show what people are doing now that contributes to air pollution. The second should show how that could change to help reduce pollution. For example, you might show a student riding to school in a car in the first panel. The second panel could show the same student riding a bike to school. Add a short caption that tells how the change will reduce air pollution.

Applying Geography Skills: Sample Responses

1.

Date	River	Level of Cyanide
Jan. 31	Szamos	medium
Feb. 1	Szamos	high
Feb. 3	Szamos or Tisza	medium
Feb. 8	Tisza	medium
Feb. 13	Tisza or Danube	low
Feb. 20	Danube	low

2. In general, pollution levels are highest in a river shortly after a toxic spill. As the spill moves downstream through the river system, the levels of the toxic chemicals in the water decrease.

Exploring the Essential Question: Sample Response

Step 1: Responses will vary. A completed table should have 10 examples of everyday activities that contribute to air pollution.

Step 2: Responses will vary. Students should circle one activity and list changes that could help to reduce air pollution caused by this activity.

Step 3: Responses will vary. Cartoons should have two panels. One should show something people do that contributes to air pollution. The other should show how that activity could change. A caption should tell how this change will help reduce air pollution.

Mastering the Content Answer Key

1. B	2. C	3. D	4. B
5. C	6. D	7. B	8. A

Applying Geography Skills Scoring Rubric

Score	General Description
2	Student responds to all parts of the task. Response is correct and clear.
1	Student responds to some parts of the task. Response is mostly correct.
0	Response does not match the task or is incorrect.

Exploring the Essential Question Scoring Rubric

Score	General Description
3	Student responds to all parts of the task. Response is correct, clear, and supported by details.
2	Student responds to most or all parts of the task. Response is generally correct but may lack details.
1	Student responds to at least one part of the task. Response may contain errors and lack details.
0	Response does not match the task or is incorrect.

Act Out a Character Affected by the Chernobyl Accident

You will work in your group to bring to life a scene from the Chernobyl accident. Your teacher will assign a character to your group. When it is time, one member of your group will be selected to play that character. A reporter will interview the characters.

Step 1: Circle the character your group has been assigned:

Inspector

Driver in Car

Passenger in Car

Resident of Belarus

Resident of Lapland

Step 2: Discuss the questions below for your character. Make sure everyone in your group can answer your characters' questions so that everyone is prepared to be the actor.

- *Inspector:* Who are you? What are you holding? Why are you checking the car? How has Chernobyl's radioactive pollution changed where you live and work?

- *Driver:* Who are you? Where are you going? Why? How do you feel every time your car is checked for radiation? What do you think Chernobyl will be like 50 years from now?

- *Passenger:* Who are you? Why are you riding in this car? How was your family affected by the radioactive pollution that spread from Chernobyl? What do you think about the concrete tomb that was built around the reactor?

- *Resident of Belarus:* Who are you? Where do you live in relation to Chernobyl? How has Chernobyl's radioactive pollution affected your country? What do you think is the Soviet Union's responsibility to the residents of Belarus?

- *Resident of Lapland:* Who are you? Where do you live in relation to Chernobyl? How did you find out about the spread of the radioactive pollution? How has Chernobyl changed your people's way of life?

Step 3: Discuss how the person who is chosen to perform can make the character come alive. Collect simple props to use during the act-it-out.

Act Out a Character Affected by the Tisza-Danube Cyanide Spill

You will work in your group to bring to life scenes from the Tisza-Danube cyanide spill. Your teacher will assign a character to your group. When it is time, one member of your group will be selected to play that character. A reporter will interview the characters.

Step 1: Circle the character your group has been assigned.

Worker at the Romanian Gold Mine

Fisherman Along the Tisza River

Townsperson Along the Tisza River

Fisherman Along the Danube River

Townsperson Along the Danube River

Step 2: Discuss the questions below for your character. Make sure everyone in your group can answer your characters' questions so that everyone is prepared to be the actor.

- *Fisherman Along the Tisza River:* Who are you? Do you plan to eat the large fish stacked up here? Why or why not? What was the Tisza River like before January 2000? What was it like immediately after the incident?

- *Townsperson Along the Tisza River:* Who are you? Where do you live in relation to the Romanian gold mine? How were you and your family affected by the incident? What is the condition of the Tisza River today?

- *Worker at the Romanian Gold Mine:* Who are you? What happened at your workplace on January 30, 2000? What types of pollutants did your mine release into the river systems? Do you think this accident could have been prevented? How?

- *Fisherman Along the Danube River:* Who are you? Where do you live in relation to the Romanian gold mine? How were you and your family affected by the incident? What could have been done to prevent this tragedy?

- *Townsperson Along the Danube River:* Who are you? What types of pollution have you seen in the Danube? Describe the event you participated in on June 29, 2004. Do you think the International Commission for the Protection of the Danube River will be able to reduce transboundary pollution? Why or why not?

Step 3: Discuss how the person who is chosen to perform can make the character come alive. Collect simple props to use during the act-it-out.

16.3 The Chernobyl Radiation Accident

As you read Section 16.3, complete the map below.

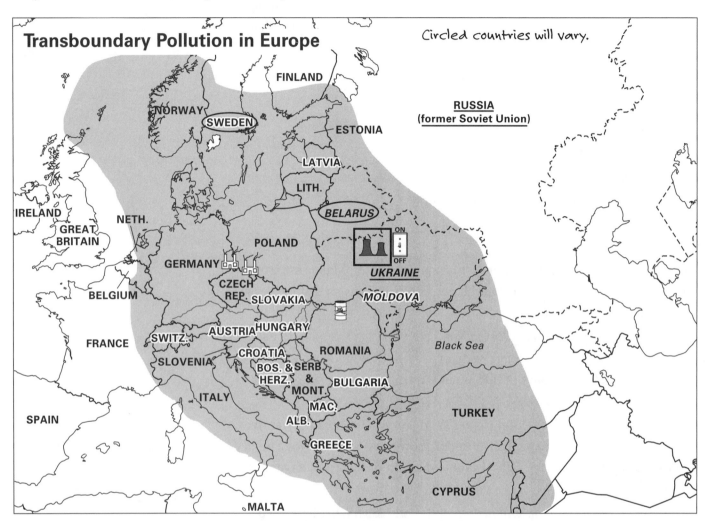

Transboundary Pollution in Europe

Circled countries will vary.

Human Error Creates a Deadly Radiation Leak

On the map, color the source of the radioactive pollution. Underline the name of the country where it is located. Then complete this sentence:

Chernobyl became a source of radioactive pollution when...
its reactor had an explosion that released a radioactive cloud.

The Radioactive Cloud Spreads Across Europe

Look at the maps your teacher is projecting. Shade your map to show the spread of radioactive pollution. Circle the names of two countries that were affected by the pollution. Then complete this sentence:

One effect of the spread of radioactive pollution across borders was...
that people outside of Ukraine had their food and water contaminated by radiation.

Efforts to Reduce Radioactive Pollution

On the map, draw one effect to reduce radioactive pollution. Then complete this sentence:

__Reactor changes__ *help to reduce radioactive pollution by...*
improving safety at nuclear power plants like making plants easier to shut down in an emergency.

16.4 The "Black Triangle" and Acid Rain

As you read Section 16.4, complete the map below.

Transboundary Pollution in Europe

Circled countries will vary.

Soot from Factories Creates Acid Rain

On the map, color the source of the acid rain. Underline the names of the countries where it is located. Then complete this sentence:

The Black Triangle became a source of acid rain when...
factories and power plants in this area burned coal.

Air Pollution Brings Acid Rain to Other Countries

Look at the map your teacher is projecting. Shade your map to show the pattern of acid rain. Circle the names of two countries affected by acid rain. Then complete this sentence:

One consequence of the spread of acid rain across borders is...
that places outside of the Black Triangle have sick trees and fish.

Efforts to Reduce Acid Rain

On the map, draw one effort to reduce acid rain. Then complete this sentence:

Smokestack scrubbers *help to reduce acid rain by...*
taking harmful substances out of the smoke from factories.

16.5 The Tisza-Danube Cyanide Spill

As you read Section 16.5, complete the map below.

Transboundary Pollution in Europe

Circled countries will vary.

A Burst Dam Releases Deadly Chemicals

On the map, color the source of the water pollution. Underline the name of the country where it is located. Then complete this sentence:

Accidental water pollution occurred when...
water laced with cyanide overflowed a pond at a mining operation.

Cyanide Flows into the Danube River System

Look at the map your teacher is projecting. Shade your map to show the spread of the water pollution. Circle the names of two countries most affected by the pollution. Then complete this sentence:

One consequence of the spread of water pollution across borders was...
that outside of Romania, 200 tons of fish were killed, water systems were shut down, and tourists canceled trips.

Efforts to Reduce Water Pollution

On the map, draw one effort to reduce water pollution. Then complete this sentence:

International commissions *help reduce water pollution by...*
having countries work together to prevent future spills.

Russia's Varied Landscape: Physical Processes at Work

Overview

In this lesson, students examine how four physical processes shape Earth's surface and identify examples of the effects of these processes on Russia's landscape. In a **Social Studies Skill Builder,** students first learn about four major physical processes by examining diagrams and conducting act-it-outs. They then use their knowledge to try to identify which physical processes are pictured in various images. Finally, they locate where in Russia each photograph was taken and place each image on a large relief map of Russia.

Objectives

Students will

- define and explain the importance of these key geographic terms: *erosion, glaciation, physical processes, tectonic movement, volcanic activity.*

- identify and analyze geographic information about Russia using relief maps, satellite images, and photographs.

- explain how physical processes such as tectonic movement, volcanic activity, erosion, and glaciation can shape the landscape.

- explain the relationship between tectonic movement and volcanic activity around the globe.

Materials

- *Geography Alive! Regions and People*
- Interactive Student Notebooks
- Transparencies 17A–17F
- Placards 17A–17L
- Information Master 17 (1 transparency)
- Student Handout 17 (1 copy for every 4 students plus 1 transparency)
- scrap paper (1 sheet per student)

Preview

1 **Have students simulate the physical process of tectonic movement.** Ask students to crumple a sheet of paper into a ball. Have them spread the crumpled paper out on their desktops without trying to flatten it entirely. Then ask,

- Look closely at what happened to the shape of your sheet of paper. What do you notice about the new shape?
- Does everyone's paper look the same? Why not?
- Thinking about the surface of Earth, what does your paper remind you of?

2 **Project** *Transparency 17A: Relief Map of Russia.* **Reveal** the upper (unlabeled) map, keeping the bottom (labeled) map covered. Have students analyze the map by asking,

- What details do you notice about this map?
- In what ways does this map resemble your crumpled sheet of paper?
- How do the parts of your crumpled paper resemble areas on this map of Russia?
- What force acted on your sheet of paper to make it look like it does?
- What kind of forces could have made the land look like it does on this map?

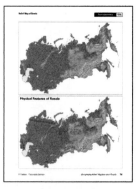

Transparency 17A

3 **Have students complete Preview 17 in their Interactive Student Notebooks.** Review the directions with them. Once students have completed Step 1 of the first part of the Preview, project the bottom map from Transparency 17A. Point out the physical features that are labeled. Have students finish the Preview, labeling the places noted on the second map and answering the two questions. Then have volunteers share their ideas.

Preview 17

4 **Explain the connection between the Preview and the upcoming activity.** Tell students that Russia is the largest country in the world, almost twice the size of the United States, and diverse in its physical features. In this lesson, students will examine how various forces, or physical processes, shape Earth and identify examples of these effects in Russia. Remind them of how they shaped a sheet of paper by crumpling it, and suggest how powerful the forces that are able to alter the Earth's surface must be. You might ask, *What kind of force would it take to crumple Earth's surface?* Also mention the fact that such forces have been acting on the Earth very slowly for millions of years. Tell students that in order to see how dramatically land can change shape, they will be examining photographs of land in Russia, some of them taken from satellites, to identify and analyze the physical processes they show.

Essential Question and Geoterms

1 Introduce Chapter 17 in *Geography Alive! Regions and People.* Explain that in this chapter students will learn about four physical processes: tectonic movement, volcanic activity, erosion, and glaciation. Have students read Section 17.1 and examine the satellite image of Russia. Then ask these questions:

- What do you see in this photograph?
- What do the different colors and shades represent?
- What might this satellite image teach us about the physical landscape of Russia?

2 Introduce the Graphic Organizer and the Essential Question. Have students examine the diagram of physical processes. Ask,

- What do you see?
- What does the map in the center tell you?
- The drawings around the map represent the four main physical processes that have shaped the land in Russia. What are they?

Have students read the accompanying text. Make sure they understand the Essential Question, *How do physical processes shape Earth's landscape?* You may want to post the Essential Question in the classroom or write it on the board for the duration of the activity.

3 Have students read Section 17.2. Then have them work individually or in pairs to complete Geoterms 17 in their Interactive Student Notebooks. Have them share their answers with another student, or have volunteers share their answers with the class.

Geoterms 17

Social Studies Skill Builder

Phase 1: Preparing and Presenting Act-It-Outs of Four Physical Processes

1 Arrange students in mixed-ability groups of four. You may want to prepare a transparency that shows them with whom they will work and where they will sit. (**Note:** If you have a small class, you may want to create groups of three.)

2 Explain Phase 1 of the activity. Tell students that in this first phase of the activity, they will read about four physical processes and examine a diagram that shows how each works. Then, in their groups, they will create a visual representation of the diagram using all four group members as "actors" who will each represent one aspect of the diagram. Various groups will be

called on to present their act-it-outs to the class for discussion.
Clarify that every group will prepare an act-it-out for each of
the four processes, but that only two groups will be called upon
for each process. Every group must be prepared to present each
time, since groups will be called upon randomly.

3 Project *Transparency 17B: Mountain Formation.* Have
students examine the diagram. Ask,

- What do you see in this diagram?
- What are some of the parts of this process?
- What might be some results or effects of this process?
- How might this process change the land?

4 Have students read Section 17.3 of *Geography Alive!
Regions and People.* This reading will give them a general
understanding of tectonic movement and how it shapes the land.

5 Have students complete Reading Notes 17 for this section.
Have groups work together to label the corresponding diagram
using the transparency and Section 17.3 as guides. Circulate to
make sure students are labeling the diagram correctly.

6 Give each group *Student Handout 17: Preparing an
Act-It-Out of a Physical Process.* Review the directions with
students, answering any questions about how to prepare the
act-it-outs. For example, to show mountain formation, one
student in a group might be the mountain, while others take on
the role of tectonic plates. The "mountain" might crouch down
until two "tectonic plates" collide and push him or her upward.

7 Circulate as groups prepare and rehearse their act-it-outs.
Remind them that they must meet these requirements:

- All group members must be involved.
- All aspects of the diagram must be represented.
- Presentations should take 30 seconds or less.

8 Call on a few groups to perform their act-it-outs. Clear a
space at the front of the room, and choose one group to perform
their act-it-out. Then ask the rest of the class to comment on
these aspects of the presentation:

- Did the group accurately re-create the physical process?
- Were there any missing elements? What?
- What was the strongest aspect of the presentation? What was
  the weakest?

Select another group to perform their act-it-out, and have the
audience analyze this performance. You may find it useful to

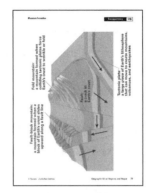

Transparency 17B

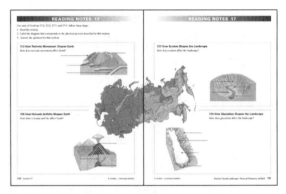

Reading Notes 17

Student Handout 17

use the command "freeze frame" during the presentation to indicate that you'd like the group to hold a certain position. As the group freezes, encourage the class to examine the parts of the physical process and determine what role each person is playing at that moment. You might also ask questions of the group to clarify what each person's role is and why he or she is doing a particular motion or action.

9 Repeat Steps 3–8 for *Transparencies 17C–17E: Volcano, Erosion,* and *Glaciation.* For each of Sections 17.5, 17.7, and 17.9, assign students to read about the physical process, label the corresponding diagram in their Reading Notes, and, with their groups, prepare an act-it-out for that process. (**Note:** Students will read Sections 17.4, 17.6, 17.8, and 17.10 in Phase 2 of the activity.)

Phase 2: Matching Images of the Russian Landscape to Physical Processes

1 **Prepare the classroom.** Post *Placards 17A–17L: Russian Landscape Images* around the room. You also may want to place a copy of *Geography Alive! Regions and People* near each placard instead of having students carry their books with them.

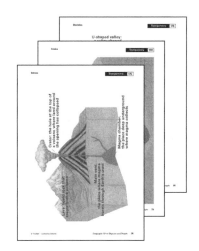

Transparencies 17C–17E

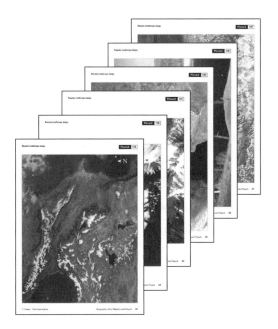

Placards 17A–17F

Placards 17G–17L

2 **Place students in mixed-ability pairs.** You may want to create a seating chart on a transparency.

3 Explain Phase 2 of the activity. Tell students that they will use their knowledge of the four physical processes to try to identify which process is at work in each of the 12 images around the room. Some images show the physical process itself; others show the effects of that process on the Russian landscape. Project *Information Master 17: Identifying and Analyzing Placards,* and review the steps for Phase 2. Information Master 17 also explains how students are to complete the second spread of Reading Notes 17.

4 Conduct the Social Studies Skill Builder. Project Information Master 17 during the activity as a reference. Instruct pairs to choose a placard to start with, with no more than two pairs at any one placard at a time. Have pairs come to you after they have identified their first placard to make sure they are completing the Reading Notes correctly. (**Note:** You may find it helpful to continue to have pairs show you their Reading Notes after they have visited each placard. Students may find that some placard images are challenging to identify; you may have to suggest they reexamine the placards if they do not identify the correct location.)

5 Conduct a wrap-up activity. After all pairs have identified all or most of the placards, hand out the 12 placards, one to each pair. Project the upper map on Transparency 17A again. One at a time, have one student in each pair tape their placard to the correct location on the projected map of Russia. Have the other student tell the class what physical process was exemplified and what landform in Russia is pictured. (See the list at right for complete descriptions.) Once all placards have been placed, ask the class,

- What physical process is most noticeable in Russia?
- What physical process changes the landscape most dramatically?
- What physical process do you think is most common worldwide?
- What physical process do you think would be most difficult for humans to adapt to?
- What are some possible effects that these processes could have on human activity worldwide?

Global Connections

1 Introduce the Global Connections. Tell students that the physical processes they have learned about are responsible for much of Earth's topography. They will now examine how tectonic plate movement has not only shaped mountains and valleys, but has also created patterns of volcanic chains across

Information Master 17

Reading Notes 17

Placard 17A	Caucasus Mountains
Placard 17B	Kliuchevskoi Volcano
Placard 17C	Kolka Glacier
Placard 17D	Sedimentation in the Caspian Sea
Placard 17E	Erosion Near the Amur River
Placard 17	Flooding of the Lena River
Placard 17G	Krenitsyn Volcano
Placard 17H	Yamal Peninsula
Placard 17I	West Sayan Mountains
Placard 17J	Mount Manaraga
Placard 17K	Troitsky Crater of the Maly Semyachik Volcano
Placard 17L	Amanauzsky Glacier in the Caucasus Mountains

Earth's surface and is responsible for large and sometimes deadly earthquakes in certain areas of the world.

2 Project *Transparency 17F: Global Connections.* Help students analyze the map by asking the questions below. Use the additional information given to enrich the discussion.

Transparency 17F

- **What does this map tell you?**
  This map shows the boundaries of the world's tectonic plates and the distribution of major earthquakes and active volcanoes. When two plates slip past each other, earthquakes can occur. In some cases, volcanoes form. The location of volcanoes is closely related to the positions and movements of the major plates. Generally, volcanoes are found within a couple of hundred miles of the sea or in areas of recent fold mountains.

- **What do the colored regions represent?**
  The colored regions are the world's major tectonic plates. The plates move due to currents in the magma of Earth's mantle.

- **What does each red triangle represent? Each black dot?**
  Each triangle represents an active volcano. Each dot represents a significant earthquake.

- **What does this map tell us about the relationship between volcanoes, earthquakes, and tectonic movement?**
  The map illustrates that volcanoes and earthquakes are closely tied to the movements of plates on Earth's crust. Specifically, volcanoes and earthquakes occur when two tectonic plates slide past each other.

3 Have students compare the map of the world's hot spots to a map of the world's physical features. Point out that the continents are visible under the tectonic plates. Have students turn to the physical map of the world in the atlas at the back of *Geography Alive! Regions and People* and examine the physical features shown on the map. Use these questions to lead a class discussion:

- **What do you notice about the locations of some of the world's largest mountains in relationship to plate boundaries? Why would this be?**
  Many of the world's larger mountain ranges are situated on top of plate boundaries. For example, the Himalayas were formed about 40 to 50 million years ago when two land-masses, Eurasia and India, collided. The pressure caused the land to thrust skyward, and the jagged Himalayan peaks were formed. This collision is ongoing, and the Himalayas continue to rise slowly.

One peak in this range, Mount Everest, is, at five and a half miles high, the highest mountain in the world. Since most mountain ranges are formed when tectonic plates collide and push Earth's surface upward (folding) or when plates break apart and slide vertically away from each other (faulting), we would expect them to be located along plate boundaries.

- **Look at the maps once more. Note areas of land that are not located near a plate boundary. How might the absence of tectonic plate movement affect the land there?**
  Areas in the centers of tectonic plates might be more affected by the processes of erosion and glaciation. Mountains in these areas, such as the Appalachian range of North America, are being worn down by erosive agents while not being built up by folding or faulting.

4 **Continue the discussion of the relationship between tectonic activity and the physical world.** Place students in mixed-ability pairs and have them turn to Section 17.12. Ask them to read the text and to examine the rest of the information. Encourage them to look for relationships between the information given in the maps, the graph, and the table. Then facilitate a discussion by asking,

- **Why is the Ring of Fire located around the Pacific Ocean?**
  Because the Pacific Plate is so large and is in constant motion, tremendous pressure is created underneath the crust and a lot of activity occurs on Earth's surface.

- **Why isn't there a Ring of Fire around the edge of the Atlantic Ocean?**
  The North American and Eurasian plates meet in the middle of the ocean rather than close to land. As the plates move apart, the space between them fills with magma. Seawater cools and hardens this magma, forming a chain of underwater volcanoes and rift valleys called a mid-ocean ridge. However, these small volcanoes are much less explosive than the volcanoes in the Ring of Fire.

- **How has tectonic movement shaped human development on Earth?**
  Tectonic plates have been responsible for creating the continents that separate Earth into regions. They have also created mountains that isolate communities from each other and are sometimes used as the boundaries between nations.

Processing

1 **Help students prepare for the Processing activity.**

- Have students identify their hometown on political and physical maps of the United States.

- Have students draw an imaginary circle with a 100-mile radius around their hometown. Within that circle, have them identify three or four of the most prominent or interesting physical features. Create a master list of all these features.

- Have students sort the list of physical features by the processes that created or shaped them.

2 **Have students complete Processing 17 in their Interactive Student Notebooks.** If time permits, allow them to share the locations they have chosen and what physical process has helped to shape each location. You may also wish to open a discussion about which field trip sounds like the most fun and which chosen location is the strongest or most unique example of a physical process.

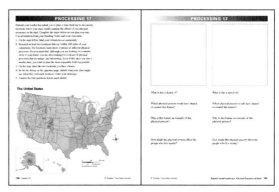

Processing 17

Online Resources

For more information on physical processes and varied landscapes, refer students to Online Resources for *Geography Alive! Regions and People* at www.teachtci.com.

Assessment

Masters for assessment appear on the next three pages followed by answers and scoring rubrics.

Mastering the Content

Shade in the oval by the letter of the best answer for each question.

1. Which of these is **most likely** to be changed by physical processes?
   ○ A. Earth's crust
   ○ B. Earth's oceans
   ○ C. Earth's climate
   ○ D. Earth's atmosphere

2. Which of these natural forces tend to wear down mountains?
   ○ A. folding and faulting
   ○ B. glaciation and erosion
   ○ C. volcanic activity and flooding
   ○ D. tectonic activity and sedimentation

3. Which of the layers of Earth shown in this diagram is made up of liquid rock called *magma*?
   ○ A. the mantle
   ○ B. the outer core
   ○ C. the inner core
   ○ D the crust

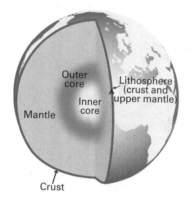

4. What is the **main** cause of major earthquakes?
   ○ A. the eruption of volcanoes
   ○ B. the movement of tectonic plates
   ○ C. the cooling of Earth's inner core
   ○ D. the weight of glaciers on Earth's crust

5. The liquid rock that erupts from a volcano is called
   ○ A. lava.
   ○ B. magma.
   ○ C. sediment.
   ○ D. precipitation.

6. Flooding often adds a fresh layer of soil to a floodplain. Which term in the diagram below **best** describes this process?

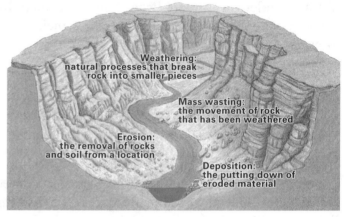

   ○ A. erosion
   ○ B. mass wasting
   ○ C. deposition
   ○ D. weathering

7. Which of these natural forces causes glaciers to move?
   ○ A. tectonic movement
   ○ B. volcanic activity
   ○ C. convection
   ○ D. gravity

8. The Ring of Fire marks a zone of volcanic activity around the edge of which ocean?
   ○ A. Arctic Ocean
   ○ B. Atlantic Ocean
   ○ C. Indian Ocean
   ○ D. Pacific Ocean

Applying Geography Skills: Analyzing a Diagram

Use the diagram and your knowledge of geography to complete the tasks below. Write your answers in complete sentences.

Mountain Building

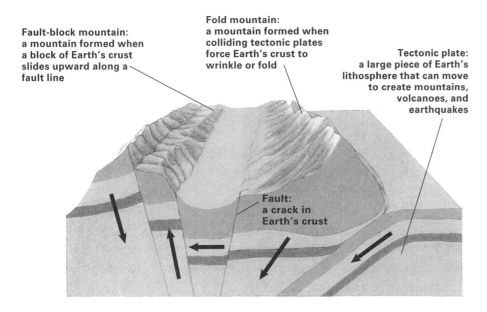

Fault-block mountain: a mountain formed when a block of Earth's crust slides upward along a fault line

Fold mountain: a mountain formed when colliding tectonic plates force Earth's crust to wrinkle or fold

Tectonic plate: a large piece of Earth's lithosphere that can move to create mountains, volcanoes, and earthquakes

Fault: a crack in Earth's crust

1. Identify the two types of mountains shown in the diagram.

2. Identify the physical process that causes both kinds of mountains to form.

3. Predict where mountain building is most likely to be going on today based on this diagram.

Test Terms Glossary

To **identify** means to tell what something is.

To **predict** means to say what is likely to happen in the future based on what you already know.

Exploring the Essential Question
How do physical processes shape Earth's landscape?

In Chapter 17, you explored how four physical processes have shaped Russia's landscape. Now you will use what you learned. Use the photographs below and your knowledge of geography to complete this task.

Ring Lake, Krenitsyn Volcano

Lena River Delta, Siberia

The Task: Analyzing Sites for a New Ecotourism Resort
You work for a hotel company in Russia. Your company is planning to build an ecotourism resort in one of two places. They are marked as Locations A and B in the photographs above. The resort will attract tourists who want to visit unique ecosystems.

Step 1: Analyze both photos. Think about the attractions of each place for tourists. Also consider the dangers of locating a resort in each location. Circle the place where you think the company should build its resort.

Step 2: Write a memo to Alexei Orlov, president of your company, explaining your choice. In your memo, be sure to do the following:

A. Begin with a memo heading using this form:
   Date: (add today's date)
   To: (add the name of the person you are writing to)
   From: (add your name)
   Subject: (tell what you are writing about)
B. State which location you think the company should choose for the new resort.
C. State two reasons you think this is the best choice. Support your argument with details from the photos.
D. State one counterargument that might be raised against your choice. Base it on your knowledge of the physical processes at work in the place you chose.
E. Respond to the counterargument by explaining why you think it should not change the president's mind.
F. Conclude by restating your recommendation.

Applying Geography Skills: Sample Responses

1. The two types of mountains shown in the diagram are fault-block mountains and fold mountains.
2. Both types of mountains are formed by the physical process of tectonic movement.
3. Mountain formation today is most likely to be going on at the edges of tectonic plates where the collision of plates forces Earth's crust to fold or along faults where blocks of crust are pushed upward.

Exploring the Essential Question: Sample Response

Step 1: Students should circle either Location A or B.

Step 2: The memo should include the elements listed in the prompt. These elements are identified by letter in the response below.

A. Date: January 20, 2007
   To: Alexei Orlov
   From: Tanya Ferrer
   Subject: Location of Ecotourism Resort
B. I recommend building our company's new resort beside Ring Lake at the Krenitsyn Volcano.
C. I chose this location because it has spectacular views for visitors to enjoy. Ring Lake will also attract people who like to fish, swim, or go boating.
D. Some may argue that building a resort so close to a volcano is dangerous because it could erupt again.
E. I would point out that being close to a volcano will attract tourists. Many people want to explore volcanic activity. Besides, we will have time to move people to safety if the volcano does erupt again.
F. I hope you will agree with me that our new resort should be built on the shores of Ring Lake.

Mastering the Content Answer Key

1. A	2. B	3. A	4. B
5. A	6. C	7. D	8. D

Applying Geography Skills Scoring Rubric

Score	General Description
2	Student responds to all parts of the task. Response is correct and clear.
1	Student responds to some parts of the task. Response is mostly correct.
0	Response does not match the task or is incorrect.

Exploring the Essential Question Scoring Rubric

Score	General Description
3	Student responds to all parts of the task. Response is correct, clear, and supported by details.
2	Student responds to most or all parts of the task. Response is generally correct but may lack details.
1	Student responds to at least one part of the task. Response may contain errors and lack details.
0	Response does not match the task or is incorrect.

Act Out a Physical Process

You have just read about a physical process that shapes Earth, and your teacher has projected a diagram of that process. You will now work with your group to re-create that diagram and demonstrate the physical process in action. Each member of your group will become a feature of the physical process.

Step 1: Assign each member of your group to a certain role in the physical process. Make sure everyone knows what feature he or she is and can answer these questions:

- What part of this physical process do you represent?
- Describe your job or function in this physical process.
- What effect do you have on the other parts of the physical process? What effect do you have on the land?

Step 2: Work together to physically re-create the diagram of the physical process. Brainstorm ideas on how each person can bring to life his or her part of the process. Talk about any motions or sounds each person could make. Is there is a particular order in which the movements or sounds should be made? Who should go first, second, or third? Or should all members begin their parts at the same time?

Step 3: Rehearse how you will bring this physical process to life in 30 seconds or less. Make your presentation as realistic and detailed as possible.

Analyze Images of Physical Processes

Work with your partner to analyze the 12 placards around the room.
For each placard, you will

- determine which physical process is represented.
- decide where in Russia the image was taken, using clues in your
  book to guide you.

Step 1: Visit one of the placards. Observe the image carefully. Talk with
your partner about these questions:

- What are some interesting details in this image?
- What are some of the physical features pictured—for example, mountains, rivers, lakes, valleys?
- Which physical processes could have played a role in shaping the land
  you see?

Step 2: Decide which physical process the image represents. With
your partner, guess which physical process—tectonic movement, volcanic
activity, erosion, or glaciation—the image represents. Then turn to the
second part of Reading Notes 17. Write the placard's letter in one of the
boxes under that heading.

**Step 3: Choose a few details from the image to explain why you think
it relates to that physical process.** List them in the box.

**Step 4: Examine the relief map of Russia, and record where you think
this image might have been taken.** Study the relief map of Russia in
Section 17.2 of your book. Using details about the land that you see in
the image, choose two to four locations where this image might have
been taken. Using the map in your Reading Notes, record the numbers of
these locations in the box.

**Step 5: Read the appropriate section (Section 17.4, 17.6, 17.8, or 17.10)
to find more clues about where this scene really exists in Russia.**
Find and read the section that matches the physical process represented
in this image. The reading describes some of the landforms in Russia.
Use this information to decide which location matches the placard.
In your Reading Notes, record the number of the location you think
definitely matches this image.

Step 6: Annotate the map of Russia in your Reading Notes. Next to
the number on the map that represents where this image was taken, write
the placard's letter and the name of the physical feature that is shown.

For each of Sections 17.3, 17.5, 17.7, and 17.9, follow these steps:

1. Read the section.

2. Label the diagram that corresponds to the physical process described in that section.

3. Answer the question for that section.

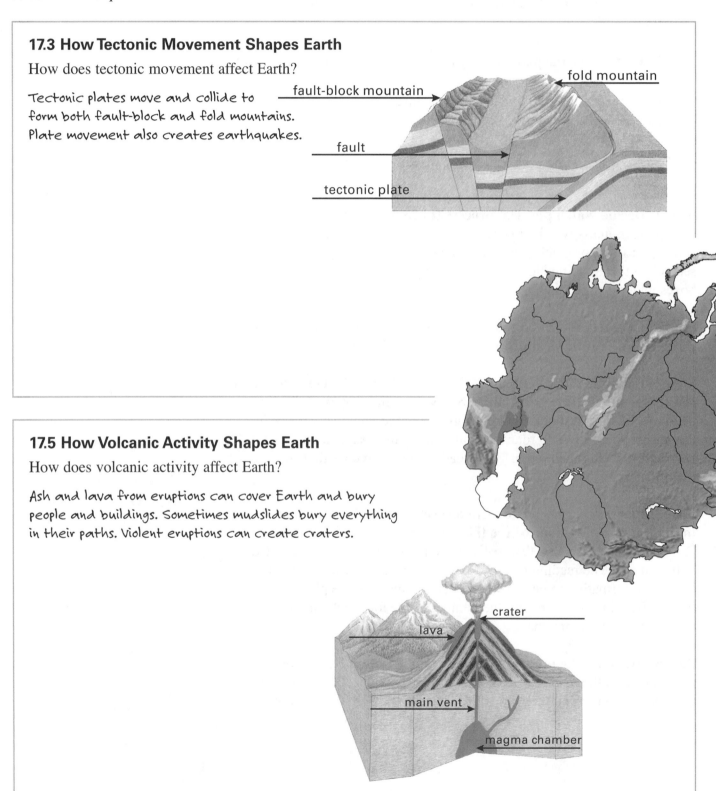

17.3 How Tectonic Movement Shapes Earth

How does tectonic movement affect Earth?

Tectonic plates move and collide to form both fault-block and fold mountains. Plate movement also creates earthquakes.

fault-block mountain

fold mountain

fault

tectonic plate

17.5 How Volcanic Activity Shapes Earth

How does volcanic activity affect Earth?

Ash and lava from eruptions can cover Earth and bury people and buildings. Sometimes mudslides bury everything in their paths. Violent eruptions can create craters.

crater

lava

main vent

magma chamber

17.7 How Erosion Shapes the Landscape

How does erosion affect the landscape?

Wind, water, ice, and gravity all erode the land. Wind carries away soil. Rivers can erode the land to form valleys. Oceans can wear away land to form banks and cliffs. Glaciers can carve out valleys and create new landforms.

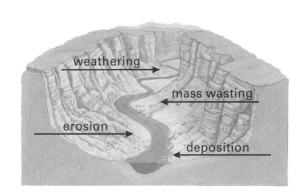

17.9 How Glaciation Shapes the Landscape

How does glaciation affect the landscape?

Glaciers can grind rock into soil and push rocks and dirt great distances. They create lakes, pointed mountain peaks called "horns," and U-shaped valleys.

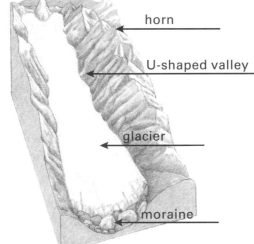

Follow the directions your teacher has projected to complete this part of your Reading Notes.

Tectonic Movement

Placard letter: A
Details you see in the image: snowcapped mountains
Possible locations of this scene (numbers from the map):
Actual location: 1, Caucasus Mountains

Placard letter: J
Details you see in the image: jagged mountain peak
Possible locations of this scene (numbers from the map):
Actual location: 4, Mount Manaraga, Ural Mountains

Placard letter: I
Details you see in the image: steep ridges and exposed rock
Possible locations of this scene (numbers from the map):
Actual location: 7, West Sayan Mountains

Volcanic Activity

Placard letter: B
Details from image: volcano ash, smoke plume

Possible locations of this scene (numbers from the map):
Actual location: 10, Kliuchevskoi Volcano

Placard letter: G
Details you see in the image: volcano, crater lake
Possible locations of this scene (numbers from the map):
Actual location: 12, Krenitsyn Volcano

Placard letter: K
Details you see in the image: crater, lake, bright blue water
Possible locations of this scene (numbers from the map):
Actual location: 11, Maly Semyachik Volcano

Placard letter: D
Details you see in the image: river, sedimentation, cloudy green water
Possible locations of this scene (numbers from the map):
Actual location: 2, Volga River/Caspian Sea

Erosion

Placard letter: E
Details you see in the image: river, eroded riverbank
Possible locations of this scene (numbers from the map):
Actual location: 6, Amur River

Placard letter: F
Details you see in the image: river

Possible locations of this scene (numbers from the map):
Actual location: 8, Lena River

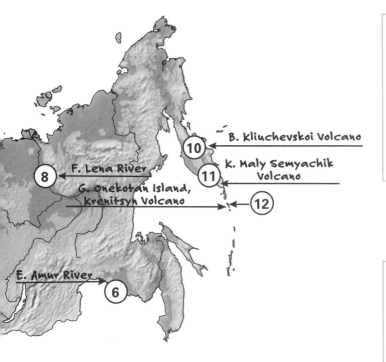

B. Kliuchevskoi Volcano
K. Maly Semyachik Volcano
F. Lena River
G. Onekotan Island, Krenitsyn Volcano
E. Amur River

Glaciation

Placard letter: H
Details you see in the image: swampy, holes filled with water
Possible locations of this scene (numbers from the map):
Actual location: 5, Yamal Peninsula

Placard letter: C
Details you see in the image: ice, snow, mountains, avalanche debris
Possible locations of this scene (numbers from the map):
Actual location: 3, Kolka Glacier

Placard letter: L
Details you see in the image: ice, snow, downward movement of snow
Possible locations of this scene (numbers from the map):
Actual location: 9, Amanauzsky Glacier

New Nation-States from the Old Soviet Empire: Will They Succeed?

Overview

To better understand why political maps can change, students analyze economic and political information about five nation-states that formed after the breakup of the Soviet Union. In a **Writing for Understanding** activity, students gather information from maps, charts, and their reading to determine which of the five nation-states are most likely to be politically and economically successful. They use this information to recommend one of these nation-states as the most promising site for a future fictitious world games competition.

Objectives

Students will

- define and explain the importance of these key geographic terms: *ethnic group, nation, nationalism, nation-state, state.*
- identify some major factors that affect whether a nation will succeed or collapse.
- analyze some of the factors that may determine the success of the nation-states that have developed out of the former Soviet Union.
- examine other regions in the world where new nations are forming.

Materials

- *Geography Alive! Regions and People*
- Interactive Student Notebooks
- Transparencies 18A–18C
- Station Directions 18 (6 copies plus 1 transparency)
- Station Masters 18A–18K (6 of each)
- Student Handout 18 (1 per student or 1 transparency)
- CD Tracks 14–19

Preview

1 **Project the first map on *Transparency 18A: Preview 18*** **and have students complete Part 1 of Preview 18 in their Interactive Student Notebooks.** Then ask students to share their ideas about the three questions in Part 1:

- What do you notice about the country on this map?
- What might be some advantages to controlling a country this large? *Possible answer: more available resources, more land for agriculture and industry, larger workforce*
- What might be some disadvantages to controlling a country this large? *Possible answer: more people who need jobs, more housing needed, more territory to maintain*

Transparency 18A   Preview 18

2 **Project the second map on Transparency 18A and have students complete Part 2 of the Preview.** Then have students share their ideas about the questions in Part 2:

- What differences do you notice between the two maps? *Possible answer: more boundary lines*
- What might have happened to cause these changes? *Possible answer: These countries declared their independence or gained independence, the Soviet Union government was overthrown, the Soviet Union collapsed.*
- How might the changes in this region affect the people living there? *Possible answer: economic hardships for these new nations as they struggle to form; political instability; more national unity in the new, smaller nations*

3 **Explain the connection between the Preview and the upcoming activity.** Tell students that in this lesson they will learn that in 1991 the Soviet Union broke apart and 15 new nation-states were formed. Since that time, however, many of these nation-states have struggled with the same issues that confronted the former Soviet Union. In this activity, students will examine those issues and evaluate which nation-states are faring better and which are struggling.

Essential Question and Geoterms

1 **Introduce Chapter 18 in *Geography Alive! Regions and People*.** Have students examine the photograph of the statue of Felix Dzerzhinsky being toppled. Ask,

- What do you see?
- Why do you think these people have gathered here? What might they be doing?
- What message do you think they are trying to send? To whom are they trying to send it?

2 Explain that in this chapter, students will learn about the collapse of the Soviet Union in 1991 and examine some of the issues confronting the new nation-states that have formed. Have students read Section 18.1. Ask them to point out details from their reading that might explain what the people in the photograph are doing and why they are doing it.

3 Introduce the Graphic Organizer and the Essential Question. Have students examine the illustration and read the accompanying text. Make sure they understand the Essential Question, *What factors contribute to the success or failure of new nation-states?* You may want to post the Essential Question in the room or write it on the board for the duration of the activity.

4 Have students read Section 18.2. Then have them work individually or in pairs to complete Geoterms 18 in their Inter-active Student Notebooks. (**Note:** Students will complete their Reading Notes for Section 18.2 during the Writing for Under-standing activity.) Have them share their answers with another student, or have volunteers share their answers with the class.

Writing for Understanding

1 Prepare materials. Before class, prepare materials and arrange the room for a "tour" of the former Soviet Union.

- Make six copies of each of *Station Masters 18A–18K* and six copies plus one transparency of *Station Directions 18: Visiting Nation-States in the Former Soviet Union.*

- Move furniture to the edges of the room.

- Create six Kazakhstan "visitor centers" by taping Station Directions 18 as well as copies of *Station Master 18A: Kazakhstan, Station Master 18B: Kazakhstan,* and *Station Master 18K: Comparative Data* to desks or walls throughout the room. Each visitor center can accommodate two groups of students.

- Set up rows of chairs in groups of three, with an aisle down the center of the rows, to resemble the seats on an airplane. All seats should have a view of the projector screen. (See the classroom diagram on the next page.)

- Divide students into mixed-ability groups of three. You may want to prepare a seating chart that shows them who is in their group and where they will sit.

Geoterms 18

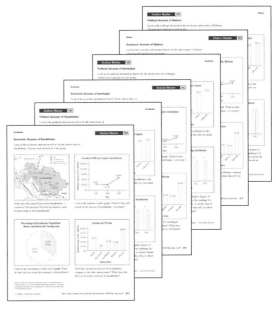
Station Masters 18A–18F

Station Directions 18

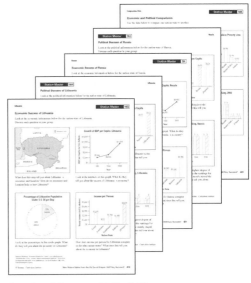
Station Masters 18G–18K

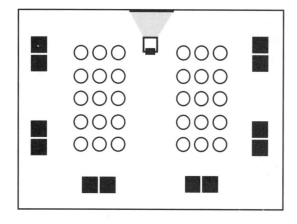

■■ Visitor center

2 **Have students board the plane as you introduce the activity.**
Have students form a single-file line on one side of the room.
You may wish to act as a flight attendant and welcome them
aboard Flight 405 to Moscow, Russia's capital city. Have them
walk down the aisle and find their seats. Explain that, as representatives of the (fictitious) International GeoGames Committee,
their job is to scout out the best possible site for a future Geo-
Games, an Olympic-type event that will host athletes from many
countries. The committee has decided to choose a site in one of
five nation-states of the former Soviet Union. Acting as representatives, students will gather enough information about each
nation-state to enable them to decide which is most successful,
both economically and politically, and would thus be the most
capable of hosting an upcoming GeoGames.

3 **Explain the activity, and have students complete the
Reading Notes for Section 18.2.** Have students turn to Reading
Notes 18. Point out the "scorecards" in Sections 18.3 to 18.7,
which they will be using to judge each nation-state. Make sure
students notice the factors listed on the scorecards for both economic and political success. Explain that students will be stopping at "visitor centers" in five cities to learn more about these
nation-states. At each stop, they will be given information about
a variety of factors that will help them decide which nation-state
they think is most successful. To be able to analyze this information, they must understand the various factors that help determine political and economic success; Section 18.2 explores this.
Have groups complete the notes for Section 18.2, and then use
Guide to Reading Notes 18 to check their answers.

Reading Notes 18

4 **Start the tour by playing CD Track 14, "Welcome to Moscow," and projecting** *Transparency 18B: The Soviet Union.* After students have listened to the recording, ask them to find Moscow and the five cities they will be visiting—Astana, Baku, Minsk, Vilnius, and Irkutsk—on the map.

5 **Project Station Directions 18, and review the directions for how students will conduct their "tour" through the nation-states of the former Soviet Union.** Answer any questions students have.

Transparency 18B

6 **Play CD Track 15, "Welcome to Kazakhstan," and have groups visit their first city.** After playing the welcoming message, explain that in a moment students will carefully disembark the plane. In their groups of three, they will go to one of the "visitor centers" set up by the local chamber of commerce, where they will learn a little more about the nation-state of Kazakhstan. Have groups go to the visitor centers, and remind them to carefully read and follow the steps on Station Directions 18. Monitor their progress by circulating while they work.

7 **Have students complete the Reading Notes for Section 18.3.** Have students retake their seats aboard the plane. Instruct them to finish their Reading Notes for this section by filling in the remainder of the scorecard, answering the two questions, and annotating the map. Point out that the projected transparency contains the directions for completing their Reading Notes. While they are working, create "new" visitor centers by replacing Station Masters 18A and 18B with *Station Master 18C: Azerbaijan* and *Station Master 18D: Azerbaijan.* Leave Station Directions 18 projected.

Reading Notes 18

8 **Repeat Steps 6 and 7 for the remaining four sites.** For each of the other sites, play the corresponding CD Track 16–19 to welcome students to that city. Have groups go to the new visitor centers and begin work on the Reading Notes for that section. Finally, have them reboard the plane to complete their notes while you replace the station masters with those for the next city.

9 **Conduct a wrap-up of the activity by having students rank their choices in order of best choice for a GeoGames site to worst choice for a GeoGames site.** Explain that they now must report back to the International GeoGames Committee about their findings. Follow these steps:

• In their groups of three, have students rank the five nation-states from best choice to worst choice as a future GeoGames site. Remind them that they are looking for nations with long-term potential, since these GeoGames may not be played for several years, and that they should consider both political and economic factors.

- Have groups write their rankings, and a short rationale for each, on a separate sheet of paper.

- Have each group select a Presenter to report the group's top choice and their rationale. If there is any variation, encourage students to engage in a debate-style discussion to try to reach a consensus. (**Note:** Expect many students to consider Lithuania the best choice, as it has little if any ethnic or religious conflict, strong economic growth, a relatively stable government, an advantageous location between Russia and Western Europe, as well as a short coastline that makes the country more accessible to trade.)

- Choose a new Presenter in each group to report the second choice and rationale. Again, if there is variation, encourage students to reach a consensus.

After the presentations, ask students to consider these questions: *What do you think was the most important factor to consider when deciding whether a nation-state was a good place to host a future GeoGames? The least important factor?*

10 Distribute or project a transparency of *Student Handout 18: Writing a Letter of Proposal,* and review the directions. Have students write their letters.

Student Handout 18

Global Connections

1 Introduce the Global Connections. Have students read Section 18.8. Then explain that they will now see how some of the issues in this activity play out on a global scale. Tell students that the factors that played a role in the breakup of the Soviet Union, and that continue to play a role in the survival of these new nation-states, have influenced the breakup and formation of other nations around the world. Where are these factors most evident in the world today? And what factors have played a role in the formation and success of recently independent nations?

2 Project *Transparency 18C: Global Connections.* Cover the table on the transparency, and help students analyze the map by asking,

- **What does this map tell you?**

- **During what time period do you notice a large increase in the number of nations in the world?**
  The 20 years between 1945 and 1965 show the greatest number of new nations, mostly in Africa as well as South and

Transparency 18C

Southeast Asia. More than 50 nations gained independence in this time span.

• **Where on the map do you notice the greatest increase in nations in the last 60 years?**
Africa and Asia have seen the greatest increase in new nations in the last 60 years.

3 Have students turn to **Section 18.9.** Independently or as a class, have them read the text on the left and analyze the other information in the section. Uncover the table on the transparency, and facilitate a class discussion by asking,

• **What were these new nation-states before they gained their independence?**

• **How did these new nation-states gain their independence?**

• **Which of these new nations are most likely to succeed?**

Processing

There is no Processing for this lesson. The proposal letter functions as the Processing assignment.

Online Resources

For more information on new nation-states, refer students to Online Resources for *Geography Alive! Regions and People* at www.teachtci.com.

Assessment

Masters for assessment appear on the next three pages followed by answers and scoring rubrics.

Assessment | 18

Mastering the Content

Shade in the oval by the letter of the best answer for each question.

1. Which of these terms refers to an independent country whose people mostly share a common identity?
   - ○ A. colonial empire
   - ○ B. ethnic group
   - ○ C. nation-state
   - ○ D. plural society

2. What is a feeling of pride and loyalty toward one's country called?
   - ○ A. pluralism
   - ○ B. nationalism
   - ○ C. self-respect
   - ○ D. cultural identity

3. Which of these is an example of a failed state?
   - ○ A. the Azerbaijan Republic
   - ○ B. the European Union
   - ○ C. the United Kingdom
   - ○ D. the Soviet Union

4. Based on the graphs below, which of these is **most likely** to be a major problem facing Kazakhstan?

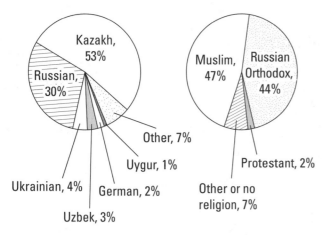

Ethnic Diversity

Kazakh, 53%
Russian, 30%
Ukrainian, 4%
Uzbek, 3%
German, 2%
Uygur, 1%
Other, 7%

Religious Diversity

Muslim, 47%
Russian Orthodox, 44%
Other or no religion, 7%
Protestant, 2%

   - ○ A. religious conflict between Muslims and Jews
   - ○ B. ethnic tension between Russians and Kazakhs
   - ○ C. the settlement of Ukrainian and Uzbek refugees
   - ○ D. the growing power of the Russian Orthodox Church

5. What natural resource has become Azerbaijan's leading export?
   - ○ A. oil
   - ○ B. coal
   - ○ C. copper ore
   - ○ D. natural gas

6. Life expectancy in Belarus has dropped since 1990. Which of these has contributed **most** to this trend?
   - ○ A. the collapse of the Soviet Union
   - ○ B. the Chernobyl power plant explosion
   - ○ C. the Chechen independence movement
   - ○ D. the conflict between Muslims and Christians

7. In 2004, Lithuania became a member of the
   - ○ A. Baltic States.
   - ○ B. Soviet Union.
   - ○ C. United Nations.
   - ○ D. European Union.

8. Which statement is **best** supported by the information on the graph below?

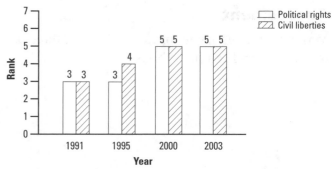

Freedom Index Ranking, Russia

☐ Political rights
▨ Civil liberties

Rank / Year

1991: 3 3
1995: 3 4
2000: 5 5
2003: 5 5

On this scale, 1 represents the highest degree of freedom, and 7 the lowest.

   - ○ A. Russia became less free between 1991 and 2003.
   - ○ B. Russia became more free between 1991 and 2003.
   - ○ C. Russia became a democracy between 1991 and 2003.
   - ○ D. Russia became a failed state between 1991 and 2003.

Applying Geography Skills:
Drawing Conclusions from Graphic Data

Use the graph, table, and your knowledge of geography to complete the
tasks below. Write your answers in complete sentences.

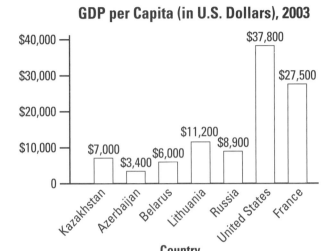

GDP per Capita (in U.S. Dollars), 2003

Life Expectancy and Infant Mortality, 2003

Country	Life Expectancy (years)	Infant Mortality (deaths per 1,000 births)
Kazakhstan	63	59
Azerbaijan	63	82
Belarus	68	14
Lithuania	70	14
Russia	68	20
United States	77	7
France	79	4

1. Identify the country in which GDP per capita is closest to that of the
   United States.

2. Compare life expectancy and the infant mortality rate in Belarus
   and France.

3. Compare life expectancy in Azerbaijan to that of the other countries
   on the table and graph. Also compare the infant mortality rate and
   GDP per capita. Summarize what you see in one sentence.

4. Draw a conclusion about the relationship between the data in the table
   and the data in the graph.

Test Terms Glossary
To **summarize** means
to briefly present the
main points.

A **conclusion** is a
judgment reached after
looking at the facts.

Exploring the Essential Question

What factors contribute to the success and failure of new nation-states?

In Chapter 18, you learned that many factors can play a role in the success or failure of new countries. Now you will use what you learned. Use the information in the table below and your knowledge of geography to complete this task.

Country Comparison: Eritrea and Slovakia

	Infant Mortality Rate, 2005	Life Expectancy at Birth, 2005	GDP per Capita, 2004	Ethnic Groups, 2001	Freedom Index Ranking, 2005
Eritrea	75 deaths per 1,000 births	52 years	$900	Tigrinya, 50% Tigre & Kunama, 40% Afar, 4% Saho, 3% Other, 3%	political rights, 7 civil liberties, 7
Slovakia	7 deaths per 1,000 births	75 years	$14,500	Slovak, 86% Hungarian, 10% Roma, 2% Other, 2%	political rights, 1 civil liberties, 1

The Task: Comparing Two New Countries' Chances of Success

This table shows data for two nation-states that became independent in 1993. Your task is to decide which one is more likely to succeed.

Step 1: Compare life expectancy and infant mortality rate for the countries. Circle the figures that indicate a better quality of life.

Step 2: Compare the GDP figures. Circle the per capita GDP of the country with the stronger economy.

Step 3: Compare the ethnic makeup of each country. Circle the single largest ethnic group in terms of percent of the country's population.

Step 4: Compare the Freedom Index Rankings of the countries. On this scale, 1 represents the highest degree of freedom, and 7 the lowest. Circle the rankings that indicate a free country.

Step 5: Write a paragraph comparing these two countries and their chances for success. Your paragraph should have these elements:

A. a title that identifies your topic
B. a topic sentence that states your thesis, or position. This thesis statement should tell the reader which country you think has the better chance of success.
C. body sentences that use data from the table to support your thesis
D. a concluding sentence that restates your thesis

Writing Tips: Drafting a Thesis Statement
A thesis statement is a sentence that tells what you plan to prove or explain. It usually appears at the beginning of a paragraph or essay. It should give readers a clear idea of what to expect when they read your piece.

Example: *Eritrea and Slovakia both became nation-states in 1993, but their chances of success are very different.*

Applying Geography Skills: Sample Responses

1. France is the country with a per capita GDP closest to that of the United States.
2. Belarus has a higher infant mortality rate and a lower life expectancy than France.
3. Azerbaijan has the highest infant mortality rate, the lowest life expectancy, and the lowest GDP per capita of the seven countries.
4. As GDP per capita increases in a country, life expectancy increases and the infant mortality rate decreases.

Exploring the Essential Question: Sample Response

Step 1: Students should have circled the life expectancy and infant mortality rate of Slovakia.

Step 2: Students should have circled the GDP per capita of Slovakia.

Step 3: Students should have circled the Slovak ethnic group, which makes up 86 percent of the population of Slovakia.

Step 4: Students should have circled the rankings of 1 for Slovakia.

Step 5: The paragraph should include the elements listed in the prompt.

Two New Countries' Chances of Success

Both Eritrea and Slovakia became nation-states in 1993, but their chances of success are very different. Slovakia has a healthy population and a good economy. Its infant mortality rate is low. Its people live long lives. In contrast, Eritrea is a very poor nation. Its infant mortality rate is high. Life expectancy is just 52 years. Most people living in Slovakia belong to a single ethnic group. Eritrea has two large ethnic groups. This could lead to ethnic tensions there. Slovakia's government respects the rights of its people. This is not true of Eritrea's government. For all of these reasons, Slovakia is more likely to succeed than Eritrea.

Mastering the Content Answer Key

1. C	2. B	3. D	4. B
5. A	6. B	7. D	8. A

Applying Geography Skills Scoring Rubric

Score	General Description
2	Student responds to all parts of the task. Response is correct and clear.
1	Student responds to some parts of the task. Response is mostly correct.
0	Response does not match the task or is incorrect.

Exploring the Essential Question Scoring Rubric

Score	General Description
3	Student responds to all parts of the task. Response is correct, clear, and supported by details.
2	Student responds to most or all parts of the task. Response is generally correct but may lack details.
1	Student responds to at least one part of the task. Response may contain errors and lack details.
0	Response does not match the task or is incorrect.

Gather Information About Nation-States

Follow these steps for each nation-state you visit:

1. With your group, go to a visitor center in this nation-state's capital city.

2. Locate the section of your Reading Notes for this nation-state.

3. Examine the information and discuss the questions on the two station masters for this nation-state. Use Station Master 18K to compare this nation-state to other nation-states.

4. Read the related section of Chapter 18 in *Geography Alive! Regions and People*. Then talk about these questions with your group:
   - What new information did you learn about this nation-state?
   - With everything you've learned, do you feel more positive or more negative about this nation-state?

5. The scorecard lists several factors for both economic and political success. Give this nation-state a score of 1, 2, 3, 4, or 5 for each factor. A score of 1 is the highest.

6. Return to your seat on the plane. Work with your group to complete this section of Reading Notes. Give each nation-state an "overall" score in both economic and political success. Add comments to explain each of your overall scores. Include information from at least two factors you analyzed. Then answer the two questions under the scorecard.

7. On the map in your Reading Notes, draw and label *three* new important facts about the political or economic success of this nation-state. For example, if you learned that this nation-state exports a lot of diamonds, which would help its economy, you might draw a diamond on the map and label it "diamond exports."

Economic Success of Kazakhstan

Look at the economic information below for the nation-state of Kazakhstan. Discuss each question in your group.

What does this map tell you about Kazakhstan's resources? Its location? How do its resources and location help or hurt Kazakhstan?

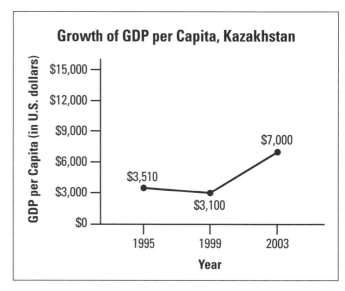

Look at the numbers on this graph. What do they tell you about the success of Kazakhstan's economy?

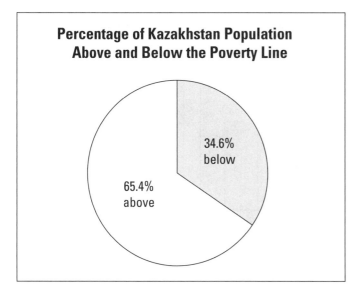

Look at the percentages in this circle graph. What do they tell you about the economy in Kazakhstan?

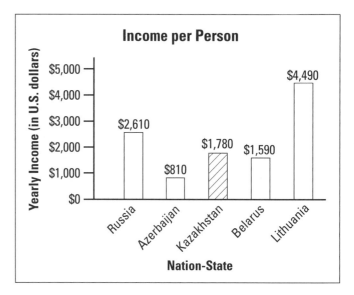

How does income per person for Kazakhstan compare to the other nation-states? What does this tell you about the economy in Kazakhstan?

Sources: *Infoplease,* "Economic Statistics by Country," www.infoplease.com. *The World Bank Group,* "Country Statistical Information Database," "2004 World Development Indicators,"www.worldbank.org. *The World Factbook* 1995, 1999, Central Intelligence Agency.

Station Master | **18B**

Political Success of Kazakhstan

Look at the political information below for the nation-state of Kazakhstan. Discuss each question in your group.

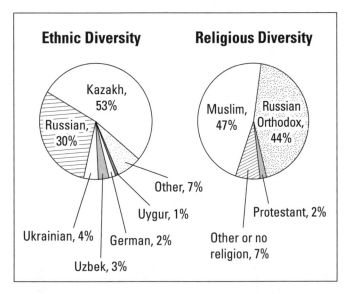

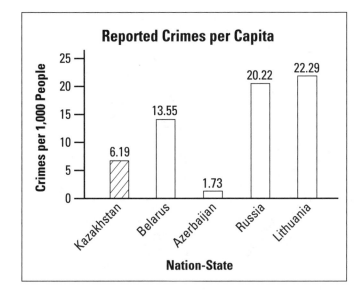

Look at these circle graphs. What do they tell you about possible ethnic and religious tension in Kazakhstan?

Compare the level of crime in Kazakhstan to the other nation-states. What might this tell you about security in Kazakhstan?

Life Expectancy and Infant Mortality in Kazakhstan

Year	Life Expectancy (years)	Infant Mortality Rate (deaths per 1,000 births)
1995	68	40
1999	63	59
2003	63	59

Notice how the numbers change in this table. What might this tell you about quality of life for people in Kazakhstan?

On this scale, 1 represents the highest degree of freedom, and 7 the lowest. Have the rankings for Kazakhstan gone up, gone down, or mostly stayed the same over time? What does this tell you about rights and freedoms in Kazakhstan?

Sources: *Freedom House,* "Freedom in the World Country Scores: 1972–2003," www.freedomhouse.org. *United Nations Office on Drugs and Crime,* "The Seventh United Nations Survey on Crime Trends and the Operations of Criminal Justice Systems (1998–2000)," www.unodc.org/unodc. *The World Factbook 1995, 1999, 2003,* Central Intelligence Agency.

Economic Success of Azerbaijan

Look at the economic information below for the nation-state of Azerbaijan. Discuss each question in your group.

What does this map tell you about Azerbaijan's resources? Its location? How do its resources and location help or hurt Azerbaijan?

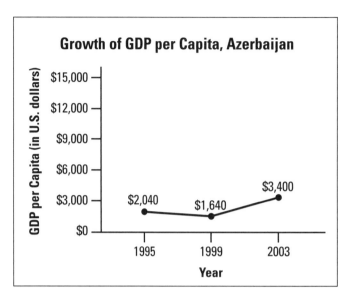

Look at the numbers on this graph. What do they tell you about the success of Azerbaijan's economy?

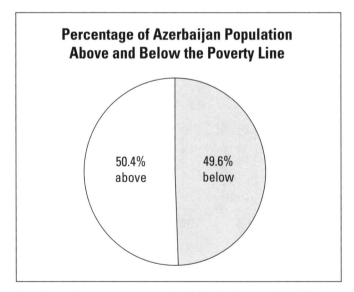

Look at the percentages in this circle graph. What do they tell you about the economy in Azerbaijan?

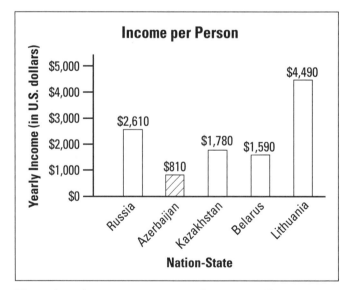

How does income per person for Azerbaijan compare to the other nation-states? What does this tell you about the economy in Azerbaijan?

Sources: *Infoplease*, "Economic Statistics by Country," www.infoplease.com. *The World Bank Group*, "Country Statistical Information Database," "2004 World Development Indicators,"www.worldbank.org. *The World Factbook* 1995, 1999, Central Intelligence Agency.

Political Success of Azerbaijan

Look at the political information below for the nation-state of Azerbaijan.
Discuss each question in your group.

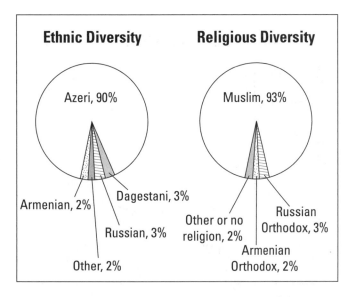

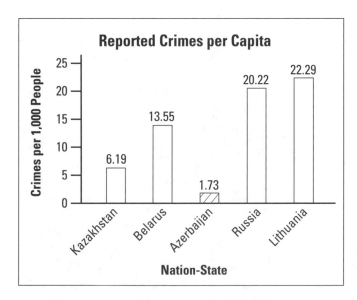

Look at these circle graphs. What do they tell you about possible ethnic and religious tension in Azerbaijan?

Compare the level of crime in Azerbaijan to the other nation-states. What might this tell you about security in Azerbaijan?

Life Expectancy and Infant Mortality in Azerbaijan

Year	Life Expectancy (years)	Infant Mortality Rate (deaths per 1,000 births)
1995	71	35
1999	63	83
2003	63	82

Notice how the numbers in this table change. What might this tell you about quality of life for people in Azerbaijan?

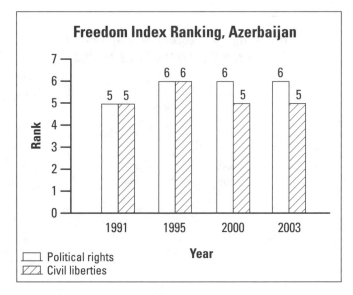

On this scale, 1 represents the highest degree of freedom, and 7 the lowest. Have the rankings for Azerbaijan gone up, gone down, or mostly stayed the same over time? What does this tell you about rights and freedoms in Azerbaijan?

Sources: *Freedom House,* "Freedom in the World Country Scores: 1972–2003," www.freedomhouse.org. *United Nations Office on Drugs and Crime,* "The Seventh United Nations Survey on Crime Trends and the Operations of Criminal Justice Systems (1998–2000)," www.unodc.org/unodc. *The World Factbook 1995, 1999, 2003,* Central Intelligence Agency.

© Teachers' Curriculum Institute

Economic Success of Belarus

Look at the economic information below for the nation-state of Belarus.
Discuss each question in your group.

What does this map tell you about Belarus's resources? Its location? How do its resources and location help or hurt Belarus?

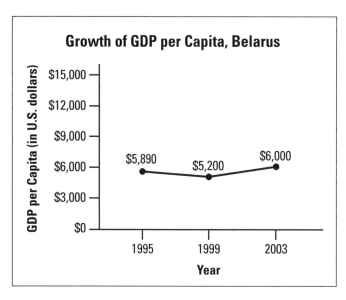

Look at the numbers on this graph. What do they tell you about the success of Belarus's economy?

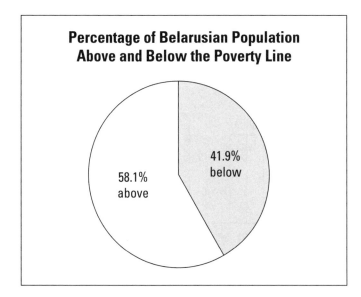

Look at the percentages in this circle graph. What do they tell you about the economy in Belarus?

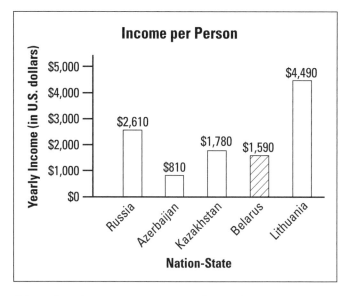

How does income per person for Belarus compare to the other nation-states? What does this tell you about the economy in Belarus?

Sources: *Infoplease*, "Economic Statistics by Country," www.infoplease.com. *The World Bank Group*, "Country Statistical Information Database," "2004 World Development Indicators," www.worldbank.org. *The World Factbook* 1995, 1999, Central Intelligence Agency.

Political Success of Belarus

Look at the political information below for the nation-state of Belarus.
Discuss each question in your group.

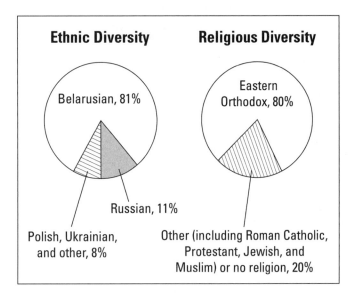

Look at these circle graphs. What do they tell you about possible ethnic and religious tension in Belarus?

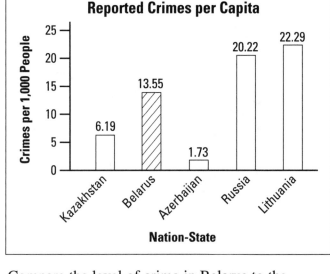

Compare the level of crime in Belarus to the other nation-states. What might this tell you about security in Belarus?

Life Expectancy and Infant Mortality in Belarus

Year	Life Expectancy (years)	Infant Mortality Rate (deaths per 1,000 births)
1995	71	19
1999	68	14
2003	68	14

Notice how the numbers in this table change. What might this tell you about quality of life for people in Belarus?

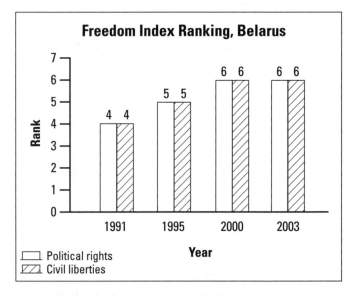

On this scale, 1 represents the highest degree of freedom, and 7 the lowest. Have the rankings for Belarus gone up, gone down, or mostly stayed the same over time? What does this tell you about rights and freedoms in Belarus?

Sources: *Freedom House*, "Freedom in the World Country Scores: 1972–2003," www.freedomhouse.org. *United Nations Office on Drugs and Crime*, "The Seventh United Nations Survey on Crime Trends and the Operations of Criminal Justice Systems (1998–2000)," www.unodc.org/unodc. *The World Factbook 1995, 1999, 2003*, Central Intelligence Agency.

Economic Success of Lithuania

Look at the economic information below for the nation-state of Lithuania.
Discuss each question in your group.

What does this map tell you about Lithuania's resources and location? How do its resources and location help or hurt Lithuania?

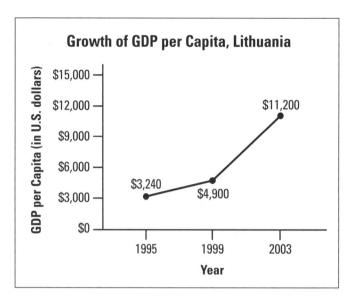

Look at the numbers on this graph. What do they tell you about the success of Lithuania's economy?

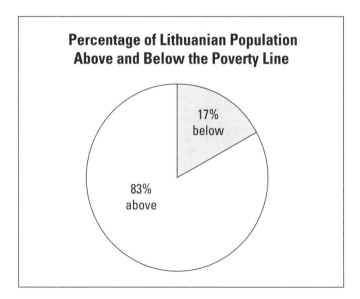

Look at the percentages in this circle graph. What do they tell you about the economy in Lithuania?

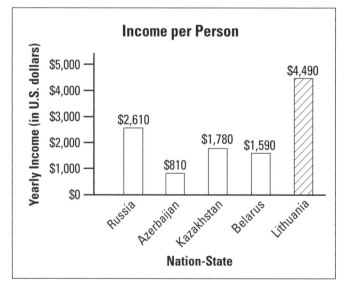

How does income per person for Lithuania compare to the other nation-states? What does this tell you about the economy in Lithuania?

Sources: *Infoplease*, "Economic Statistics by Country," www.infoplease.com. *The World Bank Group*, "Country Statistical Information Database," "2004 World Development Indicators,"www.worldbank.org. *The World Factbook* 1995, 1999, Central Intelligence Agency.

Station Master | **18H**

Political Success of Lithuania

Look at the political information below for the nation-state of Lithuania.
Discuss each question in your group.

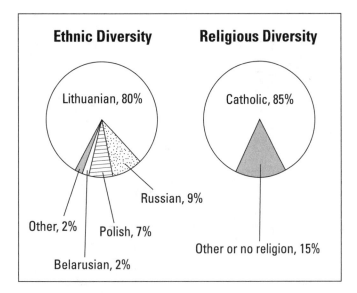

Look at these circle graphs. What do they tell
you about possible ethnic and religious tension
in Lithuania?

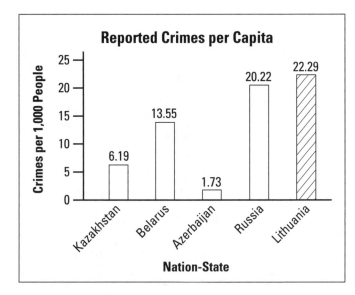

Compare the level of crime in Lithuania to the
other nation-states. What might this tell you
about security in Lithuania?

Life Expectancy and Infant Mortality in Lithuania

Year	Life Expectancy (years)	Infant Mortality Rate (deaths per 1,000 births)
1995	71	17
1999	69	15
2003	70	14

Notice how the numbers in this table change.
What might this tell you about quality of life
for people in Lithuania?

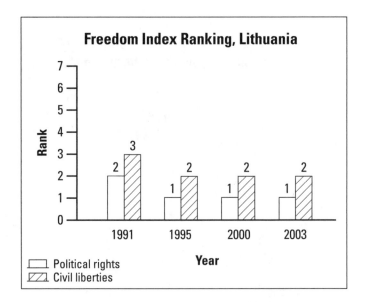

On this scale, 1 represents the highest degree of
freedom, and 7 the lowest. Have the rankings for
Lithuania gone up, gone down, or mostly stayed
the same over time? What does this tell you about
rights and freedoms in Lithuania?

Sources: *Freedom House*, "Freedom in the World Country Scores: 1972–2003," www.freedomhouse.org.
United Nations Office on Drugs and Crime, "The Seventh United Nations Survey on Crime Trends and
the Operations of Criminal Justice Systems (1998–2000)," www.unodc.org/unodc. *The World Factbook
1995, 1999, 2003*, Central Intelligence Agency.

Economic Success of Russia

Look at the economic information below for the nation-state of Russia.
Discuss each question in your group.

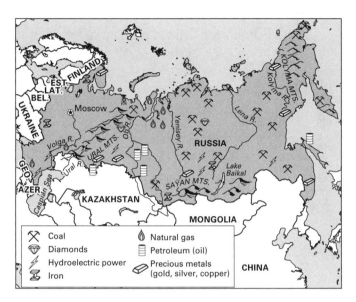

What does this map tell you about Russia's resources? Its location? How do its resources and location help or hurt Russia?

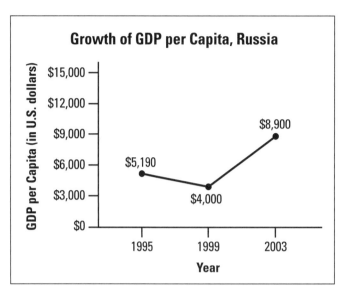

Look at the numbers on this graph. What do they tell you about the success of Russia's economy?

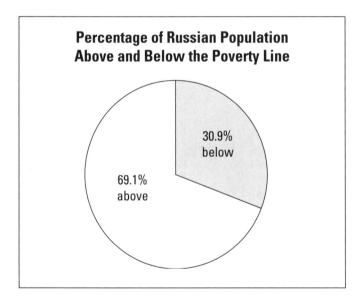

Look at the percentages in this circle graph. What do they tell you about the economy in Russia?

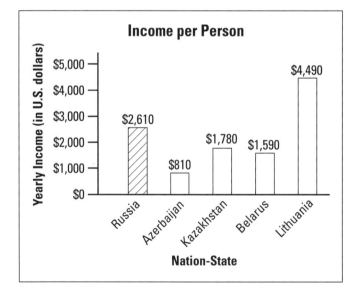

How does income per person for Russia compare to the other nation-states? What does this tell you about the economy in Russia?

Sources: *Infoplease*, "Economic Statistics by Country," www.infoplease.com. *The World Bank Group*,
"Country Statistical Information Database," "2004 World Development Indicators,"www.worldbank.org.
The World Factbook 1995, 1999, Central Intelligence Agency.

Political Success of Russia

Look at the political information below for the nation-state of Russia.
Discuss each question in your group.

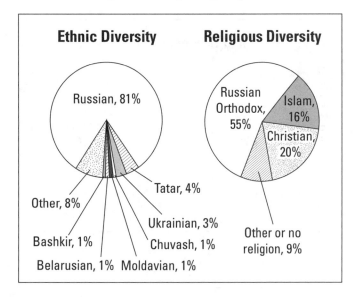

Look at these circle graphs. What do they tell you about possible ethnic and religious tension in Russia?

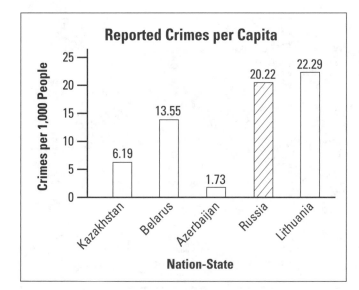

Compare the level of crime in Russia to the other nation-states. What might this tell you about security in Russia?

Life Expectancy and Infant Mortality in Russia

Year	Life Expectancy (years)	Infant Mortality Rate (deaths per 1,000 births)
1995	69	27
1999	65	23
2003	68	20

Notice how the numbers in this table change. What might this tell you about quality of life for people in Russia?

On this scale, 1 represents the highest degree of freedom, and 7 the lowest. Have the rankings for Russia gone up, gone down, or mostly stayed the same over time? What does this tell you about rights and freedoms in Russia?

Sources: *Freedom House*, "Freedom in the World Country Scores: 1972–2003," www.freedomhouse.org.
United Nations Office on Drugs and Crime, "The Seventh United Nations Survey on Crime Trends and the Operations of Criminal Justice Systems (1998–2000)," www.unodc.org/unodc. *The World Factbook 1995, 1999, 2003*, Central Intelligence Agency.

Economic and Political Comparisons

Use the data below to compare one nation-state to another.

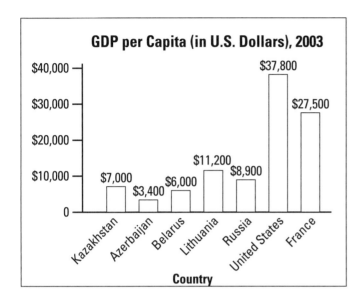

GDP per Capita (in U.S. Dollars), 2003

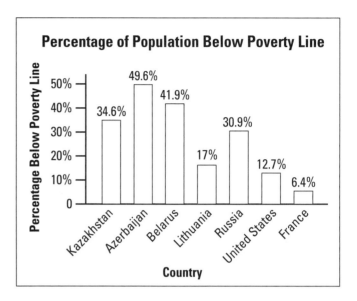

Percentage of Population Below Poverty Line

Life Expectancy and Infant Mortality, 2003

Country	Life Expectancy (years)	Infant Mortality (deaths per 1,000 births)
Kazakhstan	63	59
Azerbaijan	63	82
Belarus	68	14
Lithuania	70	14
Russia	68	20
United States	77	7
France	79	4

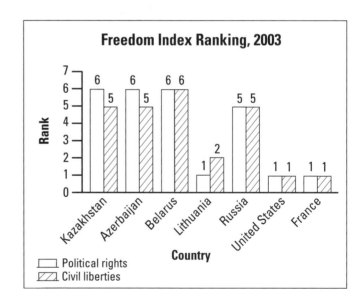

Freedom Index Ranking, 2003

Sources: *Freedom House*, "Freedom in the World Country Scores: 1972–2003," www.freedomhouse.org. *Infoplease*, "Economic Statistics by Country," www.infoplease.com. NationMaster, "France: Economy," "United States: Economy," www.nationmaster.com. The World Bank Group, "2004 World Development Indicators," www.worldbank.org. *The World Factbook 2003*, Central Intelligence Agency.

Write to the International GeoGames Committee

You have just visited five nation-states that were once a part of the Soviet Union. Write a letter to the International GeoGames Committee. Tell them which nation-state you think is the best site of a future GeoGames. Also advise the committee which nation-state you think is the worst site.

Your letter must include

- a date and a proper heading.

- an introduction that briefly describes your tour. Mention where you visited and your impressions of the nation-states. Tell what kind of information you gathered.

- your recommendation for the *best* nation-state as a site of a future GeoGames. Give three reasons for your choice.

- your recommendation for the *worst* nation-state as a site of a future GeoGames. Give three reasons for your choice.

- a concluding statement. Summarize your arguments and restate your opinion.

Your letter should be at least one page in length. Type it or write it neatly in ink.

18.2 The Geographic Setting

What are the five basic factors that affect the success of a nation-state?

The five basic factors affecting a nation-state's success are security, political freedom, economic growth, quality of life, and national unity.

What are some key ways that a nation-state can keep its people secure?

A nation-state can protect its people from foreign enemies and from crime.

What is GDP? Along with GDP, what two other factors might indicate whether a nation-state is experiencing economic growth?

GDP, or gross domestic product, is the total value of goods and services produced within a nation-state in a year. Income and poverty levels might also indicate whether a nation-state is experiencing economic growth.

How can a government improve its citizens' quality of life? What are two measures of quality of life within a nation-state?

A government can improve its citizens' quality of life by providing safe food, clean water, and good medical care. Life expectancy and death rate of babies are two indicators of quality of life within a nation-state.

What is nationalism? In what ways can it both foster and work against unity within a nation-state?

Nationalism is a feeling of pride and loyalty toward one's nation. In countries with many ethnic groups, nationalism can create a sense of unity. Ethnic group nationalism sometimes works against unity if ethnic groups decide they would be better off as independent nations.

What does the organization Freedom House do? What two kinds of rights does it examine for each country?

Freedom House is an organization that rates countries on how free they are. It looks at a country's protection of political and civil rights.

Nation-States of the Former Soviet Union

18.3 Kazakhstan: A Central Asian Giant

1. Complete this scorecard for Kazakhstan. Follow your teacher's directions.

Nation-State Scorecard				
Factors to Consider for Economic Success		**Factors to Consider for Political Success**		
FACTOR	SCORE	FACTOR	SCORE	
Location, available resources	Answers will vary.	Possible ethnic or religious conflict	Answers will vary.	
GDP growth		Crimes reported		
Poverty		Life expectancy, infant mortality		
Income level		Freedom Index ranking		
Overall success		Overall success		
Comments:		Comments:		

2. Answer these questions:

   Suppose you choose Kazakhstan to host a GeoGames. What is the biggest disadvantage?

   Possible answers: ethnic and religious tensions, slow economic growth, split between northern and southern Kazakhstan, high poverty, low rank on the Freedom Index, low per capita income, environmental problems

   What is the biggest advantage?

   Possible answers: rich in mineral and oil reserves, plenty of agriculture in the northern region, excellent relative location, plenty of opportunity for future economic growth, GDP growth, low crime rate

3. What *three* new important things have you learned about the political or economic success of Kazakhstan? On the map, draw and label them.

   Answers will vary.

18.4 Azerbaijan: Where Europe Meets Asia

1. Complete this scorecard for Azerbaijan. Follow your teacher's directions.

Nation-State Scorecard			
Factors to Consider for Economic Success		**Factors to Consider for Political Success**	
FACTOR	SCORE	FACTOR	SCORE
Location, available resources	*Answers will vary.*	Possible ethnic or religious conflict	*Answers will vary.*
GDP growth		Crimes reported	
Poverty		Life expectancy, infant mortality	
Income level		Freedom Index ranking	
Overall success		Overall success	
Comments:		Comments:	

2. Answer these questions:

   Suppose you choose Azerbaijan to host a GeoGames. What is the biggest disadvantage?

   Possible answers: ethnic and religious conflict, slow economic growth, high poverty, low rank on the Freedom Index, declining life expectancy, increasing infant mortality rate

   What is the biggest advantage?

   Possible answers: plentiful oil reserves in the Caspian Sea, good relative location, possibility for economic growth in the future, some GDP growth, low crime rate

3. What *three* new important things have you learned about the political or economic success of Azerbaijan? On the map, draw and label them.

   Answers will vary.

18.5 Belarus: Between Europe and Russia

1. Complete this scorecard for Belarus. Follow your teacher's directions.

Nation-State Scorecard				
Factors to Consider for Economic Success			**Factors to Consider for Political Success**	
FACTOR	SCORE		FACTOR	SCORE
Location, available resources	Answers will vary.		Possible ethnic or religious conflict	Answers will vary.
GDP growth			Crimes reported	
Poverty			Life expectancy, infant mortality	
Income level			Freedom Index ranking	
Overall success			Overall success	
Comments:			Comments:	

2. Answer these questions:

Suppose you choose Belarus to host a GeoGames. What is the biggest disadvantage?

Possible answers: landlocked nation-state, environmental problems left from the Chernobyl disaster, relies heavily on Russia for fuel and trade, low rank on the Freedom Index, high poverty

What is the biggest advantage?

Possible answers: close ties to Russia might make it more politically stable, possible lower possibility of ethnic conflict

3. What *three* new important things have you learned about the political or economic success of Belarus? On the map, draw and label them.

Answers will vary.

18.6 Lithuania: One of Three Baltic States

1. Complete this scorecard for Lithuania. Follow your teacher's directions.

Nation-State Scorecard			
Factors to Consider for Economic Success		**Factors to Consider for Political Success**	
FACTOR	SCORE	FACTOR	SCORE
Location, available resources	*Answers will vary.*	Possible ethnic or religious conflict	
GDP growth		Crimes reported	
Poverty		Life expectancy, infant mortality	
Income level		Freedom Index ranking	
Overall success		Overall success	
Comments:		Comments:	

2. Answer these questions:

   Suppose you choose Lithuania to host a GeoGames. What is the biggest disadvantage?

   Possible answers: few fossil fuel resources, higher crime rate

   What is the biggest advantage?

   Possible answers: strategic location between Russia and Europe, fertile soil for agriculture, some availability of minerals, strong feeling of nationalism, strong economic growth, membership in EU and NATO, high rank on Freedom Index, low poverty, declining infant mortality rate

3. What *three* new important things have you learned about the political or economic success of Lithuania? On the map, draw and label them.

   Answers will vary.

18.7 Russia: The Largest Nation on Earth

1. Complete this scorecard for Russia. Follow your teacher's directions.

Nation-State Scorecard			
Factors to Consider for Economic Success		**Factors to Consider for Political Success**	
FACTOR	SCORE	FACTOR	SCORE
Location, available resources	Answers will vary.	Possible ethnic or religious conflict	Answers will vary.
GDP growth		Crimes reported	
Poverty		Life expectancy, infant mortality	
Income level		Freedom Index ranking	
Overall success		Overall success	
Comments:		Comments:	

2. Answer these questions:

Suppose you choose Russia to host a GeoGames. What is the biggest disadvantage?

Possible answers: low percentage of land suitable for farming, many failed businesses, high crime rate, high poverty, high housing costs, pollution, drop in birth rate, ethnic group nationalism, ethnic tensions in Chechnya

What is the biggest advantage?

Possible answers: plenty of resources, steady economic growth, strong oil exports, decrease in infant mortality

3. What *three* new important things have you learned about the political or economic success of Russia? On the map, draw and label them.

Answers will vary.

Options for Students
with Special Needs

The diverse needs of students are inherently addressed in the pedagogy of the TCI Approach, which taps multiple intelligences, creates cooperative interaction, and spirals learning from basic knowledge to higher-order thinking. Still, there may be times when an individual or a group of students would benefit from differentiated instruction during portions of the lessons in this program. Read through the following tips for ways to adapt the lesson activities in *Geography Alive! Regions and People* to suit the particular special needs of your students.

The Tools of Geography

English Language Learners

Help students with new vocabulary. When introducing the Essential Question and the Geoterms, point out that Geoterms appear in blue type. With students, find the Geoterms in the glossary and read the definitions aloud. Then read the sentence in the chapter that uses each Geoterm. Have students work with a partner to complete Geoterms 1 in their Interactive Student Notebooks.

Simplify the reading for each phase of the Social Studies Skill Builder. Have students read one paragraph or subsection at a time, and give them the card or cards from Student Handouts 1F–1K that match the content they've just read. Have them follow the directions on the card to complete that part of their Reading Notes. Then have them move on to the next subsection of the text.

Learners Reading and Writing Below Grade Level

Have students help you create an outline of the chapter using the section heads and subheads. Explain that this outline is a preview of the chapter's main ideas and that the section heads and subheads will help guide them while they're reading. If they get confused while reading, they can read the outline for a reminder of the main ideas.

Point out the illustrations in the chapter, and read a few of the caption titles. Remind students that illustrations and captions can also help them better understand the main ideas of the reading.

Learners with Special Education Needs

Model each geographic skill as you introduce or review it. As you use the transparencies in each phase of the Social Studies Skill Builder, circulate around the room to make sure students are following the discussion. Help individuals as necessary by pointing to items on their maps as volunteers respond to the questions.

Advanced Learners

In the Processing assignment, students create a map of their classroom with a title, legend, compass rose, grid, and scale. Instead, consider using a larger area—such as the school or a neighborhood—that would require more detail for the legend and more challenge in calculating an accurate scale.

Seeing the World Like a Geographer

English Language Learners

In the Preview assignment, students create an ad encouraging people to move to their town or city. Instead of designing the ad for the place where they currently live, students could choose another location with which they are familiar, such as their birthplace.

In the Processing assignment, for Lines 3 through 6 of the poem, provide an illustrated word bank of appropriate adjectives and phrases to help students compose these lines. Use terms such as the following, along with simple illustrations as cues to help students understand and learn the vocabulary.

Line 3: *cool, cold, warm, hot, rainy, snowy, dry*
Line 4: *tropical, green, grassy, forested, flowering, fertile, empty*
Line 5: *dense, crowded, spread out, lonely, urban, rural*
Line 6: *agricultural, industrial, many resources*

Learners Reading and Writing Below Grade Level

As students complete their Reading Notes in Step 2 of each phase of the Visual Discovery activity, have them use color to help them remember each thematic map's unique terminology. Ask students to outline each item's box in a color similar to that used for that item in the key of the thematic map.

Learners with Special Education Needs

In Step 3 of Phase 1 of the Visual Discovery activity, assign one student in each group to be the "sound effects technician" who will make sound effects during the act-it-out. This option works well with features that have recognizable sounds, such as bodies of water. Alternatively, assign one student in each group to be a narrator. During the act-it-out, the narrator can read clues from an index card to help the audience correctly name the physical feature.

Have students use the bulleted points in Step 3 on Student Handouts 2B and 2C to create three cue cards for the second and third act-it-outs. Each cue card should contain simple words and phrases to help groups remember their main points during the act-it-outs. A cue card for the economic activity act-it-out might read as follows:

See: open blue sea, large nets, sails
Hear: roaring of waves, seagulls, running motors
Smell: salty air

Advanced Learners

In place of the seven-line poem for the Processing assignment, have students design a continent with at least 15 of the physical features shown in Section 2.3. Then have students create at least one other specialty map (climate, vegetation, population density, or economic activity) for their continent. Remind them to consider the influence of physical features on the patterns seen on these maps. All maps should have a title, legend, compass rose, and scale.

Settlement Patterns and Ways of Life in Canada

English Language Learners

Encourage students to use color to complete their Reading Notes. Provide students with photocopies of Sections 3.4 to 3.8 of the textbook. Read the text aloud as students read along with you and highlight information that pertains to each region, using different colors. For example, in all five sections, students might highlight information about the Atlantic region in yellow. They might also highlight in yellow the heading for the Atlantic region on their Reading Notes. Prompt for the highlighting as needed. You may find it helpful to restate the main points for students with beginning or intermediate English skills.

Learners Reading and Writing Below Grade Level

Provide students with a partial copy of Guide to Reading Notes 3. Block out two or three answers for each topic in the Guide to Reading Notes. For example, you might block the answers for "Population" in the Atlantic and Pacific regions and the answers for "Language" or "Climate" in the core and prairie regions. Have students fill in the missing information as they complete their Reading Notes.

The night before the activity, encourage students to preread the sections of text you will be covering in the *Where in Canada?* game the following day. Do not, however, have them complete the Reading Notes ahead of time.

Learners with Special Education Needs

Assign students who are physically unable to participate in the Preview to a partner. Have each pair discuss where they would stand on the floor map of Canada, and have the partner stand in the appropriate location. Call on the student who is not on the game board to explain the pair's location.

Advanced Learners

In addition to the Processing assignment, have students compare where they live to another area in the United States. Beneath their Processing assignment, have students write the name of another location in the United States—a place they have lived, visited, or are interested in learning more about. Then have them write a paragraph explaining how and why their life might be different if they lived there.

The Great Lakes: The U.S. and Canada's Freshwater Treasures

English Language Learners

Have the class create and display a poster with definitions for difficult vocabulary. Before beginning this activity, post a large sheet of butcher paper on the wall of your classroom. Place a marker nearby. On the left side of the paper, write some of the more challenging vocabulary in the chapter, including the Geoterms. Tell students that these are words they will learn in the activity and that the class will work together to find and post definitions for each word. During the activity, ask students to raise their hands when they encounter these words. Then ask for volunteers to write definitions or draw pictures for each word. Offer the option for students to explain the term in their own words as you add their definitions to the poster. Correct grammar and restate definitions for students as necessary.

Learners Reading and Writing Below Grade Level

Simplify the writing requirements for this activity. Instead of having students write the editorial described on Student Handout 4, ask them to write postcards from the Great Lakes. Direct them to download and print an appropriate image of the Great Lakes and affix it to an index card. Then have them write a note from their "recent visit" to the lakes on the reverse side. The postcard should include these things:

- the date and a proper salutation
- a description of what the lakes look like from a particular location
- two positive statements about the current condition of the Great Lakes
- two negative statements about the current condition of the Great Lakes

Learners with Special Education Needs

Follow these steps to simplify the activity:

1. Complete the Preview and read Sections 4.1 and 4.2 as a class.

2. Have students listen to CD Track 3, "The Sad State of Our Once-Great Lakes."

3. Put students in mixed-ability pairs to create a poster. On the left side of the poster, ask students to write words and draw illustrations that show the condition of the Great Lakes in 1969. On the right side, ask them to write words and draw illustrations that show the condition of the lakes today. Tell them to use Sections 4.3 to 4.6 as evidence for their posters.

4. Ask students to display their posters, and lead a debriefing using these questions: *How did human activity affect the Great Lakes by 1969? In what ways are the Great Lakes better off today? Are there any ways that the Great Lakes are worse off today? What might people do to better manage the Great Lakes?*

Advanced Learners

Encourage students to research how editorials are submitted and published in newspapers and on radio and television. After students have completed the editorials described on Student Handout 4, ask them to research the names of newspapers and radio and television stations in the Great Lakes region. Have them research how they might submit their editorials to the media, and encourage them to follow through.

Urban Sprawl in North America: Where Will It End?

English Language Learners

Partner students who may struggle with this activity with students who have strong verbal linguistic skills. When assigning roles, assign one role to a pair of students. Have each pair share presentation responsibilities for their role during the policy-planning group discussions during Step 3 on Information Master 5.

Consider making a transparency of the Preview and modeling the activity with students. This should help students better understand the Preview and prepare them for completing the Reading Notes.

Learners Reading and Writing Below Grade Level

Have students work in groups to complete the Reading Notes. Allow policy-planning groups to complete their Reading Notes as a group, during Steps 1 and 6 on Information Master 5. (**Note:** Students already complete part of their Reading Notes with their interest group in Step 2 on Information Master 5.)

Learners with Special Education Needs

Place students with physical disabilities in a location conducive to movement between groups. Place students who will have a difficult time moving between groups in the policy-planning group located closest to their interest group. See the classroom map in Step 1 of the Experiential Exercise for additional guidance.

Ensure that students are prepared to participate by explaining the activity to them ahead of time. Have them read over their role cards from Student Handout 5 as well as the arguments for and against urban sprawl in Section 5.3 of the text. Also, if possible, have an aide provide these students with additional help they may need during the activity.

Advanced Learners

Assign students extra responsibilities during the activity. Consider giving advanced learners the role of Planning Commissioner. In addition to presenting the plan itself, require them to present the *reasoning* that went into the plan their policy-planning group developed for each city.

National Parks: Saving the Natural Heritage of the U.S. and Canada

English Language Learners

Have students preread Sections 6.1 and 6.2 prior to participating in the Preview activity. Help these students build background knowledge about what national parks are, why they were created, and what they might see if they were to visit one.

Have students also preread the appropriate sections of the text before working on their tour plans.

Learners Reading and Writing Below Grade Level

Provide photocopies of Sections 6.3, 6.4, and 6.5 from the textbook. As students read these pages, have them highlight or underline key features that will help them plan their tours. Suggest that they use blue for flora found in the park, red for fauna, and green for physical features. Point out that this will help them find the information they need to complete their Reading Notes.

Learners with Special Education Needs

Consider providing magnifying glasses to allow students to read the topographic maps more easily and to help them interpret the contour lines.

To make the activity more straightforward, give students a copy of the topographic map of each park with a tour route already drawn on it. Have students complete the Reading Notes accordingly. You might also want to make calculators available to help them determine elevation changes along their tour routes.

Advanced Learners

Expand the Processing assignment by having students create a guidebook that covers the three national parks highlighted in the activity. Students might create their guidebooks from a standard size sheet of paper, trifolded, or some other format of their design. Guidebooks should have the following:

- a cover that includes pictures and an appropriate title
- a brief history of each national park and why these areas have been set aside
- the key features of each park with explanations of what makes each park unique and worth preserving

Consumption Patterns in the United States: The Impact of Living Well

English Language Learners

In Step 1 of the Response Group activity, create some groups of five, adding one English language learner to a group of four. Have that student share presenting responsibilities with another student for one of the questions during the activity.

Learners Reading and Writing Below Grade Level

Model good note-taking skills by making a transparency of the Reading Notes. As you discuss the cartogram with the class and encourage students to share their answers to the questions for each section, fill in the Reading Notes with appropriate student responses.

Learners with Special Education Needs

Provide assistance for the Processing assignment by having students dictate their cartoon ideas and captions to a teacher, classroom aide, or partner.

Advanced Learners

As an extension of Processing 7, have students create two political cartoons from different perspectives. One should support the idea that high levels of global consumption have a positive impact, and the other should depict increasing consumption levels as having a negative impact.

Migration to the United States: The Impact on People and Places

English Language Learners

Provide additional support during the interview segment of the Experiential Exercise. Before Step 3 of Phase 2, prepare picture cards for possible push and pull factors revealed in each interview. As students listen to the immigrants share their answers to each question, have them choose the picture card that matches each response. Model or prompt as necessary. Picture cards might include these topics:

Push Factors
- war
- military takeover
- persecution
- natural disaster
- human-made disaster
- low-paying work
- shortage of jobs and food

Pull Factors
- the "American Dream"
- safety
- freedom
- good job/pay
- improved living standard
- reunited with family
- education

Learners Reading and Writing Below Grade Level

Using Guide to Reading Notes 8, block out key words from each of the examples in Sections 8.3, 8.4, 8.5, and 8.6. Make photocopies of these partially completed Reading Notes, and have students complete the unfinished parts as they read each section.

Learners with Special Education Needs

Allow students who may be uncomfortable with the roles in this activity to choose to be co-interviewers or observers. In Phase 1 of the Experiential Exercise, allow students to become a third member of a pair. During Phase 2, have some students travel with an interviewer and either share the responsibility of asking the immigrant questions or quietly observe the interview. Also, consider explaining to students what will happen in the Experiential Exercise the day before you plan to execute it.

Advanced Learners

Extend the Processing assignment by having students interview a second immigrant. Then ask them to create a Venn diagram and record at least three similarities and three differences between the two migration stories they heard.

Spatial Inequality in Mexico City: From Cardboard to Castles

English Language Learners

To complete Part 2 of the Reading Notes, students listen to a recording to answer survey questions. Use Guide to Reading Notes 9 to identify which three survey questions will not be answered for each neighborhood visit. Before students listen to the recording, have them cross out those sections of the survey so they know they do not have to listen for those answers.

Learners Reading and Writing Below Grade Level

In Phase 2 of the Writing for Understanding activity, help students create a simple outline for writing the newspaper article. Use the bullet points found on Information Master 9. An outline might look as follows:

I. Title of my article
II. Introduction to Mexico City
  A. Two important geographic facts
  B. Two important historical facts
III. Life in one neighborhood
  A. Description
  B. Two facts from the survey that support my description
IV. Life in another neighborhood
  A. Description
  B. Two facts from the survey that support my description
V. Conclusion
VI. "Photographs"
  A. Caption 1
  B. Caption 2

Learners with Special Education Needs

Consider shortening the writing assignment. Instead of having students write a several-paragraph newspaper article describing life in Mexico City, provide a partially complete outline of an article on this topic. Have students complete the outline orally or in writing as their abilities allow.

Advanced Learners

In the Global Connections, students examine a world map of Human Development Index rank by country. Individually or in small groups, have students select one country for each level of HDI rank: very high, high, medium, low, and very low. Have students use the Global Data Bank to research the life expectancy, per capita GDP, and literacy rate for each of these countries. Then ask them to discuss the differences they see among the countries researched.

Indigenous Cultures: The Survival of the Maya of Mesoamerica

English Language Learners

Before projecting the image in the Preview, review the concepts of "traditional" and "modern" by having students reflect on their own families. Have them discuss or write about aspects of their family life that reflect "traditional" culture, such as special holiday practices, and those that show adaptation to "modern" life, such as how technology has affected their families.

Learners Reading and Writing Below Grade Level

Provide additional support to help students complete the Reading Notes. Give them photocopies of Sections 10.3 to 10.7, and have them use two colors to highlight text as they read. They should use one color to highlight details that show preservation of traditional culture and a second color to highlight adaptations to modern life. Explain that this will help them complete their Reading Notes.

Learners with Special Education Needs

Before the Problem Solving Groupwork activity, examine Student Handout 10 with students and encourage them to choose a role they feel comfortable with. Help them choose roles that match their unique learning styles and individual strengths. In some situations, you might set up a group of five and allow two students to share a role, or make one student an assistant to another for one of the roles. Also make sure that students understand all of the steps involved in preparing their dramatizations.

In the Processing, students revisit the photograph from the Preview to annotate it with details that they learned in the lesson. Provide additional structure by providing a checklist that students can follow as they complete the assignment. Also consider using the checklist to reduce the number of details required to complete the assignment. For example, a checklist might look as follows:

Preserving traditional culture (circle two): *community, home and family, work, market day, traditions*

- Color or draw a detail for each.
- Write a brief caption for each: *The _____ shows that this highland Maya family has preserved its traditional culture. It shows this because _____.*

Adapting to modern life (circle two): *community, home and family, work, market day, traditions*

- Color or draw a detail for each.
- Write a brief caption for each: *The _____ shows that this highland Maya family has adapted to modern life. It shows this because _____.*

Advanced Learners

To extend the Global Connections, have students create a collage about one of the indigenous peoples portrayed on the world map. Individually, or in groups of two or three, have students select one indigenous group to research. Students should focus on finding information that shows ways in which this group is preserving its traditional culture and ways in which it is adapting to modern life. As a final product, have students create a collage of images, words, and phrases that show what they have learned.

Dealing with Extreme Weather: Hurricanes in the Caribbean

English Language Learners

In Step 2 of the Visual Discovery activity, as an alternative to having students read Section 11.3 individually, use the two maps to review the content of this section. Use the "Prevailing Winds Around the World" map to introduce and point out the influence of the Coriolis effect. Use the "Cyclones Around the World" map to highlight the geographic origins of tropical cyclones and the various names of the storms in different parts of the world.

Learners Reading and Writing Below Grade Level

To support students as they complete their Reading Notes, introduce and use the following SQ3R reading strategy before students begin reading:

- **S**urvey. Preview the section by looking at the title, subheads, and illustrations. Read the first paragraph.

- **Q**uestion. Turn the title and subhead into questions to focus your reading. Look up the meaning of new vocabulary.

- **R**ead. Search for answers to your questions.

- **R**ecite. Recite the answers to your questions aloud or in writing. Reread if you have any unanswered questions.

- **R**eview. Look over the section and summarize what you have learned by completing the Reading Notes.

Learners with Special Education Needs

For Sections 11.4 and 11.6 to 11.8, students summarize what they've read using a word bank. Block out the underlined word bank terms in each of these sections of Guide to Reading Notes 11, and photocopy the altered pages for students. Have students use the word bank to fill in the words as they read each section.

Advanced Learners

As an alternative to the Processing activity, which involves creating a pamphlet to teach people about hurricanes, have students research and create a pamphlet about other extreme weather events. Use the bulleted list in the Processing to provide guidelines for the assignment. Have students choose from the following extreme weather events: *blizzards, drought, floods, freezes, heat waves, ice storms, nor'easters, severe thunderstorms, tornadoes.*

Land Use Conflict in the Amazon Rainforest

English Language Learners

In Phase 2 of the Response Group activity, groups discuss a series of critical thinking questions. For each question, groups can record their answers on an index card, or "presenter-response" card. Allow the Presenters time to practice reading through this completed response card several times before you call on them to share their group's ideas.

A presenter-response card for Question 1 might look like this:

> *We think that [first group] and [second group] have the most legitimate claims to decide what should happen to the resources of the rainforest.*

> *We think that [first group] has the most legitimate claim because (list one or two reasons):*

> *We think that [second group] has a legitimate claim because (list one or two reasons):*

> *We think that [last group] has the least legitimate claim because (list one or two reasons):*

Learners Reading and Writing Below Grade Level

Before each group presents their news report to the class in Phase 1 of the Response Group activity, give students a copy of Guide to Reading Notes 12 that corresponds to the news report being presented. Allow time for students to read through the answers. Then, when the rest of the class is completing their Reading Notes, have these students highlight information they heard in the news report on their copy of the Guide to Reading Notes. As the news reports continue, consider including progressively less information on the Guide to Reading Notes by blocking out different sections when you copy it. By the final (sixth) news report, students may be able to complete all of the notes.

Learners with Special Education Needs

In Phase 2 of the Response Group activity, adapt the amount of information that each Presenter needs to share with the class. For example, instead of having Presenters share which two groups have the strongest case and which have the weakest, have the Presenter share just which two groups (or one group) have the strongest case. Alternatively, have students co-present their group's information along with another member of their group, so that they are responsible for sharing only one piece of information.

Advanced Learners

In Phase 1 of the Response Group activity, assign one group of students to research, prepare, and present a news report for an additional rainforest group that is not included in the chapter, such as builders of hydroelectric power projects. For this group, key words include *Tucurui Dam, Belo Monte Dam, Eletronorte, Amazon River, hydroelectric power*. Also ask students to create additional statements for Student Handout 12A.

Life in the Central Andes: Adapting to a Mountainous Region

English Language Learners

In Step 5 of the Social Studies Skill Builder, students visit three stations to view placards with assorted graphics and categorize the graphics by elevation zone. When students visit the stations for the first time, circulate around the room to make sure they are making correct connections between the images and the categories.

Learners Reading and Writing Below Grade Level

In Part 1 of the Reading Notes, students read about and take notes on the physical characteristics of each elevation zone. Provide photocopies of Sections 13.3 to 13.6 of the textbook. As students read these pages, have them highlight or underline important details they will need to complete Part 1 of the Reading Notes.

In the Processing, instead of having students read and respond to researched articles about mountainous regions around the world, have them create a cover for a magazine about life in the central Andes. Have them follow these guidelines:

- Create an imaginative subtitle.
- Include three pictures of human adaptations from at least two elevation zones.
- Write a brief caption for each picture explaining what the adaptation is and why it is important.
- Add creative touches to make the magazine cover catch people's attention.

Learners with Special Education Needs

For the Processing assignment, instead of having students research to find an article about life in a mountain range of their choice, provide a selection of screened articles from which they can choose.

Advanced Learners

After the Social Studies Skill Builder, have pairs of students actually create the feature article, following these guidelines:

- Create an imaginative title and introduction.
- Include one page for each elevation zone: *tierra helada, tierra fría, tierra templada,* and *tierra caliente.* Each page should have one paragraph about the physical characteristics of the zone and one paragraph about human adaptations to the zone.
- Include at least two pictures for each page. Students can use the ones from the activity or create their own. Each picture should be accompanied by a brief caption.
- Add creative touches to make the article appealing to readers.

Supranational Cooperation in the European Union

English Language Learners

As an alternative for completing the Processing assignment, students might show their ideas with drawings or with a combination of words and drawings. Or they might dictate their comparison to a classroom aide or partner who can then help them write their comparison.

Learners Reading and Writing Below Grade Level

Provide students with additional support for the Reading Notes by making a copy of Sections 14.3 to 14.5 from *Geography Alive! Regions and People* for students to highlight as they read. Point out that each section discusses centripetal forces under the first subhead and centrifugal forces under the second subhead. Encourage students to highlight main ideas about centripetal forces in one color and centrifugal forces in another before completing the Reading Notes.

Learners with Special Education Needs

Provide more structure for Phases 2 and 3 of the Experiential Exercise. Place some students in mixed-ability pairs for this activity, with one student shadowing the other.

Also consider creating checklists on index cards for each role in this activity. For example, the checklist for a Customs Agent in Phase 2 might include the following:

- Check the passport of each Tourist.
- Have the Tourist say "Hello" in your country's language.
- Write your initials in one of the "Passport Checks" boxes.

The checklist for a Tourist in Phase 3 might include the following:

- Walk into a country.
- If you have different money from the country you are visiting, go to the Currency Exchanger to get the right currency.
- If you have the same money as the country you are visiting, go right to the Merchant.
- Give the Merchant one coin to buy a bumper sticker.
- Travel to another country and repeat these steps.

Advanced Learners

Extend the Global Connections by having students research one of the international organizations represented on the map. Have them begin by using the map to list every country that is a member of the organization they have been assigned. Then encourage students to use the Internet or other sources to discover the centripetal and centrifugal forces of that organization.

Extend the Processing assignment by having students read about current issues in the European Union in newspapers or on the Internet. Require them to include one of these issues in their annotated simile of the EU as a neighborhood.

Population Dilemmas in Europe

English Language Learners

Assign students a peer tutor. Peer tutors can help with the following aspects of this lesson:

- Helping to explain population pyramids in the Preview.

- Working through Student Handout 15A during Phase 1 of the Response Group activity.

- Completing the Reading Notes during Phase 2 of the Response Group activity.

- Assisting with the questions in the Processing assignment.

Learners Reading and Writing Below Grade Level

Provide students with additional support for Reading Notes 15 by giving them a copy of Guide to Reading Notes 15 with the answers to Step 3 for each dilemma omitted. Before students begin reading, slightly change the directions for Step 2 under each dilemma. For example, on the first page of Reading Notes, the new directions could read:

- *As you read Section 15.4, highlight each cause listed below after you have read about it in your book.*

Once students have finished reading the section and highlighting answers, have them complete the sentence in Step 3 on their own.

Learners with Special Education Needs

Simplify Student Handout 15A used in Phase 1 of the Response Group activity. Draw in the missing age bands for each pyramid before giving the handout to students. Then have students focus on Step 2 of the directions and color the appropriate parts of each age band pink or blue.

For the Preview and Response Group portions of this lesson, get students actively involved in analyzing the population pyramids. Have students become "human pointers" for the transparencies by letting them come up to the screen to point out specific details.

Advanced Learners

Revise Student Handout 15A used in Phase 1 of the Response Group activity to make it more challenging. Omit the partially drawn pyramid on each page of the handout before distributing the handout, and ask students to create the population pyramids using the data in the tables.

Invisible Borders:
Transboundary Pollution in Europe

English Language Learners

Provide students with additional support for the Reading Notes. Instead of having them work in pairs, allow them to get in their groups of four from the act-it-outs and complete one copy of the Reading Notes together. Then make copies of the completed Reading Notes for all group members.

Learners Reading and Writing Below Grade Level

Provide additional support for students during the Visual Discovery activity by doing the following:

- Give students copies of the questions you will ask about each transparency. Students can then read along as you ask these spiral questions.

- Have students make cue cards for use during the act-it-outs. As groups prepare answers to their characters' questions on Student Handouts 16A and 16B, have students take notes on index cards for use during the act-it-out.

Reduce the written directions for creating act-it-outs on Student Handouts 16A and 16B. Rather than have students read the full page of directions, read the directions aloud to the class. Then give each group the questions for their character only.

Learners with Special Education Needs

Use Guide to Reading Notes 16 to provide partial answers for the Reading Notes. Consider the following changes to each page:

- *Left column:* Provide students with the source of the pollution already colored and the sentence completed. Highlight the second sentence of the directions. Block out the lines under the country names, and have students focus on underlining the source country or countries only.

- *Center column:* Provide students with the maps already showing the spread and the sentence completed. Highlight the third sentence of the directions. Block out or omit the circles around the country names, and have students focus on

circling the names of two countries that were most impacted by the pollution.

- *Right column:* Provide students with the sentence completed, and have them focus on drawing an effort to reduce the pollution on their maps.

Advanced Learners

Enrich this lesson by using the Preview activity to have students create maps of how the confetti spread in their classroom. Ask students to create a map of the transboundary pollution they experienced by doing the following:

- Draw a map of the classroom as it was set up at the beginning of the Preview. (**Note:** You may want to provide a copy of the classroom map in the Lesson Guide as a model.)

- Draw in the source of the pollution and label it.

- Use a highlighter to show how the confetti spread in Round 1 of the activity. Use a different colored highlighter to show how the confetti spread in Round 2.

- On the map, draw one effort that could be made to reduce the spread of the confetti. Then complete the following sentence below your map:
  _____ *could help reduce the spread of confetti by* _____ .

Russia's Varied Landscape: Physical Processes at Work

English Language Learners

For Phase 2, Step 3, of the Social Studies Skill Builder, give students their own copy of Information Master 17 with the most important directions highlighted. Underline such words as *visit, examine,* and *read* to cue students what they should be doing at each step. Model the steps as necessary.

Learners Reading and Writing Below Grade Level

Photocopy Sections 17.4, 17.6, 17.8, and 17.10 of the text for students. As students complete Step 5 of Information Master 17, encourage them to highlight clues that might help them match the placards with their physical features. Specifically, have them look for directional clues, such as *flows northward through Siberia,* that will help them correctly place each placard on the map, as well as descriptive phrases, like *jagged mountain ridges,* that might help them determine whether this physical feature matches the placard image.

Learners with Special Education Needs

For the act-it-outs in Phase 1 of the Social Studies Skill Builder, encourage some groups to choose a Host to introduce the physical process the group will be acting out, as well as to identify what each student's role is during the act-it-out. Hosts could prepare a cue card to read before the group presents their act-it-out. For example, a cue card might read as follows:

> *My group is going to act out [physical process]. Playing the part of the [one feature of the physical process] is [student]. Playing the role of the [second feature of the physical process] is [student]. And finally, playing the role of the [third feature of physical process] is [student].*

Advanced Learners

To extend Processing 17, have students research at least four locations in the United States where the physical processes they learned about have helped to shape the land. Encourage them to find examples for each of the four processes—erosion, glaciation, tectonic movement, and volcanic activity—and to look beyond the 100-mile radius specified in the Processing directions. Have them examine a physical map of the United States and use the Internet to find as many locations as possible. Students can list each location, sketch the physical feature, identify the physical process that is responsible, and explain how people living nearby might be affected.

New Nation-States from the Old Soviet Empire: Will They Succeed?

English Language Learners

Provide students with their own copies of Station Directions 18. Underline or highlight key words in the directions that may help students focus on what is being asked of them, such as *locate, read, answer,* and *draw and label*. Provide a small symbol that students can use to better understand each direction.

Learners Reading and Writing Below Grade Level

Give students an altered copy of Guide to Reading Notes 18 to use as a model for taking notes.

- For Section 18.2, omit key words from each of the answers for students to fill in as they read.

- For Sections 18.3 and 18.4, provide students with cloze sentences for Question 2, such as:

  Most of Kazakhstan is too _____ for agriculture. Also, religious and cultural differences divide the _____ and the _____. Settlement in Kazakhstan has created a serious _____ in the country. Finally, Kazakhstan faces serious _____ problems.

- For Sections 18.5 and 18.6, provide students with sentence starters to guide them as they read those sections in the text.

- For Section 18.7, ask students to complete the answers to the questions unassisted.

Learners with Special Education Needs

Reduce the number of stations students visit from five to two or three. Allow them to choose the stations they wish to visit and complete only those Reading Notes. Consider helping them fill in their Reading Notes for the stations they do not visit, using a copy of Guide to Reading Notes 18 for reference.

Consider shortening the writing assignment. Instead of having students write a letter of proposal arguing their choices, allow them to rank three of the five sites on a spectrum from best to worst. For each site, have them write, in bulleted or sentence form, one or two reasons why that site is a good choice (if highly ranked) or a poor choice (if ranked low on the list).

Advanced Learners

To extend the Writing for Understanding activity, have students use the Global Data Bank to analyze the success of four or five other newer nations (for example, Croatia, East Timor, Micronesia, Namibia, Palau, and Yemen). Encourage them to find data in these areas:

- ethnic or religious diversity
- Freedom Index Ranking
- infant mortality or life expectancy
- GDP per capita
- poverty level

Have students create scorecards for each of these nations and evaluate which might be good or poor choices as a future GeoGames site.

Correlation to National Geography Standards

Geography for Life Standards	Geography Alive! Regions and People
The World in Spatial Terms	
1. How to use maps and other geographic representations, tools, and technologies to acquire, process, and report information from a spatial perspective.	Lessons 1, 2, 6, 7, 9, 11, 17, 18, 27, 34 Introducing the Region, Units 2–8 Mapping Labs: Canada and the United States, Latin America, Europe and Russia, Africa, Southwest and Central Asia, Monsoon Asia, Oceania and Antarctica
2. How to use mental maps to organize information about people, places, and environments in a spatial context.	Lessons 8, 11, 34 Introducing the Region, Units 2–8 Mapping Labs: Canada and the United States, Latin America, Europe and Russia, Africa, Southwest and Central Asia, Monsoon Asia, Oceania and Antarctica
3. How to analyze the spatial organization of people, places, and environments on Earth's surface.	Lessons 1, 2, 3, 5, 9, 13, 16, 22, 31, 32 Introducing the Region, Units 2–8 Mapping Labs: Canada and the United States, Latin America, Europe and Russia, Africa, Southwest and Central Asia, Monsoon Asia, Oceania and Antarctica
Places and Regions	
4. The physical and human characteristics of places.	Lessons 2, 3, 5, 6, 9–11, 13, 15, 17, 19–22, 24, 25, 29–31, 33–35 Introducing the Region, Units 2–8 Mapping Labs: Canada and the United States, Latin America, Europe and Russia, Africa, Southwest and Central Asia, Monsoon Asia, Oceania and Antarctica
5. That people create regions to interpret Earth's complexity.	Lessons 2, 13, 14, 20, 22, 24, 32, 34 Introducing the Region, Units 2–8 Mapping Labs: Canada and the United States, Latin America, Europe and Russia, Africa, Southwest and Central Asia, Monsoon Asia, Oceania and Antarctica
6. How culture and experience influence people's perceptions of places and regions.	Lessons 7, 8, 14, 22, 23, 28 Introducing the Region, Units 2–8 Mapping Labs: Canada and the United States, Latin America, Europe and Russia, Africa, Southwest and Central Asia, Monsoon Asia, Oceania and Antarctica

Geography for Life Standards	Geography Alive! Regions and People
Physical Systems	
7. The physical processes that shape the patterns of Earth's surface.	Lessons 2, 17, 19, 20, 24, 27, 34, 35 Introducing the Region, Units 2–8 Mapping Labs: Canada and the United States, Latin America, Europe and Russia, Africa, Southwest and Central Asia, Monsoon Asia, Oceania and Antarctica
8. The characteristics and spatial distribution of ecosystems on Earth's surface.	Lessons 2, 6, 12, 13, 16, 19, 20, 33, 35 Introducing the Region, Units 2–8 Mapping Labs: Canada and the United States, Latin America, Europe and Russia, Africa, Southwest and Central Asia, Monsoon Asia, Oceania and Antarctica
Human Systems	
9. The characteristics, distribution, and migration of human population on Earth's surface.	Lessons 2, 5, 8–10, 15, 23, 30, 31, 33, 34 Introducing the Region, Units 2–8 Mapping Labs: Canada and the United States, Latin America, Europe and Russia, Africa, Southwest and Central Asia, Monsoon Asia, Oceania and Antarctica
10. The characteristics, distribution, and complexity of Earth's cultural mosaics.	Lessons 3, 8, 10, 14, 18, 22, 23, 25
11. The patterns and networks of economic interdependence on Earth's surface.	Lessons 2, 7, 14, 21, 24, 28, 32 Introducing the Region, Units 2–8 Mapping Labs: Canada and the United States, Latin America, Europe and Russia, Africa, Southwest and Central Asia, Monsoon Asia, Oceania and Antarctica
12. The processes, patterns, and functions of human settlement.	Lessons 2, 3, 5, 9, 10, 25, 31, 34
13. How the forces of cooperation and conflict among people influence human control of Earth's surface.	Lessons 12, 14, 18, 23, 24
Environment and Society	
14. How human actions modify the physical environment.	Lessons 4–7, 12, 13, 16, 19, 20, 25, 26, 29–31, 35
15. How physical systems affect human systems.	Lessons 4, 11, 13, 19, 20, 26, 27, 29, 33, 34

Geography for Life Standards	Geography Alive! Regions and People
Environment and Society (cont.)	
16. The changes that occur in meaning, use, distribution, and importance of resources.	Lessons 2, 4, 7, 23, 24, 30
The Uses of Geography	
17. How to apply geography to interpret the past.	Lessons 16, 18, 25, 30, 32
18. How to apply geography to interpret the present and plan for the future.	Lessons 6, 7, 11, 15, 27, 28, 30, 35

Lesson Analysis of Essential Knowledge, Skills, and Strategies

Lesson Title and Essential Question	National Standards	Geography and Critical Thinking Skills	Key Geography Concept and Geoterms	TCI Teaching Strategy
Unit 1: The Geographer's World				
Lesson 1: The Tools of Geography How do geographers show information on maps?	1, 3	Creating maps Using latitude and longitude Using scale Using tables, diagrams, and graphs Identifying points of view	*Mapping the Earth* absolute location distortion map projection relative location	Social Studies Skill Builder
Lesson 2: Seeing the World Like a Geographer Why do geographers use a variety of maps to represent the world?	1, 3, 4, 5, 7, 8, 9, 11, 12, 16	Analyzing maps Determining patterns on maps Interpreting images Identifying cause-and-effect relationships Making valid generalizations Synthesizing information	*Thematic Maps* climate economic activity landform physical feature population density region thematic map vegetation	Visual Discovery
Unit 2: Canada and the United States				
Mapping Lab: Canada and the United States	1, 2, 3, 4, 5, 6, 7, 8, 9, 11	Making mental maps Determining patterns on maps Creating maps Using latitude and longitude Drawing inferences Synthesizing information		
Lesson 3: Settlement Patterns and Ways of Life in Canada How does where you live influence how you live?	3, 4, 10, 12	Determining patterns on maps Interpreting images Using tables, diagrams, and graphs Drawing conclusions Making valid generalizations Decision making	*Settlement Patterns* ecumene plural society rural urban	Social Studies Skill Builder
Lesson 4: The Great Lakes: The U.S. and Canada's Freshwater Treasures How can people best use and protect Earth's freshwater ecosystems?	8, 16	Interpreting images Using tables, diagrams, and graphs Identifying cause-and-effect relationships Decision making Synthesizing information Supporting a position	*Ecosystems* ecosystem food chain food web freshwater watershed	Writing for Understanding
Lesson 5: Urban Sprawl in North America: Where Will It End? How does urban sprawl affect people and the planet?	3, 4, 9, 12, 14	Using scale Finding main ideas and supporting details Identifying points of view Identifying bias Decision making Problem solving	*Urban Sprawl* metropolitan area rural fringe suburb urban core urban fringe urban sprawl	Experimental Exercise

Lesson Title and Essential Question	National Standards	Geography and Critical Thinking Skills	Key Geography Concept and Geoterms	TCI Teaching Strategy
Lesson 6: National Parks: Saving the Natural Heritage of the U.S. and Canada What features make national parks special and worth preserving?	1, 4, 8, 14, 18	Determining patterns on maps Interpreting images Using tables, diagrams, and graphs Drawing conclusions Making valid generalizations Decision making	*Natural Heritage* conservationist fauna flora topographic map	Response Group
Lesson 7: Consumption Patterns in the United States: The Impact of Living Well How do American consumption patterns affect people and the planet?	2, 6, 9, 10	Using tables, diagrams, and graphs Drawing conclusions Synthesizing information Comparing and contrasting Summarizing Transferring information from one medium to another	*Resource Consumption* consumption developed country developing country gross domestic product (GDP) per capita	Response Group
Lesson 8: Migration to the United States: The Impact on People and Places How does migration affect the lives of people and the character of places?	2, 6, 9, 10	Analyzing maps Creating maps Determining patterns on maps Finding main ideas and supporting details Identifying cause-and-effect relationships Identifying points of view	*Migration* emigrate immigrate migration stream pull factor push factor refugee	Experiential Exercise
Unit 3: Latin America				
Mapping Lab: Latin America	1, 2, 3, 4, 5, 6, 7, 8, 9, 11	Making mental maps Determining patterns on maps Creating maps Using latitude and longitude Drawing inferences Supporting a position		
Lesson 9: Spatial Inequality in Mexico City: From Cardboard to Castles Why does spatial inequality exist in urban areas?	1, 3, 4, 9, 12	Determining patterns on maps Using tables, diagrams, and graphs Finding main ideas and supporting details Analyzing primary sources Making valid generalizations Using reliable information	*Spatial Inequality* rural decline spatial inequality standard of living urbanization	Writing for Understanding
Lesson 10: Indigenous Cultures: The Survival of the Maya of Mesoamerica How do indigenous peoples preserve their traditional culture while adapting to modern life?	4, 9, 10, 12	Analyzing maps Interpreting images Identifying cause-and-effect relationships Drawing inferences and conclusions Synthesizing information Comparing and contrasting	*Indigenous Cultures* adaptation indigenous peoples subsistence farming traditional culture	Problem Solving Groupwork

Lesson Title and Essential Question	National Standards	Geography and Critical Thinking Skills	Key Geography Concept and Geoterms	TCI Teaching Strategy
Lesson 11: Dealing with Extreme Weather: Hurricanes in the Caribbean What causes extreme weather, and how do people deal with it?	1, 4, 15, 18	Making mental maps Creating tables, diagrams, and graphs Sequencing Making valid generalizations Summarizing Predicting consequences	*Extreme Weather* El Niño extreme weather meteorology natural disaster tropical cyclone	Visual Discovery
Lesson 12: Land Use Conflict in the Amazon Rainforest How should the resources of rainforests be used and preserved?	8, 13, 14, 16, 18	Making mental maps Using tables, diagrams, and graphs Identifying points of view Sequencing Decision making Supporting a position	*Land Use Conflict* biodiversity carbon-oxygen cycle deforestation sustainable development tropical rainforest	Response Group
Lesson 13: Life in the Central Andes: Adapting to a Mountainous Region How do people adapt to living in a mountainous region?	3, 4, 5, 8, 14, 15	Interpreting images Analyzing primary sources Decision making Comparing and contrasting Predicting consequences Using reliable information	*Human Adaptation* altitudinal zonation snow line terracing tree line vertical trade	Social Studies Skill Builder
Unit 4: Europe and Russia				
Mapping Lab: Europe and Russia	1, 2, 3, 4, 5, 6, 7, 8, 9, 11	Making mental maps Determining patterns on maps Creating maps Using latitude and longitude Drawing inferences Synthesizing information		
Lesson 14: Supranational Cooperation in the European Union What forces work for and against supranational cooperation among nations?	5, 11, 13	Analyzing maps Creating tables, diagrams, and graphs Identifying cause-and-effect relationships Summarizing Comparing and contrasting Supporting a position	*Supranational Cooperation* centrifugal force centripetal force common market supranational cooperation	Experiential Exercise
Lesson 15: Population Dilemmas in Europe How do population trends affect a country's future?	4, 9, 18	Interpreting images Creating tables, diagrams, and graphs Making valid generalizations Decision making Predicting consequences Transferring information from one medium to another	*Population Trends* demography dependency ratio life expectancy replacement rate total fertility rate (TFR)	Response Group

Lesson Title and Essential Question	National Standards	Geography and Critical Thinking Skills	Key Geography Concept and Geoterms	TCI Teaching Strategy
Lesson 16: Invisible Borders: Transboundary Pollution in Europe Why can one country's pollution be another country's problem?	3, 8, 14, 16	Analyzing maps Determining patterns on maps Identifying cause-and-effect relationships Drawing inferences and conclusions Synthesizing information Predicting consequences	*Transboundary Pollution* acid rain nuclear radiation river system transboundary pollution	Visual Discovery
Lesson 17: Russia's Varied Landscape: Physical Processes at Work How do physical processes shape Earth's landscape?	1, 4, 7,	Analyzing maps Interpreting images Using tables, diagrams, and graphs Identifying cause-and-effect relationships Drawing inferences and conclusions Summarizing	*Physical Processes* erosion glaciation physical processes tectonic movement volcanic activity	Social Studies Skill Builder
Lesson 18: New Nation-States from the Old Soviet Empire: Will They Succeed? What factors contribute to the success or failure of new nation-states?	4, 5, 13	Analyzing maps Using tables, diagrams, and graphs Sequencing Synthesizing information Comparing and contrasting Supporting a position	*Nation-States* ethnic group nation nationalism nation-state state	Writing for Understanding
Unit 5: Africa				
Mapping Lab: Africa	1, 2, 3, 4, 5, 6, 7, 8, 9, 11	Making mental maps Determining patterns on maps Creating maps Using latitude and longitude Drawing inferences Supporting a position		
Lesson 19: The Nile River: A Journey from Source to Mouth How do rivers change as they flow across Earth's surface?	4, 7, 8, 14, 15	Using latitude and longitude Using tables, diagrams, and graphs Summarizing Sequencing Predicting consequences Using reliable information	*River System* hydroelectric potential perennial irrigation river basin water cycle	Social Studies Skill Builder
Lesson 20: Life in the Sahara and the Sahel: Adapting to a Desert Region How do people adapt to living in a desert region?	4, 5, 7, 8, 14, 15	Analyzing maps Interpreting images Drawing inferences and conclusions Problem solving Comparing and contrasting Predicting consequences	*Human Adaptation* desertification drought marginal land pastoral nomads	Response Group

Lesson Title and Essential Question	National Standards	Geography and Critical Thinking Skills	Key Geography Concept and Geoterms	TCI Teaching Strategy
Lesson 21: Micro-entrepreneurs: Women's Role in the Development of Africa How are women micro-entrepreneurs in developing countries changing their communities?	4, 11	Analyzing maps Determining patterns on maps Using tables, diagrams, and graphs Identifying cause-and-effect relationships Making valid generalizations Transferring information from one medium to another	*Microentrepreneurship* gender-based division of labor informal economy micro-enterprise micro-entrepreneur	Writing for Understanding
Lesson 22: Nigeria: A Country of Many Cultures How can dividing a diverse country into regions make it easier to understand?	3, 4, 5, 6, 10	Interpreting images Analyzing primary sources Sequencing Decision making Comparing and contrasting Using reliable information	*Regions* colonialism cultural region ethnic diversity linguistic group	Social Studies Skill Builder
Lesson 23: Resources and Power in Post-apartheid South Africa How might ethnic group differences affect who controls resources and power in a society?	6, 9, 10, 13, 16	Finding main ideas and supporting details Identifying points of view Identifying bias Using reliable information Transferring information from one medium to another Supporting a position	*Resource Distribution* apartheid distribution multiracial segregation	Visual Discovery
Unit 6: Southwest and Central Asia				
Mapping Lab: Southwest and Central Asia	1, 2, 3, 4, 5, 6, 7, 8, 9, 11	Making mental maps Determining patterns on maps Creating maps Using latitude and longitude Drawing inferences Synthesizing information		
Lesson 24: Oil in Southwest Asia: How "Black Gold" Has Shaped a Region How might having a valuable natural resource affect a region?	4, 5, 7, 11, 13, 16	Interpreting images Using tables, diagrams, and graphs Sequencing Comparing and contrasting Predicting consequences Supporting a position	*Natural Resources* crude oil nonrenewable resource oil reserves renewable resource	Response Group
Lesson 25: Istanbul: A Primate City Throughout History Where are primate cities located, and why are they important?	4, 10, 12, 14, 17	Analyzing maps Creating maps Determining patterns on maps Summarizing Synthesizing information Comparing and contrasting	*Primate City* capital city primate city site situation	Experiential Exercise

Lesson Title and Essential Question	National Standards	Geography and Critical Thinking Skills	Key Geography Concept and Geoterms	TCI Teaching Strategy
Lesson 26: The Aral Sea: Central Asia's Shrinking Water Source How are humans affected by changes they make to their physical environment?	14, 15	Creating maps Finding main ideas and supporting details Identifying points of view Sequencing Synthesizing information Transferring information from one medium to another	*Human-Environment Interaction* environmental degradation groundwater salinization water stress	Problem Solving Groupwork
Unit 7: Monsoon Asia				
Mapping Lab: Monsoon Asia	1, 2, 3, 4, 5, 6, 7, 8, 9, 11	Making mental maps Determining patterns on maps Creating maps Using latitude and longitude Drawing inferences Supporting a position		
Lesson 27: Waiting for the Rains: The Effects of Monsoons in South Asia How does climate influence human activity in a region?	4, 7, 15	Using latitude and longitude Determining patterns on maps Creating tables, diagrams, and graphs Problem solving Comparing and contrasting Transferring information from one medium to another	*Impact of Climate on Human Activity* atmospheric pressure monsoon orographic effect rain shadow	Social Studies Skill Builder
Lesson 28: Tech Workers and Time Zones: India's Comparative Advantage What factors give some countries a comparative advantage in the global IT revolution?	6, 11, 18	Analyzing maps Using tables, diagrams, and graphs Finding main ideas and supporting details Making valid generalizations Summarizing Synthesizing information	*Comparative Advantage* comparative advantage information technology (IT) outsource time zone	Writing for Understanding
Lesson 29: Mount Everest: Climbing the World's Tallest Physical Feature How can people both experience and protect the world's special places?	4, 14, 15	Analyzing maps Drawing inferences and conclusions Summarizing Synthesizing information Comparing and contrasting Predicting consequences	*Extreme Physical Geography* acclimatize carrying capacity exposure World Heritage site	Experiential Exercise
Lesson 30: China: The World's Most Populous Country How does a country meet the challenges created by a large and growing population?	4, 5, 9, 16, 17, 18	Using tables, diagrams, and graphs Decision making Problem solving Predicting consequences Using reliable information Supporting a position	*Population Growth* doubling time famine rate of natural increase zero population growth	Response Group

Lesson Title and Essential Question	National Standards	Geography and Critical Thinking Skills	Key Geography Concept and Geoterms	TCI Teaching Strategy
Lesson 31: Population Density in Japan: Life in a Crowded Country How does population density affect the way people live?	3, 4, 9, 12, 14	Interpreting images Determining patterns on maps Using tables, diagrams, and graphs Finding main ideas and supporting details Identifying cause-and-effect relationships Drawing inferences and conclusions	*Population Density* arable land arithmetic population density physiologic population density population distribution	Experiential Exercise
Lesson 32: The Global Sneaker: From Asia to Everywhere What is globalization, and how does it affect people and places?	3, 5, 11, 16	Analyzing maps Creating maps Using scale Interpreting images Identifying cause-and-effect relationships Making valid generalizations	*Globalization* economic interdependence free trade globalization multinational corporation	Visual Discovery
Unit 8: Oceania and Antarctica				
Mapping Lab: Oceania and Antarctica	1, 2, 3, 4, 5, 6, 7, 8, 9, 11	Making mental maps Determining patterns on maps Creating maps Using longitude and latitude Drawing inferences Synthesizing information		
Lesson 33: Relative and Absolute Location: What Makes Australia Unique? How does a country's location shape life within its borders?	4, 8, 9, 15	Analyzing maps Using latitude and longitude Using tables, diagrams, and graphs Identifying cause-and-effect relationships Making valid generalizations Comparing and contrasting	*Effects of Relative and Absolute Location* continental drift theory endangered species exotic species native species threatened species	Social Studies Skill Builder
Lesson 34: The Pacific Islands: Adapting to Life Surrounded by Ocean How do people adapt to life in an island region?	7, 8, 18	Creating maps Interpreting images Making mental maps Sequencing Summarizing Transferring information from one medium to another	*Human Adaptation* atoll continental island lagoon volcanic island	Problem Solving Groupwork
Lesson 35: Antarctica: Researching Global Warming at the Coldest Place on Earth How might global warming affect the environment in the world's coldest places?	4, 7, 8, 14, 18	Interpreting images Identifying points of view Predicting consequences Using reliable information Transferring information from one medium to another Supporting a position	*Global Warming* biome global warming greenhouse effect ice shelf	Writing for Understanding

Credits

Lesson Guide

Cover
background: Yann Arthus-Bertrand/Corbis. **insets,** Krahmer/Corbis. **center left:** Ludovic Maisant/Corbi Olivier Coret/Corbis. **center right:** Carl Purcell/Corbis ©Joseph Sohm-Visions of America/Corbis.

Lesson 1
p. 23: Qin Zhong Yu. **p. 24:** Qin Zhong Yu. **p. 29:** Qin Zhon

Lesson 2
p. 52, top: Qin Zhong Yu.

Lesson 3
p. 80, top right, center left: Qin Zhong Yu. **p. 80, bottom right:** L Ebert. **p. 82, icons:** Len Ebert. **p. 82, graphs:** Qin Zhong Yu. **p. 86:** Qin Zhong Yu. **p. 87:** Qin Zhong Yu. **p. 88:** Len Ebert.

Lesson 4
p. 104: Qin Zhong Yu. **p. 105:** Qin Zhong Yu. **p. 106:** Len Ebert. **pp. 114–116:** Len Ebert.

Lesson 5
pp. 134, 136, 138: Len Ebert.

Lesson 7
p. 163: Qin Zhong Yu. **p. 165:** Qin Zhong Yu. **p. 166:** Qin Zhong Yu.

Lesson 10
p. 238: Len Ebert. **p. 256:** Jeremy Horner/Corbis.

Lesson 11
p. 263, center: Qin Zhong Yu. **p. 268:** Qin Zhong Yu. **p. 279, right:** Qin Zhong Yu.

Lesson 12
p. 290: Siri Weber Feeney. **pp. 291, 292, icons:** Len Ebert. **pp. 294–297:** Len Ebert.

Lesson 13
p. 305, top left: Qin Zhong Yu.

Lesson 14
p. 326: Clay Bennett © 2002 The Christian Science Monitor.

Lesson 16
p. 374: Len Ebert.

Lesson 18
p. 408: Qin Zhong Yu. **p. 409:** Qin Zhong Yu. **p. 413, top right, bottom:** Qin Zhong Yu. **p. 414:** Qin Zhong Yu. **p. 415, top right, bottom:** Qin Zhong Yu. **p. 416:** Qin Zhong Yu. **p. 417, top right, bottom:** Qin Zhong Yu. **p. 418:** Qin Zhong Yu. **p. 419, top right, bottom:** Qin Zhong Yu. **p. 420:** Qin Zhong Yu. **p. 421, top right, bottom:** Qin Zhong Yu. **p. 422:** Qin Zhong Yu. **p. 423:** Qin Zhong Yu.

al Biological Service. **4A, top right:** ttom left and right: . **4B, background:** Getty Sea Grant Program. **4B,** re, Univ. of Syracuse at U/NOAA. **4C, bottom** bottom left: EPA. **4D,** /GLRO. **4E, top right:** Univ. of Toledo/ ong Yu. **4F, top** **top right:** Great Mahan/ gital Library. ions. **4F, bot-**

, **bottom** rbis. **13B, top** Craig Lovell/Corbis. rbis. **13C, top left, bottom** 3C, **top right:** Carl Purcell/Corbis.

Le
17A B: NASA. **17C:** NASA. **17D:** NASA. **17E:** Kristi Bress Index Stock Imagery. **17F:** NASA. **17G:** Lutz Kirchner. **17H:** Jacques Langevin/Corbis Sygma. **17I:** William Sokolenko. **PL17J:** TASS/Sovfoto. **17K:** Lutz Kirchner. **17L:** TASS/Sovfoto.

Lesson Guide Notes
Lesson 8
p. 184: The passage "The 'Lost Boys of Sudan'" was based on the article "Refugee Students Among 'Lost Boys of Sudan' Graduate from HACC," Jan. 3, 2005, *HACC Public Relations Office,* www.hacc.edu. **pp. 190–191:** The biography of Ricardo Flores was based on the article "The Mexican Laborer," in "The New Americans," *PBS,* www.pbs.org.

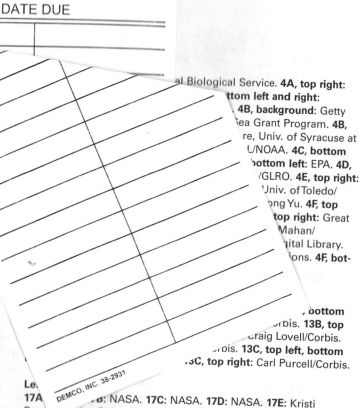